Lecture Notes in Computer Science 5100

Commenced Publication in 1973
Founding and Former Series Editors:
Gerhard Goos, Juris Hartmanis, and Jan van Leeuwen

Kurt Jensen   Wil M.P. van der Aalst
Jonathan Billington (Eds.)

Transactions on Petri Nets and Other Models of Concurrency I

Editor-in-Chief

Kurt Jensen
University of Aarhus
Faculty of Science
Department of Computer Science
IT-parken, Aabogade 34, 8200 Aarhus N, Denmark
E-mail: kjensen@cs.au.dk

Guest Editors

Wil M.P. van der Aalst
Technical University of Eindhoven
Department of Mathematics and Computer Science
Den Dolech 2, 5612 AZ Eindhoven, The Netherlands
E-mail: w.m.p.v.d.aalst@tue.nl

Jonathan Billington
University of South Australia
School of Electrical and Information Engineering
Mawson Lakes Campus, Mawson Lakes, South Australia 5095, Australia
E-mail: jonathan.billington@unisa.edu.au

Library of Congress Control Number: Applied for

CR Subject Classification (1998): D.2.2, I.6, F.4, H.2.3

LNCS Sublibrary: SL 1 – Theoretical Computer Science and General Issues

ISSN 0302-9743 (Lecture Notes in Computer Science)
ISBN-10 3-540-89286-9 Springer Berlin Heidelberg New York
ISBN-13 978-3-540-89286-1 Springer Berlin Heidelberg New York

springer.com

Typesetting: Camera-ready by author, data conversion by Scientific Publishing Services, Chennai, India
Printed on acid-free paper SPIN: 12568871 06/3180 5 4 3 2 1 0

Preface by Editor-in-Chief

This is the first volume in a new Journal entitled "LNCS Transactions on Petri Nets and Other Models of Concurrency (ToPNoC)". The volume contains revised and extended versions a selection of the best papers from the workshops at the "28th International Conference on Application and Theory of Petri Nets and Other Models of Concurrency", which took place in Siedlce, Poland, June 25–29, 2007.

As Editor-in-Chief of ToPNoC, I would like to thank the two editors of this special issue: Wil van der Aalst and Jonathan Billington. Moreover, I would like to thank all authors, reviewers, and the organizers of the workshops that served as a basis for this first ToPNoC volume.

August 2008

Kurt Jensen
Editor-in-Chief
LNCS Transactions on Petri Nets and Other Models of Concurrency (ToPNoC)

LNCS Transactions on Petri Nets and Other Models of Concurrency: Aims and Scope

ToPNoC aims to publish papers from all areas of Petri nets and other models of concurrency ranging from theoretical work to tool support and industrial applications.

The foundation of Petri nets was laid by the pioneering work of Carl Adam Petri and his colleagues in the early 1960s. Since then, an enormous amount of material has been developed and published in journals and books and presented at workshops and conferences.

The annual International Conference on Application and Theory of Petri Nets and Other Models of Concurrency started in 1980. The International Petri Net Bibliography maintained by the Petri Net Newsletter contains close to 10,000 different entries, and the International Petri Net Mailing List has 1,500 subscribers. For more information on the International Petri Net community, see: http://www.informatik.uni-hamburg.de/TGI/PetriNets/

All issues of ToPNoC are LNCS volumes. Hence they appear in all large libraries and are also accessible in LNCS Online (electronically). Simultaneously the ToPNoC volumes form a Journal, and it is possible to subscribe to ToPNoC without subscribing to the rest of LNCS.

ToPNoC contains:

- Revised versions of a selection of the best papers from workshops and tutorials at the annual Petri net conferences
- Special sections/issues within particular subareas (similar to those published in the *Advances in Petri Nets* series)
- Other papers invited for publication in ToPNoC
- Papers submitted directly to ToPNoC by their authors

Like all other journals, ToPNoC has an Editorial Board, which is responsible for the quality of the journal. The members of the board assist in the reviewing of papers submitted or invited for publication in ToPNoC. Moreover, they may make recommendations concerning collections of papers proposed for inclusion in ToPNoC as special sections/issues. The Editorial Board consists of prominent researchers within the Petri net community and in related fields.

Topics

System design and verification using nets; analysis and synthesis, structure and behavior of nets; relationships between net theory and other approaches; causality/partial order theory of concurrency; net-based semantical, logical and algebraic calculi; symbolic net representation (graphical or textual); computer tools for nets; experience with using nets, case studies; educational issues related to nets; higher level net models; timed and stochastic nets; and standardization of nets.

Applications of nets to different kinds of systems and application fields, e.g.: flexible manufacturing systems, real-time systems, embedded systems, defence systems, biological systems, health and medical systems, environmental systems, hardware structures, telecommunications, railway networks, office automation, workflows, supervisory control, protocols and networks, the Internet, e-commerce and trading, programming languages, performance evaluation, and operations research.

For more information about ToPNoC, please see: www.springer.com/lncs/topnoc

Submission of Manuscripts

Manuscripts should follow LNCS formatting guidelines, and should be submitted as PDF or zipped PostScript files to ToPNoC@cs.au.dk. All queries should be addressed to the same e-mail address.

LNCS Transactions on Petri Nets and Other Models of Concurrency: Editorial Board

Preface by Guest Editors

This inaugural issue of ToPNoC contains revised and extended versions of a selection of the best papers from the workshops held at the 28th International Conference on Application and Theory of Petri Nets and Other Models of Concurrency, which took place in Siedlce, Poland, June 25–29, 2007. The best papers were selected in close cooperation with the chairs of the workshops, and their authors were invited to submit improved and extended versions. After a rigorous review process we selected the 13 papers in this first issue.

We are indebted to the Program Committees of the workshops and in particular the workshop chairs. Without their competent and enthusiastic work this volume would not have been possible. Many members of the PCs participated in reviewing the revised and extended papers considered for this issue.

Papers from the following workshops were considered when selecting the best papers:

- The Workshop on Teaching Concurrency (TeaConc'2007) organized by Luis Gomes (Portugal) and Søren Christensen (Denmark).
- The International Workshop on Petri Nets and Software Engineering (PNSE'07) organized by Daniel Moldt (Germany), Fabrice Kordon (France), Kees van Hee (The Netherlands), José-Manuel Colom (Spain), and Rémi Bastide (France).
- The Workshop on Petri Net Standards 2007 organized by Ekkart Kindler (Denmark) and Laure Petrucci (Paris).
- The International Workshop on Formal Approaches to Business Processes and Web Services (FABPWS'07) organized by Kees van Hee, Wolfgang Reisig, and Karsten Wolf.
- The Workshop on Unfolding and Partial Order Techniques (UFO'07) organized by Eric Fabre (France) and Victor Khomenko (UK).

Thanks to the support of the workshops chairs and their PC members, we were able to select a set of high-quality papers. Moreover, we also invited a paper based on the tutorial "Elasticity and Petri nets" given in Siedlce.

All invited papers were reviewed by three or four referees. We followed the principle of also asking for "fresh" reviews of the revised papers, i.e., from referees who had not been involved initially in reviewing the papers. Some papers were accepted or rejected after the first round of reviewing while the authors of others were asked to make a major revision which was then accepted or rejected after a second round of reviewing. We thank the reviewers and authors for doing an outstanding job.

In the end 13 papers were accepted out of the 17 initially considered as best papers. (Note that the workshops accepted about 50 papers in total and that the number of submissions to these workshops was considerably higher.)

The first four papers of this issue originated from the Workshop on Teaching Concurrency. "Constructive Alignment for Teaching Model-Based Design for Concurrency" by Claus Brabrand, "Teaching Modelling and Validation of Concurrent Systems using Coloured Petri Nets" by Lars Kristensen and Kurt Jensen, and "Teaching Concurrency Concepts to Freshmen" by Holger Hermanns and Christian Eisentraut provide interesting views on teaching concurrency-related topics and show that more research into the way that we teach concurrency is justified. In "TAPAs: a Tool for the Analysis of Process Algebras", Francesco Calzolai et al. present a tool for the analysis of concurrent systems and report their experiences with using this tool in teaching.

The next six papers were originally presented at the PNSE workshop. Kristian Lassen and Boudewijn van Dongen report on a new form of process discovery where explicit causalities in the form of Message Sequence Charts are taken into account in "Translating Message Sequence Charts to Other Process Languages Using Process Mining". The paper "Net Components for the Integration of Process Mining into Agent-Oriented Software Engineering", by Lawrence Cabac and Nicolas Denz, uses an original combination of two Petri-net-based tools, Renew and ProM, to link agents and mining.

Dahmani Djaouida et al. present a Petri-net variant incorporating time, give formal semantics, and propose an analysis technique in their paper "Time Recursive Petri Nets".

In "Designing Case Handling Systems" Kees van Hee et al. combine Petri nets, XML, and the relational data model to describe and enact case handling processes. Isaac Corro Ramos and his co-authors focus on testing systems with a known process structure in "Model-Driven Testing Based on Test History". They investigate both exhaustive testing and a statistical release procedure.

The paper "Assessing State Spaces Using Petri-Net Synthesis and Attribute-Based Visualization" by Eric Verbeek et al. focuses on the visualization of state spaces which are too large to show as a classical graph. Moreover, regions are used to extract the labeling structure needed for this visualization.

The next two papers were originally presented at the UFO workshop. Motivated by automated planning problems, Blai Bonet et al. present an analysis approach that combines Petri net unfolding with artificial intelligence heuristics to improve the performance of searching for a goal state in "Directed Unfolding of Petri Nets". In their paper, "McMillan's Complete Prefix for Contextual Nets", Paolo Baldan et al. present a new algorithm that allows for unfolding a larger class of contextual nets (i.e., Petri nets with test arcs) where the unfolding is again a contextual net.

Finally, "Elasticity and Petri Nets" by Jordi Cortadella et al. describes methods for modelling, performance analysis, and optimization of elastic systems using (extended) marked graphs.

The above 13 papers cover a wide range of concurrency-related topics ranging from process mining and performance analysis to verification and model checking in application domains that include the design of hardware systems and business process management. Insight is also gained into how concurrency topics can be taught at tertiary level. Therefore, this volume provides a useful blend of theory, practice and tools related to concurrency research.

August 2008

Wil van der Aalst
Jonathan Billington
Guest Editors, Inaugural Issue of ToPNoC

Organization of This Issue

Guest Editors

Wil van der Aalst, The Netherlands
Jonathan Billington, Australia

Co-chairs of the Workshops

Luis Gomes (Portugal)
Søren Christensen (Denmark)
Daniel Moldt (Germany)
Fabrice Kordon (France)
Kees van Hee (The Netherlands)
José-Manuel Colom (Spain)
Rémi Bastide (France)
Ekkart Kindler (Denmark)
Laure Petrucci (Paris)
Wolfgang Reisig (Germany)
Karsten Wolf (Germany)
Eric Fabre (France)
Victor Khomenko (UK)

Referees

Joao Paulo Barros
Remi Bastide
Carmen Bratosin
Didier Buchs
Piotr Chrzastowski-Wachtel
Gianfranco Ciardo
José-Manuel Colom
Philippe Darondeau
Jörg Desel
Boudewijn van Dongen
Christian Eisentraut
Javier Esparza
Dirk Fahland
Jorge César Abrantes de Figueiredo
Guy Gallasch
Amar Gupta
Kees van Hee
Keijo Heljanko
Holger Hermanns
Vladimir Janousek
Jens B. Jørgensen
Astrid Kiehn
Victor Khomenko
Gabriele Kotsis
Maciej Koutny
Marta Koutny
Lars Kristensen
Charles Lakos
Kristian Bisgaard Lassen
Nimrod Lilith
Johan Lilius
Robert Lorenz
Ricardo Machado
Daniel Moldt
Rocco De Nicola
Laure Petrucci
Laura Recalde
Heiko Rolke
Vladimir Rubin
Sylvie Thiebaux
Francesco Tiezzi
Ruediger Valk
Antti Valmari
Eric Verbeek
Walter Vogler
Michael Westergaard
Karsten Wolf
Jianli Xu
Alex Yakovlev
Syed Abbas Kazim Zaidi

Table of Contents

Constructive Alignment for Teaching Model-Based Design for Concurrency
(A Case-Study on Implementing Alignment in Computer Science)

Claus Brabrand

IT University of Copenhagen,
Rued Langgaards Vej 7, DK-2300 Copenhagen S, Denmark
`brabrand@itu.dk`
`http://www.itu.dk/people/brabrand/`

Abstract. *"How can we make sure our students learn what we want them to?"* is the number one question in teaching. This paper is intended to provide the reader with: (i) a general answer to this question based on The Theory of *Constructive Alignment* by John Biggs; (ii) relevant insights for bringing this answer from theory to practice; and (iii) specific insights and experiences from using constructive alignment in teaching model-based design for concurrency (as a case study in implementing alignment).

Keywords: teaching, student learning, constructive alignment, the SOLO taxonomy, model-based design for concurrency.

1 Introduction

This paper is intended to show *how* The Theory of Constructive Alignment [2] provides a compelling answer to the number one question in teaching:

"How can we make sure our students learn what we want them to?" `(Q1)`

Specifically, to illustrate *how* the theory can be used in the context of teaching model-based design for concurrency, to guide and maximize student learning; and, to provide *incentive* and *support* for student learning in a direction intentionally chosen by a teacher.

The paper is divided into two parts. Part 1 briefly gives a general introduction to The Theory of Constructive Alignment and The SOLO Taxonomy [3]. The essence of this part is also available as a 19-min award-winning short-film by the author, entitled *"Teaching Teaching & Understanding Understanding"* [5]. Part 2 is the main part and shows how to apply the theory to a specific case; namely, to teach five ECTS,[1] 7 week, undergraduate course on model-based design for

[1] European Credit Transfer and Accumulation System (one academic year is 60 ECTS).

K. Jensen, W. van der Aalst, and J. Billington (Eds.): ToPNoC I, LNCS 5100, pp. 1–18, 2008.

concurrency at the University of Aarhus, Denmark. The course has been taught four times by the author using FSP [10] for modeling, Java for implementation, and the book [10] for introducing relevant concepts, problems, and solutions. The course ran twice before the implementation of alignment (in 2004 and 2005), and twice after (in 2006 and 2007); each year with a group of 20–30 students. The paper concludes by giving a comparison of teaching the course "pre-" versus "post-alignment".

2 Part 1: The Theory of Constructive Alignment

The Theory of Constructive Alignment [2] provides a compelling answer to `(Q1)`. The theory is developed by Biggs and has its roots in *curriculum theory* and *constructivism* [11]; the idea that the learner's *actions* define what is learned and that knowledge is actively constructed by the individual through interaction with the external world (see [8,13]). It is a *systemic theory* that regards the total teaching context as a whole, as a *system*, wherein all contributing factors and stakeholders reside. To understand the system, we need to identify and understand the parts of the system and how they interact and affect one another. The Theory of Constructive Alignment provides just that for the teaching system; it provides relevant and prototypical models of the parts that ultimately enable us to *predict* how the teaching system reacts when we change various aspects of our teaching. It is also a theory of motivation and of planning that looks at teaching far beyond what goes on in the classroom and auditorium.

However, before we present constructive alignment as "the solution" to `(Q1)`, we need to look closer at (models of) the main parts of the system; the students, the teachers, and of cognitive processes.

As with all models (just like the models we use in concurrency) they might seem a bit simplistic or crude at first. Nonetheless, they are highly instructive for us to get an idea of what the system looks like and what causes and effects we may be up against as a teacher.

2.1 Student Models

In his book, *"Teaching for Quality Learning at University"* [2], Biggs has identified and personified two prototypical student models classified according to their motivation for being at university, immortalized as *"Susan and Robert"*:

Susan is *intrinsically* motivated. She likes to get to the bottom of things and often reflects on possibilities, implications, applications, and consequences of what she is learning. She uses high-level learning activities such as *reflecting*, *analyzing*, and *comparing* that continually deepen her understanding.

Robert, on the other hand, is *extrinsically* motivated. He is not interested in learning and understanding in itself; he just wants to pass exams, so that he can get a degree, so he can get a (decent) job. To this end, he will cut any corner, including sticking with lower-level learning activities, such as *identifying*, *note-taking*, and *memorizing* as long as they suffice.

It is important to note that a given student may embody any combination of these two prototypes and that it may vary according to the area of interest. For this reason it is often advantageous to think of them as *strategies* (as in *"The Susan Strategy"*), rather than actual *persons.*

As a teacher, it is not Susan we need to watch out for. Faced with a curriculum, she basically teaches herself; in fact, we almost cannot prevent her from learning. Rather, it is Robert we need to pay attention to; in particular, to the learning activities he is employing (before, during, and after teaching).

Our challenge as a teacher is to engage Robert and get him to use higher-level learning activities; i.e., make him *behave* more like Susan. The good news is that it is actually possible to do something about Robert (or rather, Robert's learning). We shall shortly explain how to, systemically speaking, positively change the system so as to (have him) change his *behavior.* But before we do that, we need to look at the situation from a teacher perspective.

2.2 Teacher Models

Biggs [2] also has a few prototypical models of the teachers; this time three (increasingly desirable) models of teachers according to their main focus in teaching, known as the *"three levels of thinking about teaching"*:

The level 1 teacher is concerned with what students *are.* He operates with a binary perspective; a student is either (inherently) good xor bad. The exam is a diagnostic means to "sort the good students from the bad" after teaching. This perspective is essentially deferring the responsibility for lack of learning; in particular, the teacher can no longer do anything about it: "it's just the way students are; either good or bad" (i.e., independent of the teaching).

The level 2 teacher is concerned with what the teacher *does.* A teacher at the second level is preoccupied with acquiring an armory of techniques, "tips'n'tricks" along with visual and technological aides, in order to enhance *his* performance. While this perspective is a dramatic improvement to the first, it is still independent of *student learning* which is incorporated directly in the third and final level.

The level 3 teacher is concerned with what a student *does* (before, during, and after teaching). He is adopting a *student-learning focus* and will judge all pedagogic dispositions according to how they affect student learning.

Again, a given teacher may embody combinations of these characteristics.

2.3 Learning Models

In 1949, one of the most influential American educators, Ralph W. Tyler said:

> *"Learning takes place through the active behavior of the student: it is what he does that he learns, not what the teacher does."*

The idea that knowledge is *transmitted* from an (active) teacher to a (passive) learner is dead. There is increasing evidence that what is learned is intimately tied to which actions are performed by the learner and that knowledge is *actively constructed* (see [8,13]). In fact, John Biggs defines good teaching [2] directly as a function of student activity:

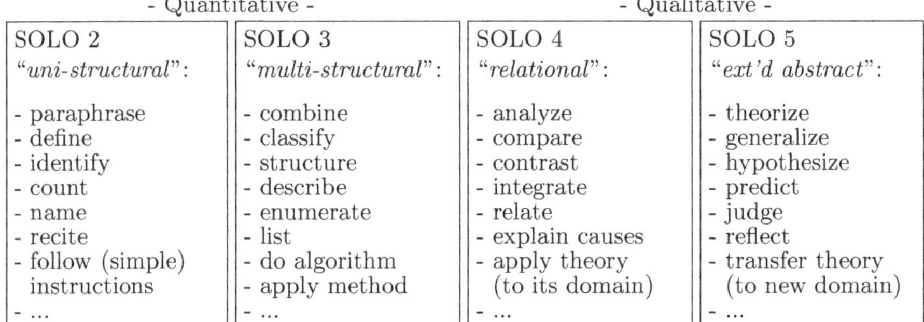

- Quantitative -
- Qualitative -
SOLO 2
"uni-structural":
- paraphrase
- define
- identify
- count
- name
- recite
- follow (simple) instructions
- ...
SOLO 3
"multi-structural":
- combine
- classify
- structure
- describe
- enumerate
- list
- do algorithm
- apply method
- ...
SOLO 4
"relational":
- analyze
- compare
- contrast
- integrate
- relate
- explain causes
- apply theory (to its domain)
- ...
SOLO 5
"ext'd abstract":
- theorize
- generalize
- hypothesize
- predict
- judge
- reflect
- transfer theory (to new domain)
- ...

Fig. 1. Sample competence verbs from *"The SOLO Taxonomy"*. Improvements in learning outcomes occur *quantitatively* at SOLO 2–3 and *qualitatively* at levels 4–5.

> *"**Good teaching** is getting most students to use the higher cognitive level processes that the more academic students use spontaneously."*

Teaching is about activating students; getting them to use *higher cognitive level processes*. For this we need a model of understanding, cognition, and quality of learning. There are many such models; e.g., *"The SOLO Taxonomy"* [3], *"The BLOOM Taxonomy"* [4],[2] and Klopfer's models of student behavior [9]. However, I have chosen to present only one of these models, namely The SOLO Taxonomy, since it has been deliberately constructed for research-based university teaching and converge on research at its fifth and highest level.

The Structure of the Observed Learning Outcome taxonomy (SOLO [3]), distinguishes five levels of cognitive processes according to the cognitive processes required to obtain them. Although there is a close relationship between the levels of the SOLO taxonomy and the levels in Jean Piaget's (hypothetical) cognitive structures, the former was designed to evaluate learning outcomes and cognitive processes, the latter for describing the developmental stages of individuals, especially children (see [3,12]). The five levels are (in increasing order of complexity, each level prerequisitionally building upon the previous):

SOLO 1 (aka. "the pre-structural level"). At the first level, the student has no understanding, uses irrelevant information, and/or misses the point altogether. Although scattered pieces of information may have been acquired, they

[2] *"The BLOOM Taxonomy"* was originally designed to guide representative *selection* of items on a test, rather than *evaluating* the quality of learning outcomes.

will be unorganized, unstructured, and essentially void of real content or relation to a relevant issue or problem.

SOLO 2 (aka. "the uni-structural level"). At the second level, a student can deal with one single aspect. A student may make obvious connections and hence have the competence to *recite*, *identify*, *define*, *follow* simple instructions, and so on.

SOLO 3 (aka. "the multi-structural level"). A student at level three can now deal with several aspects, but they are considered independently. A student may have the competence to *enumerate*, *describe*, *classify*, *combine*, *structure*, *execute* procedures, and so on.

SOLO 4 (aka. "the relational level"). At the relational level, a student may now understand relations between several aspects and understand how they may fit together to form a whole. A student may thus have the competence to *compare*, *relate*, *analyze*, *apply*, *explain* things in terms of causes and effects, and so on.

SOLO 5 (aka. "the extended abstract level"). At the fifth and highest level, a student may generalize structure beyond what was given, essentially producing new knowledge. A student may perceive structure from many different perspectives, transfer ideas to new areas, and may have the competence to *generalize*, *hypothesize*, *theorize*, and so on.

Fig. 1 shows a *non-exhaustive* list of common verbs from the SOLO taxonomy.

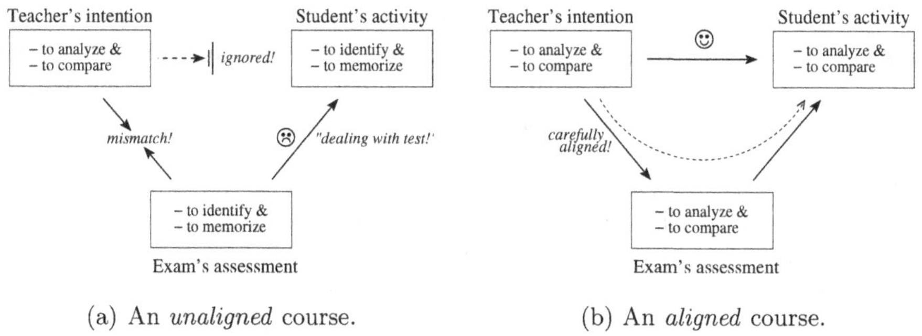

(a) An *unaligned* course.

(b) An *aligned* course.

Fig. 2. An unaligned vs. aligned course

2.4 Constructive Alignment

We now have the ingredients and models to understand the system and why constructive alignment is a compelling answer to `(Q1)`.

Definition (constructive alignment). A course is said to be *constructively aligned* [2] when:

- the *intended learning outcomes* (ILOs) are stated clearly;
- the ILOs are explicitly communicated to the students;
- the exam assessment(s) match the ILOs; *and*
- the teaching form(s) match the ILOs.

The solution is to constructively align courses (the name "alignment" comes from the fact that the following elements are all pointing in the same direction):

$$\textit{exam assessment} \;\approx\; \textit{intended learning outcomes} \;\approx\; \textit{teaching form}$$

To appreciate this solution, let us first have a look at the problems with an *unaligned course* where there is a mismatch between the intended learning outcomes and the exam assessment. After this, we will see how constructive alignment remedies this situation.

Unaligned course. Fig. 2a illustrates an example of an *unaligned* course. Here, it is the teacher's intention that the students learn how to *analyze* and *compare.* However, the nature of the exam used is such that it measures something else; in this case, the ability to *identify* and *memorize.* The problem with this arrangement is that Robert will soon realize the minimal requirements, totally ignore the teacher's intended learning outcomes, and only study for what is directly required of him on the exam. This *"backwash effect"* is appropriately referred to as Robert *"dealing with the test"*.

Aligned course. Fig. 2b depicts an *aligned* version of the course. Here, the teacher has carefully aligned the exam with the intended learning outcomes such that it assesses precisely those (in this case, the ability to *analyze* and to *compare*). We get a commuting diagram; Robert's goal of passing the course will invariably lead him past learning the intended objectives. This way, we are effectively using Robert's (extrinsic) motivation to pass courses, to make him learn.

Now Robert is *motivated* to learn, but he still needs the support. This is where the form of teaching comes in; the other aspect of constructive alignment is to also align the *teaching form* with the intended learning outcomes and exam. During a course, students would ideally "train towards the exam". The challenge then becomes choosing—perhaps several different—adequate forms of teaching in which the students best practice the skills and competences intended and measured.

In a constructively aligned course Robert now has the *support* (from the teaching form) and *incentive* (from the exam assessment) to learn like Susan.

This was a brief and general introduction to The Theory of Constructive Alignment. In the following, we will have a look at *how* these ideas can be applied to improve the teaching of a Computer Science course on Model-Based Design for Concurrency.

3 Part 2: Constructive Alignment for Teaching Concurrency

Adhering to the principle of the Chinese Proverb:

> *"Give a man a fish and he will eat for a day. Teach a man to fish and he will eat for a lifetime."*

this section will not attempt to present "*a* perfectly aligned course", but rather, to illustrate *how* the principle of constructive alignment can be useful and used for judging the relevance of and selecting different forms of assessment and teaching.

3.1 From Content to Competence

First though, I want to motivate and advocate a shift from thinking courses in terms of *content* to thinking in terms of *competence.*

Content. Traditionally, many courses specify the aims of a course as a *content description*; listing course-specific concepts that are "to be understood". This was also the case in earlier versions of my concurrency course (before exposure to the theory of alignment, that is). It essentially stated that the goal of the course was for the students to *understand* a bunch of concurrency concepts such as "interference" and "deadlock" (see Fig. 3a for the exact formulation).

The problem with general "understanding goals" via content descriptions is that teachers and students may not (in fact, usually do not) have the same *interpretation* of the intended learning outcomes. Teachers and examiners—being products of a research-based teaching tradition—will immediately agree; that what is really meant by "understanding deadlock" is, for instance, the competence to *analyze* programs for deadlock, *explain* possible causes and effects, and *predict* consequences of possible solutions. However, this is tacit knowledge. A student—unfamiliar with the traditions—is likely to interpret the same content description at an entirely different level; e.g., as the competence to *recite* conditions for deadlock and *name* standard solutions. However, even if students and teachers did agree on an interpretation, we already know from the theory of alignment, that Robert's learning activity will still ultimately be dominated by the constitutional effect of the exam (cf. Fig. 2a).

Competence is inherently operational and captured by verbs as opposed to content by nouns. Competence is knowledge plus the capacity to act upon it; to *use* attained understanding of a topic to inform behavior and act accordingly. The SOLO levels provide a taxonomy of appropriate verbs for describing intended learning outcomes as a hierarchy of competences. Thus, in our ultimate intended learning outcomes, we are not aiming for (passive) knowledge of content, but (active) competence.

Aim:
The purpose is to give the students a thorough knowledge of models, systems, and concepts in concurrency (cf. contents below), such that this may be used in the realization of solid solutions to realistic and practical problems.
Contents:
Processes, threads, interaction, interference, synchronization, monitors, deadlock, safety and liveness properties, forms of communication, and software architecture for systems and concurrency.

(a) Pre-alignment: course aims (given as a content description).

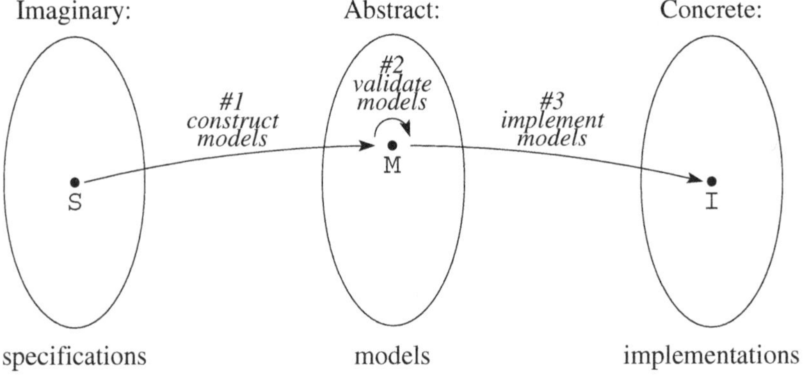

(b) Course philosophy: the model-based design process.

STEP no.	COMPETENCE: *After the course, students are expected to be able to...:*	SOLO level
n/a	• ~~*memorize*~~ content;	~~2~~
#1	• ***construct*** models from specifications;	3
	• ***apply*** standard solutions to common concurrency problems;	4
	• ***relate*** models and specifications;	4
#2	• ***test*** models w.r.t. behavior (using tool support);	2
	• ***define*** relevant safety/liveness properties for models;	2
	• ***verify*** models w.r.t. safety/liveness properties (using tools);	3
	• ***analyze*** models (and programs) w.r.t. behavior;	4
	• ***compare*** models (and programs) w.r.t. behavior;	4
#3	• ***implement*** models in familiar programming languages; *and*	3
	• ***relate*** models and implementations.	4

(c) Post-alignment: intended learning outcomes (based on the SOLO taxonomy)

Fig. 3. Pre- and post-alignment course description

3.2 Course Philosophy: Model-Based Design

There is obviously a wide spectrum of perspectives on concurrency and thus on possible concurrency courses; ranging from the study of abstract categorical frameworks for concurrency process calculi to semaphore protocol programming.

However, as hinted in the title of this paper, the overall philosophy and activity in the course investigated in this paper is centered around models, using a *model-based design* approach.

Before presenting the intended learning outcomes as competences based on The SOLO Taxonomy, I want to spend a few lines on motivation. In general, as a teacher I need to provide students with a solid answer for what they get out of following the course; what it is they will be able to *do* after the course, why that is important, and what advantages those competences will give them. Also, I need to spend time communicating this answer to the students. If I cannot "sell the course" to the students who have not actively elected the course, they will be less motivated to spend time on it. Thus, when teaching model-based design for concurrency, I need to provide my students with a solid answer to the (very appropriate) question:

"Why bother learning about model-based design for concurrency!?"

Here is a short summary of the motivational answer I give my students early on in the course, motivating a "model-based design approach" to concurrent software development. Concurrent programming is much more difficult than sequential programming; systems are inherently non-deterministic and parallel; the concurrency is conceptually harder to grasp and adds—along with complexity—a whole new range of potential errors such as interference, deadlock, starvation, un-intended execution traces, unfairness, and priority inversion. In the presence of all these errors, models come to the rescue. Models offer a means for offline reasoning through a formal modeling language to read, write, and talk about models (to gain understanding of a system), run-time testing (to gain confidence), and automatic[3] compile-time property verification (to gain safety).

The model-based design process, as depicted in Fig. 3b, advocates that systems are better built by first constructing models from specifications (step #1), then validating the models constructed (step #2), and only then implementing those validated models as concrete systems (step #3). The quality of the final resulting system constructed is, of course, tied to the "appropriateness" of the intermediary steps through the models.

3.3 Intended Learning Outcomes

With the overall philosophy of the course in place, I need to *operationalize* it and express it in terms of concrete evaluable competences. Here, one needs to carefully avoid the temptation to use so-called *understanding goals* (e.g., such as *"to understand X"*, *"be familiar with Y"*, or *"have a notion of Z"*), for the simple reason that we cannot measure them. General understanding goals should be turned into measurable competence. Note that understanding is, of course, a requisite for competence.

Fig. 3c presents the intended learning outcomes expressed as competences based on The SOLO Taxonomy and directed towards the students. The description starts with the formulation:

[3] *"Never send a human to do a machine's job"*, A. Smith (The Matrix, 1999).

"After the course, students are expected to be able to ..."

Note how this formulation places the learning focus on the students and that it is directly expressed in terms of *competence* (i.e., "to be able to..."). This line is then followed by the individual competences to be learned during the course. The first, "to memorize content" (which is at SOLO level 2) is explicitly included as a non-goal to send a clear message to the students that this competence will not help them during the course and exams.

This is followed by the ten actual intended learning outcomes for the course listed along with their corresponding SOLO level. The competences are divided into the three steps related to model-based design process (#1 to #3). Note how each competence is expressed using an active *verb* (highlighted in boldface) and a passive noun/noun-phrase, expressing: "what is it the students are expected to be able to *do* (verb) with *content* (noun)". The application of standard solutions to common concurrency problems covers issues such as semaphores, mutual exclusion, synchronization, deadlock, and the reader/writer protocol.

I will not go further into the particular choice of intended learning outcomes here, because this is not the point of this paper. Rather, the point is to show how such intended learning outcomes can be used to provide *incentive* and *support* for student learning in a direction intentionally chosen by a teacher, as explained in the following.

3.4 On Aligning the Assessment (with the ILOs)

When I learned about constructive alignment in 2005, the exam of my concurrency course consisted of a group project during the last 2 weeks of the course, and an individual multiple-choice test at the end of the course, each counting 50% towards the final grade. This happened to coincide with my preferences if I were to choose freely among all reasonable forms of evaluation for measuring the intended learning outcomes of Fig. 3c, as reported in the following along with my experiences.

On Aligning the Project. In the pre-alignment courses, it was also my intention that emphasis be placed on the model-implementation relationship which had also been clearly communicated to the students. However, since the aims of the course were given by a traditional *content description* (Fig. 3a), this was not reflected in explicit intended learning outcomes, nor was it listed as explicit criteria for project grading. In the end, I received some projects with no apparent relation between the two. It was as if the construction of the model and implementation had been approached independently and pursued in two altogether different directions, defying the whole purpose of model-based design.

In the 2006 course, I tried to apply the idea of constructive alignment. I formulated explicit intended learning outcomes around which the exam was carefully centered and on which the teaching was based. To *relate* was explicitly included as an intended learning outcome and explicitly included on the exam. The product was a project entitled "The Banana Republic" which was a synthesis-oriented project where the students had to construct a system via the model-based design paradigm. Figures 7 and 8 show the specification, task, report requirements, and evaluation criteria of the 2006 project. The project was explicitly *designed* to evaluate all the competences of Fig. 3c, except the more analytical competences; i.e., *to analyze* and *compare* models and programs. In my opinion, such competences are more appropriately evaluated in a multiple-choice test as explained below. The projects received in 2006 generally had a better correspondence between model and implementation.

On Aligning the Multiple-Choice Test. The two analytical competences not directly addressed in the project (*to analyze* and *to compare* models and programs), are more appropriately evaluated in a multiple-choice test. The main advantage is that in a multiple-choice test one is free to prefabricate (even contrived) models whose main purpose is to exhibit more interesting and challenging aspects and behaviors than the students are likely to come upon during the model-based construction process. Since I believe these two competences are important, and not guaranteed to be required in the project, I have to explicitly examine the students in them. Thus, I have devoted an independent test solely to them.

I used the multiple choice tool (MCT [7]) to automatically permute questions and choices, to evaluate the answers, and to ensure that the grading was statistically robust and based on provably sound principles.

Earlier tests asked seemingly innocent questions such as the one found in Fig. 4a. Although this seems like a perfectly reasonable question to ask and for which the students should know the answer, it has dramatic implications on learning. The problem is that it is possible to get by with *memorization.* Hence, Robert is free to "deal with the test" and direct his study effort towards memorizing content (recall Fig. 2a). Note that information about the sufficiency of surface understanding may also be rumored by former students exposed to similar questions in earlier courses.

After the introduction of alignment, later tests were carefully centered around the competence *to analyze* and *to compare* models. For examples of such questions, see Fig. 4b and 4c. (Please note that we do not expect the reader to understand the details of the FSP models; for details of the FSP modelling language, we refer to [10].) It should be obvious that these are high-level questions for which lower-level activities such as memorization no longer suffice. By construction, they depend on the capacity to analyze and compare models. Some questions were also testing the ability to analyze and compare (Java) programs.

I still use the the memorization question. However, now it instead serves as a "non-goal"; as an example of a type of question *not* appearing on the final multiple-choice exam, hence the strikeout in Fig. 3c.

What are FSP programs compiled into by the LTSA tool?:

a ☐ Stateless Machines.
b ☐ Finite State Models.
c ☐ Infinite State Models.

(a) Assesses competence: *"to **memorize** content"* (i.e., bad alignment).

Given the following FSP model `M`, *safety property* `S`, and *liveness property,* `L`:

```
RESOURCE = (get -> put -> RESOURCE).

P = (printer.get -> (scanner.get -> copy -> printer.put -> scanner.put -> P
                    |timeout -> printer.put -> P)).

Q = (scanner.get -> (printer.get -> copy -> printer.put -> scanner.put -> Q
                    |timeout -> scanner.put -> Q)).

||M = (p:P || q:Q || {p,q}::printer:RESOURCE || {p,q}::scanner:RESOURCE).

property S = (p.printer.get -> p.printer.put -> S
             |q.printer.get -> q.printer.put -> S).

progress L = {p.copy, q.copy}
```

Which of the following property relationships are satisfied?:

a ☐ $\texttt{M} \models \texttt{S}$ and $\texttt{M} \models \texttt{L}$ *(i.e., M satisfies both S and L)*
b ☐ $\texttt{M} \models \texttt{S}$ and $\texttt{M} \not\models \texttt{L}$ *(i.e., M satisfies S, but not L)*
c ☐ $\texttt{M} \not\models \texttt{S}$ and $\texttt{M} \models \texttt{L}$ *(i.e., M satisfies L, but not S)*
d ☐ $\texttt{M} \not\models \texttt{S}$ and $\texttt{M} \not\models \texttt{L}$ *(i.e., M satisfies neither S, nor L)*

(b) Assesses competence: *"to **analyze** models w.r.t. behavior"* (i.e., good alignment).

Let two FSP processes, `CRIT` and `LOCK`, be given:

```
CRIT = (acq->crit->rel->CRIT).
LOCK = (acq->rel->LOCK).
```

Now, consider the two different systems, `SYS1` and `SYS2`, defined below:

```
||SYS1 = ({x,y}:CRIT || {x,y}::LOCK).
||SYS2 = ({x,y}::CRIT || {x,y}:LOCK).
```

Which of the following traces is *invalid* for `SYS1` and *valid* for `SYS2`?:

a ☐ The empty trace (containing no actions).
b ☐ `x.acq`
c ☐ `x.acq ; x.rel`
d ☐ `x.acq ; x.crit ; x.rel`
e ☐ `x.acq ; y.crit ; x.rel`

(c) Assesses competence: *"to **compare** models w.r.t. behavior"* (i.e., good alignment).

Fig. 4. Unaligned and aligned sample multiple-choice questions (each question always has exactly one correct answer)

3.5 On Aligning the Teaching Form (with the ILOs)

In constructively aligning my form of teaching, I use a combination of five different teaching activities. Specifically, I use:

1. ***lectures*** to introduce the students to fundamental concepts and to show applications of standard solutions to common concurrency problems in terms of models and implementations (based on [10]);
2. ***modeling and programming lab*** as a means for students to gain hands-on practical experience in *constructing*, *implementing*, *testing*, and *verifying* models, *defining* properties, and *applying* standard solutions to common concurrency problems (here a TA is present and acts as a consultant);
3. ***theoretical exercise classes*** as a means for the students to learn how to *apply* variations of common solutions to standard problems (here the students get feedback from a TA who supervises and facilitates the class);
4. ***weekly hand-ins*** in the form of small compulsory exercises wherein the students are asked to *construct* and *implement* models with special emphasis on *relating* models and implementations (here the students train for the project and receive individual feedback on their hand-ins from a TA); *and*
5. ***multiple-choice sample questions*** as a means for the students to learn to *analyze* and *compare* models (here the students train for the multiple-choice exam. The questions are given without the correct answers, to maximize student activation.

Note how the real training of competences (i.e., practicing of verbs) takes place, not during the lectures, but in the four other *student-centric* learning activities. This disposition is consistent with the ideas of constructivism; that knowledge is (actively) constructed by the students themselves according to their behavior. There is a big difference between a student (passively) listening to a lecture on application and the student performing the applying himself. During the lectures, I try my best to engage and activate the students using various techniques such as 1-min papers [1], 2-min neighbor discussions, and a 3-min student structural recapitulation at the end to encourage active participation. However, such level 2 "tips'n'tricks" are beyond the scope of this paper.

Structurally, the course iterates through the model-based design process many times with the introduction of each new concurrency concept (a structure also taken in [10]). The advantage of doing it this way, rather than a division according the steps model-based design process (i.e., #1, #2 and #3), is that the students get to practise the overall process many times over and incorporate insights and feedback from previous the iterations. The project is thus essentially the last, unsupervised, iteration.

In earlier versions of the course, teaching activities (4) and (5) above were missing, along with the training in and feedback on those competences. Also, the lectures (1) were more one-way communication and did not explicitly incorporate student activation. Finally, the activities (1), (2), and (3) were never deliberately structured around intended learning outcomes (since these were never consciously established).

4 Conclusion

In the following, I attempt to compare "pre-" versus "post-alignment" courses and report my experiences divided into subjective and objective measures. However, a few reservations should be kept in mind before attempting to reason about the causes and effects of alignment: there are many factors involved that may vary from year to year; as all teachers I gain more experience over time, the student population varies, and the "Susan/Robert ratio" may vary from year to year.

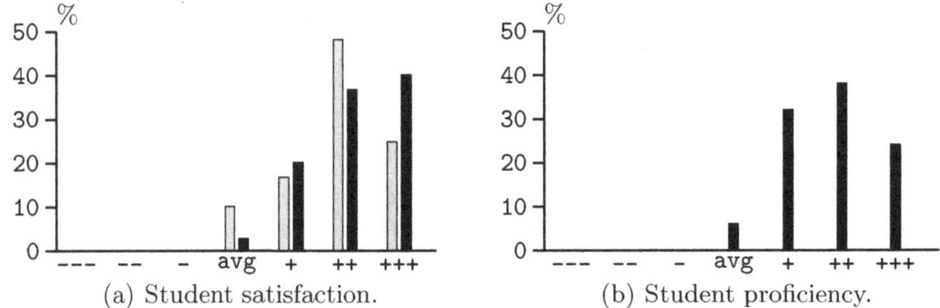

Fig. 5. Self-reported student satisfaction and confidence (on a 7-step scale): pre-alignment in gray (Concurrency 2004 and 2005); post-alignment in black (2006 and 2007). Pre-alignment data is not available for student proficiency.

Subjectively, it is my experience that the theory of constructive alignment provides a solid and constructive answer for (Q1). It provides insights on where and how to optimize the teaching system for student learning in making sure the students have the necessary *incentive* and *support* for learning. It is also my own personal experience that the course and the quality of the projects handed in by the students improved significantly with alignment. Also, before alignment, I primarily acted on my intuition, whereas alignment has influenced my behavior and I am now making conscious and informed choices. I am now aware of different pedagogical possibilities and, perhaps more importantly, of the implications different dispositions are likely to have on student learning.

Objectively, I have quantitative data from student self-evaluation questionaires, reporting on *student satisfaction* (with the teaching) both before and after the implementation of alignment:

	Year	No. of students	No. of evaluations	Percent%
Pre-alignment	2004	29	10	63
	2005	26	24	92
Post-alignment	2006	17	16	94
	2007	22	19	90

In 2004, the evaluations were conducted on the last day which featured a "bonus lecture" on concurrency abstractions in C++ which was not on the exam curriculum; hence the low attendence and number of evaluations.

Step number	Competence (abbreviated):	Pre-alignment (SOLO levels)	Post-alignment (SOLO levels)
n/a	• ~~*memorize*~~ content..	2	-
#1	• *construct* models..	3	3
	• *apply* solutions..	4	4
	• *relate* model/spec..	-	4
#2	• *test* models..	2	2
	• *define* properties..	2	2
	• *verify* models..	3	3
	• *analyze* models..	-	4
	• *compare* models..	-	4
#3	• *implement* models..	3	3
	• *relate* model/impl..	-	4

Fig. 6. Pre- versus post-alignment courses compared w.r.t. the SOLO levels directly involved. For each objective; when explicitly *tested* and *trained* for, the SOLO level of the objective is indicated (otherwise, a dash "-" is given).

Figure 5a plots student satisfaction as reported by themselves on a seven-step scale in a questionnaire at the end of the course; the gray bars depict the distribution of the answers in the pre-alignment courses (2004 and 2005), while the black bars illustrate the situation for the post-alignment courses (2006 and 2007). The students appear slightly more satisfied after alignment which can also be taken to mean that implementing alignment did not compromise student satisfaction.

However, student satisfaction should not be over-estimated; although a positive sign, it need not correlate with student learning. It is much more interesting to compare student self-reported proficiency in the area of study after the course. Unfortunately, I did not evaluate student proficiency before I got introduced to educational theories, notably to *evaluation theory* [6]. Hence, only the post-alignment (black) data is available as presented in Fig. 5b. Although generally positive, without the pre-alignment data it is hard to draw firm conclusions as to the effect of alignment from the evaluations.

If we compare the pre- and post-alignment courses with respect to the SOLO levels involved (those tested for on the exam and trained for during teaching activities), we get an interesting picture. The two rightmost columns of Fig. 6 show the SOLO levels of the learning activities involved in the pre-alignment and post-alignment courses, respectively; a dash "-" is given when the learning objectives were not *tested* and *trained* for. Evidently, alignment has facilitated a significant increase in the SOLO levels involved, in tune with Biggs' definition of "good teaching". The pre-alignment courses predominantly involved lower-level SOLO 2 and 3 activities with most of the level 4 activities completely missing. The post-alignment courses, on the other hand, managed to explicitly incorporate the intended higher-level-4 objectives (*relate*, *analyze*, *compare*, and *relate*), while discouraging the low-level memorization activity.

In 2006, one of the students wrote the following in the anonymous course evaluation which pretty much captures exactly what I was aiming (and hoping) for:

> **Overall:** *"This course has been awesome! It took me a while to be able to think in models, but I saw the light along the way."*

Teaching: *"Lectures have been great, the theoretical exercise classes have been rewarding and the feedback has been immense and insightful"*

Exercises: *"I did not have a lot of time to do the exercises, but they seemed relevant from week to week."*

Project: *"The mini project was a good and solid exercise in analyzing a problem, making a model and implementing it. A very good exercise!"*

Finally, I believe we need to move away from considering the exam a "necessary evil" to instead recognize and perceive it as a powerful pedagogical and motivational instrument.

Acknowledgments. The author would like to acknowledge John Biggs, Bettina Dahl Søndergaard, Torben K. Jensen, Anne Mette Mørcke, Mogens Nielsen, and Michael Schwartzbach for valuable comments and suggestions. Also, thanks to Jacob Andersen, Søren Besenbacher, and Martin Mosegaard, for serving as TAs on the course, providing me with continual feedback.

References

1. Angelo, T.A., Cross, P.K.: Classroom Assessment Techniques: A Handbook for College Teachers (Jossey Bass Higher and Adult Education Series), Jossey-Bass (February 1993)
2. Biggs, J.: Teaching for Quality Learning at University. The Society for Research into Higher Education and Open University Press (2003)
3. Biggs, J., Collis, K.F.: Evaluating the Quality of Learning: The SOLO Taxonomy. Academic Press, New York (1982)
4. Bloom, B.S.: Taxonomy of educational objectives: the classification of educational goals. In: Handbook 1: Cognitive Domain, David McKay Company, Inc, New York (1970)
5. Brabrand, C.: Teaching Teaching & Understanding Understanding. 19-minute (award-winning) short-film, Aarhus University Press (October 2006), Written & Directed by Brabrand, C. Produced by Brabrand, C. Andersen, J., `http://www.daimi.au.dk/~brabrand/short-film/`
6. Dahler-Larsen, P.: Den Rituelle Reflektion–om evaluering i organisationer. Syddansk Universitetsforlag (1998)
7. Frandsen, G.S., Schwartzbach, M.I.: A singular choice for multiple choice. In: ITiCSE-WGR 2006: Working Group Reports on ITiCSE on Innovation and Technology in Computer Science Education, pp. 34–38. ACM Press, New York (2006)
8. Gale, J., Steffe, L.P.: Constructivism in Education. Lawrence Erlbaum, Mahwah (1995)
9. Klopfer, L.E.: Student behavior and science content categories and subcategories for a science program. University of Pittsburgh, Learning Research and Development Center, WP-54, pp. 1–62 (1970)
10. Magee, J., Kramer, J.: Concurrency: State Models & Java Programs. John Wiley & Sons, Inc., New York (1999)
11. Marton, F., Booth, S.: Learning and Awareness. Lawrence Erlbaum, Mahwah (1997)

12. Pegg, J., Tall, D.: The fundamental cycle of concept construction underlying various theoretical frameworks. Zentralblatt für Didaktik der Mathematik (ZDM) 37(6), 468–475 (2005)
13. Piaget, J.: Genetic Epistemology. Columbia University, New York (1970)

A Project Specification

Here is the specification of the *"Banana Republic"* project, as given to the students (Figs. 7,8):

Banana Republic:

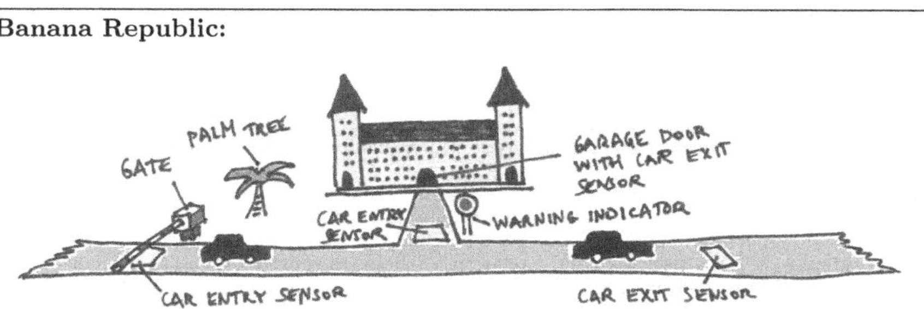

Textual specification:

A one-way road passes by the presidential palace in the *"Banana Republic"*. In order not to delay his excellency, El Presidente, and to make him avoid too close contact with the population, a gate has been mounted (to the west) so that access to the road may be restricted (by closing the gate). Underneath the gate is a car entry sensor which detects cars passing by the gate when it is open. The road also has a car exit sensor (to the east) which detects when cars exit the area in front of the palace. The garage door of the palace is equipped with a sensor to detect when the presidential car is leaving the palace; an entry sensor detects when it enters the main road, and a warning signal (`on`/`off`) indicates whether or not cars are on the road (i.e., whether or not it is safe for the president to enter the road).

You may assume that `N=4` cars drive on the main road and that they "reappear" to the west when they drive away to the east (as in the old PacMan games). Cars may overtake each other, even in the crossing area (which has a capacity of, say, `M=3` cars). You may also assume that his excellency, El Presidente, only leaves the palace and that his car reappears at the palace when he has driven off (to the east).

Your job is to make sure (using a *controller*) that no other cars are on the road in the area in front of the palace at the same time as El Presidente's. The controller receives input from the sensors and may control the gate (`open`/`close`) and warning indicator signal (`on`/`off`).

When El Presidente is nowhere in sight, the gate should be open so the cars may pass into the restricted road without delay, however when El Presidente is coming, he should be allowed to safely enter the road as soon as possible - even in congested rush-hour traffic.

(a) Specification.

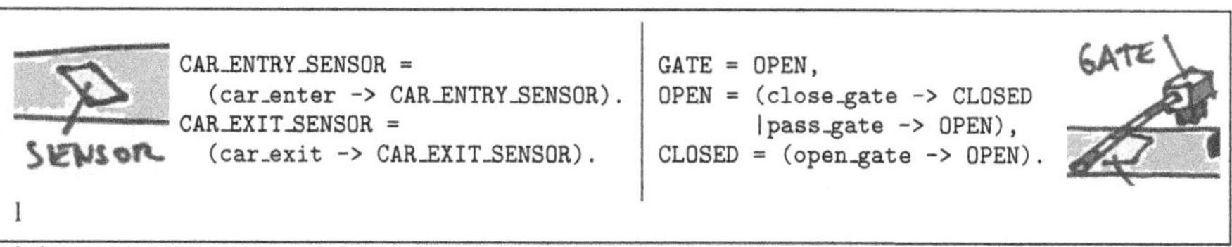

(b) Processes given. (For details of the FSP modelling language, we refer to [10].)

Fig. 7. Project specification

Your task: [specification $\mapsto$ (unsafe) model $\mapsto$ (safe) model $\mapsto$ (safe) implementation]:

(a) Construct a model of the (unsafe) `BANANA_REPUBLIC` (i.e., without a *controller*).
(b) Test your model to see that collisions with El Presidente can occur (give trace).
(c) Define a safety property, `NO_CRASH`, that can check that collisions with El Presidente can occur.
(d) Verify that collisions with El Presidente can occur (using the above safety property).
(e) Now construct a *controller* and add it to the system to model a `SAFE_BANANA_REPUBLIC` (such that collisions with El Presidente can no longer occur).
(f) Then verify formally that collisions with El Presidente can no longer occur (with the controller constraining the behavior).
(g) Subsequently add a liveness property, `LIVE_PRESIDENTE`, formally verifying that El Presidente is always eventually permitted to enter the restricted road even in congested rush-hour traffic.
(h) Finally, implement your (safe) model in Java as closely to your model as possible (and give a UML diagram of its structure).

(a) Project task.

Document everything in a small written report which should (at least) include:

(1) Discussions of relevant problematic issues;
(2) Explanations of your solutions and motivations for your solutions;
(3) For step (a), give an explanation of the meaning of all actions in terms of all processes;
(4) For step (a) & (e), a discussion of the relationship between your model and the specification.
(5) For step (h), a discussion of the relationship between your model and your implementation.

The report should be self-contained in the sense that we should be able to understand your solution and the motivations for your solution without having to look into the model or implementation. This means that it should for instance include all necessary and relevant parts of the model and implementation, underlining relevant discussions in the report.

Be concise and to the point (not necessarily "the more explanation the better"); include only issues relevant to the problem at hand (irrelevant issues may subtract points). This is what wins you points (there are no points for an unmotivated solution "out of the blue").

(b) Project report.

The grading is done relative to the *course objectives*; i.e., that you demonstrate the ability to:

- ***construct*** (unsafe and safe) models of the "Banana Republic" (from the specification);
- ***apply*** standard solutions to common concurrency problems in the "Banana Republic";
- ***relate*** your (unsafe and safe) models of the "Banana Republic" to the specification;
- ***test*** your unsafe model and exhibit a collision trace (using the LTSA tool);
- ***define*** the `NO_CRASH` and `LIVE_PRESIDENTE` properties relevant for the "Banana Republic";
- ***verify*** your (unsafe and safe) models wrt. the above properties (using the LTSA tool);
- ***implement*** your safe model in Java; *and*
- ***relate*** your implementation to your safe model.

(c) Project evaluation criteria.

Fig. 8. Project task, report, and grading

Teaching Modelling and Validation of Concurrent Systems Using Coloured Petri Nets

Lars Michael Kristensen* and Kurt Jensen

Department of Computer Science, University of Aarhus
IT-parken, Aabogade 34, DK-8200 Aarhus N, Denmark
{lmkristensen,kjensen}@daimi.au.dk

Abstract. This paper describes a course on modelling and validation of concurrent systems given by the authors at the Department of Computer Science, University of Aarhus. The course uses Coloured Petri Nets (CPNs) as the formal modelling language for concurrency, and exposes students to the benefits and applications of modelling for designing and reasoning about the behaviour of concurrent systems. After the course the participants will have detailed knowledge of CPNs and practical experience with modelling and validation of concurrent systems. The course emphasises the practical use of modelling and validation and has less focus on the formal foundation of CPNs. The course is based on a new textbook on CPNs.

1 Introduction

To cope with the complexity of modern computing systems, it is crucial to be able to debug and test the central parts of system designs prior to implementation. One way to do this is to build a prototype. Another and often faster way is to build a model. This allows the designer to inspect the model and investigate the behaviour of the system prior to implementation. In this way many design problems and errors can be discovered early in the system development phase.

The course *Coloured Petri Nets — modelling and validation of concurrent systems* discussed in this paper focuses on Coloured Petri Nets (CPNs) [14–18]. CPN is a discrete-event modelling language combining Petri nets [22] and the functional programming language CPN ML which is based on Standard ML [24]. The CPN modelling language is a general purpose graphical modelling language used for communication protocols, data networks, distributed algorithms, workflow systems, embedded systems, and systems in general where concurrency and communication are key characteristics. CPN allows system designers to build models that can be executed and analysed by a computer tool. Simulation of CPN models makes it possible to conduct a detailed investigation of the system behaviour, and to reason about performance properties (such as delays and throughput). State space analysis makes it possible to verify functional properties of the system (such as absence of deadlocks). The course introduces the

* Supported by the Danish Research Council for Technology and Production and the Carlsberg Foundation.

K. Jensen, W. van der Aalst, and J. Billington (Eds.): ToPNoC I, LNCS 5100, pp. 19–34, 2008.

participants to the CPN modelling language, its analysis methods, and supporting computer tools. It also includes presentation of industrial projects where CPNs have been used for the modelling and validation of systems.

The course is divided into two parts, each lasting 7 weeks, and participants may choose to follow only the first 7 weeks. Each part of the course corresponds to five ECTS which means that the participants are required to use 1/3 of their study-time on the course. The aim of the first part of the course is that the participants will obtain detailed knowledge of CPNs and experience with modelling and validation of small concurrent systems. The aim of the second part is that the participants will have practical experience with the application of CPNs and CPN Tools [10] for modelling and validation of larger concurrent systems. The working methods of the second part will also train the participants to plan and complete projects and to communicate professional issues.

The only prerequisite for the course is that the participants must have completed the first two short introductory programming courses of their bachelor studies. These two programming courses correspond to ten ECTS. This means that we assume that the participants are familiar with conventional programming language concepts such as variables, types, procedures, and modules. The overall approach taken in the course is to introduce the CPN modelling language in a similar way as programming languages are introduced, i.e., through concrete examples that illustrate the constructs in the modelling language and also the more general concepts of concurrency, synchronisation, and communication. The course is an optional advanced course, and the majority of the participants are in their third to fifth year of studies when taking the course. The course usually has 20 – 30 participants. It is important to emphasise that the course presented in this paper is a specialised course on the CPN modelling language and supporting computer tools. There are several other courses in the curriculum at our computer science department aimed at giving a more general introduction to the theoretical and practical aspects of concurrency. The theoretically oriented courses include courses on automata, concurrency, and model checking that introduce the students to labelled transition systems, CSP, CCS, and temporal logic. The practically oriented courses include courses on network protocols and internetworking, operating systems, and distributed systems.

In the following sections we present and discuss the intended learning outcomes of the course (Sect. 2), the teaching and assessment methods used (Sect. 3), give an example of a representative student project (Sect. 4), and present the new textbook on CPNs on which the course is based (Sect. 5). Finally, we discuss experiences and further development of the course (Sect. 6).

2 Intended Learning Outcomes

The formulation of the intended learning outcomes of the course is based upon the Structure of the observed learning outcome (SOLO) taxonomy of Biggs [1] which provides a tool and framework for specifying the learning outcomes of a course. The SOLO taxonomy has five levels (1–5) determining a hierarchy of learning competences where level 5 is the highest level:

Level 1: **Prestructural** Is the very bottom level where no competences have been obtained.
Level 2: **Unistructural** Characterised by verbs such as memorise, identify, and recognise. These verbs represent a minimalistic, but sufficient understanding of each topic viewed in isolation.
Level 3: **Multistructural** Characterised by verbs such as *classify*, *describe*, and *list*. These verbs represents solid competences within each topic and basic understanding of the boundaries for each topic.
Level 4: **Relational** Characterised by verbs such as *apply*, *integrate*, *analyse*, and *explain*. These verbs represent competences for orchestrating facts and theory, action, and purpose.
Level 5: **Extended abstract** Characterised by verbs such as *theorise*, *hypothesise*, *generalise*, *reflect*, and *generate*. These verbs represent competences at a level extending beyond what has been dealt with in the actual teaching.

The SOLO taxonomy has been adopted by the Faculty of Science at University of Aarhus as a general means for formulating learning outcomes and coincides with the introduction of a new Danish assessment scale with seven grades and an ECTS certification process currently being undertaken by the University of Aarhus. The purpose of the new grading scale is to measure more explicitly than earlier the extent to which course participants have achieved the intended learning outcomes. Within our department, a variant of the SOLO taxonomy has been developed with verbs specifically aimed at computer science competences. When specifying the intended learning outcomes for the course below, we will highlight (using bold and italics) the verbs that map into the five levels of SOLO taxonomy. The SOLO level to which a given verb belongs is written in superscript following the verb. For the first part of the course discussed in this paper six *intended learning outcomes* (ILOs) given in Table 1 have been defined. These intended learning objectives express what the participants are expected to be able to do at the end of the course. In the following we discuss each of the learning outcomes in more detail.

ILO1 is concerned with learning the constructs of the CPN modelling language which includes net structure concepts and the CPN ML inscription language, and the concepts related to hierarchical and timed CPN models. ILO1 also includes concepts such as binding elements, steps, concurrency and conflict.

In ILO2, we require the participants to be able to formally define and explain the syntax and semantics of CPNs. The purpose of ILO2 is for the participants to understand that CPNs rely on a formal foundation, and presenting the formal definitions means that participants explore CPNs from a different angle than just the example driven introduction to the language. In that sense, the formal definitions represent a complementary view of the modelling constructs that can help the participants to further consolidate their understanding. ILO2 does not

Table 1. Intended learning objectives–first part of the course

ILO1	***explain***^{4} the constructs and concepts in the CPN modelling language
ILO2	***define***^{2} and ***explain***^{4} the syntax and semantics of CPNs
ILO3	***define***^{2} and ***explain***^{4} properties for characterising the behaviour of concurrent systems
ILO4	***explain***^{4} the basic concepts and techniques underlying state space analysis methods
ILO5	***apply***^{4} CPNs and CPN Tools for modelling and validation of smaller concurrent systems
ILO6	***judge***^{4} the practical application of CPNs for modelling and validation of concurrent systems

require the participants to be able to formally define hierarchical CPN models and timed CPN models. The formal definitions for this limited subset of the CPN modelling language can be introduced using simple mathematical concepts.

In ILO3 we require the participants to be able to define and explain the standard behavioural properties of CPNs (such as boundedness properties, dead markings, and live transitions) and quantitative performance properties (such as delay, throughput, and utilisation). These concepts are used when the students work with the analysis methods of CPNs which include simulation, simulation-based performance analysis, and state space analysis.

ILO4 relates to the state space analysis methods of CPNs. Here we require the participants to be able to explain the concepts of state spaces and strongly connected component graphs. Furthermore, we require the participants to be able to explain how the standard behavioural properties of CPN models can be checked from the state space and strongly connected component graphs.

ILO5 specifies that the participants must have operational knowledge of the topics taught in the course, i.e., be able to apply the modelling language and the analysis methods in practice.

The purpose of ILO6 is that participants must be able to determine whether CPNs are an appropriate choice for modelling and validating a system within some domain, i.e., determine whether CPNs are suited for modelling the system considered given the properties to be validated.

For the second part of the course three intended learning outcomes given in Table 2 have been defined. The purpose of ILO7 and ILO8 is for the participants to be able to model and validate concurrent systems of a size and complexity that appears in representative system development projects. The purpose of ILO9 is that participants must be able to convey results and issues from modelling and validation to colleagues.

We discuss the learning outcomes further in the next section when explaining how the teaching methods have been chosen to support the participants in achieving the intended learning outcomes, and how the assessment methods have been chosen to measure whether the participants have achieved the intended learning outcomes.

Table 2. Intended learning objectives–second part of the course

ILO7	***construct***[3] and ***structure***[3] CPN models of larger concurrent systems
ILO8	***apply***[4] analysis methods for CPNs for validation of larger concurrent systems
ILO9	***discuss***[5] the application of CPNs for modelling and validation of larger concurrent systems

3 Teaching and Assessment Methods

The teaching and assessment methods used in the course have been chosen according to the theory of *constructive alignment* [1]. In short, this theory states that the intended learning outcomes should be the focus point of the course and the teaching methods and activities used should be chosen so that they support the participants in achieving the intended learning outcomes. Similarly, the assessment methods used (e.g., the form of the exam) must be chosen so that they measure the degree to which the participants have fulfilled the intended learning outcomes. The overall goal of constructive alignment is to encourage and motivate students to take a *deep approach* to learning in contrast to a *surface approach*. The surface approach is characterised by students doing the tasks with a minimum of effort using low cognitive level activities, while a deep approach to learning is characterised by students actively working with the topics using higher cognitive level activities. This means that the focus of constructive alignment is the process and products that results from the learning activities of the students. A fun and easy way to learn more about the SOLO taxonomy and the difference between surface learning and deep learning is to watch the award winning 19-min short-film *Teaching teaching and understanding understanding* [2] which is available via the Internet. Another example of applying the theory of constructive alignment in a course on concurrency can be found in [3].

As explained earlier, the course is divided into two parts. The first part of the course has a duration of 7 weeks (a so-called quarter) and is organised into 14 sessions as detailed in Table 3. Each session lasts for 2 hours. It can be seen that the course is a combination of lectures and workshops. In the three workshops, the participants work in groups of two to three persons in front of a PC using CPN Tools to solve exercises and projects. The lecturers are present to help with technical questions and issues related to the projects and exercises. In our experience, these workshops are very useful as it enables face-to-face discussions with the participants and is effective in highlighting issues that need to be discussed in more detail—and which can then be discussed on-demand at the workshops. In this respect the workshops facilitate an interactive teaching-learning environment. Furthermore, the intention of the workshops is to support the intended learning outcomes of the course, in particular learning objective ILO5, but the workshops also facilitate learning outcomes ILO1–ILO4 as it stimulates discussions among the participants of the concepts covered.

Table 3. Sessions in the first part of the course

Session	Topic	Teaching method	Material
1	Why modelling and validation?	Lecture	Chapter 1 of [17]
2	Basic concepts	Lecture	Chapter 2 of [17]
3	CPN ML programming	Lecture	Chapter 3 of [17]
4	Modelling	Workshop	Small exercises
5	Formal definition of CPNs	Lecture	Chapter 4 of [17]
6	Modelling	Workshop	Project 1
7	Hierarchical CPNs	Lecture	Chapter 5 of [17]
8	State space analysis (1)	Lecture	Chapters 7 and 8 of [17]
9	State space analysis (2)	Lecture	Chapters 7 and 8 of [17]
10	State space analysis	Workshop	Project 2
11	Timed CPNs	Lecture	Chapter 10 of [17]
12	Performance analysis	Lecture	Chapter 12 of [17]
13	Industrial applications	Lecture	Selected chapters from part II of [17]
14	Course evaluation	Discussion	

The lectures use a series of variants of the protocol system shown in Fig. 1 to introduce the modelling and analysis concepts. Protocols are used because they are easy to explain and understand, and because they involve concurrency, non-determinism, communication, and synchronisation which are key characteristics of concurrent systems. No preliminary knowledge of protocols is assumed. The protocol consists of a *sender* transferring a number of *data packets* to a *receiver*. Communication takes place over an unreliable network, i.e., packets may be lost and overtaking is possible. The protocol uses sequence numbers, acknowledgements, and retransmissions to ensure that the data packets are delivered once and only once and in the correct order at the receiving end. The protocol uses a stop-and-wait strategy, i.e., the same data packet is transmitted until a corresponding acknowledgement is received. A data packet consists of a sequence number and the data payload to be transmitted. An acknowledgement consists of a sequence number specifying the number of the next data packet expected by the receiver. The protocol is simple and unsophisticated, but yet complex enough to illustrate the CPN constructs.

There are two mandatory projects in the first part of the course: project 1 on modelling and project 2 on state space analysis. The projects are conducted in groups and are to be documented in a short five to ten pages page written report. The first project is concerned with extending the CPN model of the stop-and-wait protocol (see Fig. 1) to model a sliding window protocol. The model of the sliding window protocol must be validated using simulation. The second project is concerned with conducting state space analysis of the model developed in project 1 in order to verify the correctness of the protocol. It is interesting that 50–75% of the groups usually discover errors in their design of

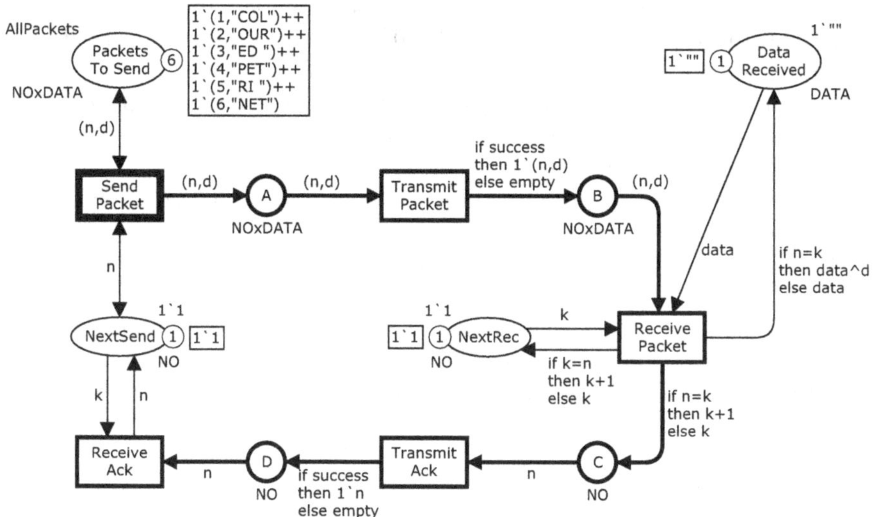

Fig. 1. Basic version of protocol model used as a running example

the sliding window protocol from project 1—errors that were not discovered by the simulation conducted as part of project 1. This means that the participants experience first-hand the power of verification techniques such as state spaces.

Both projects must be approved in order to enrol for the exam. This ensures that the participants have fulfilled learning objective ILO5 before taking the exam. The exam is a 20-min oral exam and the participants have approximately 1 week for preparation of the exam. At the exam each examinee draws one of five exam questions covering ILO1-4. ILO6 cannot be directly accessed with the current form of the mandatory projects and oral exam. Hence, it is only indirectly covered via lecture 13 on industrial applications of CPNs.

The second part of the course is organised in a different manner as the main aim is to consider modelling and validation of larger concurrent systems. In this part of the course, the participants conduct a larger modelling and validation project. There is a large degree of freedom in defining the project which is to be done in groups of two to three persons. There are no conventional lectures during this part of the course, but there are two progress workshops where the groups make a 25-min oral presentation of the current state of their project. In the first progress workshop, the focus is mainly on modelling, and the groups discuss their model with the lecturers and the other participants who provide feedback. In the second progress workshop, the focus is mainly on the validation part of the project. The project is typically based on a natural language description of a larger concurrent system. In the next section we give an example of a representative project conducted in the second part of the course. The following is a partial list of systems that have served as a basis for the project over the past three years:

- Distributed file systems. This project was based upon Chap. 8 of [8].
- Dynamic host configuration protocol (DHCP). This project was based upon the Request for Comments document [11] specifying DHCP.
- Data dissemination protocol. This project was based upon the paper [4].
- Dynamic MANET on-demand routing protocol (DYMO). This project was based upon the Internet-Draft [6] specifying DYMO.
- Internet key exchange protocol (IKE).This project was based upon the Request for Comments document [19] specifying IKEv2.
- Mutual exclusion algorithms. This project was based upon selected algorithms from the book [21].
- PathFinder scheduling mechanism. This project was based upon the description that can be found in the paper [13].
- WebPic communication protocol. This project was based upon the document [9] describing the protocol.

The participants are free to choose the system to be used as a basis for the project, but we also provide a set of five to ten project proposals. Many of the projects have focused on communication protocols and distributed algorithms, but it is possible to choose systems from other domains such as workflow systems, manufacturing systems, and embedded systems.

The assessment of this part of the course is based on an evaluation of the written report which is required to have a length of 15–20 pages, and an individual oral exam where each participant is required to make a presentation of the group project. The final grade is the average of the grade for the written report and the grade for the oral performance. The act of constructing a larger model and validating it is what supports learning outcomes ILO7 and ILO8, whereas the progress presentations support ILO9.

4 Example of a Student Project

As a representative example of a project conducted in the second part of the course, we consider a project made by a student group on modelling and validation of the DYMO [6] protocol. A mobile ad-hoc network (MANET) is an infrastructure-less wireless network consisting of a set of mobile nodes, where multi-hop communication is supported by the individual mobile nodes acting as routers. DYMO is a routing protocol being developed by the IETF MANET working group [20] and is specified in a 35-page Internet-draft giving a natural language specification of the protocol.

Figure 2 shows the top-level module of the hierarchical CPN model constructed by the student group. The CPN model is divided into four main parts represented by the four *substitution transitions* drawn as rectangles with double lines. The Application Layer represents the applications that use the multi-hop routes established by the DYMO Layer. The Network Layer models the transmission of packets over the underlying mobile network, and the Topology part models the mobility of the nodes which causes the topology of the MANET to

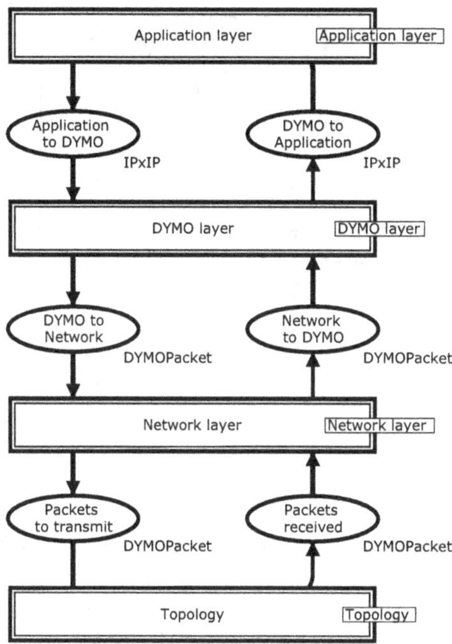

Fig. 2. Top-level module of CPN model of the DYMO routing protocol

be dynamic. The submodules associated with the substitution transitions then specify in detail the operation of the DYMO protocol and the environment in which it operates.

The complete CPN model is a medium-sized model consisting of 9 modules, 18 transitions, 45 places, 17 colour sets, and 20 CPN ML functions. Fig. 3 gives an example of one of the modules in the CPN model. It models the processing of Route Reply (RREP) messages by the mobile nodes. Messages from the underlying network arrives at the Message from network place (drawn as an ellipse) at the lower right. The module captures the two possible cases when receiving a RREP message. Either the RREP message has to be forwarded to the next mobile node on the route being established, or the mobile node is the target for the RREP. These two cases are modelled by the accordingly named transitions (drawn as rectangles). If the RREP is to be forwarded it is put on the place DYMO to network. If the mobile node is the target for the RREP, the message is put on place ReceivedRREP for further processing.

The constructed CPN model captures a large subset of the DYMO protocol specification. Through the organisation of the CPN model into a hierarchically structured set of modules, the students demonstrated that they are able to take a complex system (in this case the DYMO protocol) and construct a CPN model at a good level of abstraction (cf. ILO7). Furthermore, they showed that they can divide the CPN model into modules which naturally reflect the operation of the protocol. In the process of constructing the CPN model, the students

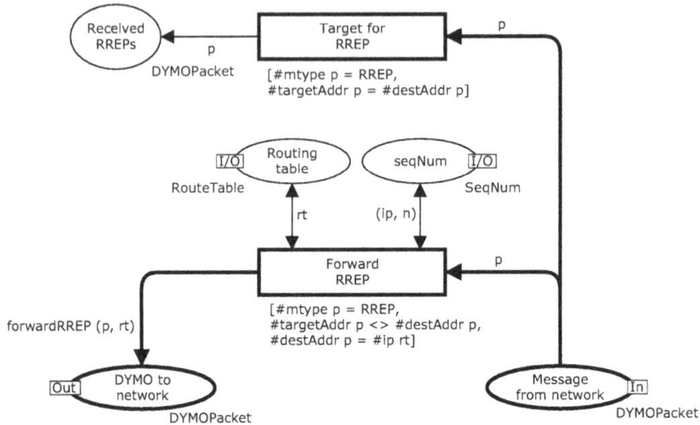

Fig. 3. Low-level module of describing processing of RREP message

discovered several ambiguities and missing parts in the DYMO specification, and they used state space analysis to investigate non-trivial issues related to the operation of the DYMO protocol (cf. ILO8). The project was documented in a 20-page written report that introduced the basic operation of the DYMO protocol, presented the CPN model and the assumptions made in the modelling, and discussed the simulation and state space analysis results obtained (cf. ILO9). A revised version of the project report was later published in [12].

5 Course Material

The course is based on a new textbook [17] that is currently being written by the authors of this paper. The book is organised into two parts. Part I introduces the constructs of the CPN modelling language and presents the analysis methods. This part provides a comprehensive roadmap to the practical use of CPNs. Part II presents a collection of case studies illustrating the practical use of CPN modelling and validation for design, specification, simulation, and verification in a variety of application domains. Most of the examples in Part II are taken from industrial projects. The book is aimed at both university courses and self-study. The book contains more than enough material for a one semester course at an undergraduate or graduate level. A typical course will cover Part I on the basics of CPNs and then select appropriate chapters in Part II depending on the aim of the course. The following is a brief description of chapters contained in Part I of the textbook:

Chapter 1: *Introduction to modelling and validation.* This chapter gives a motivation for modelling and validation of concurrent systems and explains how they can be used in system development projects. It also discusses the benefits and limitations of the techniques, and provides a very brief overview of CPNs and CPN Tools.

Chapter 2: *Basic concepts.* This chapter introduces the building blocks of the CPN modelling language, including net structure (places, transitions, and arcs), inscriptions (colour sets, initial marking, arc expressions, and guards), and enabling and occurrence of binding elements and steps.

Chapter 3: *CPN ML programming.* This chapter presents the CPN ML programming language for defining colour sets and functions, declaring variables, and writing inscriptions in CPN models. This chapter provides a comprehensive introductory road map to the CPN ML programming language.

Chapter 4: *Formal definition of Coloured Petri Net.* This chapter gives a formal definition of the syntax and semantics of the CPN modelling language as informally introduced in Chap. 2. The chapter formally defines multi-sets and associated operations, the elements of a CPN model, and the enabling and occurrence rules. It also introduces and explains the diamond rule specifying that a step can be divided into substeps, and that executing all substeps (in any order) results in the same marking as executing the original step.

Chapter 5: *Hierarchical Coloured Petri Nets.* This chapter shows how a CPN model can be organised as a set of modules, which is similar to how programs are organised into modules. It introduces the concept of modules, port and socket places, substitution transitions, and module instances. It also introduces fusion places and fusion sets.

Chapter 6: *Formal definition of hierarchical Coloured Petri Nets.* This chapter formally defines the syntax and semantics of hierarchical CPN models as informally introduced in Chap. 5.

Chapter 7: *State space analysis and behavioural properties.* This chapter introduces the basic state space method of CPNs and shows how it can be used to investigate the behavioural properties. The chapter introduces the concepts of state spaces, strongly connected component graphs, and reachability, boundedness, home, liveness, and fairness properties.

Chapter 8: *Advanced state space methods.* This section gives a brief survey of and introduction to a number of state space methods applicable in the context of CPNs for alleviating the state explosion problem.

Chapter 9 *Formal definition of state space analysis and behavioural properties.* This chapter formally defines state spaces and behavioural properties informally introduced in Chap. 7.

Chapter 10: *Timed Coloured Petri Nets.* This chapter shows how timing information can be added to CPN models. This makes it possible to evaluate how efficiently a system performs its operations, as well as model and validate real-time systems, where the correctness of the system relies on the proper timing of the events. The chapter introduces the concepts of time inscriptions, time stamps, global clock, and the enabling and occurrence rules for timed CPN models.

Chapter 11: *Formal definition of timed Coloured Petri Nets.* This chapter formally defines timed CPN models as informally introduced in Chap. 10.

Chapter 12: *Simulation-based performance analysis.* This chapter shows how the performance of systems can be investigated using simulation. It introduces performance measures, data collection, simulation replications, and statistical processing of the collected data.

Chapter 13: *Behavioural Visualisation.* This chapter discusses the use of visualisation that allows for the presentation of design ideas and analysis results using concepts from the application domain. This is particularly important in discussions with people and colleagues unfamiliar with CPN models.

The book is primarily aimed at readers interested in the practical use of CPNs. This is reflected in the presentation of the material. All concepts and constructs are informally introduced through examples followed by the formal definition of the concept. We have decided to include the formal definitions of the CPN modelling language and analysis methods for the following reasons. Firstly, including the formal definitions resolves any ambiguity that may be left in the informal explanations. Secondly, it means that the book can be used by readers interested in studying the underlying theory of CPNs. The material is, however, organised such that the practically-oriented reader can skip the chapters containing the formal definitions. This underpins the important property that CPNs can be taught and learned without studying the associated formal definitions.

The book can be seen as an update of the three-volume book *Coloured Petri Nets. Basic concepts, analysis methods, and practical use* authored by Kurt Jensen in 1992-1997 [14–16]. The CPN language and analysis methods described in the new book are very close to those presented in the earlier three-volume book. The new book gains from the experience on teaching [7, 23] and using CPNs over the last 10 years—by the research group of the authors and by the more than 5,000 people who have licences for CPN Tools.

6 Experiences and Outlook

The course and the textbook have been developed over the last three years where the course discussed in this paper has been given four times (2005, 2006, 2007, and 2008). Throughout this period we have gradually refined and revised the course material and textbook based upon the feedback received from the course participants and our own experiences.

At the end of both parts of the course we use approximately 30-min together with the participants on evaluating and discussing the course in an informal way. This informal evaluation is supplemented by a more formal on-line evaluation of the course organised by the Faculty of Science. Table 4 provides a summary of the evaluation for the version of the course that was given in the spring of 2007. Altogether there were eight participants that filled out the on-line evaluation form and each "*" in a table entry represents the feedback of one participant. This means that a single participant represents 12, 5% of the replies and the evaluation results should therefore be interpreted with some care. Still, the feedback provides a useful indication of the participants' view on the course.

Table 4. Summary of on-line participant evaluation–spring 2007

	To a very large extent	To a large extent	To some extent	To a lesser extend	Not at all
Were course goals achieved	*	*******			
Did content match description	**	*****	*		
Was the course interesting	*	*****	**		
Was the course difficult			***	****	*
	<4	5–8	9–12	13–16	17–20
Hours used		***	*****		
	Very good	Good	Either way	Bad	Very bad
Learning outcome	*	******		*	
Lectures	*	*****	**		
Workshops	*	***	****		
Textbook	*	******	*		
Overall evaluation	*	*******			

The evaluations that we have received are in general very positive. In terms of achieving the course goals, content, and level of interest the participants are positive. It is also interesting to observe that the participants do not find the course to be particularly difficult. Participants are also positive with respect to learning outcomes, lectures, workshops, and the textbook. The participants are expected to use about 1/3 of their study time on the course which is approximately 45h, but the feedback shows that they use slightly less. This is probably related to the participants not finding the course difficult which in turn may be related to the workshops, where the participants can work on their project under our supervision and issues that may arise can thereby be resolved quickly. The overall evaluation of the course is also positive.

A main difference compared to [14–16] and how we have taught CPNs earlier, has been to add more material on the CPN ML programming language. Mastering the CPN ML programming language is important in order to apply the CPN modelling language successfully for modelling and validation of concurrent systems. Experience has shown that this is a non-trivial task. The main reason is that CPN ML (which is based on Standard ML) is a functional programming language and therefore has a different conceptual basis than traditional languages such as C, Java, and C++ that the participants are familiar with.

Our teaching activities rely heavily on the integrated use of CPN Tools. This choice is deliberate as it is, in our view, a very motivating factor for the participants and it encourages the participants to work actively with the topics. We have also made the deliberate choice of introducing CPNs directly without first introducing ordinary Petri nets (e.g., place/transitions nets). The main benefit of this is that it immediately enables us to use realistic model examples from the beginning of the course without having to model data manipulation in an unnatural way using net structure. This is possible because the data manipulation can be modelled using very simple CPN ML inscriptions. Demonstrating that realistic examples can be modelled using relatively simple constructs is also a factor which contributes to the motivation of the participants.

A key characteristic of CPNs is that the language has few but powerful modelling constructs. This is an advantage from a teaching perspective since there are relatively few concepts that have to be introduced and mastered. It is also to some extent a disadvantage in practical modelling since certain parts of systems cannot be modelled in a straightforward way. A further development of the CPN modelling language and CPN Tools to include constructs such as queueing places, capacities, and module parametrisation is therefore of interest also from a teaching perspective and would improve the modelling convenience.

The first part of the course relies heavily on the protocol model used as a running example. In the second part of the course, we have observed that it takes some effort from the participants to get started on their own modelling project which is concerned with a different system and sometimes within a different application domain. We plan to improve on this in the next version of the course by integrating more of the examples from part II of the textbook in the first part of the course. Similarly, we plan to have some lectures also in the second part of the course devoted to presenting some larger examples of CPN models. Altogether, this would give the participants a broader perspective on CPN modelling which will be useful when the participants are actively working on their larger project, and hence are facing the challenges of modelling a larger system. This would also further contribute to the learning goals concerned with being able to judge the practical application of CPNs. Finally, we also consider adding a third project on performance analysis in the first part of the course.

We have recently adapted the theory of constructive alignment and the SOLO taxonomy of [1] at our department for describing course aims and learning outcomes. This has not prompted major changes to the way that the course is being taught, but it has been very helpful in making the learning outcomes of the course much more explicit than earlier. The SOLO taxonomy and constructive alignment provides in our opinion, a very good and practically applicable framework for reflecting upon teaching and assessment methods used in a course.

We expect the new textbook to be completed by 2008. Slide sets, CPN models, and suggestions for exercises and projects are available from the course web pages [5]. All of the material is in English. These web pages will eventually evolve into a set of web pages accompanying the textbook. Teachers interested in evaluating and/or using our course material are most welcome to contact us and obtain a draft of the textbook.

Acknowledgments. The authors wish to thank Kristian L. Espensen and Mads K. Kjeldsen for letting us use their CPN model as the representative project example in Sect. 4. The authors also wish to thank the anonymous reviewers for their constructive comments that have helped us to improve the paper.

References

1. Biggs, J.: Teaching for Quality Learning at University, 2nd edn. The Society for Research into Higher Education and Open University Press (2003)
2. Brabrand, C.: Teaching Teaching and Understanding Understanding, `http://www.daimi.au.dk/~brabrand/short-film/`
3. Brabrand, C.: Constructive alignment for teaching model-based design for concurrency. In: Gomes, L., Christensen, S. (eds.) Proc. of 2nd Workshop on Teaching Concurrency (TeaConc 2007), pp. 1–18. University of Podlasie (2007)
4. Brøndsted, J., Kristensen, L.M.: Specification and performance evaluation of two zone dissemination protocols for vehicular ad-hoc networks. In: Proc. of 39th Annual Simulation Symposium, pp. 68–79. IEEE Computer Society, Los Alamitos (2006)
5. Coloured Petri Nets Course–Home page, `http://www.daimi.au.dk/~kris/CPN/`
6. Chakeres, I.D., Perkins, C.E.: Dynamic MANET On-demand (DYMO) Routing. Internet-Draft. Work in Progress (July 2007), `http://www.ietf.org/internet-drafts/draft-ietf-manet-dymo-10.txt`
7. Christensen, S., Jørgensen, J.B.: Coloured Petri Nets: Examples of courses and lessons learned. In: Desel, J., Reisig, W., Rozenberg, G. (eds.) Lectures on Concurrency and Petri Nets. LNCS, vol. 3098, pp. 402–412. Springer, Heidelberg (2004)
8. Colouris, G., Dollimore, J., Kindberg, T.: Distributed Systems–Concepts and Design. Addison-Wesley, Reading (2001)
9. I/O Consulting. Software manual for the webpic evaluation board
10. CPN Tools Homepage, `http://www.daimi.au.dk/CPNTools`
11. Droms, R.: Dynamic Host Configuration Protocol. Request for Comments 2131 (March 1997)
12. Espensen, K.L., Kjeldsen, M.K., Kristensen, L.M.: Towards modelling and verification of the dymo routing protocol for mobile ad-hoc networks. In: Proc. of Workshop on Practical Use of Coloured Petri Nets and the CPN Tools, pp. 243–262 (2007)
13. Holzmann, G., Najm, E., Serhrouchni, A.: SPIN model checking: an introduction. International Journal on Software Tools for Technology Transfer 2, 321–327 (2000)
14. Jensen, K.: Coloured Petri Nets. Basic Concepts, Analysis Methods and Practical Use. Basic Concepts. Monographs in Theoretical Computer Science, vol. 1. Springer, Heidelberg (1992)
15. Jensen, K.: Coloured Petri Nets. Basic Concepts, Analysis Methods and Practical Use. Analysis Methods. Monographs in Theoretical Computer Science, vol. 2. Springer, Heidelberg (1994)
16. Jensen, K.: Coloured Petri Nets. Basic Concepts, Analysis Methods and Practical Use. Practical Use. Monographs in Theoretical Computer Science, vol. 3. Springer, Heidelberg (1997)
17. Jensen, K., Kristensen, L.M.: Coloured Petri Nets–Modelling and Validation of Concurrent Systems. Textbook. Springer, Heidelberg (to appear, 2008)

18. Jensen, K., Kristensen, L.M., Wells, L.: Coloured Petri Nets and CPN Tools for Modelling and Validation of Concurrent Systems. Int. Journal on Software Tools for Technology Transfer (STTT) 9(3-4), 213–254 (2007)
19. Kaufman, C.: Internet Key Exchange (IKEv2) Protocol. Request for Comments 4306 (December 2005)
20. IETF MANET Working Group, `http://www.ietf.org/html.charters/manet-charter.html`
21. Raynal, M.: Algorithms for Mutual Exclusion. North Oxford Academic, New York (1986)
22. Reisig, W.: Petri Nets–An Introduction. EATCS Monographs on Theoretical Computer Science, vol. 4. Springer, Heidelberg (1985)
23. Mortensen, K.H., Christensen, S.: Teaching Coloured Petri Nets–a gentle introduction to formal methods in a distributed systems course. In: Azéma, P., Balbo, G. (eds.) ICATPN 1997. LNCS, vol. 1248, pp. 290–309. Springer, Heidelberg (1997)
24. Ullman, J.D.: Elements of ML Programming. Prentice-Hall, Englewood Cliffs (1998)

Teaching Concurrency Concepts to Freshmen

Christian Eisentraut and Holger Hermanns

Department of Computer Science, Saarland University,
Campus Saarbrücken, 66123 Saarbrücken, Germany
{eisentraut,hermanns}@cs.uni-sb.de

Abstract. Concurrency phenomena are omnipresent in everyday computer practice and their understanding must therefore become a prime focus of contemporary academic education in computer science. This paper devises a concept suitable for teaching concurrency theory to first year Bachelor students in computer science. It is based on Robin Milner's Calculus of Communicating Systems, which is smoothly integrated in an introductory functional programming course. We report on a concrete instantiation of this concept in an introductory course held at Saarland University in winter 2005/2006.

1 Introduction

Concurrent computing is pervading the world and one cannot underestimate its importance in the future. With the arrival of multicore processor desktop systems concurrency needs to be thoroughly understood by every computer scientist in order to use present systems skillfully. This is evident for instance in the *Java* way of dealing with shared memory [12]. Also other disciplines like bio-informatics have started to use ideas from concurrency theory to model enzyme reactions via stochastic process calculi [8,28]. So concurrency theory will be far more widespread in the future then it already is nowadays.

The important role concurrency plays is reflected in the curricula at Saarland University. In our mainly research-oriented Master's and the Bachelor's programs in computer science and bio-informatics, there are a number of courses in which concurrency phenomena arise naturally, and their proper understanding is practically relevant. Examples include principle courses on "Data networks", "Operating Systems, "Verification", and "Database systems". All of these courses are not only found at Saarland University, but are present in the core curriculum of computer science in almost every university in similar form. However, teaching the theoretical basis of concurrency is usually only done — if at all — at a late point in the curriculum. Since concurrency is notoriously difficult to understand, it is kept implicitly in most courses or only dealt with intuitively and not put on a formal basis. This leads to a fractal and shallow understanding of concurrency and students may not be aware of the principal difficulties that come with it. Furthermore, the trend towards multicore system architectures and multithreaded program design is promoted by the soft- and hardware industry. Yet only the benefits of concurrency are exhibited alluringly, neglecting new causes of error

K. Jensen, W. van der Aalst, and J. Billington (Eds.): ToPNoC I, LNCS 5100, pp. 35–53, 2008.

that are very hard to detect — such as deadlocks caused by badly scheduled resource competitions. Universities owe the education of computer scientists that are capable of dealing with the challenges of today and tomorrow! And concurrency definitively is one of them. Our starting point therefore has been to start teaching the foundations of concurrency as early as possible in our curricula.

In this paper, we report on an elaborated approach to put concurrency theory right in the first year of the Bachelor curriculum. At Saarland University, the very first course for starting computer science Bachelor students is called *Programming 1*. Despite its title, the concept of this course does not aim at teaching practical usage of programming languages like *Java* or *C*, but rather focuses on the theoretical foundations needed to understand the principles of computer programming. The course provides students with basic knowledge in important mathematical and algorithmic concepts needed for their further studies such as set theory, discrete mathematics, algorithms and complexity, correctness proofs for programs, formal syntax and semantics of programming languages. Therefore, the course uses Standard-ML (SML) [21], a powerful functional programming language, as a vehicle to introduce the above concepts in the form of "executable mathematics" in a practical environment. The original course has been designed by Smolka [24], and is one of the highest ranked courses according to student feedback.

As it is common to almost all introductory computer science courses, also this course has so far entirely ignored concurrency and instead only focused on aspects of sequential computing. In the sequel, we present how we modified this course to introduce freshmen to concurrency theory, while keeping the flavour of the course of being "executable mathematics". This was put into practise in the course *Programming 1* held in winter 2005/2006.

In a nutshell, we introduce a simplified version of Robin Milner's Calculus of Communicating Systems (CCS) [1,20] together with its underlying operational semantics. The latter is presented as an executable mapping on variations of graphs — after these have been introduced. We make the students implement parts of the semantics in SML, and let them then explore simple CCS examples of mutual exclusion or readers–writers problems. To round off the theoretical concepts, different notions of process equivalences (trace and bisimulation equivalence) are discussed, together with practical aspects sharpening the students awareness of concepts like deadlock-sensitivity and resource contentions in the presence of composition.

To the best of our knowledge this is the first attempt to teach concurrency theory as part of a computer science introductory course, aiming at the students' understanding of a formal model of concurrency, non-determinism and the general problems arising in concurrent computing. Other work so far has concentrated on teaching programming of parallel algorithms [2,5,10,15] or they described complete courses to teach a broad spectrum of concurrency topics, that we consider beyond the scope of first year studies [3,4,19].

This paper is organised as follows. In Section 2 we explain the context in which our teaching efforts are embedded. Section 3 gives a detailed account of the contents we taught to the students in class. Section 4 describes how the developed theory was integrated with practical experiments and programming work. Section 5 reflects on the experiences we gained when teaching, and reports about feedback received from students and colleagues.

2 Context

This section develops the background necessary to understand the way we introduced concurrency. It first provides a short overview of the curricular contents in the first semester of the Bachelor's of Science in computer science at Saarland University, and then details the original setup of the introductory course we started from. Almost all courses are worth 9 ETCS credit points which corresponds[1] to about 270 working hours of the average student. Typically, such a course comprises 4h of lecture and 2h of tutorials per week. The academic year at Saarland University is split into two terms: a winter term followed by a summer term. Each of them comprises a lecture period of 13–14 weeks.

Curricular context. There are no entrance level requirements for the Bachelor programme in computer science at Saarland University, apart from a general university-entrance diploma (German "Abitur" or equivalent). First year students are supposed to have basic knowledge in calculus and linear algebra upon entering the university, but skills in other fields of mathematics or computer science are not demanded or expected. However, the department offers a dedicated preparatory course to bridge from mathematics taught in high school to mathematics relevant for computer science.

The mandatory introductory course in the computer science Bachelor curriculum at Saarland University is *Programming 1.* This course coins the students' perception of computer science and prepares their way through the further course of study. The mathematical basics needed for computer science are introduced in three consecutive courses *Mathematics 1–3* held in the first three teaching terms.

Introductory course. Computer science students at Saarland University usually get in touch with computer science in the course "Programming 1" for the first time. In the following, we give an overview of the contents of this course. In "Programming 1" formal aspects of computer programming are taught using the functional programming language SML as a vehicle for the practical assimilation of the theoretically acquired matters. Originally, the course had the following structure.

- The first part of the course focuses on an introduction to important data structures like lists, trees and graphs and some important algorithms (list and tree traversal, sorting, ...). This is accompanied by practical experiments with their concrete realisations in SML.

[1] Each 30h of student work of the average student is worth one ETCS credit point.

- The second part of the course teaches a mathematically rigorous approach to basic considerations of program verification and (run-time) analysis of programs, based on axiomatic set theory. Program correctness is presented as an integral part of program design, and mainly obtained by induction over well-founded sets combined with termination proofs.
- The third part of the course is dedicated to formal syntax and semantics of programming languages. First, the differences between abstract and concrete syntax of a language are developed. Then, the course focuses on type checking and semantics of programming languages. For illustration, a simple subset of SML is formally specified and serves as a working base. Students are guided through the development of an interpreter for it, which includes *lexing* and *parsing*, *type checking*, *semantics* together with the appropriate data structures, all realised in SML.
- The last part of the course is devoted to the realisation of a virtual machine in SML as well as a compiler from a high-level *imperative* language to the virtual machine's assembler code. The virtual machine and the assembler are again simple, but allow for most elementary features: arithmetic operations, jumps, dynamic heap memory allocation, (recursive) procedure definitions and calls.

The course is one of the highest ranked courses according to the feedback of the students. It is generally considered a challenging but worthwhile and inspiring endeavour. The success ratio among first year students is in the order of 50–70%. Remarkably, it is lower for students who need to retake the course, which might likely be a consequence of the absence of entrance-requirements with respect to mathematic skills. Data collected from questionnaires suggest, passing the course "Programming 1" is strongly related to participation in the optional preparatory course on mathematics, but not related to previous programming experiences of the students outside the university.

3 Course Contents

When we decided to teach the introductory course in computer science in 2005, we considered concurrency theory to be underrepresented in the basic curriculum, despite its increasing impact on the theoretical and practical work of future computer scientists. This was confirmed in discussions inside the faculty, where colleagues from *databases*, *computer graphics*, and *computer architecture* all encouraged us to tackle this problem. We thus decided to extend or modify the freshmen education by a substantial introduction to concurrency theory.

3.1 Pedagogical Considerations

Teaching concurrency to freshmen is not straightforward and we needed to make the following considerations:

- Which aspects of concurrency theory are of maximal benefit to the students for the subsequent courses?

- How can we use general concepts already taught during the preceding parts of the course effectively in order to build up a theory of concurrency?
- Do we need to sacrifice other parts of the course we are focusing on?
- Do we manage to keep the overall flavour of the course?

Given that the introductory course "Programming 1" initiates the students to the world of computer science by advocating the concept of "executable mathematics", we were determined to keep this flavour in our approach. At the same time, the foundational education is at this point not very deep. The students learn about graphs and relations, but have no deep understanding of them yet, and are struggling with the difference between the syntax of an (SML-)program and its semantics.

After some deliberation, we felt that introducing a *basic process calculus* as a *language mapping on graphs* might be a good — and executable — approach. Based on this idea, the other ideas then followed. We decided to incrementally introduce a process calculus of communicating systems. If well - prepared, the students were deemed to be able to implement parts of the semantic mapping themselves in SML. This would enable them to explore classical concurrency examples, such as the dining philosophers problem in their own implementation.

These considerations led us to choosing Robin Milner's CCS [20] with its underlying semantic notion of labelled transition systems (LTS) as a model of concurrency. Labelled transitions systems are a foundational model in computer science, also outside the core world of concurrency. As a pragmatic side effect, since both SML and CCS are originating in Robin Milner's work, the students had few problems to believe that both fit together well.

When we then further shaped the contents we felt that we can only successfully teach this material towards the end of the course, when the first three quarters of the original course material have been covered. We finally decided to branch off the original course setup in the middle of the third part, right after lexer and parser were discussed. This decision lead to the following revision.

Course modification. Instead of studying type checking and semantics and their implementation for a subset of SML as an example programming language, we take fragments of CCS in a step-by-step fashion, always linking to lexing, parsing and semantics. The fourth part, where originally a virtual machine for a simple imperative programming language was to be developed, is in principle kept by us, but in a radically simplified form, in the sense that now the virtual machine is just a CCS interpreter.

All in all, this strategy allowed us to keep most of the original course contents in place, except for (1) diving deeply in aspects of type checking and semantics in the presence of recursive functions and (2) exposing the students to simple imperative programming. At the same time, we managed to teach theoretically important concepts, such as concurrency, non-determinism, interaction, operational semantics, trace and bisimulation equivalence, and compositionality.

At the point where we branch off from the original course contents, the students are already familiar with the following mathematical and programming principles, most of which will be used in the continuation of our course: *basic axiomatic set theory* introducing Boolean algebra, relations, functions, recursion, and inductive proofs; *principal concepts of programming languages* including grammars, type checking, semantics, inference rule and trees; *properties of programs* including termination and correctness, semantical equivalences of programs, time complexity; *basic data structures* such as lists, trees, graphs and their representation in SML; *principles of recursive algorithms* such as list and tree traversals, sorting, divide-and-conquer; *SML basics* and some advanced features (such as polymorphism). We proceed in three steps when introducing the notations to our students.

- In a first step, we familiarise the students with the model of labelled transition systems (LTS), as a mild extension of directed graphs.
- We then introduce a language (a subset of CCS) used to describe these models, illustrating LTS as the genuine interpretation (i.e., semantics). We call elements of this language *processes.*
- In a third step, we teach concurrency via the composition of processes interacting on complementary signals, yielding full CCS.

We think that proceeding this way appears very natural to the students, as soon as they are familiarised with the fact that processes (in their view: computer programs) can be described by states and the accomplishable transitions between states.

3.2 Graphs as a Model for Concurrency

We embark on our endeavour of teaching concurrency to freshmen by introducing labelled transition systems, in the following called labelled graphs, as a way to model the communicative aspects of programs, which abstracts away from other (internal) computations. However, the introduction at this point in the course is only very intuitive and not detailed and serves merely as a motivation. Experience has shown, that students without a decent background in concurrency theory are generally not aware of the fact, that many everyday systems, like mobile phones, vending machines, etc. are indeed communicating systems. Moreover, they are mostly completely unaware of the enormous complexity that communication adds to systems and that their analysis demands special methods. However, after this affirmative motivation we focus on the notion of a labelled graph as a minor extension to directed graphs, which have already been introduced in the course. We use the following definition:

Definition 1. *A (directed) labelled graph G is a triple (V, M, E) with V an arbitrary set of vertices, M an arbitrary set of labels, and $E \subseteq V \times M \times V$ a set of directed labelled edges.*

We only use labelled graphs where V is countable and M is finite. Now a process is easily defined as a graph together with an initial vertex, intuitively denoting the initial state of the process, which is in turn represented by the graph.

Definition 2. *A process is a pair (G, v) where $G = (V, M, E)$ is a graph and $v \in V$ is vertex of G representing the initial vertex.*

We avoid at this point to emphasise the meaning of labelled graphs as a model of concurrency, instead treat it more as an academic object. The students are already familiar with graphs and can reuse acquired knowledge. We only provide hints that a process might be an abstract view on what a computer program does. Giving this motivation allows the students to see that the previously introduced rather abstract concept of graphs has concrete applications in computer science.

3.3 Graph Languages

We now introduce our language CCS in three steps: (1) L_0, a language for acyclic processes; (2) L, a language for processes; (3) CCS, a language for communicating processes.

The semantics of L_0 maps terms to directed labelled graphs over label set M *without* cycles. The reason why L_0 does not allow for cycles is that cycles correspond to recursive process definitions and recursion is generally hard to understand, especially for beginners. Therefore at first we leave it out, and discuss some language properties and examples, before including recursive expressions (in L), and then communication, concurrency and interaction (in CCS).

Our presentation of the syntax of L_0 is at the same time used to introduce the notion of *abstract grammar*. The abstract grammar of L_0 is

$$P \in L_0 \quad = \quad 0 \mid a.P \mid P + P$$

where $a \in M$. In terms of processes, 0 intuitively denotes a processes, that cannot perform any action. $a.P$ denotes a process that can perform the action a and then behaves like P. The term $P + Q$ denotes a process that non-deterministically behaves either like P or Q. The formal semantic definition we used is as follows: Let

$$\mathcal{G}_{L_0} = \{(L_0, M, E) \mid E \subseteq L_0 \times M \times L_0\}$$

be the set of all graphs over M with vertex set L_0. The function

$$[\![\ \_\ ]\!] \in L_0 \to \mathcal{G}_{L_0} \times L_0 \ \text{ where } \ [\![\ P\ ]\!] = ((L_0, M, \to), P)$$

defines the semantics of L_0 by associating each process term with a state in the transition graph. More formally, the semantics function maps every process term P to a labelled graph, consisting of states L_0, a set of labels M, and the transition relation $\to\ \subseteq L_0 \times M \times L_0$, together with an distinguished initial state, which is P itself. $\to$ is given by the smallest relation satisfying the inference rules below in SOS-style (cf. [23]). A rule $\frac{premise}{conclusion}$ is to be read as: *conclusion* holds whenever *premise* holds. We abbreviate $(P, a, P') \in\to$ by $P \xrightarrow{a} P'$ for arbitrary L_0-terms P and P' and $a \in M$.

$$\text{prefix} \ \frac{}{a.P \xrightarrow{a} P} \qquad \text{choice\_l} \ \frac{P \xrightarrow{a} P'}{P + Q \xrightarrow{a} P'} \qquad \text{choice\_r} \ \frac{Q \xrightarrow{a} Q'}{P + Q \xrightarrow{a} Q'}$$

At this point we exploit the fact that the students have already seen a small static type system defined using inference rules. Therefore, they are used to building proof trees and are able to deduce, for instance the graphical representation of the process denoted by $(a.0 + 0) + b.(0 + 0)$ as displayed below.

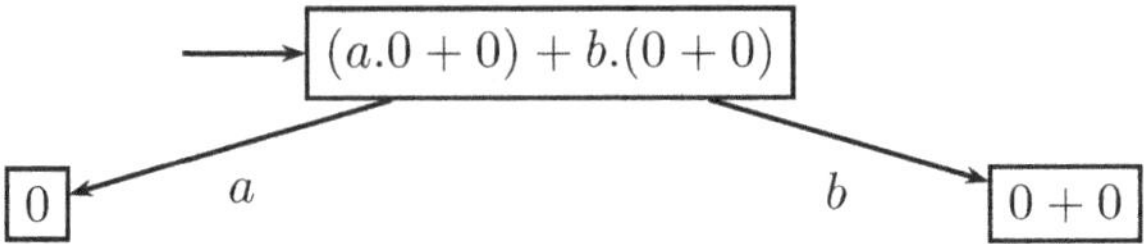

The only apparent difficulties for the students are (1) to accept that the vertices of the graph are expressions of the language, and (2) what it means that the relation defined by these rules is the *smallest* such relation.

In a next step we enhance the expressiveness of our language to allow for cyclic graphs, which correspond to *recursive* processes. The language L has means to deal with recursion via process variables. Processes are specified by a set Γ of defining equations and an initial process term as before. In Γ all equations have the form $X = E$ where X is a process variable and E is an arbitrary term of the language that may contain arbitrary variables. The terms of L are built according to the following abstract grammar:

$$P \in L \quad = \quad 0 \mid a.P \mid P + P \mid X$$

The semantics of L is obtain from the semantics of L_0 by adding one additional rule that deals with recursion:

$$\mathsf{rec} \quad \frac{\Gamma(X) = P \quad P \xrightarrow{a} P'}{X \xrightarrow{a} P'}$$

Note that the semantics of a term is now dependent on the environment Γ. Usually, Milner's CCS expresses recursion via the *rec*-operator. For example $recX.E$ corresponds to the process $(X = E, X)$ in our setting.

To use the *rec*-operator is mathematically more elegant (since several equations can be encoded in a single term), but looks frightening to beginners. We decided not to use this operator in our language, since the use of defining equations is easier to understand, especially since the students are already familiar with defining equations from various other fields of mathematics, and also from defining functions in SML.

The languages L_0 and L are our way of presenting the fragment of CCS that allows for the description of non-deterministic finite state sequential processes. They cannot yet express actual communication or interaction via parallel composition.

3.4 Interacting Processes: CCS

This part of the course introduces many important ideas and notions of concurrency theory and can be considered the core of our introduction to concurrency. For the first time, the students will see how concurrency, communication and interaction of processes are dealt with in a formal mathematical framework.

Therefore special care has to be put on this part of the course in order to communicate these principles of concurrency theory to the students effectively. For further reading, two textbooks [1,20] are recommended to the students. The preceding part of the course has already introduced a subset of CCS that allows for important aspects of concurrent processes like action prefix and non-deterministic choice via the languages L_0 and L. Therefore the students are already familiar with the syntax of processes and can rely on labelled graphs as a valid intuition for the interaction structure of processes, which in turn allows us to communicate ideas in a way that is based on a firm formal basis, but is still intuitive and motivating. As a running example we use a simple "cruise control system" drawing some inspiration from [18]. In the following, we present (a translation of) the example as used in our course notes [14], where actions appear as pairs of sending ('!') and receiving ('?') activities.

A Cruise Control System. To explain the main ideas of concurrency and interaction, we shall study a cruise control system, as it is found in many contemporary cars. We will first concentrate on the central component of the system, the *controller*. In the following, we give an informal — and strongly simplified — description of its behaviour.

- In state *IDLE* the *controller* waits for activation (*on*?).
- Successful activation is acknowledged by the *controller* via *ok*! (and the target speed is set to the current speed).
- By using the brake (*brake*?) the cruise controller gets deactivated temporarily. The *controller* changes its state to *SUSPEND*.
- While in state *SUSPEND* it is possible to resume (with target speed set to the value before suspending). This is being acknowledged by an *ok*! from the *controller*.
- Switching off the *controller* is possible at any time and leads to state *IDLE*.

We can describe the intended behaviour of the *controller* by the following defining equations (where we ignore the target speed settings):

$$\begin{aligned} IDLE &= on?.ON + off?.IDLE \\ ON &= ok!.(off?.IDLE + brake?.SUSPEND) \\ SUSPEND &= resume?.ON + off?.IDLE \end{aligned}$$

The semantics of L (*CCS* is yet to be introduced) gives us the process depicted below, where we abbreviated one state by "...".

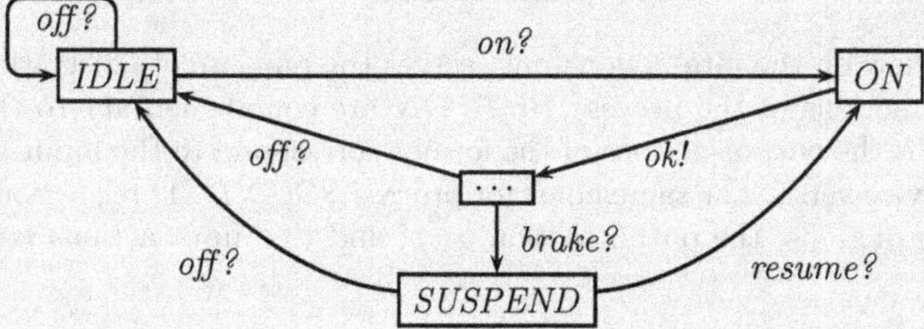

So far, this example is not more than a repetition of the syntax and semantics of L, but the actions considered have more structure: they are post-fixed with "!" or"?", representing the distinction into complementary actions typical of CCS. We motivate them as follows to the students.

In the above example we have made a natural distinction between these actions that have been initiated directly by the controller (marked by "!") and those that represent reactions to interactions with the environment (marked by "?"). We will call the former *output*-actions and the latter *input*-actions of the process.

The *controller* interacts with the environment. In our example, the environment consists of a switch in the dash board of the car. The process $BUTTON$ interacts with the *controller* in a simple way: $BUTTON$ activates ($on!$) and deactivates ($off!$) the cruise controller from time to time. We describe this behaviour with the following equation:

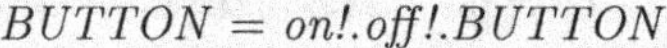

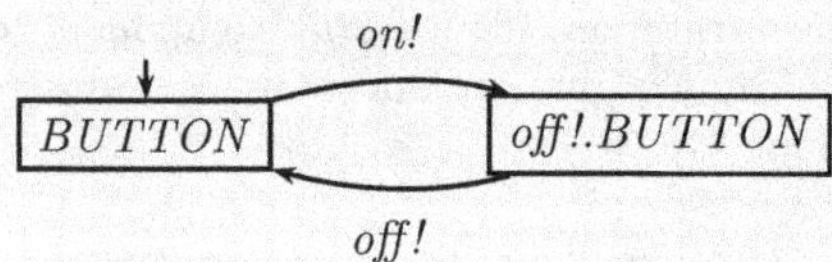

In addition, there is an acoustic *beep!*-signal, which signals the reception of $ok?$.

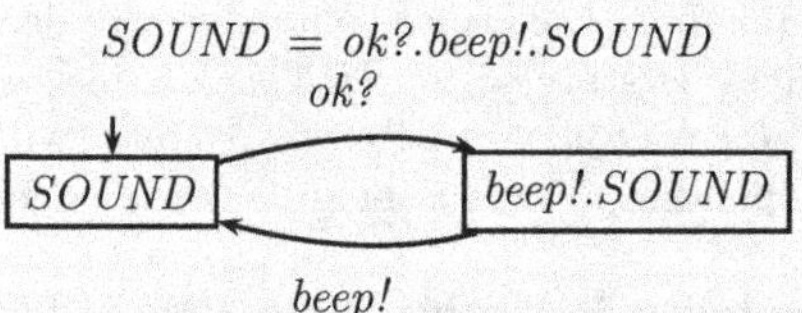

For the moment we will only consider these three processes in our example. In order to understand how the actions of the processes $SOUND$, $BUTTON$, and $CONTROLLER$ are related, we use the following illustration [18]:

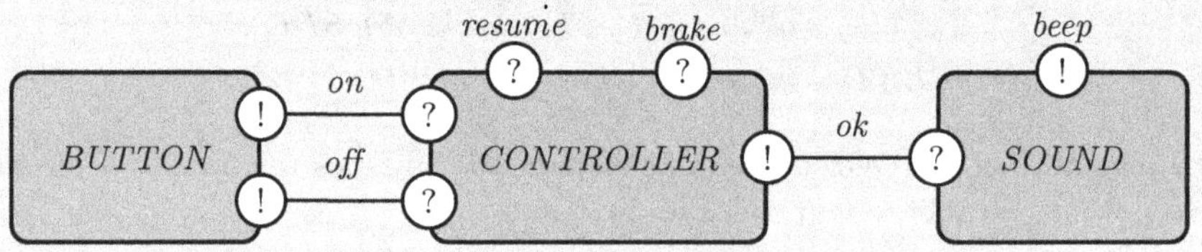

This schematic view on the interactions only serves the purpose of illustration: We can see that the actions of the process $BUTTON$ are complementary to those of $CONTROLLER$; the output-actions of the former correspond to the input-actions of the latter and vice versa. The same holds for process $SOUND$. Three actions have no corresponding actions: the output-action *beep*! and the input-actions $resume$? and $brake$?.

Once this pictorial representation is fully understood, we take the students on a quest for operators that allow us to express the pictorially represented correlation in a language, and then to equip the language operators with a semantics.

Looking at this example, we observe the following principal phenomena:

Concurrency: Let us first consider the processes $SOUND$ and $BUTTON$ and assume that $CONTROLLER$ is not present. There is no interdependence between the two processes and we may assume that each one can perform its actions independently from the other process and thereby changing its states. This is called *concurrency.*

Synchronisation: Also the processes $CONTROLLER$ and $SOUND$ are independent to a large extent. The only exception is the input/output action *ok*. This action can be performed by both processes at the same instant thereby performing a simultaneous change of state. This is called *synchronisation* of processes.

A synchronisation of processes can take place when pairs of complementary input and output actions occur.

We end this exemplary discussion with the following observation: Hitherto we only considered single processes (in form of labelled and rooted graphs) and developed a corresponding language. Now it is time to develop a language for communicating and concurrent processes and provide it with semantics.

After this introduction we postulate the following principles of concurrency which have been extensively motivated in the preceding example:

- Real-life processes have states. They can change states via certain actions.
- Actions are atomic, and their purpose is inter-process communication.
- Distinct processes can exist concurrently and perform actions.
- Inter-process communication can be performed whenever pairs of complementary input and output actions occur at the same time. This yields process synchronisation, i.e., a simultaneous change of states.

Using this motivation as a background, we add a small intermezzo on the different ways how inter-process communication might be formally captured (binary vs. multiway, directed vs. undirected, buffered vs. handshake), with a particular focus on Hoare's CSP. For further studies on CSP the students are referred to [16]. We stay on a very informal level in this intermezzo, before we return to the above example, which makes a clear case for binary, handshake, directed communication. We can thus easily motivate the formal semantic rules for the parallel composition operator | of CCS as given below. Only the usage of the distinguished internal action τ in the synchronisation rule needs further motivation in the course.

$$\mathsf{par\_l}\ \frac{P \overset{m}{\to} P'}{P \mid Q \overset{m}{\to} P' \mid Q} \quad \mathsf{par\_r}\ \frac{P \overset{m}{\to} P'}{Q \mid P \overset{m}{\to} Q \mid P'} \quad \mathsf{sync}\ \frac{P \overset{\alpha}{\to} P' \quad Q \overset{\overline{\alpha}}{\to} Q'}{P \mid Q \overset{\tau}{\to} P' \mid Q'}$$

The following example captures the essence of communication in CCS. The two parallel processes $a!.0$ and $a?.0$ can either synchronise on a both reaching a terminal state, or they can perform their respective actions independently and in sequence, eventually reaching the same state.

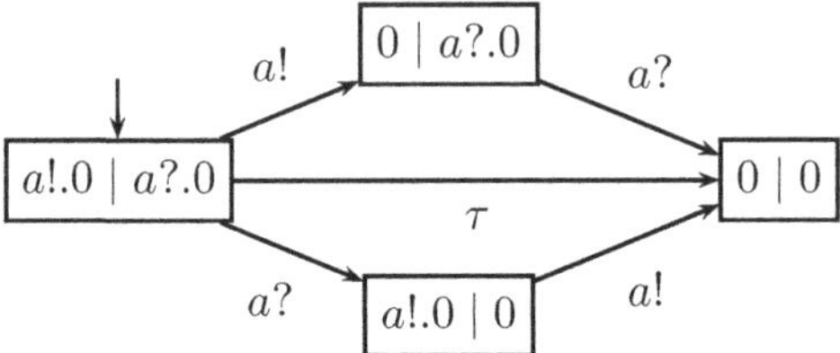

Completing our tour through CCS, we finally introduce the students to the standard rules for the restriction operator $\setminus H$, used to enforce synchronisation between actions in H.

This part of the course has introduced concurrent processes, synchronisation, etc., and the process algebra CCS (relabelling is moved as an exercise to the students). As already mentioned above, we only deviate from Milner's original CCS in the way we represent recursion.[2]

3.5 Semantic Equivalence

The question when two processes should be considered semantically equivalent is one of the most interesting ones in concurrency theory, but also one with many diverse answers, discriminating various desired or undesired properties of concurrent processes, such as deadlock, divergence, branching structure, etc. [25,26].

An introductory course to computer science is surely not the right place for an exhaustive discussion of this topic. However, we felt the need to shed some light on this, by reviewing *graph isomorphism*, *trace equivalence*, and *bisimulation equivalence*.

The topic of equivalence appears at various points in our course, always under the slogan: "When should two processes be considered equivalent?" We initially motivate this question by pointing out that in classical algebra, two arithmetic expression in one variable may *syntactically* look rather different, still *semantically* describing the same polynome.

After accepting trace equivalence as the weakest common criterion for any reasonable notion of equivalence,[3] the students learn that the process' *branching structure must be preserved* (isomorphism or bisimulation) by a reasonable equivalence notion, so as to avoid deadlocks in the context of parallel composition, and they learn that it should be a *congruence for the operators of the language* (trace equivalence or bisimulation). In summary, the students understand that for CCS bisimulation equivalence is the central notion of equivalence.

---

[2] Both representations are equally expressive, since for every expression P in our representation of CCS there is an expression Q in Milner's original representation, such that the reachable subsets of the graphs $[\![P]\!]$ and $[\![Q]\!]$ are isomorphic, and vice versa.

[3] Trace equivalence also serves as an appetiser for language equivalence from automata theory which is only taught in the second year.

```
CCS> Environment:                          |  8.) --tau-->    ((X | 0) | Z)
 X=a!.Z,                                   |  9.) --tau-->    ((X | Z) | 0)
 Y=((a?.Z + a!.0) + b!.X),                 |  10.) --tau-->   ((Z | Y) | Z)
 Z=Y                                       |
       Process:                            |  CCS- succ 6
                        ((X | Y) | Z)      |  CCS> 6-th successor via action a!:
CCS- steps                                 |                  ((X | Y) | 0)
CCS> All successors:                       |  CCS- steps
0.) --a!-->         ((Z | Y) | Z)          |  CCS> All successors:
1.) --a?-->         ((X | Z) | Z)          |  0.) --a!-->     ((Z | Y) | 0)
2.) --a!-->         ((X | 0) | Z)          |  1.) --a?-->     ((X | Z) | 0)
3.) --b!-->         ((X | X) | Z)          |  2.) --a!-->     ((X | 0) | 0)
4.) --tau-->        ((Z | Z) | Z)          |  3.) --b!-->     ((X | X) | 0)
5.) --a?-->         ((X | Y) | Z)          |  4.) --tau-->    ((Z | Z) | 0)
6.) --a!-->         ((X | Y) | 0)          |
7.) --b!-->         ((X | Y) | X)          |  CCS-
```

Fig. 1. A sample run of CCI, where "`CCS-`" is the prompt of the interpreter, "`steps`" asks the tool to list all possible next steps, and "`succ` i" selects i-th step thereof

4 Students Interacting with Processes

Our introduction to CCS is accompanied by intensive practical work. To make this possible we have beforehand implemented the semantics of L_0 and L, and CCS in an exemplary way in SML. The code is written only using concepts the students have learnt about before. The resulting tool, CCS interpreter (CCI), can best be described as an interactive exploration tool where the state space of a CCS-process is explored in a stepwise manner. An example run of CCI can be found in Fig. 1.

CCI enables the students to experiment with concurrent processes in a playful way. The usage of CCI improves the way the students dealt with CCS and allowed for an appealing way to discover interesting phenomena of concurrency interactively. In the following we present two exercises, where the students are asked to explore the system state space. The first is a typical example of resource contention.

Exercise 135. Consider the following set of recursive equations Γ.

$$
\begin{aligned}
CDWriter &= getW?.putW?.CDWriter \\
CDReader &= getR?.putR?.CDReader \\
User1 &= getR!.getW!.rip!.burn!.putW!.putR!.User1 \\
User2 &= getW!.getR!.rip!.burn!.putR!.putW!.User2
\end{aligned}
$$

Explore $Reach([\![(CDReader \mid CDWriter \mid User1 \mid User2) \setminus H]\!]_\Gamma)$, where H contains all actions except $rip!$, $rip?$, $burn!$ and $burn?$. What do you observe when you explore the process up to depth 3?

The system may run into a deadlock. Our second example introduces the famous *dining philosophers* problem.

$$
\begin{array}{lll}
\textit{steps}\ \Gamma\ 0 & = \emptyset & \\
\textit{steps}\ \Gamma\ m.P & = \{(m,P)\} & \\
\textit{steps}\ \Gamma\ X & = \textit{steps}\ \Gamma\ (\Gamma X) & \\
\textit{steps}\ \Gamma\ (P+Q) & = (\textit{steps}\ \Gamma\ P) \cup (\textit{steps}\ \Gamma\ Q) & \\
\textit{steps}\ \Gamma\ (P|Q) & = \{(m,P'|Q) & |\ \ (m,P') \in \textit{steps}\ \Gamma\ P\} \\
 & \cup\, \{(m,P|Q') & |\ \ (m,Q') \in \textit{steps}\ \Gamma\ Q\} \\
 & \cup\, \{(\tau,P'|Q') & |\ \ \exists\alpha:\ (\alpha,P') \in \textit{steps}\ \Gamma\ P \wedge (\overline{\alpha},Q') \in \textit{steps}\ \Gamma\ Q\} \\
\textit{steps}\ \Gamma\ (P \setminus H) & = \{(m,P' \setminus H) & |\ \ (m,P') \in \textit{steps}\ \Gamma\ P \wedge m \notin H\}
\end{array}
$$

Fig. 2. Defining equations of *steps*

Exercise 136. Consider the following set of recursive equations Γ.

$$
\begin{aligned}
Fork1 &= getF1?.putF1?.Fork1 \\
Fork2 &= getF2?.putF2?.Fork2 \\
Fork3 &= getF3?.putF3?.Fork3 \\
\\
PhilA &= getF1!.getF2!.eat!.putF1!.putF2!.think!.PhilA \\
PhilB &= getF2!.getF3!.eat!.putF2!.putF3!.think!.PhilB \\
PhilC &= getF3!.getF1!.eat!.putF3!.putF1!.think!.PhilC
\end{aligned}
$$

Use *Google* to learn about the "dining philosophers". Explore

$$Reach([\![\ (Fork1 \mid PhilA \mid Fork2 \mid PhilB \mid Fork3 \mid PhilC\ ]\!]_{\Gamma}) \setminus H$$

where H contains all actions except *eat*!, *eat*?, *think*! and *think*? . After which trace will the philosophers have to starve.

In the sequel, after the relevant theory of CCS is fully developed and experimented with, the students are supposed to understand how this tool is actually implemented in SML. We follow two goals with this: The students learn how one can derive a usable implementation of a formally specified language, including all necessary intermediate steps like syntax parsing, applying inference rules, execution. Furthermore, the students deepen their understanding of the CCS semantics by implementing it.

The core of our implementation — realising the semantics of CCS — is the function *steps*. It derives the set of all immediate successor of a CCS term reachable via a given action relative to the set of defining equations Γ. An implementation independent definition of this procedure is provided in Fig. 2 by a set of defining equations. Note that the function *steps* implicitly implements the complete semantics of CCS, which is given by labelled graphs over the vertex set CCS. *steps* gives us all successors of a vertex (dependent of the label/action) and hence uniquely determines the corresponding graph. Readers familiar with SML might find it interesting to see some detailed fragments of the implementation of CCS semantics (cf. Fig. 3). We do not present other parts of the implementation like, e.g., syntax parsing.

```
datatype lab = In of
name | Out of name | Tau type labset = lab list

datatype ccs = Stop                        (* stop *)
             | Var of var                  (* process variable *)
             | Pre of lab * ccs            (* prefix *)
             | Chc of ccs * ccs            (* choice *)
             | Par of ccs * ccs            (* parallel *)
             | Res of ccs * labset         (* restriction *)

(* lab -> (lab * ccs) list -> ccs list *)
fun successors act sl = ...

(* lab -> lab *)
fun complement (In a)  = ...
  | complement (Out a) = ...
  | complement Tau     = ...


(* env -> ccs -> (lab * ccs) list  *)
fun steps env Stop              = []
  | steps env (Var X)           = steps env (env X)
  | steps env (Pre (u,P))       = ...
  | steps env (Chc (P,Q))       = (steps env P) @ (steps env Q)
  | steps env (Par (P,Q))       = (map (fn (a,G) => (a,Par(G,Q)))
                                                 (steps env P))@
                                  (map (fn (a,G) => (a,Par(P,G)))
                                                 (steps env Q))@
                                  (foldl (fn ((a,P'), l1) =>
                                    ((map (fn (Q')=> (Tau,Par(P',Q')))
                                      (successors (complement a)
                                                  (steps env Q))
                                     )
                                         handle TauComplement => [])@l1
                                         )
                                    nil (steps env P)
                                  )
  | steps env (Res (G, set)) = ...
```

Fig. 3. Implementation of *steps*

The code made available to the students is for the language L. It is deliberately left incomplete in a way similar to what is depicted in Fig. 3, and it is left as an exercise to the students to fill the holes. With the implementation of *steps*, the student have learnt how to implement semantics. In a series of accompanying exercises and recommended readings in [24], the students finally are able to implement other parts of CCI, like syntax parsing, etc., and hence implement a complete interpreter for CCS from the incomplete one for L.

One fine point might be noteworthy: the function *steps* does not terminate if the environment Γ contains equations where structural recursion immediately reduces a variable X to itself, as in $X = X$, $X = a.X + X$ or $X = X|a.X$. At least in the presence of the parallel operator there is no way to circumvent this without changing the semantics, because processes may have a (countably) infinite number of successors that can be obtained by a repeated application of the recursion rule. This phenomenon was not discussed thoroughly in our introductory course, but we sensitised the students to this problem by means of an exercise, where we pointed out the problem and proposed the following solution: we replace the expression X by $u.X$ in the abstract grammar. Thus structural recursion never yields the same term again (the students were actually asked to prove this). Note that this change alters the semantic expressivity of the language. Now for every process expression P the corresponding labelled graph $[\![P]\!]$ is guaranteed to be finitely branching!

5 Lessons Learnt

This paper has described an approach to teaching the principles of concurrency theory to first year Bachelor students. We focused on the basic theory of CCS, which the students were made to experiment with, exploring examples like the dining philosophers with their own implementation of the CCS semantics. We also exposed them to some more advanced topics such as bisimulation and congruence relations.

Our approach replaces the last third of an SML-based introductory course to computer science and computer programming. The integration of the new material into the existing course turned out to be rather seamless. We managed to keep the flavour of the course of being "executable mathematics".

With the implementation of CCI the students learn to implement their first non-trivial SML program and to apply various concepts they studied in the lectures. They thus develop a deeper understanding of the semantics of CCS, and the intricacies of concurrency on pertinent examples.[4]

The students reaction on the course, and in particular the new part was encouraging. They generally found it challenging, interesting and enlightening. Similar comments were made about the entirety of the course, but it was explicitly acknowledged that the new part was having an obvious practical motivation. Of course, some students (especially those who had failed before and thus had to repeat the course) were irritated by the fact that we modified a generally well-accepted course. The student success ratio for this course edition turned out to be very much in line with earlier versions of the course. To pass the course, students had to succeed in two out of three written exams of 150 min length each.

More generally, we feel that the material we cover can also be added to other early courses in computer science curricula in a similar way. This paper has identified the base requirements needed, and we expect them to be part of the genuine first term education in computer science. Only the SML part is specific

[4] The source code of CCI is available from the authors upon request.

to our setup, but other, e.g., *Java*-based versions seem equally well possible to us, however, without the flair of "executable mathematics".

With respect to the general question whether to teach functional languages early or late within computer science curricula, we feel that the early approach implemented in Saarbrücken is a good one, in particular because it aligns the student skills to the required level of mathematics right from the start of their education, and is a clear indication — if not a roadblock — for those students who hope to be able to avoid mathematics. This appears as an important aspect since no specific entrance level requirements are imposed for Bachelor students.

One may wonder whether other models of concurrency, in particular Petri nets [11] would work equally well - or even better - in such a teaching context as CCS did. We are unable to contribute substantially to such a general debate. For our specific context, the choice of a CCS-like language was instrumental since it appeared as a very natural extension to the course contents, and it allowed to initiate awareness of principal and advanced concurrency phenomena.

In the meanwhile the awareness of concurrency has further grown within our faculty, and it has been decided that more time should be devoted to concurrency theory and practise. Therefore, the topic of *Concurrent Programming* has been promoted to a new course (with 6 ETCS credit points), mandatory for all Bachelor students. In this new course, the CCS material we developed is the nucleus of its first third, but enriched with other educational material [6,7,9,22]. The second third will be devoted to a more general introduction to models of concurrency, covering Petri nets [11], event structures [27], sequence diagrams [17] and also transaction level modelling, as used in the hardware industry nowadays [13]. We plan to discuss their respective semantic fine-points on the basis of semantic mappings onto transition system — apart from the true-concurrency aspects, which will get explicit attention. In the final third of this new course, the problem of concurrency will be reflected on from a practical programming perspective. In this part we are going to teach multithreaded imperative programming, in both *Java* and *C++*. The course *Concurrent Programming* is scheduled in the second term of the first or second year of the Bachelor curriculum. The second year option is due to organisational constraints (averaging workload per term), and is deemed late by many colleagues. Good students are encouraged to take the course right after "Programming 1", which maintains its original contents. The first edition of this course is scheduled to start April 2008.

Acknowledgments. This work is supported by the DFG as part of the Transregional Collaborative Research Center SFB/TR 14 AVACS and by the European Commission under the IST framework 7 project QUASIMODO.

References

1. Aceto, L., Ingolfsdottir, A., Larsen, K.G., Srba, J.: Reactive Systems–Modelling, Specification and Verification. Cambridge University Press, Cambridge (2007)
2. Adams, J., Nevison, C., Schaller, N.C.: Parallel computing to start the millennium. In: SIGCSE 2000: Proceedings of the Thirty-First SIGCSE Technical Symposium on Computer Science Education, pp. 65–69. ACM, New York (2000)

3. Ben-Ari, M.: A suite of tools for teaching concurrency. SIGCSE Bull. 36(3), 251 (2004)
4. Ben-Ari, M.: Teaching concurrency and nondeterminism with spin. In: ITiCSE 2007: Proceedings of the 12th Annual SIGCSE Conference on Innovation and Technology in Computer Science Education, pp. 363–364. ACM, New York (2007)
5. Ben-Ari, M., Kolikant, Y.B.-D.: Thinking parallel: the process of learning concurrency. SIGCSE Bull. 31(3), 13–16 (1999)
6. Brabrand, C.: Using constructive alignment for teaching model-based design for concurrency. In: Proceedings of TeaConc 2007, The 2nd Workshop on Teaching Concurrency, pp. 1–17. Publishing House of University of Podlasie, Siedlce (2007)
7. Brabrand, C., Mosegaard, M.: The bisimulation game (2006), `http://www.brics.dk/bisim`
8. Calder, M., Gilmore, S., Hillston, J.: Modelling the influence of rkip on the erk signalling pathway using the stochastic process algebra pepa. In: Priami, C., Ingólfsdóttir, A., Mishra, B., Riis Nielson, H. (eds.) Transactions on Computational Systems Biology VII. LNCS (LNBI), vol. 4230, pp. 1–23. Springer, Heidelberg (2006)
9. Calzolai, F., De Nicola, R., Loreti, M., Tiezzi, F.: TAPAs: a tool for the analysis of process algebras. In: Proceedings of TeaConc 2007, The 2nd Workshop on Teaching Concurrency, pp. 51–66. Publishing House of University of Podlasie, Siedlce (2007)
10. Cunha, J.C., ao Lourenço, J.: An integrated course on parallel and distributed processing. SIGCSE Bull. 30(1), 217–221 (1998)
11. Desel, J., Reisig, W., Rozenberg, G. (eds.): Lectures on Concurrency and Petri Nets. LNCS, vol. 3098. Springer, Heidelberg (2004)
12. Gosling, J., Joy, B., Steele, G., Bracha, G.: The Java Language Specification, 2nd edn. Addison-Wesley, Boston (2000)
13. Grötker, T., Liao, S., Martin, G., Swan, S.: System Design with SystemC. Springer, Heidelberg (2002)
14. Hermanns, H., Eisentraut, C.: Addendum zum Skript, `http://depend.cs.uni-sb.de/ProgI05/script.php`
15. Higginbotham, C.W., Morelli, R.: A system for teaching concurrent programming. In: SIGCSE 1991: Proceedings of the Twenty-Second SIGCSE Technical Symposium on Computer Science Education, pp. 309–316. ACM, New York (1991)
16. Hoare, C.A.R.: Communicating Sequential Processes. Prentice-Hall, Englewood Cliffs (1985)
17. Geneva ITU-TS. ITU-TS Recommendation Z.120: Message Sequence Chart (MSC) (1996)
18. Magee, J., Kramer, J.: Concurrency: State Models & Java Programs. John Wiley & Sons, Inc., Chichester (1999)
19. McDonald, C.: Teaching concurrency with joyce and linda. SIGCSE Bull. 24(1), 46–52 (1992)
20. Milner, R.: Communication and Concurrency. Prentice-Hall, Englewood Cliffs (1989)
21. Milner, R., Tofte, M., Harper, R., MacQueen, D.: The Definition of Standard ML–Revised. MIT Press, Cambridge (1997)
22. Olszewski, J.: CSP laboratory. In: SIGCSE 1993: Proceedings of the Twenty-Fourth SIGCSE Technical Symposium on Computer Science Education, pp. 91–95. ACM Press, New York (1993)
23. Plotkin, G.D.: A structural approach to operational semantics. Technical Report DAIMI FN-19, University of Aarhus (1981)

24. Smolka, G.: Programmierung–Eine Einführung in die Informatik mit Standard ML. Oldenbourg Wissensch. Vlg. (2008)
25. van Glabbeek, R.J.: The linear time-branching time spectrum (Extended Abstract). In: Baeten, J.C.M., Klop, J.W. (eds.) CONCUR 1990. LNCS, vol. 458, pp. 278–297. Springer, Heidelberg (1990)
26. van Glabbeek, R.J.: The linear time-branching time spectrum II. In: Best, E. (ed.) CONCUR 1993. LNCS, vol. 715, pp. 66–81. Springer, Heidelberg (1993)
27. Winskel, G.: Event structures. In: Brauer, W., Reisig, W., Rozenberg, G. (eds.) APN 1986. LNCS, vol. 255, pp. 325–392. Springer, Heidelberg (1987)
28. Wolf, V.: Modelling of biochemical reactions by stochastic automata networks. Electr. Notes Theor. Comput. Sci. 171(2), 197–208 (2007)

TAPAs: A Tool for the Analysis of Process Algebras

Francesco Calzolai, Rocco De Nicola, Michele Loreti, and Francesco Tiezzi

Dipartimento di Sistemi e Informatica, Università degli Studi di Firenze
Viale Morgagni 65, 50134 Firenze, Italy
{calzolai,denicola,loreti,tiezzi}@dsi.unifi.it

Abstract. Process algebras are formalisms for modelling concurrent systems that permit mathematical reasoning with respect to a set of desired properties. TAPAs is a tool that can be used to support the use of process algebras to specify and analyze concurrent systems. It does not aim at guaranteeing high performances, but has been developed as a support to teaching. Systems are described as process algebras terms that are then mapped to labelled transition systems (LTSs). Properties are verified either by checking equivalence of concrete and abstract systems descriptions, or by model checking temporal formulae over the obtained LTS. A key feature of TAPAs, that makes it particularly suitable for teaching, is that it maintains a consistent double representation of each system both as a term and as a graph. Another useful didactical feature is the exhibition of counterexamples in case equivalences are not verified or the proposed formulae are not satisfied.

Keywords: concurrency, property verification, process algebras, bisimulation, behavioural equivalences, modal logics.

1 Introduction

Process algebras are a set of mathematically rigorous languages with well-defined semantics that permit describing and verifying properties of concurrent communicating systems. They can be seen as mathematical models of processes, regarded as agents that act and interact continuously with other similar agents and with their common environment. The agents may be real-world objects (even people), or they may be artefacts, embodied perhaps in computer hardware or software systems.

Process algebras provide a number of constructors for system descriptions and are equipped with an operational semantics that describes systems evolution. Moreover, they often come equipped with observational mechanisms that permit identifying (through behavioural equivalences) those systems that cannot be taken apart by external observations. In some cases, process algebras have also complete axiomatizations, that capture the relevant identifications.

There has been a huge amount of research work on process algebras carried out during the last 25 years that started with the introduction of CCS [18,19], CSP [6] and ACP [4]. In spite of the many conceptual similarities, these process algebras have been developed starting from quite different viewpoints and have given rise to different approaches: CCS relies on an observational bisimulation-based theory starting from an operational viewpoint. CSP was motivated as the theoretical version of a practical

K. Jensen, W. van der Aalst, and J. Billington (Eds.): ToPNoC I, LNCS 5100, pp. 54–70, 2008.

language for concurrency and is still based on an operational intuition which, however, is interpreted w.r.t. a more abstract theory of decorated traces. ACP started from a completely different viewpoint and provided a purely mathematical algebraic view of concurrent systems: ACP processes are the solutions of systems of equations (axioms) over the signature of the considered algebra; operational semantics and bisimulation (in this case a different notion of bisimulation — branching bisimulation — is considered) are seen as just one of the possible models over which the algebra can be defined and the axioms can be applied. At first, the different algebras have been developed completely separately. Slowly, however, their strict relationships have been understood and appreciated, nevertheless in university courses they have been taught separately. Thus we have seen many books on CCS [19], CSP [15,22,23], ACP [3,11], Lotos [5] but not a book just on process algebras aiming at showing the underlying vision of the general approach. We feel that it is time to aim at teaching the general theory of process algebras and seeing the different languages as specific instances of the general approach. The tool we describe in this paper aims at supporting such courses.

The main ingredients of a specific process algebra are:

1. A minimal set of well thought operators capturing the relevant aspect of systems behavior and the way systems are composed.
2. A transition system associated with the algebra via structural *operational semantics* to describe the evolution of all systems that can be built from the operators.
3. An equivalence notion that permits abstracting from irrelevant details of systems descriptions.

Often process algebras come also equipped with:

4. Abstract structures that are compositionally associated with terms to provide *denotational semantics*.
5. A set of laws (axioms) that characterize behavioural equivalences to obtain a so called *algebraic semantics*.

Verification of concurrent system within the process algebraic approach is performed either by resorting to behavioural equivalences for proving conformance of processes to specifications that are expressed within the notation of the same algebra or by checking that processes enjoy properties described by some temporal logic's formulae [7,16].

In the former case two descriptions of a given system, one very detailed and close to the actual concurrent implementation, the other more abstract describing the abstract tree of relevant actions the system has to perform are provided and tested for equivalence.

In the latter case, concurrent systems are specified as terms of a process description language while properties are specified as temporal logic formulae. Labelled transition systems (LTS) are associated with terms via a set of structural operational semantics rules and model checking is used to determine whether the transition systems associated with those terms enjoy the property specified by the given formulae.

In both approaches LTSs play a crucial role; they consist of a set of states, a set of transition labels and a transition relation. States correspond to the configurations systems can reach. Labels describe the actions systems can perform to interact with the environment. Transition relation describes systems evolution as determined by the execution of specific actions. Temporal logic formulae are a mix of logical operators and modal operators. The former are the usual boolean operators, while the latter are those that permit reasoning about systems evolution in time and to deal with the dynamic aspects of LTSs.

LTSs are also the central ingredient of TAPAs, the software tool that we have implemented to support teaching of process algebras. Indeed, the main components of TAPAs are those permitting to minimize LTSs, to test their equivalence and to model check their satisfaction of temporal formulae. By relying on a sophisticated graphical user interface TAPAs permits:

- Understanding the meaning of the different process algebras operators by showing how these operators can be used to compose terms and the changes they induce on the composed transition systems.
- Appreciating the close correspondence between terms and processes by consistently updating terms when the graphical representation of LTS is changed and redrawing process graphs when terms are modified.
- Evaluating the different behavioural equivalences by having them on a single platform and checking the different equivalences by simply pushing different buttons.
- Studying model checking via a user friendly tool that, in case of failures, provides appropriate counterexamples that help debugging the specification.

The rest of the paper is organised as follows. In Sect. 2, we provide an overview of the front end of TAPAs and show how it can be used for specifying behaviours of concurrent systems. In Sect. 3, we describe the components that can be used for verifying systems behaviours. In Sect. 4, we consider a more elaborate case study dealing with mutual exclusion algorithm. The final section contain a few concluding remarks and gives a brief account of related tools.

2 Textual and Graphical Representation of Processes

TAPAs[1] [1] is a graphical tool, developed in JAVA, which aims at simplifying the specification and the analysis of concurrent systems described by means of process algebras. This tool has been used for supporting teaching Theory of Concurrency in a course of the Computer Science curriculum at 'Università degli Studi di Firenze'. TAPAs architecture is outlined in Fig. 1. It consists of five components: an editor, a run-time environment, a model checker, an equivalence checker and a minimizer. TAPAs editor permits specifying concurrent systems as terms of a process algebra: terms can be inserted into the system by using either a textual representation or a graphical notation. The run-time environment permits generating the Labelled transition system corresponding to a given specification. Model checker and equivalence checker can be used for analyzing system behaviours. The former permits verifying whether a specification satisfies

[1] TAPAs is a free software; it can be redistributed and/or modified under the terms of the GNU General Public License as published by the Free Software Foundation.

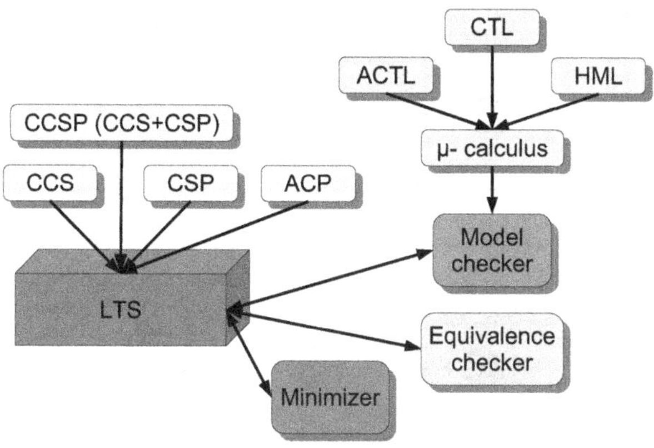

Fig. 1. TAPAs Architecture

a logic formula of modal μ-calculus [16], the latter permits verifying whether two implementations of the same system are equivalent or not. Finally, the minimizer permits reducing the size of LTS with large number of states while preserving the intended behaviour.

In TAPAs concurrent systems are described by means of *processes*, which are non-deterministic descriptions of system behaviours, and *process systems*, which are obtained by process compositions. Notably, processes can be defined in terms of other processes or other process systems. Processes and process systems are composed by means of the operators of a given process algebra. For instance, in the case of CCS, a process system can be obtained by parallel composition with binary synchronisation, relabelling and restriction of processes, while in case of CSP a process system can be also obtained by using parallel composition with multi-party synchronisation, internal and external choice operators and hiding.

The TAPAs editor permits defining processes and process systems by using both graphical and textual representations. A process is graphically represented by a graph whose edges are labeled with the actions it can perform. The same process can be represented (textually) by a term of a specific process algebra. A user can always change the process representation: TAPAs guarantees the synchronization between the graph and the corresponding term. TAPAs does not rely on specific process algebra to be used for the systems specification. Currently, we are using CCSP[2] a process algebra obtained from CCS by incorporating some operators of CSP. However, thanks to the modular implementation of TAPAs, other process algebras can be easily added. Specifically, adding a new process algebra to TAPAs requires developing two JAVA packages: one for modelling the operational semantics of the operators and the other for defining the graphical representation of the operators.

Figure 2 shows two TAPAs processes that are the graphical representations corresponding to the following CCSP processes:

[2] Although the name is borrowed from [21] our variant is slightly different from the one considered by Olderog [21] and the one proposed by van Glabbeek and Vaandrager [24] due to the different mix of operators.

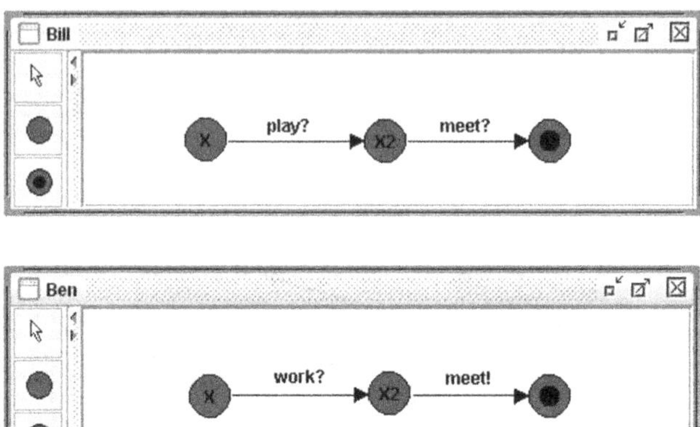

Fig. 2. Processes Bill and Ben

```
process Bill:
    X1 = play?.Bill[X2]
    X2 = meet?.nil
end
```

```
process Ben:
    X1 = work?.Ben[X2]
    X2 = meet!.nil
end
```

Process Bill can perform an input on channel play and continue with an input on meet, while process Ben can perform first an input on work and then an output on meet.

Process systems, like processes, are represented both graphically and textually. In the first case, a system is represented by a box containing a set of elements. The process system corresponding to the parallel composition of the processes Bill and Ben is shown in the left hand side of Fig. 3. To guarantee synchronization between Bill and Ben, channel meet is restricted. This is represented graphically by a black barrier around parallel composition. The textual representation of BillBen process system is the following:

```
system BillBen:
    restrict {meet} in
        Bill[X1] | Ben[X1]
    end
end
```

The LTS generated by the run-time component, corresponding to the above process system is reported on the right hand side of Fig. 3. To help the user to analyze the generated graph, TAPAs provides visualization algorithms for drawing LTSs; new algorithms for drawing graphs can be easily plugged into TAPAs. When a LTS is generated starting from a system process, TAPAs will check satisfaction of the syntactic conditions that guarantee finiteness of the generated graph. When finiteness is not guaranteed, a warning message is displayed.

2.1 Textual Specification of Terms

The TAPAs run-time environment takes as input a textual specification, written in some process algebra, and generates the corresponding LTS, which can be used by the other

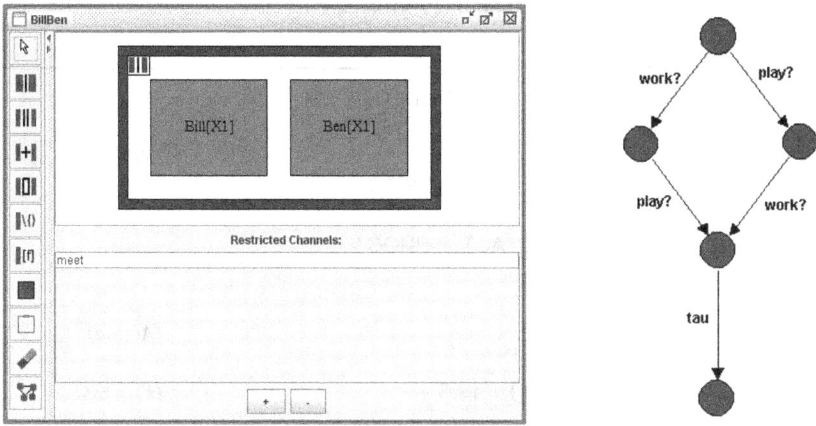

Fig. 3. Process system `BillBen` and the corresponding LTS

components for model and equivalence checking. Currently, the only process algebra that can be used to specify concurrent systems with TAPAs is CCSP. Its set of operators is not intended to be minimal. Redundancy is tolerated for making it easier to specify systems specifications while keeping them understandable. In this section, we present the syntax and the operational semantics of the CCSP terms accepted by the run-time environment.

Basic elements of CCSP processes, as in most process calculi, are *actions*. Intuitively, actions represent atomic computational steps, that can be internal or external. All internal actions are rendered as the silent action `tau`, while external actions are input/output operations on *channels* (i.e., communication ports), and represent potential interactions with the external environment.

CCSP syntax: The syntax of a CCSP module is given in Table 1; there we have used $\sum_{i\in I} \mathsf{ACT}^i_j \,.\, \mathsf{PROC}^i_j$ for $\mathsf{ACT}^1_j \,.\, \mathsf{PROC}^1_j + \cdots + \mathsf{ACT}^n_j \,.\, \mathsf{PROC}^n_j$ if $I = \{1, \ldots, n\}$. The set of names $\mathcal{N} = \mathcal{PN} \cup \mathcal{XN} \cup \mathcal{CN} \cup \mathcal{SN}$ contains (non-empty finite) sequences of alphanumeric characters (including the symbol _) where:

- P ranges over the set of *process names* $\mathcal{PN}$,
- X ranges over the set of *state names* $\mathcal{XN}$,
- c ranges over the set of *channel names* $\mathcal{CN}$,
- S range over the set of *system names* $\mathcal{SN}$.

A CCSP module is a sequence of process declaration and system declarations. Processes are defined by "*state_name* = $\sum_{i\in I}$ *action. process*", where an action can be the silent action `tau` (where `tau` $\notin \mathcal{CN}$), an output `c!` or an input `c?` on a channel `c`, while a process can be the empty process `nil` (which cannot perform any actions), a reference `P[X]` to the state `X` of the process `P` or a reference to a system `S`. Systems are defined as the composition via parallel operator (i.e., `|`), external and internal choice operators (i.e., `[]` and `(+)` respectively) of elements called *components* . These can be processes or the result of applying an operation (multi-synchronization operation `sync`, renaming operation `rename`, restriction operation `restrict`) processes. The multi-synchronization construct is inspired by the parallel operator of CSP and allows

Table 1. CCSP syntax

M	::=	PROC_DEC | SYS_DEC | M M	*(Module)*

PROC_DEC	::=	`process P :`
		$X_1 = \sum_{i \in I_1}$ ACT$^i_1$. PROC$^i_1$
		...
		$X_n = \sum_{j \in I_n}$ ACT^j_n . PROC^j_n
		`end`
			(Process dec.)

ACT	::=	`tau` | `c!` | `c?`	*(Action)*
PROC	::=	`nil` | `P[X]` | `S`	*(Process)*
SYS_DEC	::=	`system S :` COMP `end`	*(System dec.)*
COMP	::=	C | C$_1$ (+) C$_2$ | C$_1$ [] C$_2$ | C$_1$ | C$_2$	*(Components)*
C	::=	PROC | `sync on` CS `in` C$_1$ | C$_2$ `end` | `rename [F] in` COMP `end` | `restrict` CS `in` COMP `end`	*(Component)*
CS	::=	`*` | {c_1 , ... , c_n}	*(Channel set)*
F	::=	c/c' | F, F	*(Renaming fun.)*

parallel components to synchronize on any channel of the specified set when all of them can perform the same action. Renaming and restriction are the standard CCS operators; the former permits changing channel names, while the latter is used for delimiting their scope. For multi-synchronization and restriction operations, we use the wildcard symbol * to indicate $\mathcal{CN}$, i.e., the set of all channel names.

***CCSP operational semantics*:** CCSP operational semantics is defined only for *well-formed* modules, i.e., modules where all used states, processes and systems have corresponding declarations. Moreover, it is assumed that states and systems names are distinct, well-formedness check can be statically performed. CCSP semantics is provided relatively to a module M that contains the necessary definitions. It is described as a labelled transition relation $\xrightarrow{\mu}$ over components induced by the rules in Table 2, where μ is generated by the following grammar:

$$\mu \ ::= \ \texttt{tau} \ \mid \ \alpha \qquad\qquad \alpha \ ::= \ \texttt{c!} \ \mid \ \texttt{c?}$$

The meaning of labels is the following: `tau` represents internal computational steps, while `c!` and `c?` denote execution of output and input actions on channel `c`, respectively. An input and output on the same channel are called *complementary labels*. We will use $\bar{\alpha}$ to denote the complement of α (i.e., $\overline{\texttt{c!}} = \texttt{c?}$ and $\overline{\texttt{c?}} = \texttt{c!}$), and *act*(CS) to denote

Table 2. CCSP operational semantics w.r.t. module M

$$(P_{ref})\quad \frac{(\texttt{process}\ \mathtt{P}\ :\ \ldots\ \mathtt{X}_i = \sum_{j\in I} \mathsf{ACT}_i^j\,.\,\mathsf{PROC}_i^j \ldots\ \texttt{end}) \in \mathsf{M}}{\mathtt{P}[\mathtt{X}_i] \xrightarrow{\mathsf{ACT}_i^k} \mathsf{PROC}_i^k}\quad (k \in I)$$

$$(S_{ref})\quad \frac{(\texttt{system}\ \mathtt{S}\ :\ \mathsf{COMP}\ \texttt{end}) \in \mathsf{M} \qquad \mathsf{COMP} \xrightarrow{\mu} \mathsf{COMP}'}{\mathtt{S} \xrightarrow{\mu} \mathsf{COMP}'}$$

$$(Broad_1)\quad \frac{\mathsf{C}_1 \xrightarrow{\mu} \mathsf{C}' \qquad \mu \notin act(\mathsf{CS})}{\texttt{sync on}\ \mathsf{CS}\ \texttt{in}\ \mathsf{C}_1 \mid \mathsf{C}_2\ \texttt{end} \xrightarrow{\mu} \texttt{sync on}\ \mathsf{CS}\ \texttt{in}\ \mathsf{C}' \mid \mathsf{C}_2\ \texttt{end}}$$

$$(Broad_2)\quad \frac{\mathsf{C}_2 \xrightarrow{\mu} \mathsf{C}' \qquad \mu \notin act(\mathsf{CS})}{\texttt{sync on}\ \mathsf{CS}\ \texttt{in}\ \mathsf{C}_1 \mid \mathsf{C}_2\ \texttt{end} \xrightarrow{\mu} \texttt{sync on}\ \mathsf{CS}\ \texttt{in}\ \mathsf{C}_1 \mid \mathsf{C}'\ \texttt{end}}$$

$$(Broad_3)\quad \frac{\mathsf{C}_1 \xrightarrow{\alpha} \mathsf{C}_1' \qquad \mathsf{C}_2 \xrightarrow{\alpha} \mathsf{C}_2' \qquad \alpha \in act(\mathsf{CS})}{\texttt{sync on}\ \mathsf{CS}\ \texttt{in}\ \mathsf{C}_1 \mid \mathsf{C}_2\ \texttt{end} \xrightarrow{\alpha} \texttt{sync on}\ \mathsf{CS}\ \texttt{in}\ \mathsf{C}_1' \mid \mathsf{C}_2'\ \texttt{end}}$$

$$(Ren)\quad \frac{\mathsf{COMP} \xrightarrow{\mu} \mathsf{COMP}'}{\texttt{rename}\ [\,\mathsf{F}\,]\ \texttt{in}\ \mathsf{COMP}\ \texttt{end} \xrightarrow{\mathsf{F}(\mu)} \texttt{rename}\ [\,\mathsf{F}\,]\ \texttt{in}\ \mathsf{COMP}'\ \texttt{end}}$$

$$(Res)\quad \frac{\mathsf{COMP} \xrightarrow{\mu} \mathsf{COMP}' \qquad \mu \notin act(\mathsf{CS})}{\texttt{restrict}\ \mathsf{CS}\ \texttt{in}\ \mathsf{COMP}\ \texttt{end} \xrightarrow{\mu} \texttt{restrict}\ \mathsf{CS}\ \texttt{in}\ \mathsf{COMP}'\ \texttt{end}}$$

$$(Sync)\quad \frac{\mathsf{C}_1 \xrightarrow{\alpha} \mathsf{C}_1' \qquad \mathsf{C}_2 \xrightarrow{\bar{\alpha}} \mathsf{C}_2'}{\mathsf{C}_1 \mid \mathsf{C}_2 \xrightarrow{\texttt{tau}} \mathsf{C}_1' \mid \mathsf{C}_2'}$$

$$(Inter_1)\quad \frac{\mathsf{C}_1 \xrightarrow{\mu} \mathsf{C}_1'}{\mathsf{C}_1 \mid \mathsf{C}_2 \xrightarrow{\mu} \mathsf{C}_1' \mid \mathsf{C}_2} \qquad\qquad (Inter_2)\quad \frac{\mathsf{C}_2 \xrightarrow{\mu} \mathsf{C}_2'}{\mathsf{C}_1 \mid \mathsf{C}_2 \xrightarrow{\mu} \mathsf{C}_1 \mid \mathsf{C}_2'}$$

$$(Int.\ choice_1)\quad \mathsf{C}_1(+)\mathsf{C}_2 \xrightarrow{\texttt{tau}} \mathsf{C}_1 \qquad\qquad (Int.\ choice_2)\quad \mathsf{C}_1(+)\mathsf{C}_2 \xrightarrow{\texttt{tau}} \mathsf{C}_2$$

$$(Ext.\ choice_1)\quad \frac{\mathsf{C}_1 \xrightarrow{\alpha} \mathsf{C}'}{\mathsf{C}_1[\,]\mathsf{C}_2 \xrightarrow{\alpha} \mathsf{C}'} \qquad\qquad (Ext.\ choice_2)\quad \frac{\mathsf{C}_2 \xrightarrow{\alpha} \mathsf{C}'}{\mathsf{C}_1[\,]\mathsf{C}_2 \xrightarrow{\alpha} \mathsf{C}'}$$

$$(Ext.\ choice_3)\quad \frac{\mathsf{C}_1 \xrightarrow{\texttt{tau}} \mathsf{C}'}{\mathsf{C}_1[\,]\mathsf{C}_2 \xrightarrow{\texttt{tau}} \mathsf{C}'[\,]\mathsf{C}_2} \qquad\qquad (Ext.\ choice_4)\quad \frac{\mathsf{C}_2 \xrightarrow{\texttt{tau}} \mathsf{C}'}{\mathsf{C}_1[\,]\mathsf{C}_2 \xrightarrow{\texttt{tau}} \mathsf{C}_1[\,]\mathsf{C}'}$$

the set of actions corresponding to the channels of CS (i.e., tau $\notin$ *act*(CS), while c!, c? $\in$ *act*(CS) if either c $\in$ CS or CS $= *$).

Rule (P_{ref}) states that process P[X] evolves by performing one of the actions that P can execute from state X; the actual choice is nondeterministic. A system name evolves according to the actions of the body of the corresponding declaration, rule (S_{ref}). Rules for renaming, restriction, parallel composition, internal and external choice are standard (see [6,18]). Finally, rules $(Broad_1)$ and $(Broad_2)$ permit the interleaving of the actions of parallel components when actions outside the specified channel set are performed, rule $(Broad_3)$ allows multiple synchronization of processes on one of the synchronization channels.

2.2 Graphical Specification of Terms

In this section, we present the graphical formalism used for defining *processes* and *prosess systems*. TAPAs editor provides two separate kind of windows that can be used to draw processes and process systems (see Fig. 4).

Generally, the graphical representation of processes is independent from a specific process algebra, except for the labels corresponding to the actions of the algebras. A process is rendered as a graph; its edges describe the performed actions and their effect, while its nodes represent systems configurations. We have four kinds of nodes:

1. **Terminal** identify a terminal state (e.g. the empty process nil) and are represented as a red circle with a black dot.
2. **State Reference** identify states defined within the considered process, and are represented as a red circle. Only this kind of nodes can have outgoing edges.
3. **Process Reference** identify states defined in another processes, and are represented as a red box.
4. **System Reference** identify systems, and are represented as a white box.

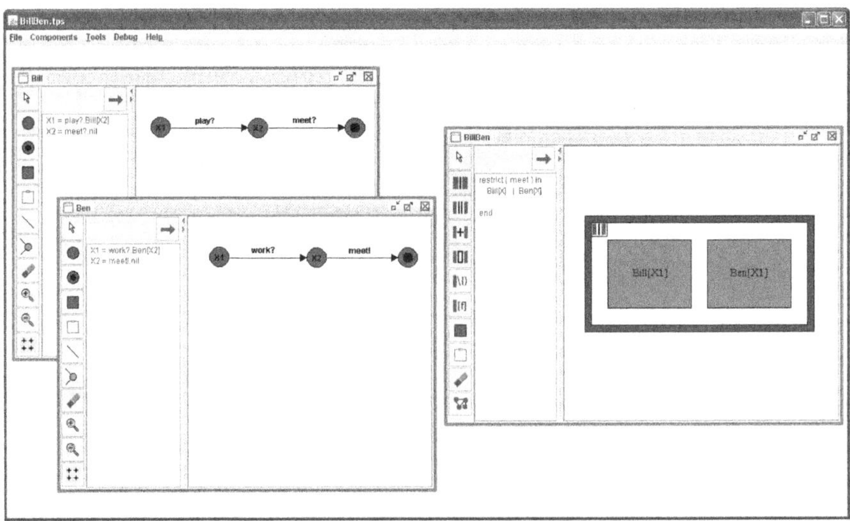

Fig. 4. A TAPAs screenshot

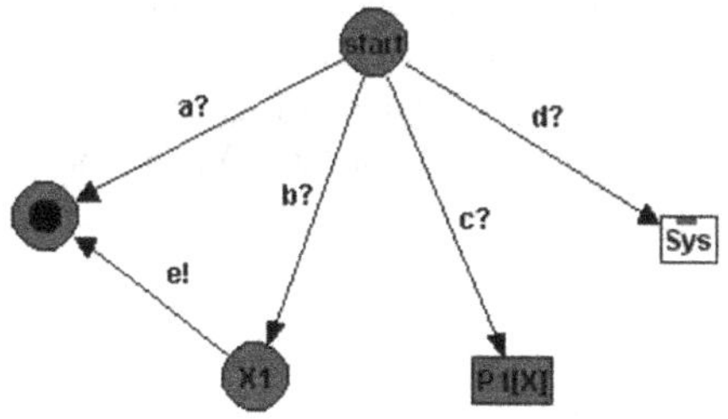

Fig. 5. Graphical representation of TAPAs nodes

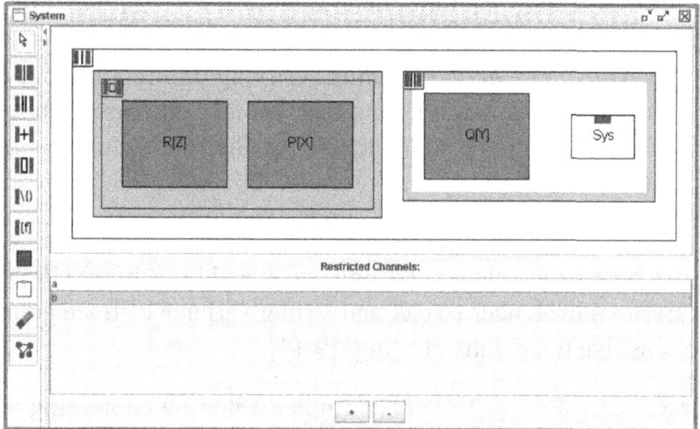

Fig. 6. Graphical representation of a process system

Figure 5 shows the graphical representation of the process below, if P1 is a process and Sys is a system.

```
process P2:
    start = a?.nil + b?.P2[X1] + c?.P1[X] + d?.Sys
    X1 = e!.nil
end
```

Process systems are graphically represented via nested boxes; each box represents either one of the system operators or a reference to a process or to a process system. For the sake of clarity, each system operator has a specific graphical box.

Figure 6 reports the graphical representation of the following process system:

```
restrict {a,b} in
  R[Z] [] P[X]
end
|
sync on {a,c} in
  Q[Y] | Sys
end
```

The outermost enclosing box represents the top level operator that, in this case, is parallel composition while its arguments are drawn as inner boxes. There are two inner components, one is a restriction the other is a multi-synchronization. Restriction is rendered as a box surrounded by a black barrier and contains an external choice between processes `R[Z]` and `P[X]`. Multi-synchronization is rendered as a box with a yellow frame that contains process `Q[Y]` and system `Sys`. When a box is selected, other parameters of the corresponding operator, such as restricted names, are shown in a separate table.

3 Verification of Process Properties

The LTS generated by the run-time environment can be used by the other TAPAs components to analyze the corresponding concurrent systems. The analysis can be performed either by an equivalence checker or by a model checker.

The TAPAs *Equivalences Checker* permits verifying different kind of equivalences between pairs of systems. It is worth noting that, if other process algebras (e.g. value-passing CCS, ACP, ...) were to be added to TAPAs, their integrations with the equivalence checker would be seamless.

Currently, TAPAs permits checking two kinds of equivalences:

1. Bisimulations based equivalences (strong, weak and branching) [19,26];
2. Decorated trace equivalences (weak and strong variants of trace completed trace, divergence sensitive trace, must, testing) [9,14].

Decorated trace equivalences have been implemented by combining a set of flags, which enable or disable checking specific properties (see Fig. 7 left side). Flags, and their meanings, are the following:

- WEAK: weak equivalences;
- CONV: convergence sensitive equivalences;
- FINL: equivalences sensitive to final states;

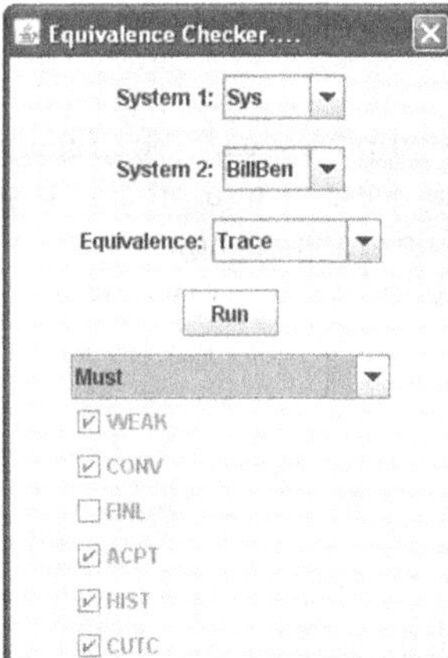

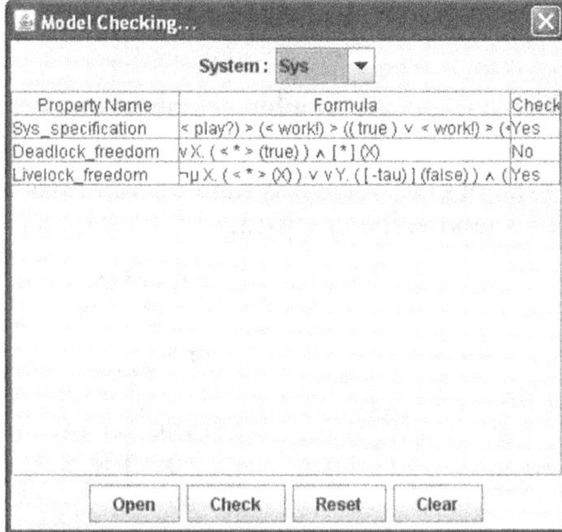

Fig. 7. Equivalence and Model Checker panels

- ACPT: equivalences sensitive to acceptance sets;
- HIST: equivalences that consider past divergences as catastrophic;
- CUTC: equivalences that ignore all behaviours after divergent nodes.

As an example, weak trace equivalence is obtained by enabling only the WEAK flag, the completed trace equivalence is obtained by enabling the FINL flag, and the weak completed trace is obtained by enabling the WEAK and the FINL flags.

Whenever an equivalence check turns out to be unsuccessful, TAPAs provides counterexamples, i.e., evidences that the analysed systems do behave differently. Hennessy-Milner logic [13] formulae that capture a property satisfied only by one of the two in-equivalent processes are exhibited.

Equivalence checker algorithms are also used for implementing a LTSs *Minimizer*. This module allows users to minimize LTSs with large number of states while preserving strong, weak or branching bisimulation.

TAPAs can be used to analyze concurrent systems also by verifying satisfaction of properties, expressed as logical formulae. This task can be achieved by using the *Model Checker* that implements a Local Model Checking Algorithm [27], and permits verifying satisfaction of modal logic formulae by system processes (Fig. 7 right side).

For efficiency reasons, the model checker takes as input only μ-calculus formulae [16]. However, TAPAs can be easily extended to accept also formulae from other logics like, for instance, Action Computation Tree Logic (ACTL) [10] that turns out to be more user friendly. Formulae of the new logics will have to be translated in equivalent μ-calculus ones and their verifications will be performed on the outcome of the translation.

4 The Study of a Mutual Exclusion Algorithm

In this section we present the *mutual exclusion problem*, one of the simpler examples that are used for supporting concurrency theory courses.

Mutual exclusion algorithms are used in concurrent programming to avoid that pieces of code, called *critical sections*, simultaneously access a common resource, such as a shared variable. We consider Peterson's algorithm, that allows two processes to share a single-use resource without conflicts. The two processes, P1 and P2, are defined by the following symmetrical pieces of pseudocode:

```
P1
while true do {
   <noncritical section>
   B1 = true;
   K = 2;
   while (B2 and K==2) do skip;
   <critical section>
   B1 = false;
}
```

```
P2
while true do {
   <noncritical section>
   B2 = true;
   K = 1;
   while (B1 and K==1) do skip;
   <critical section>
   B2 = false;
}
```

The two processes communicate by means of three shared variables, B1, B2 and K. The first two are boolean variables and are true when the corresponding process wants

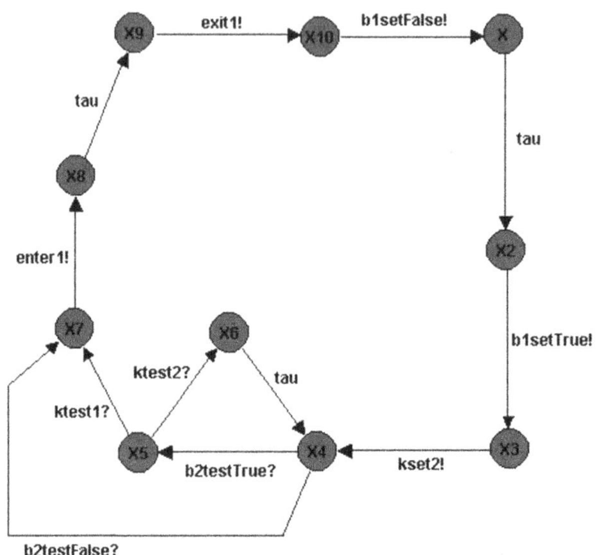

Fig. 8. Process P1

to enter the critical section. The last variable contains the identifier of the process (i.e., 1 or 2) whose turn it is. The algorithm guarantees mutual exclusion: `P1` and `P2` can never be in their critical sections at the same time.

The three variables can be easily modelled in TAPAs as two-states processes, where each state represents a value that the variable can assume. Similarly, processes `P1` and `P2` can be modelled as TAPAs processes. Since the two processes are symmetric, Fig. 8 shows only one of them (i.e., `P1`). The complete process system, reported in Fig. 9, is obtained by putting the five processes in parallel and by restricting the synchronization channels; it has the following textual representation:

```
system Sys:
    restrict { ktest1, kset2, ktest2, b1setFalse, b1testFalse,
               kset1, b2testFalse, b2testTrue, b1testTrue,
               b1setTrue, b2setTrue, b2setFalse } in
        B1[true] | B2[true] | K[1] | P1[X] | P2[X]
    end
end
```

`Sys` can interact with the external environment only by means of channels `enter1`, `enter2`, `exit1` and `exit2`, that represent entering and exiting of the two processes from the critical sections.

Generally, after showing this example, we ask to students to try to find an alternative solution of the *mutual exclusion problem*. For instance we could ask to provide an alternative formalization that does not rely on shared variables. A possible solution is that based on the multi-synchronization operator. The algorithm that uses the multi-synchronization operator is reported in Fig. 10.

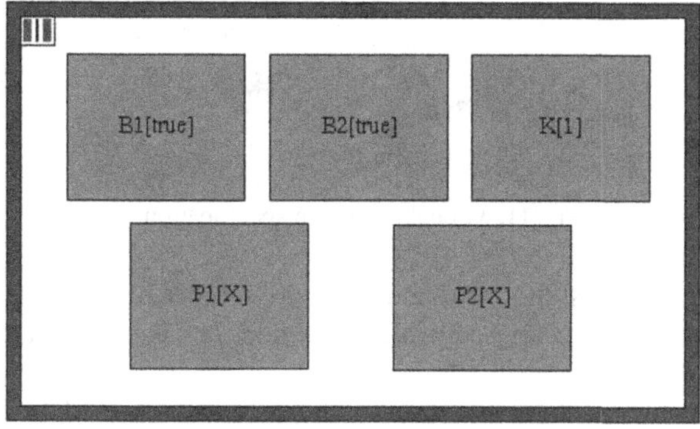

Fig. 9. The process system Sys

```
process P1:
  X -> enter1!.P1[X2] + enter2!.P1[X3]
  X2 -> tau.P1[X4]
  X3 -> exit2!.P1[X]
  X4 -> exit1!.P1[X]
end
```

```
process P2:
  X -> enter2!.P2[X2]
       + enter1!.P2[X3]
  X2 -> tau.P2[X4]
  X3 -> exit1!.P2[X]
  X4 -> exit2!.P2[X]
end
```

```
system BroadSys:
    sync on {enter1, enter2, exit1, exit2} in
        P1[X] | P2[X]
    end
end
```

Fig. 10. The CCSP representation of the Mutual exclusion algorithm using broadcast

There, `enter1` and `enter2` are synchronization channels; therefore the two processes `P1` and `P2` have to perform the same actions; if `enter1!` is the performed action, then `P1` can enter its critical section and `P2` must wait until `P1` exits; if `enter2!` is the performed action, then `P2` can enter its critical section and `P1` must wait until `P2` exits. This simple example is useful for showing that different primitives (multicast messages or singlecast messages) permit developing different solutions.

Using TAPAs students can verify properties of the systems. By means of the equivalence checker, equivalence of the system's implementation and the mutual exclusion specification reported in Fig. 11 can be tested. Process `Spec` models the cyclical behaviour of entering and exiting of `P1` and `P2` (without distinction between them) from their critical sections. In this way it is specified that they can never be in the critical sections at the same time: two consecutive actions `enter!` cannot be performed. Notably, at this level of abstraction it is not necessary to identify the actual process that is using its critical section. Thus, before executing the test, `Sys` and `BroadSys` must be slightly modified as follows:

```
rename [enter/enter1, enter/enter2, exit/exit1, exit/exit2] in
    Sys/BroadSys
end
```

Fig. 11. Mutual exclusion specification

The processes we have just modified and `Spec` are weakly bisimilar. However, due to busy-waiting, `Sys` is not testing equivalent to `Spec`, because `Sys` can diverge while `BroadSys` cannot.

The behaviour of the systems specified so far can also be verified through the TAPAs model checker. For instance, it can can be verified that the implementations of Peterson's algorithm and the one based on multi-synchronization enjoy the following relevant properties specified in μ-calculus [16].

- *Deadlock-freedom.* In each state, the system can perform at least one action:

$$\nu X.\langle - \rangle \texttt{true} \wedge [-]X$$

- *Livelock-freedom.* The system cannot reach a state where it can perform only infinite sequences of internal actions:

$$\neg \mu X.\langle - \rangle X \vee \nu Y.[-\tau]\texttt{false} \wedge \langle \tau \rangle \texttt{true} \wedge [\tau]Y$$

- *Starvation-freedom.* If a process wants to enter its critical section, eventually it succeeds:

$$\mu X.[-]X \vee \langle \texttt{enter i!} \rangle \texttt{true}$$

At the end of the academic course we assign to students a case study and they have to specify and verify it using TAPAs. We have noticed that, at first, students try to specify all the features of the system, even those redundant and not necessary. Often, after experiencing problems related to the state space explosion they understand the need of abstract description. Thus, they reduce the number of the states by simplifying the system omitting the unnecessary aspects, to capture only the interesting behaviour of the analysed system. In some case they also use the minimisation facility to reduce the size of the components before actually composing them to obtain systems.

5 Conclusions and Related Work

We have introduced TAPAs, a tool for the specification and the analysis of concurrent systems. TAPAs has been designed to support teaching concurrency and one of its distinguishing feature is the independence from specific process algebras and logics, that is guaranteed by its generic graphical formalism. TAPAs assigns a central role to LTS. By considering the LTS associated to the different terms students can appreciate similarities and differences between the operators. Moreover, by studying the effect of some of the most important equivalences over LTS, students can appreciate their impact on specific calculi and gain insight into the nature of their nature.

By comparing the lectures where TAPAs was used as teaching support with the 'classical' ones, we have noticed that the students got significantly more interested in the subject. The students that have developed simple (but realistic) case studies using TAPAs, have shown a deeper understanding of process algebras, behavioural equivalences and model checking. In spite of its didactical nature, TAPAs has also been used to deal with more complex systems and we plan to use it to gently expose researchers from industry to the use of formal methods.

In the last years many other tools were developed, but, generally, they are not intended to support teaching: some tools have not a graphical user interface, others do not support the process algebras commonly used in the academic courses (CCS, CSP) and just few tools allow the graphical specification.

One of the most used tool for teaching concurrency, that follows a process algebraic approach, is LTSA [17]. It permits generating LTS starting from a term written in a simple process algebra (named FSP), but it does not allows a direct graphical specification of terms. LTSA allows the verification of systems properties by reachability analysis based on formulae of a Linear Time Temporal logic (named Fluent LTL), and it generates traces leading to failures whenever the specified property is not satisfied. Differently from TAPAs, LTSA does not provide an equivalence checker.

Another well-known tool for process algebras is CADP [12]: it offers a wide set of functionalities, ranging from step-by-step simulation to massively parallel model-checking, but it does not allow the graphical specification and the systems descriptions have to be written in LOTOS [25] that is not a widely used process algebra.

CWB [20] and CWB-NC [2] are very efficient tools that permit specifying and verifying properties of concurrent systems. These tools support many process algebras and can be used for checking many behavioural equivalences. However, both CWB and CWB-NC do not provide a graphical interface that can be used for describing concurrent systems. Clearly, this can make difficult to use tools in academic course for introducing theory of concurrency.

As a future work, we plan also to continue the development by adding modules to deal with other process algebras, such as value-passing CCS [19] and LOTOS, and with other logics. Moreover, we will add other analysis tools, such as a simulator that allows "animating" the system showing the possible interactions between its components. We plan also to improve the TAPAs back end in order to support systems with a larger state space. Moreover we plan to enrich TAPAs along the lines of PAC [8] to permit users to define their own operators and to generate the LTS associates to terms containing these new operators.

Acknowledgments. We would like to thank Fabio Collini, Massimiliano Gori, Stefano Guerrini and Guzman Tierno for having contributed with their master theses to the development of key parts of the software at the basis of TAPAs.

References

1. TAPAs: a Tool for the Analysis of Process Algebras, `http://rap.dsi.unifi.it/tapas`
2. Alur, R., Henzinger, T.: The NCSU Concurrency Workbench. In: CAV 1996. LNCS, vol. 1102, pp. 394–397. Springer, Heidelberg (1996)

3. Baeten, J.C.M., Weijland, W.P.: Process algebra. Cambridge Tracts in Theoretical Computer Science, vol. 18. Cambridge University Press, Cambridge (1990)
4. Bergstra, J.A., Klop, J.W.: Process algebra for synchronous communication. Information and Control 60(1-3), 109–137 (1984)
5. Bowman, H., Gomez, R.: Concurrency Theory: Calculi. an Automata for Modelling Untimed and Timed Concurrent Systems. Springer, Heidelberg (2006)
6. Brookes, S.D., Hoare, C.A.R., Roscoe, A.W.: A theory of communicating sequential processes. J. ACM 31(3), 560–599 (1984)
7. Clarke, E.M., Emerson, E.A.: Design and synthesis of synchronization skeletons using branching-time temporal logic. In: Proceedings of Logic of Programs, pp. 52–71. Springer, Heidelberg (1982)
8. Cleaveland, R., Madelaine, E., Sims, S.: A front-end generator for verification tools. In: Brinksma, E., Steffen, B., Cleaveland, W.R., Larsen, K.G., Margaria, T. (eds.) TACAS 1995. LNCS, vol. 1019, pp. 153–173. Springer, Heidelberg (1995)
9. De Nicola, R., Hennessy, M.: Testing equivalences for processes. Theor. Comput. Sci. 34, 83–133 (1984)
10. De Nicola, R., Vaandrager, F.W.: Action versus state based logics for transition systems. In: Guessarian, I. (ed.) Semantics of Systems of Concurrent Processes. LNCS, vol. 469, pp. 407–419. Springer, Heidelberg (1990)
11. Fokkink, W.: Introduction to Process Algebra. Springer, Heidelberg (2000)
12. Garavel, H., Lang, F., Mateescu, R.: An overview of CADP 2001. In: European Association for Software Science and Technology (EASST). Newsletter, vol. 4, pp. 13–24 (2002)
13. Hennessy, M., Milner, R.: Algebraic laws for nondeterminism and concurrency. J. ACM 32(1), 137–161 (1985)
14. Hoare, C.A.R.: A model for communicating sequential processes. In: On the Construction of Programs, pp. 229–254. Cambridge University Press, Cambridge (1980)
15. Hoare, C.A.R.: Communicating Sequential Processes. Prentice-Hall, Englewood Cliffs (1985)
16. Kozen, D.: Results on the propositional μ-calculus. Theor. Comput. Sci. 27, 333–354 (1983)
17. Magee, J., Kramer, J.: Concurrency: State Models and Java Programs. John Wiley and Sons Inc., Chichester (2006)
18. Milner, R.: A Calculus of Communication Systems. LNCS, vol. 92. Springer, Heidelberg (1980)
19. Milner, R.: Communication and Concurrency. Prentice-Hall, Inc., Upper Saddle River (1989)
20. Moller, F., Stevens, P.: Edinburgh Concurrency Workbench User Manual, `http://homepages.inf.ed.ac.uk/perdita/cwb/`
21. Olderog, E.-R.: Operational Petri net semantics for CCSP. In: Rozenberg, G. (ed.) APN 1987. LNCS, vol. 266, pp. 196–223. Springer, Heidelberg (1987)
22. Roscoe, A.W.: The Theory and Practice of Concurrency. Prentice-Hall, Englewood Cliffs (1997)
23. Schneider, S.A.: Concurrent and Real-Time Systems: The CSP Approach. Wiley & Sons, Chichester (1999)
24. van Glabbeek, R.J., Vaandrager, F.W.: Bundle event structures and CCSP. In: Amadio, R., Lugiez, D. (eds.) CONCUR 2003. LNCS, vol. 2761, pp. 57–71. Springer, Heidelberg (2003)
25. van Eijk, P.H.J., Vissers, C.A., Diaz, M.: The Formal Description Technique LOTOS. Elsevier Science Publishers B.V., Amsterdam (1989)
26. van Glabbeek, R.J., Weijland, W.P.: Branching time and abstraction in bisimulation semantics. J. ACM 43(3), 555–600 (1996)
27. Winskel, G.: Topics in Concurrency. Lecture notes, University of Cambridge (2008), `http://www.cl.cam.ac.uk/~gw104/TIC08.ps`

Translating Message Sequence Charts to other Process Languages Using Process Mining

Kristian Bisgaard Lassen[1] and Boudewijn F. van Dongen[2]

[1] Department of Computer Science, University of Aarhus, IT-parken, Aabogade 34, DK-8200 Aarhus N, Denmark
k.b.lassen@daimi.au.dk

[2] Department of Computer Science, Eindhoven University of Technology P.O. Box 513, NL-5600 MB, Eindhoven, The Netherlands
b.f.v.dongen@tue.nl

Abstract. Message Sequence Charts (MSCs) are often used by software analysts when discussing the behavior of a system with different stakeholders. Often such discussions lead to more complete behavioral models in the form of, e.g., Event-driven Process Chains (EPCs), Unified Modeling Language (UML), activity diagrams, Business Process Modeling Notation (BPMN) models, Petri nets, etc. Process mining on the other hand, deals with the problem of constructing complete behavioral models by analyzing event logs of information systems.

In contrast to existing process mining techniques, where logs are assumed to only contain implicit information, the approach presented in this paper combines the explicit knowledge captured in individual MSCs and the techniques and tools available in the process mining domain. This combination allows us to discover high-quality process models.

To constructively add to the existing work on process mining, our approach has been implemented in the process mining framework ProM (www.processmining.org).

Keywords: message sequence charts, process mining, synthesis of scenarios-based models.

1 Introduction

Message Sequence Charts (MSCs) [26, 29] are a well-known language to specify communication between processes, and are supported by many tools, standards, and approaches, e.g., the Object Management Group (OMG) has decided to adapt a variant called sequence charts in the UML notational framework [21]. In this paper we look at MSCs that are restricted to (using) agents and messages. We do not consider structured language features such as choice and iteration introduced by the UML 2.0 standard, i.e., we consider basic MSCs rather than high-level MSCs.

When developing a system it is often useful to describe requirements for the system by MSCs were each MSC depicts a single scenario. For example, in a

K. Jensen, W. van der Aalst, and J. Billington (Eds.): ToPNoC I, LNCS 5100, pp. 71–85, 2008.

recent project, the staff and software developers at a hospital were asked to capture the requirements for a new pervasive health care system [20]. The strength of MSCs is that each MSC depicts a single scenario using an intuitive notation. Therefore, they are easy to understand. However, at the same time, this strength can be considered a weakness, since it is not clear how to consolidate several scenarios describing the same system. For example, two MSCs may be similar up to a certain point, after which they diverge. At the point where they diverge, a decision was made (either by the environment or by a person involved in the process). However, identifying the exact diversion point, the underlying semantics of the decision can only be done by analyzing the two MSCs together, and not in isolation. Hence, to get a good understanding of the system modeled by the individual MSCs, one needs to consider all of them together, i.e., a single process model needs to be *synthesized* from individual MSCs. For an elaborate overview of the related work in this area, we refer to Sect. 5 of [10].

Considerable work has been done on the synthesis of scenario-based models such as MSCs (see [19] for an overview). Existing approaches are very different and typically have problems dealing with concurrency. Moreover, the majority of approaches uses explicit annotations to "glue" MSCs together in a single model. For example, high-level MSCs are used [18, 30, 31], but also "precharts", "state conditions" and similar concepts to explicitly relate MSCs [12, 24, 25]. Other problems are related to performance, implied scenarios (i.e., the model allows for more behavior than what has actually been observed), and consistency (e.g., the synthesized model contains deadlocks) [6, 7].

The research area of process mining [2, 3, 4, 11, 14, 16, 27] focuses on the synthesis or process models from event logs, which in the process mining domain is usually referred to as *control flow discovery*. Most existing control flow discovery algorithms assume event logs to only contain the events as logged by an information system, i.e., without any explicit information about the relation between events. Therefore, these algorithms usually first abstract from the log to identify these relations and then use this abstraction for constructing a process model, represented using languages such as Event-driven Process Chains (EPCs), Petri nets, Yet Another Workflow Language (YAWL) [1], or even Business Process Execution Language (BPEL) [9].

In this paper, we present an approach to combine the synthesis of MSCs and control flow discovery, by adapting process mining algorithms to take into account the explicit information about relations between events present in MSCs. Our approach is fully implemented in the process mining framework ProM [17,32] which supports a wide variety of process modeling languages (Petri nets, EPCs, YAWL, BPEL, transition systems, heuristics nets, etc.). Using ProM the process mining results can be mapped on any of these languages.

This paper is organized as follows. First, in Sect. 2, we introduce MSCs and a running example that we will use throughout the paper. In Sect. 3 we give an overview of two existing process mining algorithms that we use in our approach. Then, in Sect. 4, we show how to use the information contained in MSCs to extend the two algorithms presented. Finally, we conclude the paper in Sect. 5.

2 Message Sequence Charts and Online Bookstore Example

As mentioned in Sect. 1, several variants of MSCs exists, such as UML 2.0 sequence charts [19] and live sequence charts [21]. In this paper we focus on MSCs with only two syntactical constructs, i.e., agents and messages. Agents can be used to denote a wide variety of entities ranging from software components and Web services to people and organizations. A message is passed from one agent to the other and therefore each message has a, (not necessarily different) sending and receiving agent. An agent has a lifeline representing the sequence of messages of which that agent is the sender or the receiver.

In this paper we will use a running example of an online bookstore, to explain the various aspects of our approach. We modeled a process of ordering a book at the bookstore in 20 different MSCs, containing 23 different messages. The example refers to the following four types of agents:

Customer. A person that wants to buy a book.
Bookstore. Handles the customer request to buy a book. The virtual bookstore always contacts a publisher to see if it can handle the order. If the bookstore cannot find a suitable publisher, the customer's order is rejected. If the bookstore finds a publisher, a shipper is selected and the book is shipped. During shipping, the bookstore sends a bill to the customer.
Publisher. May or may not have the book that the customer wants to buy.
Shipper. May or may not be able to carry out the shipping order.

Figure 1 shows two examples where the customer orders a book at the bookstore. In the first MSC the `Customer` sends a message `place_c_order`, which is received by the `Bookstore`. The `Bookstore` then sends a message to itself, signified by the box on the lifeline. Then the bookstore sends the message `place_b_order` to the `Publisher`, and so on. The overall behavior is that the customer orders a book, after which the bookstore asks two publishers if they can deliver the book. Since none of them have it in stock, the bookstore has to reject the customer's order. The second MSC describes a similar scenario, but here the customer actually receives the book.

We use the bookstore process as a running example in this paper, and in Sect. 4, we show some models obtained through process mining. Note that the agents in our example MSCs do not represent physical entities, i.e., in real life, there might be multiple bookstores that do business with multiple publishers and shippers. However, for process mining, this would only be important if the organizational perspective is considered, which, in this paper, we do not.

3 Process Mining

The goal of process mining, or more specifically control flow discovery is to extract information about processes from event logs, such that the control flow

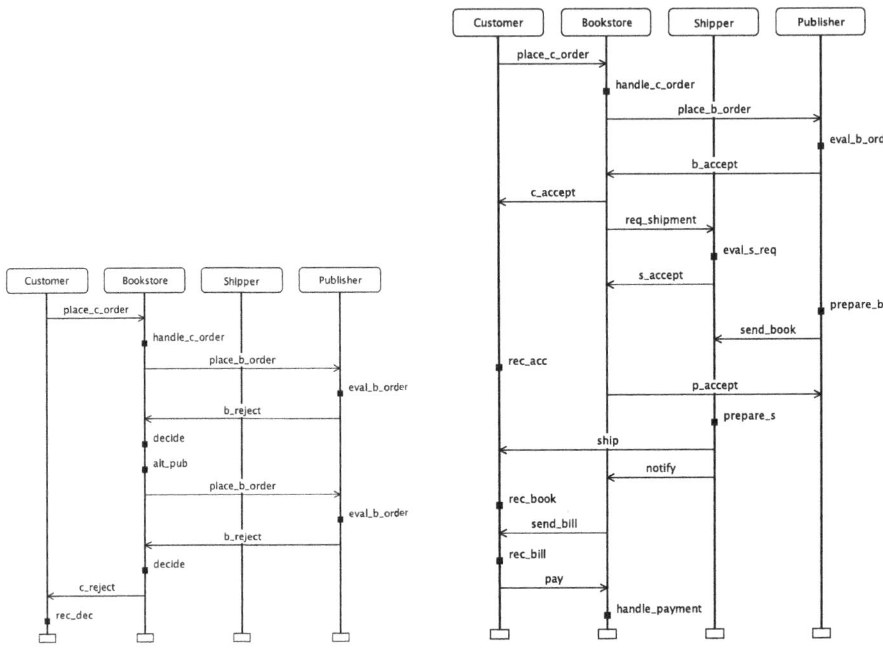

Fig. 1. Two MSCs of scenarios in our bookstore example

of a process is captured in a process model. In process mining an *activity* refers to an atomic part of a process, which may be executed over any length of time and by anyone. We refer to a *case* (we also refer to it as a *process instance*) as the execution trace of a process.

The starting point for control flow discovery is an event log that contains events such that:

1. Each event refers to an *activity* (i.e., a well-defined step in the process),
2. Each event refers to a *case* (i.e., a process instance) and
3. Events are totally ordered (for example by a timestamp).

Table 1 shows an example of a log involving 19 events and 5 activities. This event log also contains information about the people executing the corresponding activities (cf. the originator field Table 1). Often logs also contain information about data associated to events, but for the work presented in this paper, this information can be ignored.

Figure 2 shows some examples of process mining results that can be obtained using an event log of Table 1. This figure clearly shows that process mining is not limited to control flow discovery, i.e., the roles of the actors in the process, as well as their social relations can be discovered as well. However, in this paper, we only focus on the control flow, which is shown as a Petri net in Fig. 2.

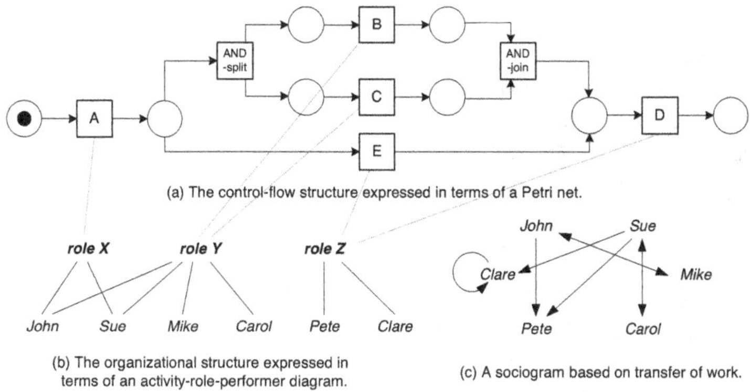

Fig. 2. Some mining results from different perspectives

The (Pro)cess (M)ining framework *ProM* has been developed as a completely plug-able environment for process mining and related topics. Currently, over 230 plug-ins have been added. For more information on process mining and the ProM framework, we refer to [17,32] and the Website `www.processmining.org`. A screenshot of ProM, showing results of analysis of our bookstore example from different perspectives is shown in Fig. 3.

ProM uses a standard log format, named MXML as described in [15] for storing process logs, such as the one in Table 1. In the context of the ProMimport framework [23], several adaptors have been developed to map logs from different information systems onto MXML (e.g., Staffware, FLOWer, MS Exchange, MQSeries, etc.).

In this paper, we show that we can use the ProM framework to analyze MSCs, by adapting two mining plug-ins to use the explicit information about the relation between events contained in MSCs. However, before describing the necessary changes to the α *Miner* and the *Multi-phase Miner*, we first introduce these algorithms in some detail.

Table 1. An event log (audit trail)

Case id	Activity id	Originator	Case id	Activity id	Originator
Case 1	Activity A	John	Case 5	Activity A	Sue
Case 2	Activity A	John	Case 4	Activity C	Carol
Case 3	Activity A	Sue	Case 1	Activity D	Pete
Case 3	Activity B	Carol	Case 3	Activity C	Sue
Case 1	Activity B	Mike	Case 3	Activity D	Pete
Case 1	Activity C	John	Case 4	Activity B	Sue
Case 2	Activity C	Mike	Case 5	Activity E	Clare
Case 4	Activity A	Sue	Case 5	Activity D	Clare
Case 2	Activity B	John	Case 4	Activity D	Pete
Case 2	Activity D	Pete			

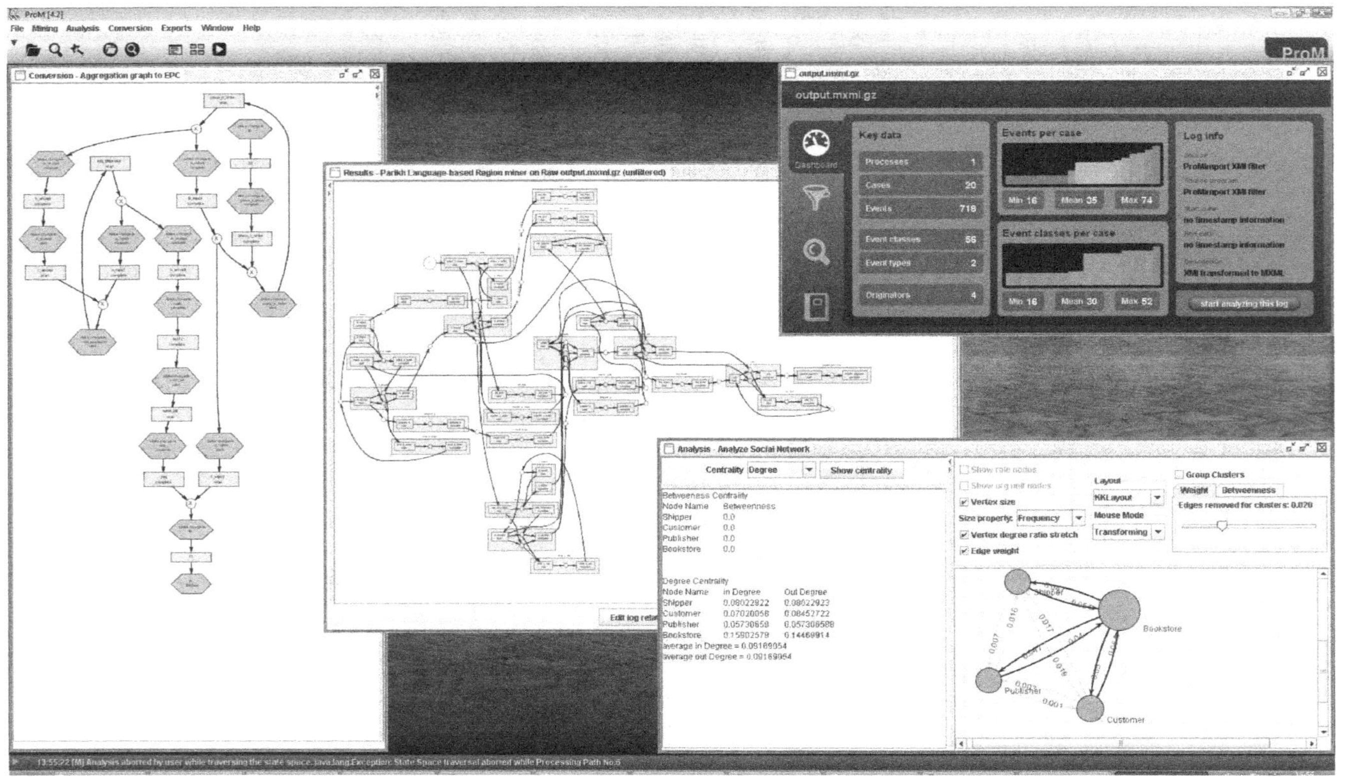

Fig. 3. ProM showing analysis of the bookstore example. The external behavior of the bookstore on the left, a summary of the log on the top right, the social network (handover of work) on the bottom right and the full process as a free-choice elementary net in the middle.

3.1 The "α Miner"

The α-miner provides an implementation of one of the earliest mining algorithms [3] and some extensions [8]. As mentioned in Sect. 1, most algorithms use an abstraction step to abstract from the event log. The abstraction made by the α-algorithm is the following. First, the event log is analyzed and for each pair of activities, it is determined whether or not they succeed each other directly, which is expressed by a $>$ relation (e.g., if one case shows that activity A is directly followed by activity B, then $A > B$).

Using the $>$ relation, two more informative relations between activities are determined, usually referred to as *ordering relations*:

- Activity B is considered to causally follow activity A (denoted by $A \rightarrow B$), if and only if $A > B$ and *not* $B > A$, i.e., in at least one case, activity A was directly succeeded by activity B, but never the other way around,
- Activities A and B are considered to be *in parallel* (denoted by $A \| B$)if and only if both $A > B$ and $B > A$, i.e., activities A and B can occur in the same case, directly succeeding each other, but the order in which they appear is arbitrary,

In a final step, the α algorithm determines the places of a Petri net model, solely based on the causal and parallel dependencies between activities.

3.2 The "Multi-phase Miner"

A slightly more advanced plug-in is the *Multi-phase Miner*. This plug-in implements a collection of algorithms [14, 16]. The first step of these algorithms is similar to the first step of the α algorithm, i.e., first the $>$ relation is built, after which the causal dependencies between activities are determined ($\rightarrow$ relation).

However, the causal dependencies between activities are not directly used to construct a process model from an event log. Instead, these relations are used to translate each case in the log into a partial order on its events, a so-called *instance graph* [14]. By introducing this partial order on a case level, each individual case now contains explicit information about parallelism and causality. Note that the information about parallelism is not derived from the $>$ relation.

In the final step of the multi-phase miner, the partially ordered cases or instance graphs are aggregated into a single process model or *aggregation graph*, for which translations are provided into EPCs and Petri nets.

In the next section, we provide the two different ways in which MSCs can be added to algorithms presented in this section. We start with the latter algorithm, as MSCs are closely related to the instance graphs used there.

3.3 Mining XML

The input language for ProM is called Mining XML (MXML) [23]. This is a simple XML language that specifies a workflow log.

Although MXML may seem fixed it is possible to extend the language, as we will see later, by extending the various data entities. These entities allow any information to be added that do not fit into the rest of the language, and are basically just pairs of named strings.

4 Generating Process Models from MSCs

This section presents two approaches for aggregating a set of MSCs into a single process model. We first present how we extended ProM such that it is capable of importing MSCs, since we want to consider MSCs in the same way as event logs are considered (i.e., as input for mining plug-ins). As the first step in process mining often is to filter the log so that it shows only relevant information, we provide the details on how to do that for partially ordered logs. Finally, we present how the MSCs are used by the two plug-ins implementing the algorithms mentioned before.

4.1 MSCs to Annotated MXML

For the conversion of *any* event log format to MXML, the ProMimport framework has been developed. For our approach, we have chosen to use XML Metadata Interchange (XMI) [22], the Object Management Group (OMG) standard interchange format, as our input format for MSCs, and to implement the translation in a plug-in for the ProMimport framework.

In this ProMimport plug-in, each MSC is translated into one case. The reason for this is simple. Since each MSC describes one possible execution scenario of the system, it corresponds to the notion of a case, which is also referred to as *process instance*.

Within each MSC, all messages are translated into *two* events, or *audit trail entries*; one referring to the sending of the message and one referring to the receiving of the message. To accomplish this, we make sure that both events refer to the same activity (i.e., the message). The event that refers to the sending of the message has event type `start`. Receiving audit trail entries have type `complete`.

To incorporate the information about agents in MXML, we use the originator field of each event in a trivial way. If the agent `Customer` sends the message `place_c_order` to the `Bookstore` agent, then the originator field of the event relating to the sending of the message equals `Customer` and the originator field of the event relating to the receiving of the message equals `Bookstore`. As mentioned before, we do not consider instances of the same agent type here, i.e., there is only one publisher agent and one bookstore agent. However, if necessary (e.g., when applying social network analysis) each instance could uniquely be identified.

Finally, we add data to each event, so that each event has a unique label within a case. Using these labels, the partial order information is stored, by providing the set of predecessors and successors of each event that we have observed in the MSC. Consider for example the MSC of Fig. 1, where the first three events are: (1) the sending of message `place_c_order` by `Customer`, (2) the receiving of message `place_c_order` by `Bookstore` and (3) the sending of message `handle_c_order` by `Bookstore`.

The relations between events stored in the data part of MXML, are built in a trivial way. If an event refers to the sending of a message, the preset of that event is the event that happened before it on the lifeline of the corresponding agent. If the event refers to the receiving of a message, the preset *also* contains the event referring to the sending of the same message. The postsets are build in a similar fashion.

Figure 4 shows a part of an annotated MXML file illustrating how MSCs are stored. It contains a `isPartialOrder` flag for the process instance to denote the fact that partial order information is present. Furthermore, it shows the identifiers and pre- and postsets for the events.

4.2 Filtering a Partially Ordered Log

Through the annotated MXML format, the MSCs can be used directly in process mining. However, our experience is that the first step in process mining is usually to focus on a subset of the information in the log, i.e., by *filtering* the log, for example by only considering the completion of activities, or the activities executed by a specific person. For this purpose, ProM is equipped with log filters.

Log filters typically remove events that are not of interest. If events are totally ordered, then this is easy to do without disturbing the ordering between events. In case of partially ordered events however, it is less trivial to remove events without disturbing the ordering relation. In fact, events can only be removed if the partial order is first *transitively closed.*

For this purpose, we implemented two log filters in ProM. The first one transitively closes the partial order. Then already existing filters can be applied and afterwards our second plug-in transitively reduces the partial order[1]. In the examples presented in the remainder of this section, we use these filters in practice.

It is important to realize that the transitive reduction of an MSC is not the MSC itself. For example, in Fig. 1, the path between the sending of message `place_c_order` by `Customer` and the receiving of message `c_reject` by the same agent is lost. However, in the remainder of this section, we show that this is an advantage for the usability of existing mining algorithms.

4.3 MSCs in the Multi-phase Miner

In Sect. 4.1 we provided a way to import MSCs into ProM and in Sect. 4.2 we provided a way to filter them as one usually would a linearly ordered event log. In this section, we show how MSCs seamlessly integrate into the first of two existing process discovery algorithms.

As stated in Sect. 3.2, the multi-phase miner implements a two-stage process. On a linearly ordered event log, it first translates each case (or process instance)

[1] The idea of transitive reduction is that an edge between two nodes in a graph is removed if there is a different path from the source node to the target node. Since partial orders are a-cyclic, the transitive reduction is unique [5].

into a partial order. Such a partial order is called an instance graph and each instance graph satisfies the following two requirements [14]:

Partial orders are minimal. The aggregation algorithm presented in [16] assumes that the partial orders used as input are minimal, i.e., there are no two paths between two nodes.

Input and output sets are uniquely labeled. The second requirement for the aggregation algorithm is that no single event is preceded or succeeded by two events with the same label twice.

The first of the two requirements is clearly not met by our MSCs, i.e., if `Customer` sends message `place_c_order` to `Bookstore` and then gets message `c_reject` back from `Bookstore` there are several paths between the event referring to the sending of message `place_c_order` and the event referring to the receiving of message `c_reject` (see Fig. 1). The first path is the trivial path directly from the sending `place_c_order` event to receiving `c_reject` event, and the other paths are those which include the receive `place_c_order` event. Therefore, it is necessary to *transitively reduce* each MSC, before applying the aggregation algorithm. To transitively reduce the partial order, we make use of the advanced filtering capabilities of ProM, which we discussed in Sect. 4.2. In the left example MSC of Fig. 1, the result of reduction is simply the sequence `place_c_order`, receive `place_c_order`, ..., send `c_reject`, receive `c_reject`; i.e., a single event occurrence path.

The second requirement is harder to satisfy. Consider Fig. 5, where the start event of message `order` by `Bookstore` is followed by two complete events of the same message, i.e., the one coming in from `Customer` and the one going to `Shipper`. Note that this situation would not occur if message `order` is first sent by `Customer` to `Bookstore` and then by `Bookstore` to `Shipper`, or if these messages would be labelled differently, as is the case in our example, where they are labelled `place_c_order` and `place_b_order`. Furthermore, our experience has shown that such situation is unlikely to occur in practice and if it does, it can be resolved by adding an internal message on the lifeline of `Bookstore`.

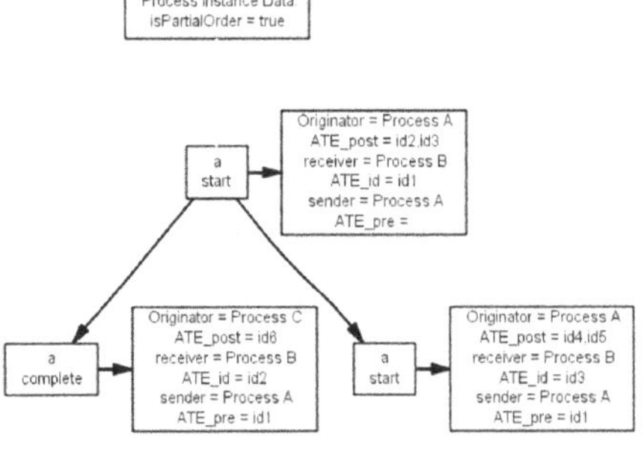

Fig. 4. A partially ordered MXML snapshot in ProM

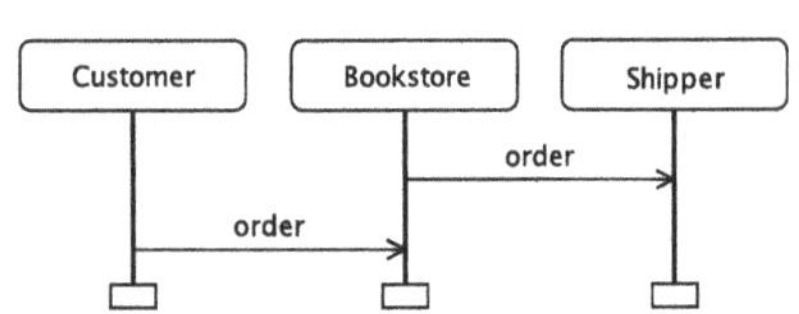

Fig. 5. An MSC that leads to problems in the aggregation

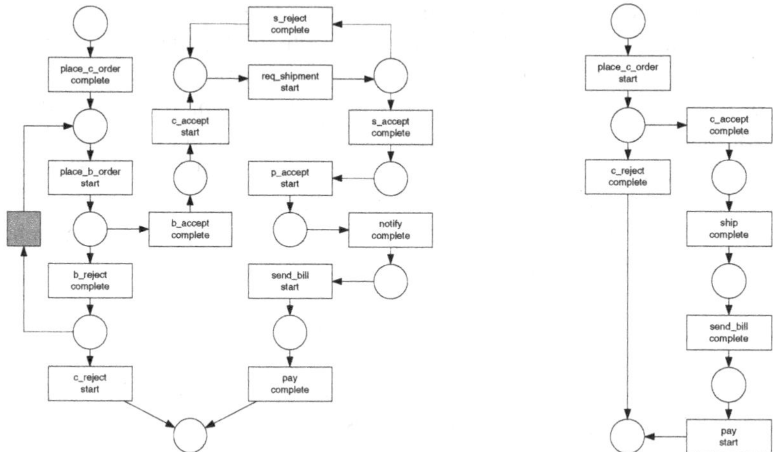

Fig. 6. Petri net showing the external behaviour of the bookstore

Fig. 7. The external behavior of the customer

In a second step, the multi-phase miner takes a collection of instance graphs (or transitively reduced MSCs) and aggregates them into a so-called aggregation graph, which in turn can be translated into an EPC or Petri net. This procedure is described in detail in [16]. In essence, an aggregation graph is a straightforward sum over a set of partial orders, with two unique nodes t_s and t_f in such a way that t_s is the only source node and t_f is the only sink node. The labels of nodes and edges represent the number of times it was visited in some partial order.

Figure 6 shows the external behavior of the bookstore from our example, obtained using the multi-phase miner. To obtain this result, we first projected the MSCs onto the audit trail entries where `bookstore` is described in the `originator` field, i.e., we focussed on the lifeline of `bookstore`. Furthermore, we removed all internal messages, i.e., messages for which the sender equals the receiver. The result is a Petri net, which shows the behavior of the bookstore as defined in the MSCs. Note that, according to this Petri net, the bookstore always finds a shipper, i.e., after sending the message `req_shipment` (transition $\texttt{req\_shipment}_{start}$), the message `s_accept` will eventually be received. This might be true in real life, but this might also indicate that not all possible behavior has been captured in MSCs yet.

Finally, each of these aggregation graphs can be translated into an EPC, i.e., into a human-readable format. This is where the requirements where the MSCs are minimal and where the in- and output sets are uniquely labeled are important, since the translation depends on the labels of nodes and edges. In short, if a node has the same label as each of its input edges, it is an AND-join, if a node has a label that equals the sum of the labels of all input edges it is an XOR-join and otherwise an OR-join and symmetrically for the split type.[2]

[2] If one of the two requirements of the input is violated, these translation rules may not be valid and the result may contain too many OR connectors.

Since the multi-phase miner already used partial orders internally, its application to MSCs was a logical choice. However, when an aggregation graph is translated to a Petri net, the result is often a model which allows for much more behavior than seen in the log. This property has been explained in detail in Sect. 6.6 of [13], where it is also shown that the resulting Petri net can reproduce the partial orders given as input. Furthermore, in [13] is was also shown that an EPC representation of a process is correct if the Petri net translation thereof is relaxed sound, which is the case for the Petri nets generated by our approach, when using the restriction process described in [16] to reduce the number of invisible transitions.

Opposite to the multi-phase miner, the α-algorithm results in more restrictive Petri nets, without "invisible" transitions, but the result might be too restrictive, i.e., the resulting Petri net cannot reproduce the log. However, we still feel that it is an important algorithm to be applied to MSCs.

4.4 The α-algorithm on Partial Orders

In Sect. 3.1, we stated that the α-algorithm first translates an event log into a set of ordering relations before constructing a Petri net. Recall that these ordering relations are traditionally based on the linear ordering of events in the log, i.e., the $>$ relation mentioned before.

To extend the α-algorithm to work with partial orders, we simply redefine the $>$ relation. For two events A and B, we say it holds that $A > B$ if there is an edge between events A and B in the partial order. In other words, we say that activities A and B could directly follow each other, if and only if there is an edge between them in an MSC. Note that this indeed holds for all messages, i.e., the sending of a message can directly be followed by the receiving of that message. For the subsequent events on a lifeline however, this is not necessarily the case, i.e., the sending of message `place_c_order` by `Customer` in the first MSC in Fig. 1 is never *directly* followed by the receiving of message `c_reject` by the same agent since other events occur in between. Therefore, in case of the α-algorithm, it is also important to look at the transitive reduction of the MSC.

Figure 7 shows the external behavior of the customer from our example, obtained using the α-algorithm. To obtain this result, we first projected the MSCs onto the audit trail entries where `customer` is described in the `originator` field and again, we removed all internal messages. The result is a Petri net, which shows the behavior of the customer as defined in the MSCs. From a customer perspective, this seems a desirable process, i.e., he places an order, after which the order is rejected or accepted. If the order was accepted, a shipment is received (containing the book) and a bill is sent *afterwards*. The process only ends when the customer sends the payment.

4.5 Other Process Mining Techniques

In Fig. 2, we presented an overview of applying mining algorithms from different perspectives. By enabling these techniques to be applied to MSCs, many useful insights can be gained into a process described by a collection of MSCs. Unfortunately, we do not have the space to elaborate on all of them. Therefore, we show a screenshot of the process mining framework ProM (see Fig. 3). The ProM framework can be downloaded from `www.processmining.org` and can freely be used (it is open source software). The reader is invited to experiment with the plug-ins and many others reported in this paper and apply it to MSCs expressed in the OMG's XMI format.

5 Conclusions

This paper presented a new approach to synthesize a process model from MSCs. The approach uses ideas from the process mining community and adapts these to incorporate the explicit causal dependencies present in MSCs. The approach has been fully implemented in ProM, by extending the MXML language with the notion of partial orders, and developing an import plug-in to convert XMI to MXML, and a partial order aggregator to generate the process models from the MXML. See Fig. 3 for a screenshot of the application.

We showed how an existing process mining algorithm can be adapted to exploit causal dependencies and that the discovered model can be represented in different notations, e.g., EPCs, Petri nets, BPEL, and YAWL. Moreover, the ideas are not limited to MSCs and can be applied to other event logs containing explicit causal dependencies, e.g., collaboration diagrams, groupware products, document management systems, case handling systems, product data management systems, etc.

The techniques introduced in this paper also applies to UML 2.0 Sequence Charts, since the structured constructs such as parallel routing, iteration, choice, etc., can initially be unfolded to the MSCs we use in this paper [28], and then mined using the techniques we present in this paper. Although high-level features may be interesting for specifying systems (and as [28] shows we are able to handle these) our intention with this paper is to show how to support modelers that use MSCs to model example scenarios. By providing a translation, we help them make a move forward, from a collection of MSCs, to a single coherent model. This model may eventually be developed into a specification of the system, or it may simply be used to give a more intelligible behavior description than the MSCs.

Acknowledgments. We would like to thank the reviewers of ToPNoC, as well as the editors, for their fruitful comments to improve this paper.

References

[1] van der Aalst, W.M.P., ter Hofstede, A.H.M.: YAWL: yet another workflow language. Information Systems 30(4), 245–275 (2005)

[2] van der Aalst, W.M.P., van Dongen, B.F., Herbst, J., Maruster, L., Schimm, G., Weijters, A.J.M.M.: Workflow mining: a survey of issues and approaches. Data and Knowledge Engineering 47(2), 237–267 (2003)

[3] van der Aalst, W.M.P., Weijters, A.J.M.M., Maruster, L.: Workflow mining: discovering process models from event logs. IEEE Transactions on Knowledge and Data Engineering 16(9), 1128–1142 (2004)
[4] Agrawal, R., Gunopulos, D., Leymann, F.: Mining Process Models from Workflow Logs. In: Schek, H.-J., Saltor, F., Ramos, I., Alonso, G. (eds.) EDBT 1998. LNCS, vol. 1377, pp. 469–483. Springer, Heidelberg (1998)
[5] Aho, A., Garey, M., Ullman, J.: The transitive reduction of a directed graph. SIAM Journal on Computing 1(2), 131–137 (1972)
[6] Alur, R., Etessami, K., Yannakakis, M.: Inference of message sequence charts. IEEE Transactions on Software Engineering 29(7), 623–633 (2003)
[7] Alur, R., Etessami, K., Yannakakis, M.: Realizability and verification of MSC Graphs. Theoretical Computer Science 331(1), 97–114 (2005)
[8] Alves de Medeiros, A.K., van Dongen, B.F., van der Aalst, W.M.P., Weijters, A.J.M.M.: Process mining: extending the α-algorithm to mine short loops. BETA Working Paper Series, WP 113. Eindhoven University of Technology, Eindhoven (2004)
[9] Andrews, T., Curbera, F., Dholakia, H., Goland, Y., Klein, J., Leymann, F., Liu, K., Roller, D., Smith, D., Thatte, S., Trickovic, I., Weerawarana, S.: Business process execution language for web services, version 1.1. Standards proposal by BEA Systems. International Business Machines Corporation, and Microsoft Corporation (2003)
[10] Bisgaard Lassen, K., van Dongen, B.F., van der Aalst, W.M.P.: Translating message sequence charts to other process languages using process mining. BETA Working Paper Series, WP 207. Eindhoven University of Technology, Eindhoven (2007)
[11] Cook, J.E., Wolf, A.L.: Discovering models of software processes from event-based data. ACM Transactions on Software Engineering and Methodology 7(3), 215–249 (1998)
[12] Damm, W., Harel, D.: LSCs: Breathing life into message sequence charts. Formal Methods in System Design 19(1), 45–80 (2001)
[13] van Dongen, B.F.: Process Mining and Verification. PhD thesis, Eindhoven University of Technology, Eindhoven, The Netherlands (2007)
[14] van Dongen, B.F., van der Aalst, W.M.P.: Multi-phase process mining: building instance graphs. In: Atzeni, P., Chu, W., Lu, H., Zhou, S., Ling, T.W. (eds.) ER 2004. LNCS, vol. 3288, pp. 362–376. Springer, Heidelberg (2004)
[15] van Dongen, B.F., van der Aalst, W.M.P.: A meta model for process mining data. In: Missikoff, M., De Nicola, A. (eds.) EMOI-INTEROP, CEUR Workshop Proceedings. CEUR-WS.org, vol. 160 (2005)
[16] van Dongen, B.F., van der Aalst, W.M.P.: Multi-phase Process mining: Aggregating Instance Graphs into EPCs and Petri Nets. In: PNCWB 2005 Workshop, pp. 35–58 (2005)
[17] van Dongen, B.F., Alves de Medeiros, A.K., Verbeek, H.M.W., Weijters, A.J.M.M., van der Aalst, W.M.P.: The ProM framework: a new era in process mining tool support. In: Ciardo, G., Darondeau, P. (eds.) ICATPN 2005. LNCS, vol. 3536, pp. 444–454. Springer, Heidelberg (2005)
[18] Foster, H., Uchitel, S., Magee, J., Kramer, J.: Tool support for model-based engineering of web service compositions. In: Proceedings of 2005 IEEE International Conference on Web Services (ICWS 2005), Orlando, FL, USA, pp. 95–102. IEEE Computer Society, Los Alamitos (2005)
[19] Object Management Group. OMG Unified Modeling Language 2.0. OMG (2005), http://www.omg.com/uml/

[20] Object Management Group. XML Meta Interchange (2006), http://www.omg.org/technology/documents/formal/xmi.htm
[21] Günther, C.W., van der Aalst, W.M.P.: A Generic Import Framework for Process Event Logs. In: Eder, J., Dustdar, S. (eds.) BPM Workshops 2006. LNCS, vol. 4103, pp. 81–92. Springer, Heidelberg (2006)
[22] Harel, D.: From play-in scenarios to code: an achievable dream. Computer 34(1), 53–60 (2001)
[23] Harel, D., Kugler, H., Pnueli, A.: Synthesis revisited: generating statechart models from scenario-based requirements. In: Kreowski, H.-J., Montanari, U., Orejas, F., Rozenberg, G., Taentzer, G. (eds.) Formal Methods in Software and Systems Modeling. LNCS, vol. 3393, pp. 309–324. Springer, Heidelberg (2005)
[24] Harel, D., Thiagarajan, P.S.: Message Sequence Charts. UML for Real: Design of Embedded Real-time Systems (2003)
[25] Herbst, J.: A machine learning approach to workflow management. In: Lopez de Mantaras, R., Plaza, E. (eds.) ECML 2000. LNCS, vol. 1810, pp. 183–194. Springer, Heidelberg (2000)
[26] Lassen, K.B.: Translating UML 2.0 sequence charts into coloured Petri net using process mining. Technical report, Department of Computer Science at the University of Aarhus (2007)
[27] Liang, H., Dingel, J., Diskin, Z.: A comparative survey of scenario-based to state-based model synthesis approaches. In: Proceedings of the 2006 International Workshop on Scenarios and State Machines: Models, Algorithms, and Tools (SCESM 2006), pp. 5–12. ACM Press, New York (2006)
[28] Machado, R., Lassen, K.B., Oliveira, S., Couto, M., Pinto, P.: Requirements validation: execution of UML models with CPN tools. International Journal on Software Tools for Technology Transfer (STTT) 9(3), 353–369 (2007)
[29] Rudolph, E., Grabowski, J., Graubmann, P.: Tutorial on message sequence charts. Computer Networks and ISDN Systems 28(12), 1629–1641 (1996)
[30] Sgroi, M., Kondratyev, A., Watanabe, Y., Lavagno, L., Sangiovanni-Vincentelli, A.: Synthesis of Petri nets from message sequence charts specifications for protocol design. In: Design, Analysis and Simulation of Distributed Systems Symposium (DASD 2004), Washington DC, USA, April 2004, pp. 193–199 (2004)
[31] Uchitel, S., Kramer, J., Magee, J.: Synthesis of behavioral models from scenarios. IEEE Transactions on Software Engineering 29(2), 99–115 (2003)
[32] Verbeek, H.M.W., van Dongen, B.F., Mendling, J., van der Aalst, W.M.P.: Interoperability in the ProM Framework. In: EMOI-INTEROP (2006)

Net Components for the Integration of Process Mining into Agent-Oriented Software Engineering

Lawrence Cabac and Nicolas Denz

Department of Informatics, ASI / TGI, University of Hamburg
Vogt-Kölln-Straße 30, 22527 Hamburg, Germany
{cabac,denz}@informatik.uni-hamburg.de

Abstract. Process mining is increasingly used as an analysis technique to support the understanding of processes in software engineering. Due to the close relation to Petri nets as an underlying theory and representation technique, it can especially add to Petri net-based approaches. However, the complex analysis techniques are not straightforward to understand and handle for software developers with little data mining background. In this paper, we first discuss possibilities to integrate process mining into our Petri net-based agent-oriented software engineering approach. As the main contribution, we focus on enhancing its usability and introduce a technique and tool for visually modeling process mining algorithms with net components. These can be used to build new complex algorithms as a patch-work of existing procedures and new compositions. Furthermore, they allow for an easy integration with standard tools such as ProM.

Keywords: Petri nets, net components, process mining chains, modeling.

1 Introduction

Process mining is a subfield of data mining concerned with the reconstruction of process models from log data [41]. During the last years, the scope of research has been extended from mere business process analysis towards several areas related to processes in general. An active research field is the application of process mining to software engineering. Current approaches focus on analyzing software development processes on the one hand [9, 31] and the behavior of complex software artifacts such as Web services [12] or agents [5, 42] on the other hand.

Despite this progress, the applicability of process mining to software engineering suffers from two problems. Firstly, it is not straightforward to feed the information gathered through mining back into a conventional code-centric or semi-formal software engineering approach. Secondly, the selection and application of appropriate mining techniques is not trivial for the normal software developer without a strong data mining background. This is due to the high complexity and limited reliability of the techniques.

In this paper, we address the first problem by presenting software engineering based on reference nets as an appropriate foundation for the integration of

K. Jensen, W. van der Aalst, and J. Billington (Eds.): ToPNoC I, LNCS 5100, pp. 86–103, 2008.

process mining. On the one hand, Petri nets are a common means for result representation in process mining. On the other hand, the reference net formalism and the agent-oriented structure provided by the related MULAN [30] architecture allow to build large executable software systems based on Petri nets. Process mining techniques can be applied to aid the modeling, debugging, and validation of these systems. Furthermore, they can be integrated into the Petri net-based software agents to improve their adaptability.

As the main contribution of this paper, we address the second problem by presenting net components for the Petri net-based modeling of the process mining techniques themselves, which enhances their re-usability, validation, and documentation. Our specific *mining components* receive data from different sources of the development environment, process it, and transfer the resulting data to the next component or to sinks allowing for a feedback into the observed system. Several types of mining components can be assembled to so-called *process mining chains*.[1] Mining components can be implemented as *Java* Code or as sub-nets. The former allows to re-use algorithms implemented in standard tools such as WEKA [15] or ProM [43].

While the modeling of process mining chains fits the context of Petri net-based software engineering very well, the approach is not limited to this domain. Since there are no restrictions on the applied algorithms and on the processed data, the proposed modeling technique can also be used in further applications of process mining or other data intensive domains such as image processing.

The paper is organized as follows: In Sect. 2 we review related work on process mining in software engineering and on the explicit modeling of mining procedures. In Sect. 3 we discuss possibilities and requirements for the integration of process mining into the Petri net-based, agent-oriented software engineering life-cycle. We then introduce reference nets, net components, and the MULAN framework as an appropriate basis in Sect. 4. Section 5 focuses on the modeling of process mining procedures by a set of generic as well as specialized net components. Furthermore, it is shown how plugins of the process mining tool ProM can be integrated into our framework. Finally we present an example application of the mining components to the reconstruction of agent interaction protocols from message logs. Section 6 concludes the paper and provides an outlook towards future prospects of the presented techniques and tools.

2 Related Work

Process mining has already been applied to software engineering several times. One direction of research focuses on the analysis of software development processes (which we will call *software development process mining*). The goal is to retrieve control-flow and organizational aspects of software development cycles

[1] To be more precise we should talk about *mining processes* instead of *mining chains*. However, this would lead to the confusing term *process mining processes*. Also for historic reasons we stick to the term mining chain, which other authors use as well (see e.g. the implementation of the *Process Mining Workbench* described in [32]).

from available data sources such as CVS repositories. In contrast, the second direction of research uses mining to analyze software artifacts in order to support tasks like debugging or validation (which we will call *software process mining*)[2].

Early work on software development process mining was carried out by Cook and Wolf [9], who reconstruct models of software development processes from event-based logs and use conformance checking techniques to compare actual development activities with specified process models. They also present a tool implementing their techniques within a software development environment. Christley and Madey [8] apply social network mining and grammar inference to the analysis of open source projects. Rubin et al. [31] introduce a general framework for process mining of software development processes. They consider several aspects including specific data sources, algorithms, and perspectives, and propose the ProM framework [43] as a supporting toolset.

Software process mining is concerned with the reconstruction of abstract models of software systems from their execution traces. Dustdar and Gombotz [12] present techniques for the analysis of operational, interaction-, and workflow-related aspects of Web-service behavior. Dallmeyer et al. [11] apply grammar inference to the state-based analysis of basic software objects in order to support testing. Dongen et al. [42] present a case example of process mining in agent-based simulation and propose to build adaptive Petri net agents. Szirbik and colleagues build adaptive Petri net agents with neural networks and propose process mining as an alternative [27,35].

In our own previous work [5], we have embedded techniques for the reconstruction of interaction protocol models into our Petri net-based agent platform MULAN/CAPA [13]. We have also described a conceptual framework for process mining in agent-oriented software engineering and simulation in [4,21]. To our impression, two aspects have not received enough attention in the literature so far. The first is a unified view including all variants of process mining in software engineering. The second is the seamless integration of process mining into actual *software development frameworks or environments.*

An integration of process mining into software engineering should also consider techniques to improve the handling of mining algorithms for software developers. Knowledge discovery processes are often complex and exhibit a module-like structure where several processing stages (selection, preprocessing, transformation, mining, visualization, and interpretation, [22, p.54]) are consecutively or concurrently applied to the input data. This structure is well expressed using notations for *data flow networks.* Semi-formal data flow notations are also occasionally used in process mining to visualize mining procedures on a conceptual level [32, p.166], [33, p.99], but not for their implementation and execution.

Several existing data analysis environments allow for the visual composition of data processing algorithms from existing and user-defined components in order to support re-use, debugging, and documentation. Examples include the scientific computing environment *Simulink* [26], the image processing system *VisiQuest* [1], the data mining tool *WEKA* [15] together with the modeling

[2] In contrast, Rubin et al. [31] use this term for the mining of development processes.

environment *Alpha Miner* developed at Hong Kong University [14], and the *Konstanz Information Miner (KNIME)* plugin for the Eclipse platform [6].

Though these tools offer good usability and mature graphical interfaces, they also have different drawbacks. Some of the tools are not easily extensible. Though most tools are capable of *offline analyses* (i.e., the complete data set is analyzed 'in one go'), *online analyses* (i.e., analyses performed during the continuous streaming of data items into the network) are seldom supported. Another problem is the concurrent execution of processing steps.

The *Java*-based *ProM* framework [43] is widely used in process mining due to its good extensibility and large set of available plugins. Interoperability is ensured by a large number of supported input and output formats. Though the plugin architecture of ProM resembles the idea of a processing chain with data acquisition, mining, conversion, analysis, and visualization steps, the current user interface is merely tailored towards an interactive application.

3 Process Mining in Software Engineering

The literature review shows that process mining can add to several stages of a software engineering life cycle. Figure 1 shows a selection of possible applications of process mining in the context of software development from the early to the late stages. The presented development cycle is very generic and borrows the software engineering disciplines from the Rational Unified Process [18].

In the context of Petri net-based software engineering, specific advantages become apparent: In the design phase process mining supports the understanding of a real system's structure and behavior. Process models mined from the real system form a straightforward basis for the (semi-)automated implementation of the Petri net-based software. In debugging, process mining adds valuable support when applied to large traces of a running system. In validation and testing, traces observed from the running software (or abstract Petri net models reconstructed from these traces) can (semi-)automatically be compared with the specification by means of conformance analysis techniques [39]. During the operation of the software system, process mining is suitable to support the monitoring and online optimization, which requires the mined Petri nets to be fed back into the running system.

In an agent-based context (as provided by our MULAN architecture) further integration of process mining stands to reason: Software agents can achieve a form of adaptability by inferring behavioral information from *watching* other agents act. Thus, they are able to construct a model of the behavioral patterns that are usual or useful in the system's environment. Furthermore, the use of the multi-agent system metaphor as a common abstraction for the software as well as for the development team [2] and process allows to handle the mining of constructed processes and the mining of software development processes within the same conceptual framework.

The broad applicability of process mining to software engineering is due to the genericness of the techniques, which can be applied to several types of log data

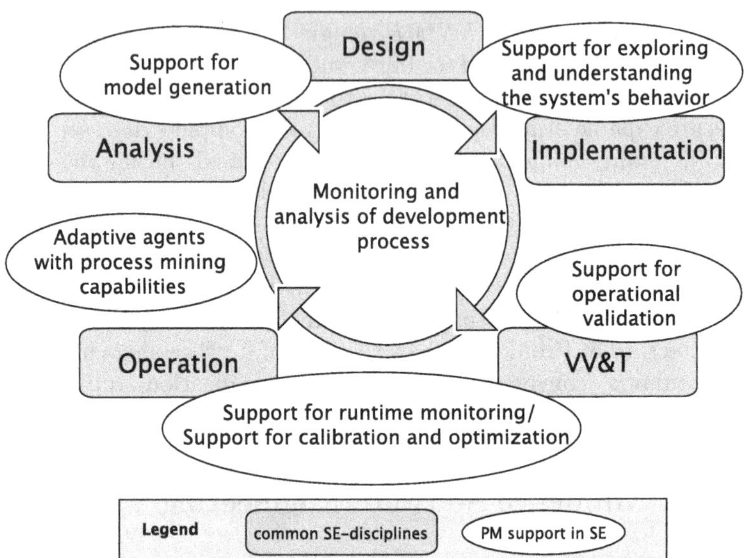

Fig. 1. Overview of process mining activities in software development processes

(for a related discussion in the context of change mining [16]). On the one hand, this includes traces of operational software systems, where the focus is either put on the behavior of single software components or on interactions including multiple objects or agents [12]. On the other hand, process mining techniques can be applied to data recorded during the execution of real world processes to gain information about the processes supported by the software under development as well as about the development process.

Especially for distributed systems process mining can add valuable information for debugging and monitoring. However, software developers have to be able to apply the techniques easily without much overhead during the development phases, and the techniques have to be tightly integrated in the usual workflows and tools. In our work we propose to apply process mining techniques through a component-based approach that allows the developer to construct complex mining algorithms by joining components together to form a data-flow network.

4 Reference Nets, Net Components and Mulan

Nets-within-nets [38] are expressive high-level Petri nets that allow nets to be nested within nets in dynamic structures. In contrast to ordinary nets, where tokens are passive elements, tokens in nets-within-nets are active elements, i.e., Petri nets. This can be regarded as token refinement. In general we distinguish between two different kinds of token semantics: value semantics and reference semantics. In value semantics tokens can be seen as direct representations of nets. This allows for nested nets that are structured in a hierarchical order because nets can only be located at one location. In reference semantics arbitrary structures of net-nesting can be achieved because tokens represent references to nets. These structures can be hierarchical, acyclic or even cyclic.

4.1 Reference Nets, Net Instances and Synchronous Channels

Reference nets [24] are an object-oriented nets-within-nets formalism with referential token semantics. In a single nesting of nets, we can distinguish between system net and object net. A token in the system net refers to an object net. Naturally, object nets can contain net tokens, and thus a system of nested nets can be obtained. The benefit of this feature is that the modeled system is modular and dynamically extensible. Furthermore, through synchronous channels [7, 23], transitions can activate and trigger the firing of transitions in other nets, just like method calls of objects.

The Petri net simulator and IDE Renew (The Reference Net Workshop [25]) combines the nets-within-nets paradigm of reference nets with the implementing power of *Java*. Tokens can be net instances, *Java*-objects or basic data types.

In comparison to the net elements of P/T-nets, reference nets offer several additional elements that increase the modeling power as well as the convenience of modeling. These additional elements include several arc types,[3] virtual places and several inscription types providing functionality for the net elements. Transitions can be augmented with expressions, actions, guards, synchronous channels and creation inscriptions while places may own type, creation and token inscriptions.

Similar to objects in object-oriented programming languages, where objects are instantiations of classes, net instances are instantiations of net templates. Net templates define the structure and behavior of nets just like classes define the structure and methods of objects. While the net instance has a marking that determines its status, the net template determines only the behavior and initial marking that is common to all net instances of one type.

In reference nets, tokens can be anonymous, basic data types, *Java* objects or net references. New net instances can be created within executing net instances similar to object creation during program execution.

For the communication between net instances, synchronous channels are used. A synchronous channel consists of two (or more) inscribed transitions. There are two types of transition inscriptions for the two ends of the synchronous channel: downlinks and uplinks. Two transitions that form a synchronous channel can only fire simultaneously and only if both transitions are activated. Downlink and uplink can belong to a single net or to different nets. In both cases any object, also another net instance, can be transferred from either transition to the other by binding them to the parameters of the synchronous channel. If two different net instances are involved, it is thus possible to synchronize these two nets and to transfer objects in either direction through the synchronous channel. For this the system net must hold the reference of the object net as token.

[3] For example, Renew offers test arcs, reserve arcs and flexible arcs. Flexible arcs are used in the example (compare Fig. 6) to gather elements from a list.

While net instance creation allows for a dynamically refinable structure of the net system through token refinement, synchronous channels allow for the communication (dynamic synchronization) between net instances, which form the different parts of the net system. Net instances and synchronous channels are also facilitated by some of the presented net components in Section 5 to allow for complex (refined) mining algorithms.

4.2 Net Components

A net component [3] is a set of net elements that fulfills one basic task. The task should be so general that the net component can be applied to a broad variety of nets. Furthermore, the net component can provide additional help, such as a default inscription or comments.

Every net component has a unique geometrical form and orientation that results from the arrangement of the net elements. A unique form is intended so that each net component can easily be identified and distinguished from the others. The geometrical figure also holds the potential to provide a defined structure for the Petri net. The unique form can be accompanied by a distinctive color choice as it has been done with the net components for process mining in Sect. 5.

Net components are transition-bordered subnets that can be composed to form a larger Petri net. To ease the practical use each output transition is supplemented with appropriate output places. Thus, the net components can be connected just by drawing arcs between such an additional output place and an input transition of another net component.

Jensen [19] describes several design rules for Petri net elements, which are based on previous work by Oberquelle [29]. These rules are concerned with the ways of drawing figures and give general advice for Petri net elements such as places, transitions and arcs. They are also concerned about combinations and arrangement of the elements.

Net components extend the rules by giving developer groups the chance to pre-define reusable structures. Within the group of developers, these structures are fixed and well known, although they are open for improvements. Conventions for the design of the code can be introduced into the development process, and for developers it is easy to apply these conventions through the net component-based construction. Furthermore, the developing process is facilitated and the style of the resulting nets is unified. Once a concrete implementation of net components has been incorporated and accepted by the developers, their arrangements (form) will be recognized as conventional symbols. This makes it easier to read a Petri net that is constructed with these net components. Moreover, to understand a net component-based net it is not necessary to read all its net elements. It is sufficient to read the substructures. Net components are used extensively and successfully for the construction of MULAN protocol nets.

4.3 Multi Agent Nets (MULAN)

MULAN [30] is a multi-agent system architecture modeled in terms of reference nets. It consists of four levels, i.e., protocols, agents, platforms, and multi-agent

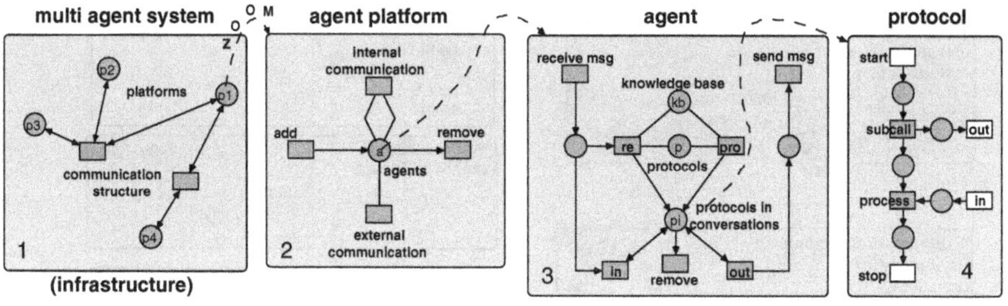

Fig. 2. The MULAN multi-agent system architecture (adapted from [30])

system infrastructure, which are related through token refinement. An agent is represented by a net that (among other aspects) provides an interface to exchange messages with its environment. The agent's range of behavior is modeled by means of workflow-like protocol nets. Depending on its knowledge an agent can instantiate a protocol net actively or reactively to perform certain tasks. Multiple agents inhabit a platform and multiple platforms can be composed in a multi-agent system infrastructure. The platforms provide internal and external (platform spanning) communication services for the agents (Fig. 2).

CAPA [13] is a FIPA-compliant implementation of the MULAN architecture based on RENEW. In the context of MULAN/CAPA some additional tools are provided through several plugins that extend the functionality of RENEW and CAPA. Some examples are the net components plugin and the MULAN components for protocol nets, the MULAN viewer, which allows to introspect the nets belonging to an agent, and the MULAN sniffer,[4] which is a message monitoring tool originally inspired by the JADE agent platform's Sniffer tool [37].

5 Net Components for Mining Chains

As part of our attempt to integrate process mining into our Petri net-based software engineering approach, we have developed a set of net components (see Sect. 4.2) to visually model process mining chains and integrate them with other parts of the software. One application is agent interaction analysis [5], where the mining chains process message logs observed during the execution of our multi-agent applications. This data has to be provided to the mining chain and the reconstructed protocol models have to be returned to the environment.

5.1 Generic Mining Components

Thus, the tasks to be supported are data acquisition, data processing, and feedback of the results into the software development or even into the running system. We have therefore identified *sources*, *processors*, and *sinks* as basic (generic)

[4] The implementation was done by Frank Heitmann and Florian Plähn.

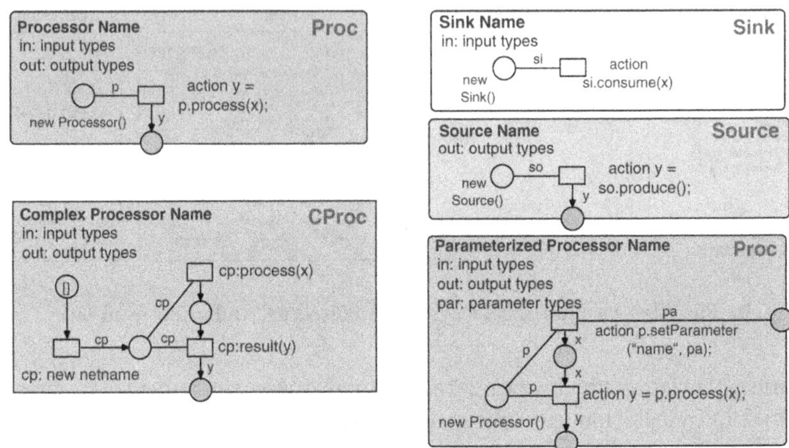

Fig. 3. Generic mining chain components

components for mining chains.[5] Figure 3 shows the generic mining components that can be used as templates to create specific ones. These net components are rather simple consisting of one place and one transition. The place holds a *Java* object that provides the respective data processing algorithm via a standardized method. The transition calls this method when a data token enters the net component. There might be an additional place and transition pair to pass parameters to the component. While processors should be implemented without side-effects, sinks and sources are explicitly introduced to interact with the surrounding software environment.

The processing method can be implemented to perform either an online or an offline analysis (see Sect. 2). In an offline analysis, one incoming token represents a whole data set (e.g. a log in process mining) that is processed at once. In an online analysis, each token represents one data element (e.g. an event in process mining) in a continuing input stream. The processing method is called on each token arrival to incrementally update the computed results based on the new data.

The reference semantics of the mining components differs from the value semantics of classical Petri net-based data flow notations [20, pp.242]. This can be an advantage but also a problem. On the one hand, it is possible to pass a reference to an object (or even to a net instance) along a chain that successively changes the object's attributes in different processing stages. On the other hand, the concurrent modification of a referenced object in different processing stages can lead to problems like race conditions. Nevertheless, the use of *Java* as an implementation allows to *clone* processed objects in order to provide independent copies.

A mining chain is composed of several net components and can also include sub-chains in a hierarchy of net instances. Also normal net elements can be used

[5] These component types are also common in other data-flow modeling tools like e.g. *KNIME* [6].

to add custom behavior. Thanks to the use of the Petri net representation, we are able not only to implement pure sequential chains. We can also model chains that own a complex control-flow including concurrency. Mining chains can in principle be implemented in any hierarchical colored Petri net formalism. However, the object-oriented structure and the *Java*-based inscription language provided by reference nets are especially well-suited to model large mining chains.

Hierarchical mining chains are realized by means of so-called *complex* sinks, sources, and processors. Here, the object providing the processing functionality is not a simple *Java* object but an instance of a sub-net. This instance receives and provides data from and to the surrounding net component via synchronous channels (see Sect. 4.1). Thereby it is possible to encapsulate a whole Petri net-based simulation model into a complex data source.

The generic as well as the interaction mining components are integrated in RENEW by a plugin (extending the net component plugin), which makes them available to the modeler as palettes of tool buttons. The user can easily build custom palettes with new mining components and use the generic components as templates.

5.2 Integration with ProM

As discussed in Sect. 2, ProM is a powerful *Java*-based process mining tool with an open plugin architecture similar to the one of RENEW. The algorithms implemented in ProM are used interactively on imported log data or process models via a GUI. Due to the simple *Java* interface provided by the mining components, an integration of both tools appears straightforward. In doing so, we can on the one hand offer Petri net-based data-flow modeling for ProM. On the other hand, we can comfortably integrate a large number of existing process mining and analysis algorithms into our Petri net-based software.

The ProM architecture distinguishes between import, export, mining, analysis, and conversion plugins. Mining result objects furthermore carry information on their visual representation (e.g. as a Petri net graph) that can be visualized by the GUI. We have straightforwardly mapped import plugins to source components and export plugins and viewers to sink components. Mining, analysis, and conversion plugins are specific kinds of processors. Based on the ProM architecture two additional component types were identified: *Filters* restrict the log to certain event types, and *interactive viewers* allow for user interactions during the mining process. The latter are implemented with the aid of so-called *manual transition* that the user fires after finishing the interaction.

Since ProM offers interfaces for each plugin type, it is not even necessary to provide an own wrapper for each algorithm. Instead, we can provide generic wrappers and pass the concrete plugin class as a parameter.

5.3 A Mining Chain for Agent Interaction Analysis

The following example shows how process mining chains can be integrated into the agent platform CAPA (see Sect. 4.3) to support the reconstruction of agent interaction protocols from message logs. Such interaction mining provides valuable

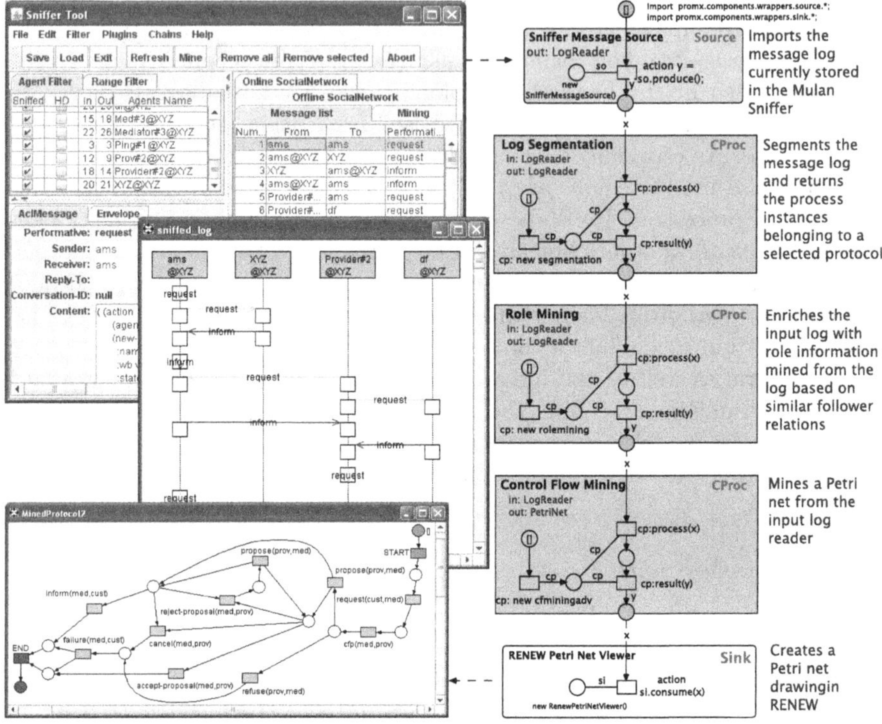

Fig. 4. Example process mining chain for agent interaction mining

hints when debugging multi-agent applications and forms a basis for autonomous protocol learning by Petri net agents [35, 42].

In [5] we have presented an interaction mining procedure that integrates and extends previous attempts from the literature [28, 33]. The procedure consists of 6 subsequent steps, i.e., log segmentation, role detection, control-flow mining, peer generation, model enrichment, and visualization.

Figure 4 shows the implementation of the first three steps by means of mining components. Each step is represented by a complex processor and refined by a sub-net. The sub-nets for the log segmentation and control flow mining steps are depicted in Figs. 5 and 6. Furthermore, there are source and sink components that help to embed the mining chain into the agent platform.

The processing starts from the *Sniffer Message Source* component that provides a message log recorded by the MULAN Sniffer. The example log was recorded during the execution of an iterated mediation protocol on the CAPA agent platform. At the end of the processing chain, the *Renew Petri Net Viewer* sink exports Petri net representations of the reconstructed interaction protocols to RENEW as new net drawings[6] that can be instantiated and executed.

[6] The graphical representation of the resulting model in RENEW is manually beautified.

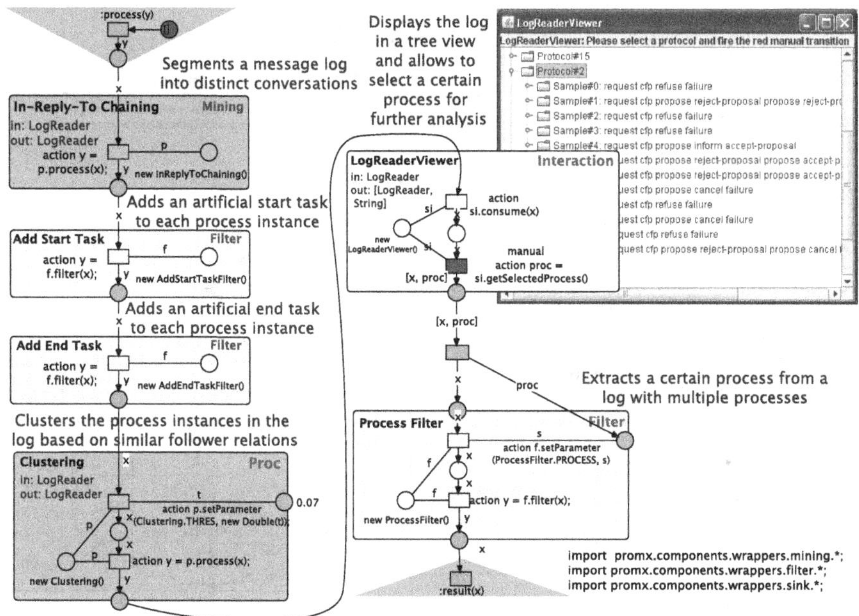

Fig. 5. A sub-chain implementing the segmentation step

Each step of the mining chain is implemented by means of several existing and new ProM plugins wrapped as mining components. The *Log Segmentation* processor depicted in Fig. 5 starts by chaining messages [39] that were sent in reply to each other into conversations. Afterwards two filters are applied that add artificial start and end events to each conversation in the log.[7]

Next, the *Clustering* component clusters the conversations in the log into protocol classes based on similar follower relations of message types (performatives). ProM includes several plugins supporting this task. The results are displayed using the *Log Reader Viewer* while the net execution waits on a manual transition. In the example, this interactive viewer lets the user select a certain protocol class for further investigation. After selecting the protocol, the manual transition is fired by the user to continue the processing. At the end of the log segmentation, a *Process Filter* restricts the log to those conversations that belong to the selected protocol.

The pre-processed log is forwarded to the *Role Mining* procedure. This step uses ProM's existing organizational miner plugin to induce the participating agents' roles from the sets of message types they send (as also proposed in [44]). The corresponding subnet is not shown here. It enriches the log with role information and forwards the enriched log to the *Control-Flow Mining* processor shown in Fig. 6.

[7] This enhances the mining results and will not be explained in detail here.

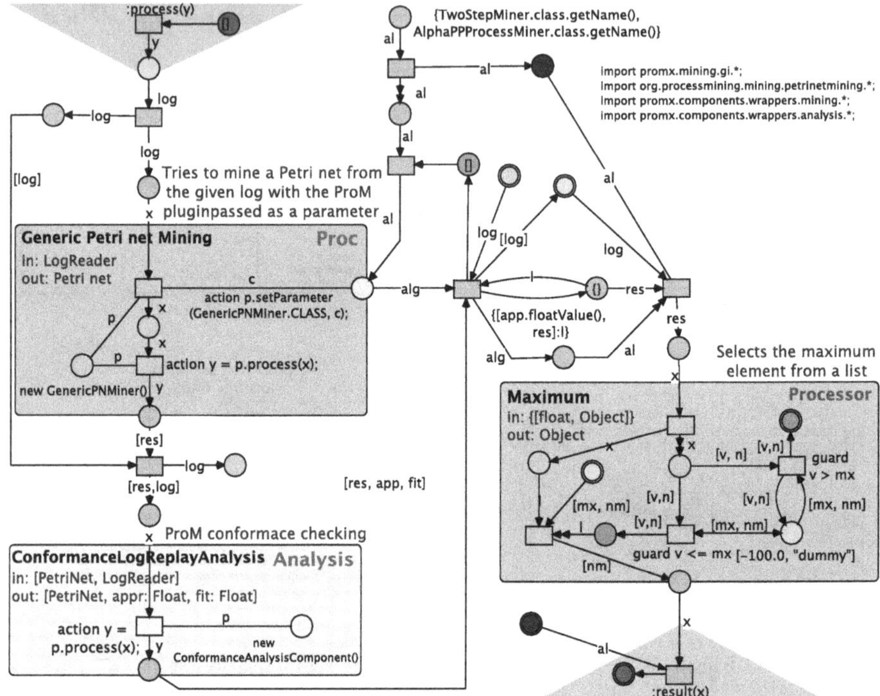

Fig. 6. A sub-chain implementing the control-flow mining step with an integrated optimization procedure

This step illustrates how mining components can be combined with custom net structures and *Java* code to build a simple optimization procedure. It also provides an example of a non linear mining chain containing cycles.

In process mining, a large number of algorithms exists for the reconstruction of control-flow, often tailored towards certain types of data. The well-known α^{++} [45] algorithm e.g. performs well on noise-free, event-based data. Other algorithms are specialized on handling circumstances like duplicate activities or noise.

Let us assume that the most appropriate algorithm for the given event log is unknown in advance. We therefore employ the generic mining component and pass a list of algorithms[8] as parameters that are applied to the same log in turn. While in the example, the algorithms are represented by *Java* objects, they could also be represented by net instances that receive and provide data via synchronous channels (see Sect. 4.1).

Subsequent to the mining we use ProM's conformance checking plugin and a custom maximizer component to identify the mining result that represents

[8] In the example, this includes the α^{++} algorithm and a two-step approach tailored towards models with duplicate activities. The latter algorithm is based on ideas from [17, 33] and presented in detail in [5]. For a related approach see also [40].

the samples in the log 'best' in terms of behavioral appropriateness.[9] The best result is finally returned to the main mining chain. A similar optimizer could be integrated into an adaptive agent in order to increase the reliability of existing process mining techniques for autonomous learning.

Summarizing, the example indicates that the mining components might indeed be a step towards tackling the two problems of integrating process mining and software engineering mentioned in Sect. 1. Concerning the first problem, the presented source and sink components provide a well-defined interface between the software development and execution environment (i.e., RENEW and CAPA) and the process mining algorithms of ProM. This allows to obtain data from and feed back results into the system. Since the mined protocols are represented as executable reference nets, they can be immediately integrated into the running Petri net simulation. In practice, the available algorithms have to be enhanced to permit the automated protocol reconstruction by adaptive agents.

Concerning the second problem, it is shown that the mining components support the creation of complex mining procedures by means of stepwise refinement. Compared to other data flow environments, the approach provides a number of advantages indicated in the example: (1) in the context of Petri net-based software engineering with RENEW, the same formalism is used to model the mining procedures *and* the analyzed software; (2) pre-defined components can be combined with custom *Java* code and net elements (e.g. to build the optimization procedure shown in Fig. 6); (3) this procedure also shows that unlike conventional hierarchical notations, reference nets allow to dynamically exchange the applied algorithms at runtime (e.g. depending on the provided data); (4) user interactions are simply included by means of manual transitions as shown in Fig. 5.

6 Conclusion and Future Work

In this paper we have discussed modeling-related aspects of the integration of process mining and software engineering. We have reviewed and summarized possible advantages of this integration and discussed the benefits of a Petri net-based approach in this context. The need to ease the handling of complex process mining algorithms and seamlessly integrate them into the development environment has been pointed out. Furthermore, we have identified data-flow networks as a common means to model data processing procedures and proposed their use for process mining in Petri net-based software engineering.

Reference nets allow to model hierarchical process mining chains as nets-within-nets. Even the processed data objects can be net instances, which suits the representation of process mining results well. Net components are a handy aid to include re-usable mining procedures in a conventionalized manner, provided through a toolbar of the Net Component Plugin of RENEW. This

[9] Of course in practice one should strive for better optimization methods than the presented brute-force approach.

technique allows for rapid prototyping, testing, refactoring and debugging of mining chains.

In a multi-agent environment such as MULAN — which is implemented in reference nets — mining chains can be executed and even composed autonomously by MULAN agents as protocols. This could lead to adaptive behavior of agents in the future. The mining components can also be straightforwardly used as wrappers for process mining plugins from the well-known interactive ProM tool. Thereby, complex process mining procedures can be set up, and a large number of available algorithms can be integrated into Petri net-based applications. We have presented a chain for agent interaction mining as an example.

In our future work we will strive to increase the usability of process mining in software engineering and validate our approach in larger case-studies of AOSE with RENEW and MULAN. Software developers will only accept process mining, if they are provided with appropriate supporting tools and techniques. While mining chains are a starting point, we can imagine several further improvements.

Mining components could e.g. be enriched with attributes that aid the selection of appropriate mining algorithms for specific situations (e.g. processing speed versus precision). Such attributes could either be presented to the user via the GUI or — given an appropriate formal representation — employed for automatic consistency checks. One might e.g. check if an algorithm applied on data provided by a certain source is really appropriate for the expected type of data.

A further objective is to enhance the integration of process mining with interactive software development environments. In our research groups, an OSGi-compliant[10] re-implementation of RENEW was prototypically integrated with a simulation environment based on the Eclipse platform[11] (see [10, 34]). This allows to utilize the mining components for the analysis of data retrieved from simulation experiments or other sources of the Eclipse development environment.

Another idea is to apply process mining to users' interactions with ProM itself. As a result, mining chains can be created from typical interactions and the user can be provided with hints for the application of algorithms based on past experiences. This technique is called *meta mining* in [36]. ProM already logs user interactions in the MXML format. For *meta mining* these should be enriched with further information like parameter settings of algorithm invocations.

Acknowledgments

We thank our colleagues, especially Dr. Daniel Moldt, for their comments and fruitful discussions as well as the anonymous reviewers, who have given us good and constructive suggestions to improve this work in their extensive comments.

[10] Open Services Gateway Initiative (`http://www.osgi.org`).

[11] Eclipse is a popular IDE that facilitates OSGi (`http://www.eclipse.org`).

References

1. Acusoft. VisiQuest, Image Processing / Visual Programming Environment (2007), http://www.accusoft.com/products/visiquest/features.asp
2. Cabac, L.: Multi-agent system: a guiding metaphor for the organization of software development projects. In: Petta, P., Müller, J.P., Klusch, M., Georgeff, M. (eds.) MATES 2007. LNCS, vol. 4687, pp. 1–12. Springer, Heidelberg (2007)
3. Cabac, L., Duvigneau, M., Rölke, H.: Net components revisited. In: Moldt, D. (ed.) Proceedings of the Fourth International Workshop on Modelling of Objects, Components, and Agents. MOCA 2006, number FBI-HH-B-272/06 in Reports of the Department of Informatics, Vogt-Kölln Str. 30, 22527, Hamburg, Germany, June 2006, pp. 87–102. University of Hamburg (2006)
4. Cabac, L., Knaak, N., Moldt, D.: Applying process mining to interaction analysis of Petri net-based multi-agent models. Technical Report 271, Department of Informatics, University of Hamburg (May 2006)
5. Cabac, L., Knaak, N., Moldt, D., Rölke, H.: Analysis of multi-agent interactions with process mining techniques. In: Fischer, K., Timm, I.J., André, E., Zhong, N. (eds.) MATES 2006. LNCS, vol. 4196, pp. 12–23. Springer, Heidelberg (2006)
6. Chair for Bioinformatics and Information Mining at Konstanz University. The Konstanz Information Miner, KNIME (2007), http://www.knime.org
7. Christensen, S., Hansen, N.D.: Coloured Petri nets extended with channels for synchronous communication. Technical Report DAIMI PB–390, Computer Science Department, Aarhus University, DK-8000 Aarhus C, Denmark (April 1992)
8. Christley, S., Madey, G.: Analysis of activity in the open source software development community. Hicss 0, 166b (2007)
9. Cook, J.E., Wolf, A.L.: Discovering models of software processes from event-based data. ACM Trans. Softw. Eng. Methodol. 7(3), 215–249 (1998)
10. Czogalla, R., Knaak, N., Page, B.: Simulating the Eclipse way - A generic experimentation environment based on the eclipse platform. In: Borutzki, W., Orsoni, A., Zobel, R. (eds.) Proceedings of the 20th European Conference on Modelling and Simulation (ECMS 2006), Bonn, September 2006, pp. 260–265 (2006)
11. Dallmeier, V., Lindig, C., Wasylkowski, A., Zeller, A.: Mining object behavior with adabu. In: WODA 2006: ICSE Workshop on Dynamic Analysis (May 2006)
12. Dustdar, S., Gombotz, R.: Discovering web service workflows using web services interaction mining. International Journal of Business Process Integration and Management, IJBPIM (2006)
13. Duvigneau, M., Moldt, D., Rölke, H.: Concurrent architecture for a multi-agent platform. In: Giunchiglia, F., Odell, J., Weiß, G. (eds.) AOSE 2002. LNCS, vol. 2585, pp. 59–72. Springer, Heidelberg (2003)
14. E-Business Technology Institute at Hong Kong University. AlphaMiner (2007), http://www.eti.hku.hk/alphaminer
15. Frank, E., Hall, M., Trigg, L.E., Holmes, G., Witten, I.H.: Data mining in bioinformatics using Weka. Bioinformatics 20(15), 2479–2481 (2004)
16. Günther, C.W., Rinderle, S., Reichert, M., van der Aalst, W.M.P.: Change mining in adaptive process management systems. In: Meersman, R., Tari, Z. (eds.) OTM 2006. LNCS, vol. 4275, pp. 309–326. Springer, Heidelberg (2006)
17. Herbst, J.: Ein induktiver Ansatz zur Akquisition und Adaption von Workflow-Modellen. PhD thesis, University of Ulm (2001)
18. Jacobson, I., Booch, G., Rumbaugh, J.: The Unified Software Development Process. Addison-Wesley, Reading (1999)

19. Jensen, K.: Coloured Petri Nets, 2nd edn., vol. 1. springer, Berlin (1996)
20. Jessen, E., Valk, R.: Rechensysteme: Grundlagen der Modellbildung. Studienreihe Informatik. Springer, Heidelberg (1987)
21. Knaak, N.: Supporting multi-agent-based simulation with data mining techniques. In: Bruzzone, A.G., Guasch, A., Piera, M.A., Rozenblit, J. (eds.) Proceedings of the International Mediterranean Modelling Multiconference (I3M 2006), Barcelona, Spain, October 2006, pp. 277–286 (2006)
22. Köster, F.: Analyse von Simulationsmodellen mit Methoden des Knowledge Discovery in Databases. Technical report, Department für Informatik, Carl von Ossietzky University of Oldenburg (2002)
23. Kummer, O.: A Petri net view on synchronous channels. Petri Net Newsletter 56, 7–11 (1999)
24. Kummer, O.: Referenznetze. PhD thesis, University of Hamburg, R35896-7. Logos-Verlag, Berlin (2002)
25. Kummer, O., Wienberg, F., Duvigneau, M., Schumacher, J., Köhler, M., Moldt, D., Rölke, H., Valk, R.: An extensible editor and simulation engine for Petri nets: Renew. In: Cortadella, J., Reisig, W. (eds.) ICATPN 2004. LNCS, vol. 3099, pp. 484–493. Springer, Heidelberg (2004)
26. MathWorks. MatLab and Simulink for Technical Computing (2007), `http://www.mathworks.com`
27. Meyer, G.G., Szirbik, N.B.: Agent behavior alignment: a mechanism to overcome problems in agent interactions during runtime. In: Klusch, M., Hindriks, K.V., Papazoglou, M.P., Sterling, L. (eds.) CIA 2007. LNCS (LNAI), vol. 4676, pp. 270–284. Springer, Heidelberg (2007)
28. Mounier, A., Boissier, O., Jacquenet, F.: Conversation mining in multi-agent systems. In: Mařík, V., Müller, J.P., Pěchouček, M. (eds.) CEEMAS 2003. LNCS, vol. 2691, pp. 158–167. Springer, Heidelberg (2003)
29. Oberquelle, H.: Communication by graphic net representations. Fachbereichsbericht IFI-HH-B-75/81, University of Hamburg, Vogt-Köllin Str. 30, 22527 Hamburg, Germany (1981)
30. Rölke, H.: Modellierung von Agenten und Multiagentensystemen–Grundlagen und Anwendungen. In: Agent Technology–Theory and Applications, vol. 2. Logos Verlag, Berlin (2004)
31. Rubin, V., Günther, C.W., van der Aalst, W.M.P., Kindler, E., van Dongen, B.F., Schäfer, W.: Process mining framework for software processes. BPM Center Report BPM-07-01.WWW, BPMcenter.org (2007)
32. Schimm, G.: Workflow Mining–Verfahren zur Extraktion von Workflow-Schemata aus ereignisbasierten Daten. PhD thesis, University of Oldenburg (2004)
33. Schütt, K.: Automated modelling of business interaction processes for flow prediction. Master's thesis, Department for Informatics, University of Hamburg (2003)
34. Simmendinger, F., Duvigneau, M., Cabac, L., Knaak, N.: Controlling osgi bundles with Petri nets. In: Moldt, D., Kordon, F., van Hee, K., Colom, J.-M., Bastide, R. (eds.) Proceedings of the Workshop on Petri Nets and Software Engineering (PNSE 2007), Siedlce (Poland), pp. 220–225. Publishing House of University of Podlaise (2007)
35. Stuit, M., Szirbik, N., de Snoo, C.: Interaction beliefs: a way to understand emergent organisational behaviour. In: Proceedings of the 2007 ICEIS Conference, Volume Software Agents and Internet Computing, pp. 241–248 (2007)
36. Syed, J., Ghanem, M., Guo, Y.: Discovery processes: representation and reuse (2002)

37. Telecom Italia. Java Agent Development Framework, JADE (2007), http://jade.tilab.com/
38. Valk, R.: Petri nets as dynamical objects. In: Agha, G., De Cindio, F. (eds.) 16th Intern. Conf. on Application and Theory of Petri Nets, Workshop proceedings, Turin, Italy, June 1995, University of Turin (1995)
39. van der Aalst, W.M.P., Dumas, M., Ouyang, C., Rozinat, A., Verbeek, H.M.W.: Choreography conformance checking: an approach based on BPEL and petri nets. Technical Report BPM-05-25.WWW, BPMcenter.org (2005)
40. van der Aalst, W.M.P., Rubin, V., van Dongen, B.F., Kindler, E., Günther, C.W.: Process mining: a two-step approach using transition systems and regions. Technical Report BPM-06-30, BPMCenter.org (2006)
41. van der Aalst, W.M.P., Weijters, A.J.M.M.: Process mining: a research agenda. Computers in Industry 53(3), 231–244 (2004)
42. van Dongen, B., van Luin, J., Verbeek, E.: Process mining in a multi-agent auctioning system. In: Moldt, D. (ed.) Proceedings of the 4th International Workshop on Modelling of Objects, Components, and Agents, Turku, June 2006, pp. 145–160 (2006)
43. van Dongen, B.F., de Medeiros, A.K.A., Verbeek, H.M.W., Weijters, A.J.M.M., van der Aalst, W.M.P.: The ProM framework: a new era in process mining tool support. In: Ciardo, G., Darondeau, P. (eds.) ICATPN 2005. LNCS, vol. 3536, pp. 444–454. Springer, Heidelberg (2005)
44. Vanderfeesten, M.: Identifying Roles in Multi-Agent Systems by Overhearing. Master's thesis, Utrecht University (2006) (in preparation)
45. Wen, L., van der Aalst, W.M.P., Wang, J., Sun, J: Mining process models with non-free-choice constructs. Technical Report BPM-06-23.WWW, BPMCenter.org (2006)

Time Recursive Petri Nets

Djaouida Dahmani[1], Jean-Michel Ilié[2], and Malika Boukala[1]

[1] LSI, Computer Science Department, USTHB
Algiers, Algeria
ddahmani2000@yahoo.com
[2] LIP6 Laboratory UPMC, Universite Paris-Descartes, France
Jean-Michel.Ilie@univ-paris5.fr

Abstract. We propose an extension of Recursive Petri Nets (TRPNs) based on the semantics of the Time Petri Nets (TPNs). TRPNs are well suited for analyzing and modeling timing requirements of complex discrete event system and allow to represent a model at different levels of abstraction. We give a formal semantics of this extended model and show that TRPNs are more expressive than TPNs. Moreover, we propose a method for building a specific state class graph that can be used to analyze timing properties efficiently.

Keywords: recursive Petri net, time Petri net, threads, recursivity.

1 Introduction

The introduction of modularity concepts in system specification is a wide research array since it eases the handling of large descriptions. Therefore, several popular models were extended, including the well-known Petri nets (PN). Hierarchy in nets makes levels of refinement and abstraction possible. Further, object Petri nets or object systems where a Petri net structure can contain Petri nets as its tokens introduce more dynamical forms of hierarchy to model processes [11]. It is now possible to use high level specification models including procedure calls, and translate it in specific Petri nets in order to be analyzed [10]. Very recently, Recursive Petri Nets (RPNs) are proposed as an alternative model to specify huge systems having dynamic structures, optionally infinite [7, 8]. They encompass the capability to model procedures since they allow to emulate dynamic creations and deaths of threads in a quite natural way. Threads in RPNs are initiated by some new kind of transitions called abstract transitions. When a thread fires an abstract transition, it consumes input tokens like an ordinary transition, and creates a new thread in addition. This latter begins its token game with a marking (which is called the starting marking of the abstract transition). The production of output tokens of the transition is delayed until the new running thread terminates (which is called a cut step of the abstract transition). RPNs have been successfully used for specifying plans of agents in a multi-agent system [9], including complex mechanisms like interruption, fault-tolerance and

K. Jensen, W. van der Aalst, and J. Billington (Eds.): ToPNoC I, LNCS 5100, pp. 104–118, 2008.

remote procedures calls. Moreover, decision procedures for some fundamental properties have been developed. In particular, the reachability, boundedness and finiteness problems remain decidable.

We propose to extend RPNs with time specification to allow the analysis of timing requirements of complex discrete event systems. There are two main extensions of PNs with time: time Petri nets (TPNs) and timed Petri Nets. It is well known that for original TPNs, a transition can fire within a time interval whereas for original timed Petri nets it has a duration and fires as soon as possible or with respect to a scheduling policy. During these last years, different flavors were proposed to improve the expressivity or the concision of these models and important efforts were produced to compare them. The TPN model, said "a la Merlin" with time intervals, strong (natural) timing semantics and mono-server approach for transitions seemed very interesting since more expressive than Timed models [5] and also exponentially more concise than its related timing semantical model, based on timed automata [2]. It is worth noting that, at the price of more intricate managements concerning timing information, a better expressivity has been demonstrated, first by allowing general time intervals and second by pushing timing information on places and, above all, on arcs [3, 4]. However, the extended models suffer from a lack of analysis tools. In contrast, TPNs (more precisely, transition-TPNs) have been widely and successfully used for the modeling and the verification of systems, since they offer a good compromise between temporal expressivity and verification tools availability (see [1] and [6] for instance).

For sake of simplicity, in this paper we will follow the original transition-TPN ideas to introduce time in our model, namely Time Recursive PN (TRPN). Actually, the above extensions would not re-open the results and originality of our approach. In contrast to TPN, a firing in a TRPN may correspond either to a transition or a cut step. So, to obtain a convenient model, we propose to attach time intervals not only to ordinary and abstract transitions but also to the cut step specifications. According to some execution in a marked TRPN, the time interval $[a_t, b_t]$ of a transition or a cut step t represents possible firing times, referring to the moment at which t was lastly enabled. If this reference occurs at time θ, then t cannot be fired before $\theta + a_t$ and must be fired before or at time $\theta + b_t$, unless it is disabled before its firing by the firing of another transition. Note that the same component description can be used (or called in a recursive manner) with different execution contexts and timing conditions. Thus it will be possible to control, in an elegant manner, both starting and ending times and durations of the threads by using TRPNs.

The next section recalls the bases of the RPN model and its state graph representation. In Sect. 3, after an intuitive presentation, we formally define the time semantics of TRPNs. The expressive powers of TRPNs and TPNs are then compared. We show how to build a state class graph for a TRPN in Sect. 4. Moreover, we demonstrate a sufficient condition to state that a TRPN is finite in Sect. 5. Section 6 is our conclusion and perspectives.

2 Recursive Petri Nets

In an ordinary PN, a single thread plays the token game by firing some transition and updating the current marking. In a RPN, there is a tree of threads and each thread has its own token game running independently on the net. As far as interleaving semantics is concerned, a step of a RPN is a step of one of its threads. In a RPN, the transitions are split in two categories: *elementary and abstract transitions*. When a thread fires an abstract transition, it consumes the tokens specified by the backward incidence matrix. This creates a new thread (called its son) which can begin its own token game, from a *starting marking* whose value is attached to the abstract transition. An indexed family of sets of final markings called termination sets are attached to the net and the indices are used to refer to them. When a thread reaches a final marking, it may terminate aborting its whole descent of threads. This operation, called a *cut step*, allows to complete the firing of the abstract transition which gave birth to it within the father-thread. Contrary to ordinary PNs, only some of the output arcs are used to produce tokens, those labeled by the index of the termination set which contains the reached final marking. So, different final markings can produce different results from the same abstract transition firing. Observe that the root thread can also reach a final marking, yielding an empty tree.

When a thread fires an elementary transition, the behavior is twofold since some abstract transitions can be under an explicit control of the elementary transition (preemption). On one hand, the thread consumes and produces tokens through the elementary transition, as usual. On the other hand, it prunes its descendants initiated by the abstract transitions to be preempted, and produces their corresponding output tokens. Here again, some (possibly additive) indices are used to specify which output arcs are used.

The next definitions formalize the model of RPNs and its associated states called *extended markings*. For sake of clarity, some concepts like test arcs and the parameterized initiation of threads are not presented (please, refer to [8] for more details).

Definition 1. *A RPN is defined by a tuple $R = \langle P, T, I, W^-, W^+, \Omega, \Upsilon, K\rangle$ where:*

1. *P is a finite set of places,*
2. *T is a finite set of transitions such that $P \cap T = \emptyset$. A transition of T can be either elementary or abstract. The sets of elementary and abstract transitions are respectively denoted by T_{el} and T_{ab},*
3. *$I = I_C \cup I_P$ is a finite set of indices, globally called termination indices, and dedicated to cut steps and preemptions respectively,*
4. *W^- is the pre function from $P \times T$ to $\mathbb{N}$,*
5. *W^+ is the post function from $P \times [T_{el} \cup (T_{ab} \times I)]$ to $\mathbb{N}$,*
6. *Ω is the starting marking function from T_{ab} to $\mathbb{N}^P$ which associates with each abstract transition an ordinary marking (i.e. an element of $\mathbb{N}^P$),*
7. *Υ is a family indexed by I_C of termination sets, Each set represents a set of final markings (i.e. elements of $\mathbb{N}^P$),*

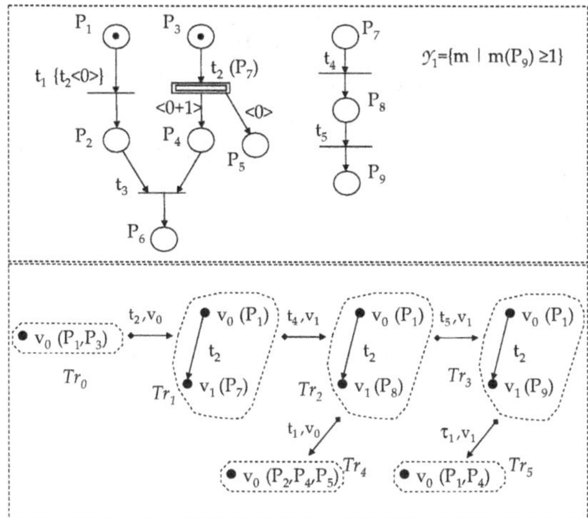

Fig. 1. A simple Recursive Petri Net and two firing sequences

8. *K is a partial control function from $T_{el} \times T_{ab}$ to I_P which allows to specify the thread preemption operations controlled by the elementary transitions.*

Let's use the net presented in the upper part of Fig. 1 to highlight RPN's graphical symbols and associated notations:

1. An abstract transition is represented by a double border rectangle; its name is followed by the starting marking $\Omega(t)$, denoted like a multi-set of places put inside brackets. For instance, t_2 is an abstract transition and $\Omega(t_2) = (P_7)$ means that any thread which is created by the firing of t_2 starts with one token put in the place P_7.
2. Any termination set can be defined concisely based on place marking conditions. A termination set indexed by i is denoted Υ_i. For instance, Υ_1 specifies the final markings of threads such that the place P_9 is marked.
3. An elementary transition t is represented by a simple bar and its name is possibly followed by a set of terms $t'\langle i' \rangle \in T_{ab} \times I_P$. Each term specifies an abstract transition t' which is under the control of t, associated with a termination index to be used when aborting t' consequently to a firing of t (i.e. $K(t, t')$ is defined and $i' = K(t, t')$). Here, t_1 is such that its firings preempt threads started by the firings of t_2 and the referred termination index is 0.
4. The set I of termination indices is deduced from the indices used to subscript the termination sets (hence, the cut steps) and from the indices bound to elementary transitions (related to preemptions). Here, we have $I = \{0, 1\}$, more precisely, $I_C = \{1\}$ and $I_P = \{0\}$.
5. Like for PN, every positive value $W^-(p, t)$ defines an input arc from the place p to the transition t and corresponds to the arc label. Graphically, the label is omitted whenever $W^-(p, t) = 1$. Similarly, every positive value $W^+(p, t)$ defines a labeled output arc from t to p, but in this case t is by definition

an elementary transition. An output arc from an abstract transition t to p depends (in addition) on the I's indices. Its label corresponds to the symbolic sum $\langle \Sigma_{i \in 2^I} W^+(p,t,i).i \rangle$, defined for the positive values $\{W^+(p,t,i) > 0\}_{i \in I}$. Graphically, the term $W^+(p,t,i).i$ is abbreviated to i whenever $W^+(p,t,i) = 1$. For instance, the label of (t_2, P_5) is $\langle 0 \rangle$, meaning that this output is used to produce 1 token according to a preemption (index 0). The output arc (t_2, P_4) is labeled by a sum of indices $\langle 0 + 1 \rangle$ since it can be involved either in a cut step (index 1) or a preemption (index 0).

In a RPN, we have two kinds of markings: extended markings and ordinary markings. An extended marking defines the state of the RPN. An ordinary marking represents an execution context of a thread.

Definition 2. *An extended marking of a RPN $R = \langle P, T, I, W^-, W^+, \Omega, \Upsilon, K \rangle$ is a labeled rooted tree directed from the root to the leaves $Tr = \langle V, M, E, A \rangle$ where:*

1. *V is the (possibly empty) finite set of nodes. When it is non empty $v_0 \in V$ denotes the root of the tree,*
2. *M is a mapping $V \to \mathbb{N}^P$ associating an ordinary marking with each node,*
3. *$E \subseteq V \times V$ is the set of edges,*
4. *A is a mapping $E \to T_{ab}$ associating an abstract transition with each edge.*

Notations and conventions:
For each node $v \in V$, we denote by $Succ(v)$ the set of its direct and indirect successors including v. Moreover, when v is not the root of the tree, we denote by $pred(v)$ its unique predecessor in the tree. The initial extended marking is denoted by Tr_0 and the empty extended marking is such that V is empty and is denoted by $\perp$. According to an extended marking, a path is denoted by $v_0 \xrightarrow{t_1} v_1 \xrightarrow{t_2} \cdots \xrightarrow{t_n} v_n$ iff $\forall i$ in $0..n-1$, (v_i, v_{i+1}) is an edge of the extended marking labeled by the abstract transition t_{i+1}. When $M(v) \in \Upsilon_i$ (with $i \in I_C$), a cut step may be performed from v. This operation is denoted by τ_i. $Reach(R, m_0)$ denotes the set of reachable extended markings of a marked RPN (R, m_0), where m_0 is the initial ordinary marking of the places of R. For concision, $V(Tr)$ denotes the set of nodes of Tr. A step (or an event) of a marked RPN may be either a firing of a transition or a cut step. The pre-set of a transition t (with $t \in T_{el} \cup T_{ab}$) is given by ${}^\bullet t = \{p \in P | W^-(p,t) > 0\}$.

Definition 3. *A transition t is enabled in a node v (or in marking $M(v)$) of an extended marking $Tr \neq \perp$ (denoted by $Tr \xrightarrow{t,v}$) if $\forall p \in P, M(v)(p) \geq W^-(p,t)$ and a cut step τ_i (with $i \in I_C$) is enabled in v (or in marking $M(v)$) (denoted by $Tr \xrightarrow{\tau_i,v}$) if $M(v) \in \Upsilon_i$.*

Definition 4. *The firing of an abstract transition t_f from a node v of an extended marking $Tr = \langle V, M, E, A \rangle$ leads to the extended marking $Tr' = \langle V', M', E', A' \rangle$ (denoted by $Tr \xrightarrow{t_f,v} Tr'$) such that:*

for v' being a fresh identifier, the five following points hold:

1. $\forall p \in P,\ M(v)(p) \geq W^-(p, t_f)$,
2. $V' = V \cup \{v'\},\ E' = E \cup \{(v, v')\},\ \forall e \in E,\ A'(e) = A(e),\ A'((v, v')) = t_f$,
3. $\forall v" \in V \setminus \{v\},\ M'(v") = M(v")$,
4. $\forall p \in P,\ M'(v)(p) = M(v)(p) - W^-(p, t_f)$,
5. $M'(v') = \Omega(t_f)$.

Definition 5. *The firing of an elementary transition t_f of T_{el} from a node v of an extended marking $Tr = \langle V, M, E, A\rangle$ leads to the extended marking $Tr' = \langle V', M', E', A'\rangle$ (denoted by $Tr \xrightarrow{t_f, v} Tr'$) such that: for $E" = \{(v, v') \in E | K(t_f, A((v, v')))$ is defined $\}$ and $V'' = \{v' \in V | (v, v') \in E"\}$, the five following points hold:*

1. $\forall p \in P,\ M(v)(p) \geq W^-(p, t_f)$,
2. $V' = V \setminus (\cup_{v' \in V''} Succ(v')),\ E' = E \cap (V' \times V')$,
3. $\forall e \in E', A'(e) = A(e)$,
4. $\forall v' \in V' \setminus \{v\},\ M'(v') = M(v')$,
5. $\forall p \in P,\ M'(v)(p) = M(v)(p) - W^-(p, t_f) + W^+(p, t_f) + \sum_{e \in E"} W^+(p, A(e), K(t_f, A(e)))$.

Definition 6. *The firing of a cut step τ_i from a node v of an extended marking $Tr = \langle V, M, E, A\rangle$ occurs when $M(v) \in \Upsilon_i$ and leads to the extended marking $Tr' = \langle V', M', E', A'\rangle$ (denoted by $Tr \xrightarrow{\tau_i, v} Tr'$) such that:*

- $(v = v_0)$ *implies* $Tr' = \bot$,
- $(v \neq v_0)$ *implies the three following points:*

1. $V' = V \setminus Succ(v)$, $E' = E \cap (V' \times V'),\ \forall e \in E',\ A'(e) = A(e)$,
2. $\forall v' \in V \setminus \{pred(v)\},\ M'(v') = M(v')$,
3. $\forall p \in P,\ M'(pred(v))(p) = M(pred(v))(p) + W^+(p, A(pred(v), v), i)$.

Example 1. Consider again the net of Fig. 1. The upper part of the Figure shows a simple recursive PN. One can notice that the RPN is disconnected; it contains two connected components. One of these components is activated by the transition t_2. Note that the transition t_2 has two different ways of completion: t_2 may terminate by reaching a final marking or may be preempted by the firing of t_1. The output tokens of t_2 are either P_4 and P_5 (corresponding to the termination index 0) or only P_4 (corresponding to the termination index 1). Two firing sequences of this net are also presented in Fig. 1. Tr_0 is the initial extended marking of this net. One can notice that the firing of the abstract transition t_2 from the node v_0 of Tr_0 leads to the extended marking Tr_1, which contains a fresh node v_1 marked by the starting marking of t_2. Then, the firing of the elementary transition t_4 from v_1 in Tr_1 leads to an extended marking Tr_2, having the same structure as Tr_1 and in particular the same set of nodes. In fact, only the ordinary marking of the node v_1 is changed by this firing. The same reasoning holds to the firing of t_5 from v_1 in Tr_2, yielding Tr_3. It is worth noting that nodes can also be removed. Thus, the node v_1 is removed either by the firing of the cut step τ_1 from the node v_1 of Tr_3 or by the firing of the transition t_1 from the node v_0 of Tr_2. In the first case, the thread, called Th, created due to the firing of t_2 has necessarily reached a final marking, i.e. an ordinary marking where the place P_9 is marked (in other terms $M(v_1)(P_9) \geq 1$). Whereas in the second case, the marking of Th is not necessarily final. Besides in both cases the suppression of v_1 corresponds to the destruction of Th and to the generation of the transition t_2's results in the execution context of the root thread represented by the node v_0 (see Tr_4 and Tr_5).

3 The Model of Time Recursive Petri Nets

A TRPN is an extended version of the RPN model, introducing timing management. Basically, TRPNs are based on the semantics of both TPN and RPN models. A *single time reference* is assumed to cadence the time specifications. In the following, the set $(T_{el} \cup T_{ab}) \cup \{\tau_i | i \in I_C\}$ is denoted by TC.

3.1 Syntactic Definition of a TRPN

A TRPN is a tuple $\langle R, Is \rangle$ where:

1. R is a RPN,
2. Is, the *static interval function*, is a mapping $TC \longrightarrow \mathbb{Q}^+ \times (\mathbb{Q}^+ \cup \{\infty\})$ (where $\mathbb{Q}^+$ is the set of positive rational numbers). The function Is associates with each element t of TC a temporal static interval. The lower and upper bounds of such an interval for t, are denoted by sEFT(t) and sLFT(t). They correspond to a static earliest firing time and a static latest firing time.

An extended marking of a TRPN is defined in a similar manner as for RPNs. The firing conditions based on markings still hold but there are augmented by timing constraints, not only for transitions but also for cut steps. Therefore a transition enabled in a node of an extended marking is not necessarily firable in the TRPN. When both enabling and timing conditions are satisfied by a transition, its firing leads to an extended marking built in similar manner as for RPNs. for pseudo RPNs.

The net of Fig. 2 illustrates the features of TRPNs. The additional items are represented as follows: the name of a transition is followed by its static firing interval, moreover the notation Υ_i:$Is(\tau_i)$ is used to represent the firing static interval of a cut step τ_i. For sake of clarity in the graphical representation, the $[0, \infty[$ firing static intervals are omitted.

The net in Fig. 2 shows the modeling of a transaction performed by a remote server. The status of the server is described by the places ON and OFF such that ON indicates that the server is operational. In this case, the server can deal with two kinds of requests (see the transitions t_1 and t_3) allowing for each one to run a transaction (see the abstract transitions t_2 and t_4 with their respective associated starting markings, including a token in P_{init}). Both transactions correspond to the same connected component (see the places P_{init} and P_{end}), except that they

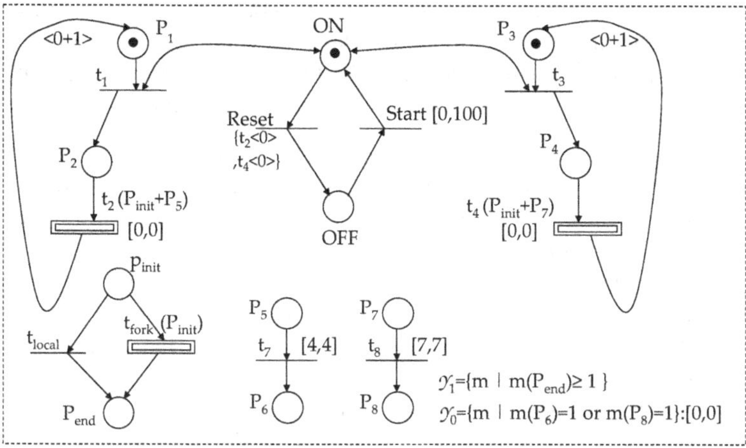

Fig. 2. A *TRPN* application

run with different timing conditions. Thus a transaction associated with a request of kind 1 (the transition t_1) must finish within 4 time units (see the transition t_7) whereas a request of kind 2 (the transition t_3) within 7 time units (see the transition t_8). A running transaction may either commit (represented by a token in the place P_{end} obtained by some firing of the transition t_{local}) or abort when its allocated time expires (represented by a token either in the place P_6 or place P_8). The corresponding final markings are represented by Υ_1 and Υ_0 respectively. Independently of the termination, a new request of any kind is possible, therefore the output arcs of t_2 and t_4 are labeled by both termination indices 0 and 1. A completion implied by a marking belonging to Υ_0 is immediate (see the timing constraint attached to Υ_0). Moreover, the server can be reset at any time (in this case, the place OFF becomes marked through the firing of the transition $Reset$). Any running transaction corresponding to t_2 or t_4 is then stopped immediately (in any case, the termination index is 0, as it is specified and attached to the transition $Reset$). The server will be operational within 100 time units (see the transition $Start$), so that new requests could be taken into account.

So, this example demonstrates the use of both external and internal preemptions (i.e. exceptions). Indeed, the firing of t_1 models a possible external preemption whereas the cut step τ_1 an internal one. The example also shows a recursive call within the transaction (see the abstract transition t_{fork} and its starting marking). Therefore, there may be infinite firing sequences due to this transition, for instance: $(t_1,t_2,t_{fork},t_{fork},t_{fork},\ldots)$. So, the *depth of the reachable extended markings is infinite* and the number of nodes in these extended markings is also infinite.

3.2 The TRPN Semantics

The semantics of TRPNs can be given in terms of Timed Transition Systems which are usual transitions systems such that the different execution sequences, called timed firing sequences, use two kinds of labels: discrete labels for events and positive real-valued labels for time elapsing. The model assumes a set of clocks, based on the same time reference, used to condition the firing from states. Main aspects of TRPN are now listed in an intuitive manner:

1. A set of positive real-valued clock(s) is associated with each reachable extended marking Tr: one for every node of $V(Tr)$ and element of TC. Actually, each element of TC may have several concurrent temporal behaviors in Tr, one per execution context (i.e., node).
2. According to a timed firing sequence, every reachable state is composed of a reachable extended marking Tr and a clock valuation $\nu c \in \mathbb{R}_{\geq 0}^{TC \times V(Tr)}$ (where $\mathbb{R}_{\geq 0}$ is the set of positive real numbers), such that $\nu c(t, v)$ represents the elapsed time since t became last enabled in the node v. Such an enabling has occurred either in Tr or in one of its predecessors in the sequence. The initial state of a TRPN is $(Tr_0, \nu c_0)$ such that $\forall t \in TC, \nu c_0(t, v_0) = 0$.
3. The firing (itself) of an element of TC from any state takes no time but it may imply a management of clocks, since nodes in the reached extended marking can be added or removed, depending on the kind of the fired element.

Like in other time PN models, we introduce a concept of "newly enabled transitions" inducing clocks to be reset. However, the concept depends now on the types of transitions.

Definition 7. *"Newly enableness of TC elements".*
Consider a firing $\langle V, M, E, A\rangle \xrightarrow{t,v} \langle V', M', E', A'\rangle$. *The TC elements newly enabled after the firing of t from v are obtained as follows:*

- $t \in T_{el}$: *only* v *may have newly enabling elements, more precisely, any element* t' *of* TC *is newly enabled in* v *after this firing iff* t' *is enabled in marking* $M'(v)$ *and, either* t' *is not enabled in* $(M(v) - {}^{\bullet}t)$ *or* $(t' = t)$.
- $t \in \{\tau_i | i \in I_C\}$: *only pred(v) may have newly enabling elements, more precisely, any element* t' *of TC is considered newly enabled in pred(v) after this firing iff* t' *is enabled in* $M'(pred(v))$ *and is not enabled in* $M(pred(v))$.
- $t \in T_{ab}$: *only the fresh node* v' *obtained in* V' *and the node* v *are concerned, more precisely, all the elements of TC are newly enabled in* v'. *Besides t may be newly enabled in v if it is enabled in the new marking of v (i.e.,* $M'(v)$*).*

Let's now give the semantics of a marked TRPN in terms of a timed transition system.

Definition 8. *"TRPN semantics"*
The semantics of a marked TRPN (R, m_0) *is a transition system* $S_{R,m_0} = (\mathbb{Q}, q_0, \mapsto)$ *where:*
For $X = TC \times V(Tr)$ *and* $Vall = (\bigcup_{Tr \in Reach(R,m_0)} V(Tr))$
- $\mathbb{Q} = Reach(R, m_0) \times (\bigcup_{Tr \in Reach(R,m_0)} \mathbb{R}_{\geq 0}^{X})$,
- $q_0 = (Tr_0, \nu c_0)$,
- $\mapsto = \mathbb{Q} \times ((TC \times Vall) \cup \mathbb{R}_{\geq 0}) \times \mathbb{Q}$ *consists of the discrete and continuous transition relations described as follows:*

1. *The discrete transition relation, denoted* $(Tr, \nu c) \mapsto^{t,v} (Tr', \nu c')$*, is defined, for any* $t \in TC$ *and* $v \in V(Tr)$*, by:*
   (a) $Tr \xrightarrow{t,v} Tr'$,
   (b) $sEFT(t) \leq \nu c(t, v) \leq sLFT(t)$,
   (c) $\forall t' \in TC$ *and* $\forall v' \in V(Tr')$, $\nu c'(t', v') = 0$ *iff* t' *is newly enabled in* $M'(v')$ *(where* $M'(v')$ *is the ordinary marking of* v' *in* Tr'*), otherwise* $\nu c'(t', v') = \nu c(t', v')$.
2. *The continuous transition relation*[1]*, denoted* $(Tr, \nu c) \mapsto^{d} (Tr', \nu c')$*, is defined, for any* $d \in \mathbb{R}_{\geq 0}$*, by:*
   (a) $Tr = Tr'$,
   (b) $\forall t \in TC$ *and* $\forall v \in V$, $\nu c'(t, v) = \nu c(t, v) + d$,
   (c) $\forall t \in TC$ *and* $\forall v \in V$, t *is enabled in* $M(v)$ *(where* $M(v)$ *is the ordinary marking of* v *in* Tr*)* $\Rightarrow \nu c'(t, v) \leq sLFT(t)$.

Example 2. Consider the net of Fig. 1 again and its extended marking sequence $Tr_0 \ldots Tr_5$. Moreover, add a timing function Is over the net, such that: $Is(t_1) = [3, 4]$, $Is(t_2) = [0, 1]$, $Is(t_3) = [0, 0]$, $Is(t_4) = [1, 1]$, $Is(t_5) = [0, \infty[$ and $Is(\tau_1) = [0, \infty[$, and consider that the clock signature of any extended marking's node v is $\nu c(v) = (x_1, x_2, x_3, x_4, x_5, r_1)$ where x_i and r_1 represent positive real values, respectively associated with transition t_i and cut step τ_1. The following timed firing sequence brings out the case where the time between two successive firings are 0 everywhere but 1 between t_2 and t_4:

$$\begin{array}{llll}
Tr_0 & \mapsto t_2, v_0 & Tr_1 & \mapsto 1 \\
\nu c(v_0) = (0,0,0,0,0,0) & & \nu c(v_0) = (0,0,0,0,0,0) & \\
 & & \nu c(v_1) = (0,0,0,0,0,0) & \\
Tr_1 & \mapsto t_4, v_1 & Tr_2 & \mapsto t_5, v_1 \\
\nu c(v_0) = (1,1,1,1,1,1) & & \nu c(v_0) = (1,1,1,1,1,1) & \\
\nu c(v_1) = (1,1,1,1,1,1) & & \nu c(v_1) = (1,1,1,1,0,1) & \\
 & & & \\
Tr_3 & \mapsto \tau_1, v_1 & Tr_5 & \\
\nu c(v_0) = (1,1,1,1,1,1) & & \nu c(v_0) = (1,1,1,1,1,1) & \\
\nu c(v_1) = (1,1,1,1,0,0) & & &
\end{array}$$

3.3 Comparing TRPN and TPN

A TRPN inherits by construction from all RPN modeling concepts [8]. In particular, the same connected component description can be used with different execution contexts, whereas an equivalent modeling by TPNs would require an explicit representation of each execution context and thus a duplication of the component. Moreover, (T)RPNs have the capability to interrupt a component under some timing conditions by firing only one elementary transition. The modeling of such an interruption by using a (T)PN is a task more complex since this

[1] W.r.t. the clocks associated with any (current) extended marking, a time elapsing step makes all the clock valuations progress synchronously. Moreover, the time progression cannot disable firings, either of transition or cut step.

requires to freeze each transition of the component. Hence, TRPN are more compact than TPN. In addition, TRPN has a better expressivity than TPN since some kinds of infinite systems can be modeled by TRPN but not by TPN. Typically, those systems whose some state must be reached from an infinite number of other states. Indeed, like in RPN, the transition system associating with a TRPN may have some states with an *infinite in-degree.*

4 Computation of the Extended State Class Graph

Time Petri Nets have a dense model of time, thus the state space is potentially infinite. Techniques for reducing the infinite state space to a finite one are necessary: several techniques have been introduced to define and compute the state class graph [1]. Here, we propose a technique for computing an extended state class graph for TRPN. Let us recall that the state of a TPN is represented by a pair called "**class**", composed of an ordinary marking and a firing domain defining possible firing times.

With regard to TRPNs, we can follow a similar approach but a class must refer to an extended marking, that means a collection of ordinary markings. We should have a firing domain attached to each of these markings. However, by assuming only one time reference for the whole model, we could gather the different firing domains of the extended marking in only one, representing the firing domain of the class. Technically, a class is now a pair $C = (Tr, D)$ such that Tr is its extended marking and D its firing domain. Actually, D is a system of inequalities that define, for every node v of Tr, the time intervals during which those transitions or cut steps enabled in v can be fired. Thus a variable of such system features a pair $< t, v >$, where t belongs to TC and v a node of Tr, namely $t.v$. Observe that $t.v$ represents the *firing date* of t from the node v of class C. Classically, such an inequality may have one of the two following forms:

1. $\alpha_v <= t.v <= \beta_v$, $\forall t \in TC$ such that t is enabled in $M(v)$, (where $M(v)$ is the ordinary marking of v in Tr)
2. $\gamma_{v,v'} <= t.v - t'.v' <= \gamma'_{v,v'}$, $\forall t, t' \in TC$ such that t is enabled in $M(v)$ and t' in $M(v')$ (where $M(v)$ and $M(v')$ are the ordinary markings of v and v' in Tr, respectively).

In these inequalities, the bounds are rational constants, $\alpha_v, \gamma_{v,v'} \in \mathbb{Q}^+$ and $\beta_v, \gamma'_{v,v'} \in \mathbb{Q}^+ \cup \{\infty\}$. Let us recall that the number of the constants $\alpha_v, \gamma_{v,v'}$, β_v and $\gamma'_{v,v'}$ which appear in the firing domains of a TPN is finite [1]; this result holds for TRPNs, since the computation of these constants is similar to that of TPNs.

4.1 Construction of the Successor Classes of a Class

The construction of the extended state class graph classically consists in determining all the reachable classes from the initial one, by inferring the firing rule until convergence is obtained, based on an equality operator on classes. The initial class of a TRPN is $C_0 = (Tr_0, D_0)$ where D_0 is defined as: $\forall t \in TC$, t enabled in $v_0 \Rightarrow sEFT(t) \leq t.v_0 \leq sLFT(t)$ is an inequality of D_0. Moreover, two classes $C_1 = (Tr_1, D_1)$ and $C_2 = (Tr_2, D_2)$ are equal iff $Tr_1 = Tr_2$ and $D_1 = D_2$. A firing from a class depends on both enabling and timing conditions.

Definition 9. *An element t of TC can be fired from a class $C = (Tr, D)$ if and only if the following two conditions hold: (i) there exists a node v of Tr such that t is enabled in v and (ii) D enriched by the inequalities of the following set $\{t.v \leq t'.v' |\ t'.v'$ is a variable of D different from $t.v\}$ has a solution. These added inequalities are called firability conditions of t and v.*

The firing of an element t of TC from a class $C = (\langle V, M, E, A\rangle, D)$ and a node v (where $v \in V$ and t is enabled in C) leads to another class $C' = (\langle V', M', E', A'\rangle, D')$. This action is denoted by $C \xrightarrow{t,v} C'$. C' is computed in the following way:
(i) $\langle V, M, E, A\rangle \xrightarrow{t,v} \langle V', M', E', A'\rangle$,
(ii) The computation of D' is carried out according the following steps:

1. $D' = D$.
2. D' is enriched by the firability conditions for t and v.
3. Remove from D' the inequalities in relation with the nodes which have been removed due to the firing of t from v.
4. If t corresponds to a transition, eliminate from D' each variable associated with a transition t' (except t) such that t and t' are in conflict in marking $M(v)$ (i.e. t and t' are enabled in $M(v)$ and $\exists p \in {}^\bullet t \cap {}^\bullet t'$, $M(v)(p) < W^-(p,t) + W^-(p,t')$).
5. In this reduced system D', substitute each variable x , with $x \neq t.v$, with $x + t.v$ and eliminate the variable $t.v$.
6. In this last step, for each node v' of V' and each element t' of TC such that t' is newly enabled in v' after the firing of t from v (see Definition 7), we introduce a new inequality $sEFT(t') \leq t'.v' \leq sLFT(t')$ in D'.

Example 3. Consider the net of the Example 2 and let us assume now that the initial marking is m_0=$(2P_1, P_3)$. One final sequence of the corresponding extended state class graph is $C_0 \xrightarrow{t_2,v_0} C_1 \xrightarrow{t_4,v_1} C_2 \xrightarrow{t_5,v_1} C_3 \xrightarrow{\tau_1,v_1} C_4 \xrightarrow{t_1,v_0} C_5 \xrightarrow{t_3,v_0} C_6 \xrightarrow{t_1,v_0} C_7$, where:

5 Some Properties of TRPNs

We now focus on boundedness and finiteness of marked TRPNs. In a RPN, the boundedness property ensures that there is a finite bound of tokens for each place, regarding all the ordinary markings of all the (reachable) extended markings. The finiteness property states that the number of reachable extended markings is finite. In Petri Nets, these two properties are equivalent and decidable. The equivalence does not hold for RPNs but decidability remains for both properties. A finite RPN is necessarily bounded but a bounded RPN is infinite when *the depth of the*

Table 1. A final sequence of the extended state class graph

Class name	Extended marking	Firing domain	Class name	Extended marking	Firing domain
C_0	$\bullet v_0\ (2P_1, P_3)$	$3 \leq t_1.v_0 \leq 4$ $0 \leq t_2.v_0 \leq 1$	C_1	$\bullet v_0\ (2P_1)$ $\downarrow t_2$ $\bullet v_1 (P_7)$	$2 \leq t_1.v_0 \leq 4$ $1 \leq t_4.v_1 \leq 1$
C_2	$\bullet v_0\ (2P_1)$ $\downarrow t_2$ $\bullet v_1\ (P_8)$	$1 \leq t_1.v_0 \leq 3$ $0 \leq t_5.v_1 \leq \infty$	C_3	$\bullet v_0\ (2P_1)$ $\downarrow t_2$ $\bullet v_1\ (P_9)$	$0 \leq t_1.v_0 \leq 3$ $0 \leq \tau_1.v_1 \leq \infty$
C_4	$\bullet v_0\ (2P_1, P_4)$	$0 \leq t_1.v_0 \leq 3$	C_5	$\bullet v_0\ (P_1, P_2, P_4)$	$3 \leq t_1.v_0 \leq 4$ $0 \leq t_3.v_0 \leq 0$
C_6	$\bullet v_0\ (P_1, P_6)$	$3 \leq t_1.v_0 \leq 4$	C_7	$\bullet v_0\ (P_2, P_6)$	

reachable extended markings is infinite. An unbounded depth can be decided as follows. The reachability graph is build until either the construction of the graph finishes or a reachable extended marking Tr is computed such that there are two fresh nodes v_1 and v_2 of Tr issued by the firings of the same abstract transition and v_1 is the ancestor of v_2. In other terms, the extended marking contains a path composed of edges labeled by the same abstract transition (label repetitions). Such a path is necessarily infinite [8] (Table 1).

Theorem 1. *The reachability and boundedness problems for TRPNs are undecidable.*

Proof. Straightforward, since TPNs are particular cases of TRPNs without abstract transitions and these properties are undecidable for TPNs.

In the following, we study conditions for a TRPN to be finite. A TRPN is finite iff the number of extended markings contained in the reachable state classes is finite.

Lemma 1. *W.r.t. a marked TRPN, the set of all the firing domains is finite iff the depth of the extended markings of the reachable state classes is finite.*

Proof. We proceed by contradiction. ($\Leftarrow$) Assume that the set of all the firing domains of the TRPN is infinite. This implies that the number of possible variables used to describe the different firing domains is infinite, since as for TPN, the number of the constants $\alpha_v, \gamma_{v,v'}, \beta_v$ and $\gamma'_{v,v'}$ appearing in all the firing domains is finite [10]. Moreover, the variables $(t.v)$ used to describe the firing domains of the reachable state classes depend on both elements of TC and nodes of the extended markings of these classes. So, we deduce that an infinite number of variables implies an infinite number of nodes in the reachable extended markings (the set TC is bounded). By consequence, the depth of the reachable extended markings is infinite.

($\Rightarrow$) Assume that the depth of the extended markings is infinite, then the number of nodes in the reachable extended markings is infinite. It is obvious that the number of variables $(t.v)$ defining all the firing domains is infinite.

Theorem 2. *A TRPN is finite if the two following points hold:*

1. *there is no reachable state class whose extended marking contains a path with at least two arcs labeled by the same abstract transition,*
2. *there is no state class $C' = (Tr', D')$ reached from another reachable state class $C = (Tr, D)$ such that a common node v satisfies $M_{Tr'}(v) > M_{Tr}(v)$ (M_{Tr} and $M_{Tr'}$ represent the ordinary marking functions of Tr and Tr', respectively).*

Proof. Assume that the TRPN is infinite, leading to an infinite number of distinct state classes. Here there are two possible cases: (i) there is an infinite number of firing domains. We deduce from Lemma 1, that the depth of extended markings contained in the reachable state classes is infinite. From [8], we know that such an infinite depth is due to an infinite path which contains labels repetitions. So, there is a state class violating the point 1 of the theorem. (ii) The number of firing domains is finite but not the number of extended markings of the reachable state classes. So, there is at least one infinite sequence in the state class graph. Let σ be the corresponding series of extended markings. By applying Lemma 1, we know that the depth of the extended markings of σ is finite (since here the number of firing domains is finite). So, the number of distinct nodes in the extended markings of σ is finite. Therefore, there is necessarily a node v which is common to an infinite number of extended markings of σ. Consequently, σ contains an infinite subsequence of extended markings, each one having a different ordinary marking for v. Since this subsequence is infinite, we can always extract a subsequence σ_1 from it, such that the marking of v is a strict increasing function. The point 2 of the theorem is then violated.

6 Conclusion

Time Recursive Petri Nets extend RPNs so that timing constraints are bound to transitions and cut steps specifications. In addition to RPN modularity, exception and preemption concepts, both delays and durations of multi-threads applications are now modeled easily. In case of infinite systems, TRPNs are more expressive than TPNs, however, we have shown that the theoretical background of TPN can be exploited for TRPNs despite the fact that the number of time variables depends now on the number of threads to be dealed with. Furthermore we have adapted the analysis tool of TPNs for TRPNs, named the state class graph, and proposed a sufficient condition of finiteness. This will allow us to investigate verification techniques based on finite systems, like model checkers. Our tool, which extends the input format of the ROMEO TPN tool, is under experiment.

References

1. Berthomieu, B., Diaz, M.: Modeling and verification of time dependent systems using time Petri nets. Journal IEEE Transactions on Software Engineering 17(3), 259–273 (1991)

2. Bouyer, P., Haddad, S., Reynier, P.A.: Extended timed automata and time petri nets. In: Proc. of ACSD: 6th Int. Conf. on App. of Concurrency to System Design, Turku, Finland (2006)
3. Bouyer, P., Haddad, S., Reynier, P.A.: Timed Petri Nets and timed automata: on the discriminating Power of Zeno Sequences. In: Bugliesi, M., Preneel, B., Sassone, V., Wegener, I. (eds.) ICALP 2006. LNCS, vol. 4052, pp. 420–431. Springer, Heidelberg (2006)
4. Boyer, M., Diaz, M.: Non equivalence between Time Petri Nets and Time Stream Petri Nets. In: Proc. of the 8th Int. Workshop on Petri Nets and Performance Modeling (PNPM 1999), Zaragoza, Spain, pp. 198–207 (September 1999)
5. Boyer, M., Roux, O.H.: Comparison of the Expressiveness of Arc, Place and Transition Time Petri Nets. In: Kleijn, J., Yakovlev, A. (eds.) ICATPN 2007. LNCS, vol. 4546. Springer, Heidelberg (2007)
6. Gardey, G., Roux, O.H., Roux, O.F.: State Space Computation and Analysis of Time Petri Nets. Journal Theory and Practice of Logic Programming (TPLP). Spec. Issue on Specification Analysis and Verification of Reactive System 6(3), 301–320 (2006)
7. Haddad, S., Poitrenaud, D.: Theoretical aspects of Recursive Petri Nets. In: Donatelli, S., Kleijn, J. (eds.) ICATPN 1999. LNCS, vol. 1639, pp. 228–247. Springer, Heidelberg (1999)
8. Haddad, S., Poitrenaud, D.: Recursive Petri Nets, an expressive model for discrete event systems. Acta Informatica (to appear, 2007)
9. Seghrouchni, A.E.F., Hadddad, S.: A recursive model for distributed planning. In: 2nd Int. Conf. on Multi-Agent Systems, Kyoto, Japan (1996)
10. Storrle, H.: Semantics of Uml 2.0 Activities with Data-Flow. In: Proc. of Int. Symp. of Visual Languages/Human Computer Centered Systems, Rome, Italy (2004)
11. Valk, R.: Object Petri Nets: Using the Nets-within-Nets Paradigm. In: Desel, J., Reisig, W., Rozenberg, G. (eds.) Lectures on Concurrency and Petri Nets. LNCS, vol. 3098, pp. 819–848. Springer, Heidelberg (2004)

Designing Case Handling Systems

Kees M. van Hee, Jeroen Keiren, Reinier Post, Natalia Sidorova, and Jan Martijn van der Werf

Department of Mathematics and Computer Science
Technische Universiteit Eindhoven
P.O. Box 513, 5600 MB Eindhoven, The Netherlands
j.j.a.keiren@student.tue.nl,
{k.m.v.hee,r.d.j.post,n.sidorova,j.m.e.m.v.d.werf}@tue.nl

Abstract. A case handling system is an information system supporting the handling of cases. The (sub) tasks for a particular case are performed by persons or software agents and the result of a task is the updating of the case data. Case handling systems consist of three parts: (1) a workflow engine that executes the process of a case, (2) a document manager that manipulates the case data and (3) a database manager for manipulation of the global data, i.e., the data that is independent of a particular case. In this paper we present a new methodology for the first four phases of the development of a case handling system: (1) user requirements, (2) functional architecture, (3) software architecture, and (4) the prototyping phase. The methodology is supported by a tool consisting of a Petri net based workflow engine, a standard document manager and a standard database system.

1 Introduction

In this paper we describe a methodology for the early stages of the development of a Case Handling System (CHS), resulting in a prototype of the system. A CHS is an information system for the support of a business process whose primary goal is the handling of *cases*. Typical examples of cases are claims in an insurance company, patients in a hospital, trip reservations in a travel agent system, sales orders in an auctioning system and orders in a manufacturing company. Thus CHSs are used in many application domains.

A case is an instance of a *case type*. A case type has two characteristics: (1) a *workflow*, i.e., a partially ordered set of *tasks* to be performed, and (2) a *case document type*, an instance of which is a *case document.* Tasks for a case are performed by *roles*, which are usually human beings, although software agents are becoming widely used as an alternative. Each task requires a particular *view* on the case data, and task execution results in updating this view. A task of the insurance company can be the registration of a claim; at a hospital it could be taking the blood pressure of a patient by a nurse. While handling the case, the case document may grow and at the end it contains all relevant information about the case.

K. Jensen, W. van der Aalst, and J. Billington (Eds.): ToPNoC I, LNCS 5100, pp. 119–133, 2008.

Case handling usually also requires data that does not depend on a particular case, so-called *global data*. Global data concerns *background* information, such as addresses or a product catalogue, and *management* information, which is aggregated information over the cases, such as the number of running cases or the total number of cases having reached a particular state.

A CHS has three main components: (1) a *workflow manager* for the execution of workflow processes, (2) a *document manager* for retrieving and updating case documents and (3) a *database manager* (DBMS) for the manipulation of global data. The workflow engine determines for each case which tasks are enabled and sends a relevant *view* of the case document and the global data to the role that will handle this task.

The design of a system requires modelling and in our situation we have to model workflow processes, case documents and the global data. The methodology we propose is a continuation of the research presented in [9] where use cases are modelled as workflows. In this paper the emphasis is on the integration with the data perspective and the use of the prototyping environment. We developed a tool specifically tuned for modelling and prototyping CHSs. The tool consists of a workflow engine YasperWE that is derived from the Petri net modelling tool Yasper [7,8], the commercial document manager Infopath (part of the MS Office suite) and a standard ODBC database manager (in our situation MySQL). The specific components of the prototyping environment are not particularly relevant but more a proof of concept of the approach, i.e., they can be replaced by similar components.

Related Work. In literature, e.g. [3], a CHS is considered to be more data-driven than a workflow management system. The authors state that too fine grained activities in workflow systems are restricting the user too much. As a solution to this problem, they propose a less granulated approach by enabling activities based on case data, and by allowing to skip or to redo activities. In our approach, the workflow manager is used to control the overall process of coarse grained activities, while the document manager regulates the operations on the case data by defining rules about data dependencies, such as mandatory or optional data elements. For example, instead of defining the addition, updating and deletion of products in an offer as different and successive activities, we consider the order creation just as one activity.

For modelling workflows the Petri net formalism is very suitable [2,13,15]. Since document handling requires data manipulation, the formalism of coloured Petri nets and their supporting tools (e.g. [1,14]) seem to be a good solution for modelling and prototyping CHSs, as proposed in e.g. [5,6]. However, handling case documents requires particular functionality that is already available in document managers. The same holds for data manipulation functions in a database manager. It is not very efficient to imitate this functionality in a coloured Petri net tool. In [11] a more general approach for information systems is described, but it does not use formal methods.

This paper is organized as follows: first we introduce basic definitions in Sect. 2. In Sect. 3 we introduce a running example. We present our design methodology in Sect. 4. In Sect. 5 we show how the tool Yasper can be used to model workflow processes. Next, in Sect. 6, we show how Infopath can be used to model case documents and how the case document and workflow processes are integrated using our tool YasperWE. Concluding remarks are given in the last section.

2 Basic Definitions

An inhibitor Petri net consists of two disjoint sets S, and T, of respectively *places* and *transitions*, a *flow function* $F : (T \times S) \cup (S \times T) \to \mathbb{N}$, and a set of *inhibitor arcs* $I \subseteq (S \times T)$. Places are depicted as circles, transitions as squares. If for a place $s \in S$ and transition $t \in T$ $F(s,t) > 0$ ($F(t,s) > 0$), an arc with multiplicity $F(s,t)$ ($F(t,s)$) is drawn between place s (transition t) and transition t (place s). An inhibitor arc is drawn as an arc with a dot at the end. Markings are states (configurations) of a net. We consider a *marking* m of N as a function $S \to \mathbb{N}$. In the graphical notation, the marking is represented by putting $m(s)$ tokens on place s. For each place $s \in S$ and transition $t \in T$, $F(s,t)$ defines the number of tokens consumed by t from s, and $F(t,s)$ defines the number of tokens produced by t to s. A transition $t \in T$ is *enabled* in marking m if $F(s,t) \leq m(s)$ for all $s \in S$, and for all s such that $(s,t) \in I$, $m(s) = 0$. An enabled transition t may *fire*. This results in a new marking m' such that $m'(s) = m(s) - F(s,t) + F(t,s)$ for all $s \in S$.

A Petri net N is a *workflow net* [2] if N has one initial place i such that $F(t,i) = 0$ for all $t \in T$, and one final place f such that $F(f,t) = 0$ for all $t \in T$, and for any node $n \in (S \cup T)$ there exists a path from i to n and a path from n to f. The initial marking of a workflow net N is the marking $\underline{m}$ with $\underline{m}(i) = 1$ and for all other $s \in S \setminus \{i\}, \underline{m}(s) = 0$. The final marking of a workflow net N is the marking $\overline{m}$ with $\overline{m}(f) = 1$ and for all other $s \in S \setminus \{f\}, m(s) = 0$. A workflow net is called *sound* [2] if the final marking can be reached from any marking reachable from the initial marking.

We extend workflow nets with a special kind of token colouring, resources, a timing mechanism and guards. In the remainder we call these nets extended Workflow nets. Our nets are a special class of timed coloured Petri nets [10]. We use colouring for giving the case tokens the *case identity.* A case identity, e.g. a natural number, is created when the first *case token* is created, and it is never changed. The only operations on this colour set are 'copy' and 'test for equality'. Besides case tokens we have 'normal' black tokens, which are treated as in classical Petri nets. A place can only store tokens of one type: either case tokens or black tokens. The places that store case tokens are called *case sensitive* places.

The firing rule is modified by adding the requirement that all case tokens consumed and produced have the same identity. In case a transition does not consume any case token, it creates a new case identity for the produced case tokens, i.e., the case tokens produced have the identity that differs from all identities of the case tokens present in the net. Such a transition is called an *emitter.* A transition with only case sensitive places as input, and not as output, is called a *collector.*

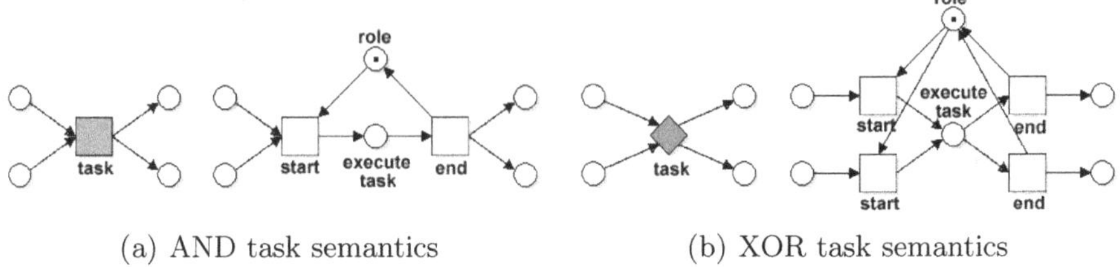

(a) AND task semantics (b) XOR task semantics

Fig. 1. Macros and their definition as Petri net

We also introduce two macros, which we call tasks: an AND task, and an XOR task (see Fig. 1). For every task, a role may be specified, which is a resource type that may execute this task. An AND task needs tokens in all its input places to be enabled, and, if fired, it produces tokens in all its output places tokens. An XOR task needs tokens in one of its input places to be enabled, and, if fired, it produces tokens in one of its output places. The choice of output place to produce in, is either randomly chosen, or it can be specified using case data. The XOR task can have an additional weight function, giving each outgoing arc a probability to be chosen as output place. Implicit choices, made by conflicts, have equal probability to be chosen (for more details see [7]).

3 Running Example

As a running example we consider the development of a generic web shop system. The web shop has to serve as a mediating party between customers and suppliers. The products the web shop offers are composed out of parts delivered by several suppliers. Different suppliers may offer the same part. Also the transportation of orders is performed by third parties. The web shop follows the "make-to-order" principle, which means that it has no stock and all components are ordered on demand at the different suppliers. Figure 2 depicts the web shop and the actors involved in the system.

The system has no domain specific information and therefore can be used in any branch. To run the system in a specific context, it has to be *configurable*. Configuration parameters are not only the name of the shop and contact information, but also the payment scheme and the information whether there are consultations with suppliers and transporters to make an offer to the customer. If a consultation is needed, also the decision which supplier and transporter are selected needs to be flexible, i.e., the lowest price or the fastest delivery time.

Customers can browse through the catalogue of the web shop and select products. These products consist of compulsory and optional parts. The customer can alter the selected product by adding and removing parts. After filling the shopping cart, the customer can request an offer for the products in its shopping cart. The web shop then contacts all suppliers that offer a part present in the offer to ask its price and delivery time in order to make a proposal to the customer, and selects the suppliers based on the system's decision rule. Also the transporters

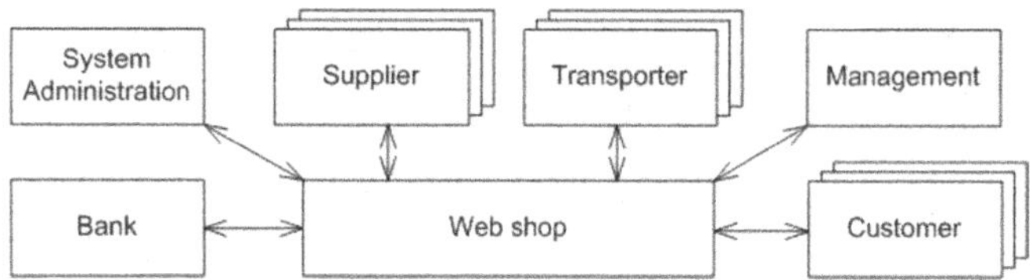

Fig. 2. The web shop and its actors

are contacted to ask when and for what price they can deliver. Based on these answers, the system composes the offer. The customer then has a choice to accept or to reject the offer. Based on the configuration, the customer may have to make an initial payment to confirm the offer acceptation. When the offer is accepted and, if required in the configuration, an initial payment has been made, the system confirms the selected offers to the chosen suppliers of the different parts, and rejects the other offers. The selected suppliers are paid according to some payment scheme. After receiving all components, the product is assembled and the transporter is contacted to send the order to the customer. The customer might have to make a payment on delivery, depending on the configuration.

4 Design Methodology

We present an approach for the first development phases of a CHS, resulting in a prototype of the system. In our approach it is important that no programming is needed to create a prototype. The development starts with the identification of the case type. In the further development we identify four phases, the *User Requirements*, the *Functional Architecture*, the *Software Architecture* and the *Prototype* phase. In the user requirements phase, the system and its functionality are identified and agreed upon with the client. These requirements are formalized into process and data models in the functional architecture phase. The created models also need to be verified in this phase, to show correctness. In the software architecture phase, the models are combined into a component model, and the case document type is formalized. The case document model, the global data model and the component model are combined into a prototype during the prototype phase. The prototype will be used to validate the user requirements in experiments with (potential) users. Figure 3 depicts the different deliverables during the phases, and how these deliverables depend on each other.

4.1 User Requirements

In the user requirements phase we focus on functional requirements. In user requirements, *actors*, persons and systems that interact with the system in development, and their *actions* with the CHS are identified. *Use cases* describe the functionality of the system. A use case is a piece of functionality involving

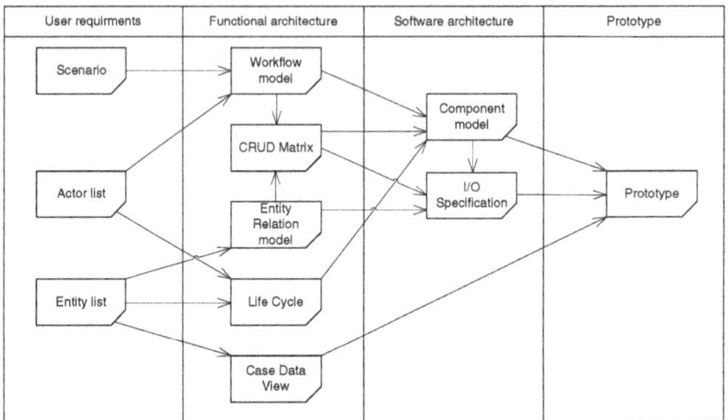

Fig. 3. Deliverables and their dependencies in the different phases

one or more actors and identified by a set of *scenarios*. A scenario is a sequence of actions; it can be either a *positive scenario*, describing the allowed behaviour, or a *negative scenario*, describing the undesired behaviour. These scenarios are often decided in consultation with the client. A natural way to model scenarios is using Message Sequence Charts (MSC) [12], to express what actions are taken by whom and in what order. In the next phase, the use cases are formalized with process models.

Part of the user requirements are the *data objects* involved in the system. These are the objects that the actors store, manipulate and retrieve with the system. In the user requirements phase, different data object types are identified and listed together with their attributes and relations.

The output of this phase is a document describing the desired functionality of the CHS in user-understandable terms, and it can be regarded as a contract between the client and the developer.

In the example, the case is the order of a customer. We can identify the actors Customer, Supplier, Transporter, Assembler, Bank and System.

A Customer can browse the catalogue, select products, add or remove parts, add a configured product to its shopping cart, request for an offer, and accept or reject an offer. The supplier can send offers to the system for a part and deliver ordered parts. The transporter can send an offer to the system, pick up orders and deliver them. The assembler assembles parts into a product. The bank can confirm and make payments.

Use cases of the web shop are e.g. the composition of a product by a customer, the request for an offer by a customer, the acceptance of an offer by a customer, the ordering of components at the suppliers, and the assembly and delivery of the product.

The use case "request for an offer by a customer" can be characterized by several scenarios. One possible scenario is a request for an order of a product consisting of three parts. The system decides not to consult the third parties. It finds the best suppliers for the three parts in the database, selects a transporter, creates an offer and sends it to the customer.

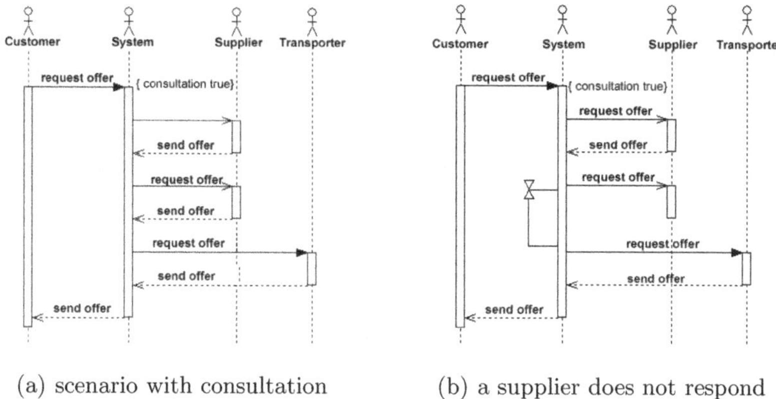

(a) scenario with consultation (b) a supplier does not respond

Fig. 4. Some scenarios of the use case "Request for an offer by a customer"

Another scenario is a request with consultation. An offer is requested for an order of a product consisting of one part. The system decides to consult the third parties. The part is provided by two suppliers, A and B. The system contacts both A and B and makes a request for the part. Both suppliers send an offer. The system selects the best supplier, and asks the transporter for what price and when it can transport the product. After the response of the transporter, the system creates an offer and sends it to the customer. This scenario is illustrated in Fig. 4a, where both suppliers respond, and in Fig. 4b, where supplier B does not respond within the defined time interval.

When specifying the scenarios, the data objects involved in the system and their relations are identified. For the web shop we can identify different actors, products and parts, configured products, configured parts, and customer, part and transporter offers.

4.2 Functional Architecture

In the functional architecture phase, the user requirements are formalized. For each use case the scenarios are combined into a workflow Petri net, such that each positive scenario is a trace of the workflow model, while each negative scenario is forbidden there. As a consequence, each action of an actor becomes a transition in the created workflow Petri net.

The objects identified in the user requirements and their relations are separated into global and case data objects. For both global and case data an Entity-relationship diagram (ERD) [4] is created, using only (zero-) one-to-many functional binary relations, labelled with a unique identifier. A special relation is the one-to-one relation, drawn with a triangle head, which is often used to express an "is-a" relation. Constraints on attributes and between objects in the data models are identified and formalized in the predicate logic. A view on the case data model is defined for each of the actions the actors can perform. For each global data object a *life cycle* is created. The life cycle of an

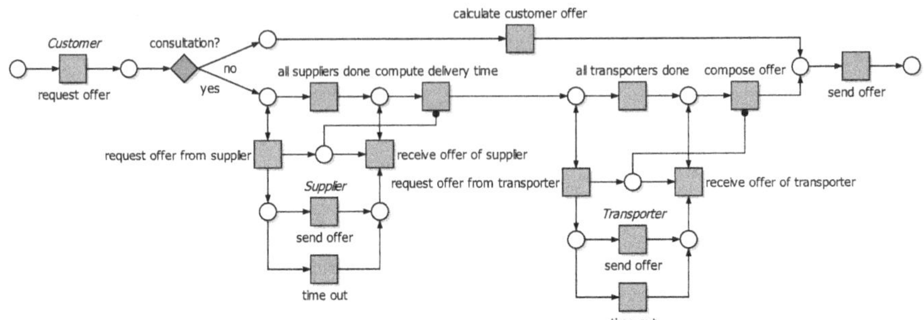

Fig. 5. The workflow that requests an offer to order a product

object defines in what states an object can be and what operations can be performed on the object. As a result of these operations, an object may go to a next state.

The actions of the actors can manipulate different objects in the system by *Create*, *Retrieve*, *Update*, and *Delete* operations. The *CRUD matrix* [9] expresses the relation between the transitions of the workflow and the operations on the objects. A transition can execute operations for different objects. However, it can only execute a single operation per object.

The developed workflow models of the use cases are then subject to analysis, i.e., property verification and performance analysis. First we check correctness properties of the workflow process, such as *soundness*. If the process satisfies correctness properties, we check its performance, i.e., the throughput of cases and utilization of resources, as will be explained in Sect. 5.

Then the CRUD matrix is verified. First, for each object in the matrix it is checked whether it is created and used, i.e., for each object there is a transition that creates the object, and there is at least one transition that retrieves or updates it. The next check is whether the retrieve and update operations are only performed between creating and deleting the object.

In our example, Fig. 5 shows the result of combining the scenarios of the use case "Request of an offer by a customer". The scenarios described in the user requirements show that *any* number of suppliers and transporters can be consulted. We create a workflow in which this feature is modelled using an inhibitor arc. All basic actions of the actors are represented by a transition. For each transition performed by an actor other than "system", the role is added in italics.

Figure 6 shows the data model of the global and case data. A product consists of parts; parts can belong to multiple products. Suppliers provide the web shop with parts. Parts can be provided by different suppliers.

An offer is an order that is not yet accepted. An order consists of a configured product, with configured components. All offers of suppliers and transporters are stored respectively in "SupplierOffer" and "TransporterOffer". For each component the best offer of the suppliers is selected (relation p in the data model). The best offer of a transporter is selected to deliver the order (relation t in the data model). A typical constraint of this model is given in Equation 1,

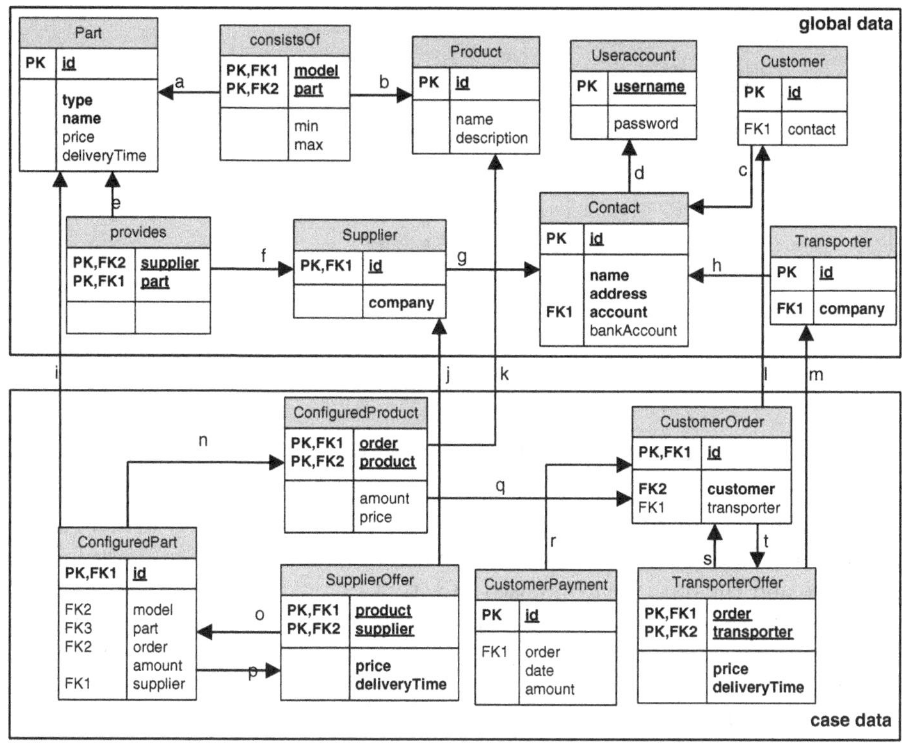

Fig. 6. The global and case data model using the technique described in Sect. 4.2. In the diagram, PK indicates a primary key, FKi indicates a foreign key.

which states that for each order, the selected transporter made an offer for that order.

$$\forall co \in \text{CustomerOrder} : \exists to \in \text{TransporterOffer} : t(co) = to \wedge s(to) = co \quad (1)$$

Each actor has its own view. The customer needs a view to create an order with products and configured components of the web shop, a view to see the offer and to accept or reject it. The supplier and transporter need a view to see the components they have to make an offer for and to notify a delivery to the system.

4.3 Software Architecture

In the next phase, the Software Architecture, a component model is created. A component consists of one process model and one data base (not necessarily realized with a DBMS). The activities of the process can only use the data elements of the data base of the component. Communication between components is modelled by the exchange of messages (represented as tokens) via places between the communicating components. A good practice is first to integrate all workflow models representing the use cases and the life cycles into one process

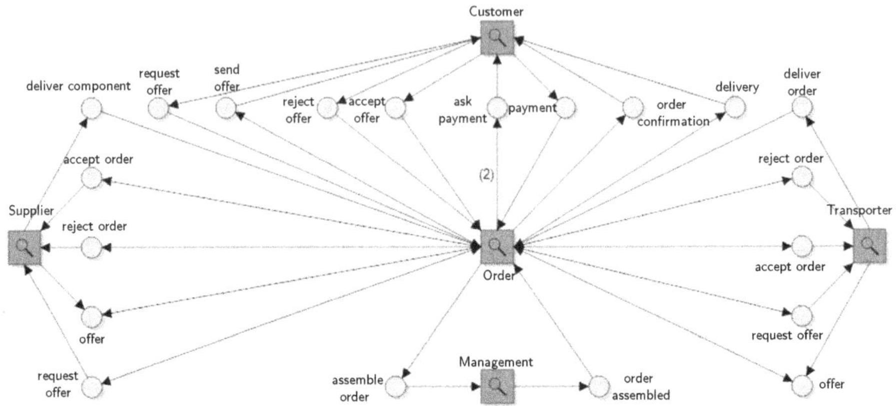

Fig. 7. Structure diagram of the Web shop system

model, and then divide these models into components. The data model can be divided over the components based on clustering, using the role types for the activities and the data elements used in activities.

The scenarios defined in the user requirements are test cases of the system. Each positive scenario should be a proper execution, while each negative scenario should not be possible. After modelling, the model is verified for correctness.

Next step in this phase is to specify the *I/O relations*; the manipulations of each transition in the integrated system on both the global and case data. For each of the I/O relations it has to be shown that it does not violate any data constraint specified in the functional architecture, and that it preserves the CRUD matrix. Using SQL, it means that each action corresponds to a query on the corresponding table of the object, i.e., each C action corresponds to an insert query, each R to a select query, each U to an update query, and each D to a delete query.

In our example, we could identify five components for our system: Customer, Supplier, Transporter, Order and Management. Figure 7 shows the components and their communication. Figure 8 shows how the use case "Request for an offer by a customer" is assigned to different components. As the transitions "request offer" and "receive offer" are actions of the customer, they are assigned to the customer component. The offer sent by the supplier and transporter are assigned respectively to the supplier component and to the transporter component.

4.4 Prototyping

In this phase the prototype of the system is created. As the complete system is specified, we would like to generate the prototype, rather than program it. By using YasperWE the prototype can be generated, as will be explained in Sect. 6. The potential user can experience how the system will behave, and validate the system to check whether the user requirements are met. Figure 10 shows a screenshot of the running prototype of the web shop.

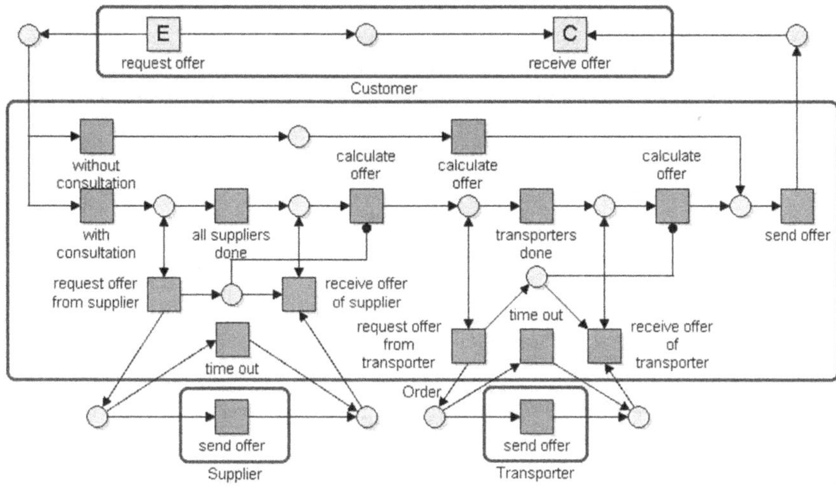

Fig. 8. The workflow of "Request for an offer by a customer" divided into components

4.5 Meta Model and Tool Support

Figure 9 depicts the meta model showing how the different elements and documents in the phases relate. The actions of actors form the scenarios of use cases. These use cases are formalized as workflow models. Data can be separated into case data, with views on this data, and global data, with life cycles. A life cycle consists of states and operations that can be performed in a state. An action of an actor has a view on the case data attached.

Different phases are supported by different tools. Yasper supports modelling and performance analysis of workflow processes (Sect. 5). For verification we use Woflan [17] and LoLA [16]. These tools are only used at design time and not during prototyping. Case documents are modelled in an easy way with Microsoft Infopath, which uses XML for documents and *forms* for views on the data (Sect. 6). For modelling scenarios and relational data schemes, many specialistic tools exist and can be used.

5 Modelling Workflows in Yasper

The tool Yasper [8,7] supports the modeling of processes described in Sect. 2. To help the end-user to validate a workflow process, Yasper has an animation mode to play the token game by hand. Each role has its own work list, containing all tasks the role can execute in the current state (marking). By clicking in the work list, the chosen task fires.

In the design of a system the performance should be analyzed in the early stages. Performance analysis in Yasper is realized by simulation. Yasper calculates the following four performance indicators: (the average) *cycle time*, (the average) *cycle*

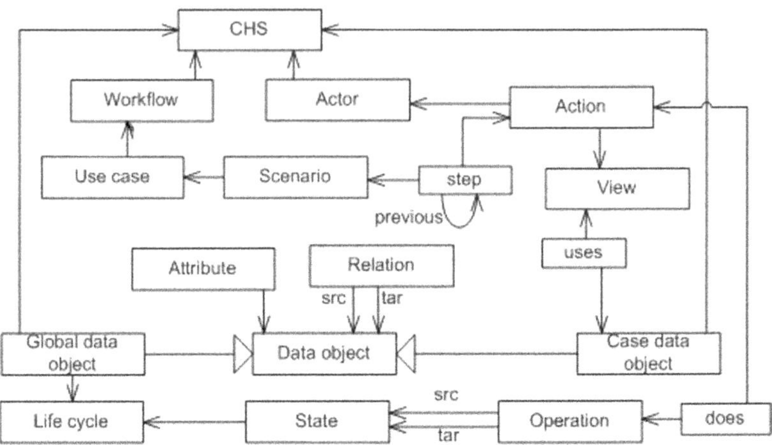

Fig. 9. Meta model of our approach in the development of a CHS, using the technique described in Sect. 4.2

costs, the (average) *cycle waiting time* and the (average) *role utilization*, where a cycle is a run of a single case. The cycle time is the time that elapses between creation of a case and the time a collector consumes the last token of this case. The cycle waiting time is defined as the time that no tasks are executed for a specific case, i.e., the time that no activity is performed on the case. The costs of a task is the sum of the fixed costs of that task and the variable costs of that task multiplied by the time units the task was running. The cycle costs is defined as the total costs of all tasks executed in the cycle. The role utilization is the fraction of time a role is involved in any task of any case.

6 Prototyping with YasperWE

In the second stage, after identifying the notion of the case, the designer starts modelling the document type. Microsoft Infopath, part of the Microsoft Office Suite, is a commercial document management system. To design CHSs, we created a generic Infopath template. This template consists of some basic case data, needed to define choices of XOR tasks in the workflow. For a particular CHS the designer only has to extend this template.

6.1 Modelling the Case Document Type in Infopath

Infopath uses XML as a data type and offers functionality to design a document as well as to fill in forms. The combination of a data definition and forms definition is the *configuration* of the document manager. In the design mode of Infopath, the designer models the case data in terms of an XML schema. In Infopath, the data is structured using *groups* and *fields*. A group is a named *container*, consisting of fields and other groups. A group can be seen as a singleton

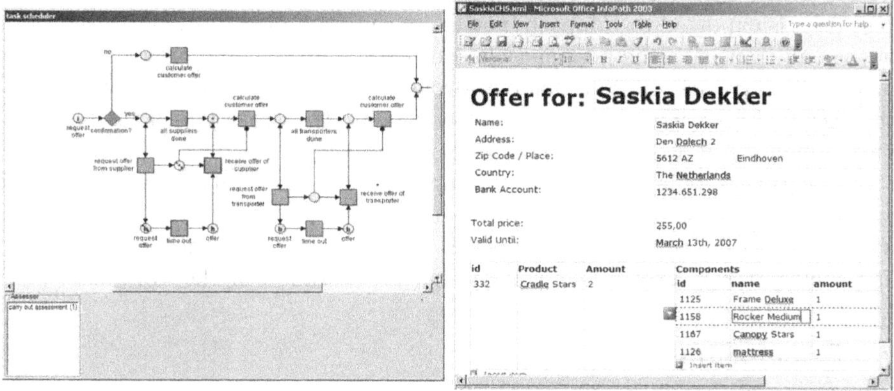

Fig. 10. YasperWE running the web shop in the running example

table definition in relational database. Multiple records of the same type can be stored by making the group a *repeating group*. Forms consist of elements from the XML schema and user interface controls, like radio buttons, check boxes, list boxes, text fields, etc., to interact with the end-user. The data end-users enter in these controls can be validated against rules, which can be set in the control. Also *constraints* on the data elements based on the case data can be expressed.

An end-user uses the document manager to fill in and alter documents. The submitted data can be saved locally, or it can be used in other systems, by submitting the data to a program, a database or web service.

6.2 Integration by YasperWE

In the prototype phase, the workflow engine (YasperWE), the document manager (Infopath) and the database manager (MySQL) are integrated to realize the component model, the case document type and the global data model. Each task performed by a role, needs a view on the case data. The designer has created the views in the previous stage in Infopath. Yasper is used as the design tool and the configuration tool for YasperWE. So the coupling of tasks to views in Infopath is specified in Yasper and the actual linking is done by YasperWE. When the designer finishes the global data model, the SQL definition of the global data needs to be integrated in YasperWE.

The querying of the case data and of the global data can be done by Infopath and MySQL separately, but in our prototyping tool we have chosen to transform the case data from XML format into the relational database, because this makes it easier to query and manipulate global and case data simultaneously. Query processing is divided into two parts, *prequeries* and *postqueries*. Prequeries are typically used to prepare the case data for presentation to the users, postqueries to process the case data after the user completed the forms. As depicted in Fig. 1, a task consists of a start transition and an end transition. Prequeries are executed with the start transition. If the task has to be performed by a role, the case data is exported to Infopath, and users can then modify it. With the firing of the end transition the postquery is executed. Note that the prequery is not a precondition (which would possibly prevent a transition to execute), but part of the executed task. The end-user can now validate the prototype of the CHS, by *animation*, like in Yasper, but now with realistic data.

YasperWE is built as a generic template Infopath solution, which can be extended for a case handling system. The solution needs the PNML file of the workflow to start YasperWE. YasperWE then shows the workflow and the work list. Picking tasks can be done using either the workflow or the work list.

7 Conclusions

Case Handling Systems form an important class of information systems and therefore it is worthwhile to have a dedicated and efficient development approach with supporting tools for them. We have presented such an approach here where we combine (an extension of) the Petri net formalism for modelling the process aspect and XML and the relational data model for the the two types of data involved in CHSs; case data and global data respectively. The approach is based on formal modelling techniques and verification methods. We also have combined and integrated existing tools to construct a prototyping tool for CHS, based on a Petri net modeler (Yasper), a document manager (Infopath) and a relational database manager (MySQL). Each of these components can be replaced by a similar one; the combination we presented here is a proof of concept.

We have done a number experiments with YasperWE in a second-year course at our university. About a 100 students divided over 20 groups had to build a prototype of the web shop presented here as running example within 10 weeks of 6h. The students modelled the complete system, from a product offer to delivery and invoice. They used YasperWE to create the prototype. All groups succeeded in showing a working prototype of the system. By following our approach they found out that there are already many hidden problems in the development of such a web shop, which they only could find out by modelling and verifying the system formally.

The experiment with students shows the applicability of the approach. However, we need to do more case studies to test and improve the approach. At this point in time, verification of the CRUD matrix, which is an important aspect of the approach, has to be done manually, which is error prone. Therefore, we want to extend the tool support in this approach, to offer automatic verification and analysis.

References

1. van der Aalst, W.M.P., et al.: ExSpect 6.4 An Executable Specification Tool for Hierarchical Colored Petri Nets. In: Nielsen, M., Simpson, D. (eds.) ICATPN 2000. LNCS, vol. 1825, pp. 455–464. Springer, Heidelberg (2000)
2. van der Aalst, W.M.P.: Verification of workflow nets. In: Azéma, P., Balbo, G. (eds.) ICATPN 1997. LNCS, vol. 1248, pp. 407–426. Springer, Heidelberg (1997)

3. van der Aalst, W.M.P., Weske, M., Grünbauer, D.: Case handling: a new paradigm for business process support. Data Knowl. Eng. 53(2), 129–162 (2005)
4. Chen, P.P.: The entity-relationship model: towards a unified view of Data. ACM Transactions on Database Systems 1, 9–36 (1976)
5. Choppy, C., Petrucci, L.: Towards a methodology for modeling with Petri nets. In: Practical Use of Coloured Petri Nets, pp. 39–56 (October 2004)
6. Günther, C.W., van der Aalst, W.M.P.: Modeling the case handling principles with Colored Petri nets. In: Practical Use of Coloured Petri Nets (2005)
7. van Hee, K.M., Oanea, O., Post, R.D.J., Somers, L.J., van der Werf, J.M.E.M.: Yasper: a tool for workflow modeling and analysis. In: ACSD 2006, pp. 279–282 (2006)
8. van Hee, K.M., Post, R.D.J., Somers, L.J.: Yet another smart process editor. In: ESM 2005 (2005)
9. van Hee, K.M., Sidorova, N., Somers, L.J., Voorhoeve, M.: Consistency in model integration. Data and Knowledge Engineering 56(1), 4–22 (2006)
10. Jensen, K.: Coloured Petri nets: basic concepts, analysis methods and practical use, vol. 2. Springer, London (1995)
11. Kurbel, N., Schnieder, K.: Integration issues of information engineering based I-CASE tools. In: ISD 1994, pp. 431–441 (1994)
12. Mauw, S., Reniers, M.A.: An algebraic semantics of Basic Message Sequence Charts. The Computer Journal 37(4), 269–277 (1994)
13. Peterson, J.L.: Petri net theory and the modeling of systems. Prentice-Hall, Englewood Cliffs (1981)
14. Ratzer, A.V., et al.: CPN tools for editing, simulating, and analysing coloured Petri nets. In: van der Aalst, W.M.P., Best, E. (eds.) ICATPN 2003. LNCS, vol. 2679, pp. 450–462. Springer, Heidelberg (2003)
15. Reisig, W.: Petri Nets: An Introduction. Monographs in Theoretical Computer Science: An EATCS Series, vol. 4. Springer, Berlin (1985)
16. Schmidt, K.: Distributed Verification with LoLA. Fundamenta Informaticae 54(2-3), 253–262 (2003)
17. Verbeek, H.M.W., Basten, T., van der Aalst, W.M.P.: Diagnosing workflow processes using Woflan. The Computer Journal 44(4), 246–279 (2001)

Model Driven Testing Based on Test History

Isaac Corro Ramos, Alessandro Di Bucchianico, Lusine Hakobyan, and Kees van Hee

Department of Mathematics and Computer Science,
Eindhoven University of Technology,
P.O. Box 513, 5600 MB Eindhoven, The Netherlands
{i.corro.ramos,a.d.bucchianico,l.hakobyan,k.m.v.hee}@tue.nl

Abstract. We consider software systems consisting of a set of components running as a sequential process. We model such software systems as a special class of transition systems. The difference with existing approaches is that we propose a test procedure based on the structure of the model and the prior test history that can be used for exhaustive testing in an efficient way. On top of that we provide a statistical stopping rule, that is independent of the underlying way of walking through the system, which allows us to stop earlier with a certain statistical reliability.

Keywords: transition systems, Petri nets, stopping criterion, software testing.

1 Introduction

Model-based testing is a software test method consisting of automatic generation of efficient test procedures using models of the system (see e.g. [1,5,11] or [16]). Formalization of testing theory was first presented in [8]. A few years later in [3] a formal theory based on abstract data type specifications was introduced, establishing the foundations of functional testing. Functional testing focuses on black-box testing since only the input–output relation is tested. We are focusing on structural testing in which we exploit the component structure of the system. However, we abstract from the testing of the components themselves (can be done by functional testing) but we concentrate on the control flow over the components. We use a model of labelled transition systems where each transition represents a component. Among the rich literature on labelled transition systems based testing we mention the early papers [7,13] and [14], and more recently [4] and [22].

In this paper, we consider a model of software systems consisting of a set of components running as one sequential process. This can be seen as a stepping stone for more realistic models with several parallel threads (cf. [17,19]). We model the components as transitions that either have a correct or an erroneous behaviour. In this context testing means executing software and observing whether it behaves correctly or not. We assume that there is a way to determine whether the execution of a transition is conforming to the specifications, for

K. Jensen, W. van der Aalst, and J. Billington (Eds.): ToPNoC I, LNCS 5100, pp. 134–151, 2008.

example by functional testing. Therefore, we define an error as a symbolic labeling of a transition that can be discovered only when the transition is fired. In literature all kind of test strategies are considered in order to avoid exhaustive testing which is not always feasible in practice (see e.g. [23]). These strategies are usually expressed in terms of coverage where a certain amount of components are covered. The difference with existing approaches (cf. [1,2,9]) is that we consider a test strategy based on the structure of the model and the test history that can be used for exhaustive testing (test all transitions in the system) in an efficient way (our algorithm reduces the labelled transition system after certain runs through the system) and on top of that we provide a statistical stopping rule, that is independent of the underlying way of walking through the system, which allows us to stop earlier with a certain statistical reliability. Hence, the statistical procedure can also be considered as a coverage method but with a statistical measure of quality. In spite of the extensive literature on statistical stopping criteria for functional (black-box) testing ([6,10,15] or [18] to mention some of them), there do not seem to be similar criteria for structural testing. Our statistical procedure should not be confused with the common statistical testing techniques developed in [21]. The term *statistical testing* is normally used for the probability of coverage (components, branches, etc...) while we are using it for the remaining number of errors in the system. Our procedure stops if the probability of having a predetermined number of remaining errors is smaller than a certain confidence limit. Our underlying test strategy is also statistically based, in the sense that the selection of the next transition to be tested is chosen at random. However, we have a reduction algorithm to reduce the model based on observed (and repaired) components.

The rest of the paper is organized as follows. An example of modelling a real system as a labelled (workflow) transition system is presented in Sect. 2. In Sect. 3 we introduce the test framework. A detailed description of the exhaustive test strategy is explained in Sect. 4. The statistical release procedure is described in Sect. 5. An example to illustrate a real application of our procedure is given in Sect. 6. Finally, in Sect. 7 we discuss the results obtained so far and future work.

2 Example of Modelling Software as a Workflow Transition System

Before formalizing our test framework in Sect. 3, we illustrate with the following example how we map the abstract model to a real application. This example represents a simplified generic medical workflow of a hospital. The business processes of the hospital are supported by an information system that is mainly used for updating the electronic patient records, the planning of activities and the protection of medical protocols. In this process the patient is central and each new illness of a patient is a new case that flows through the process. Each activity in the process is associated with a software service. The process model we use here is a Petri net (cf. [20]) with an additional construct: an or-transition,

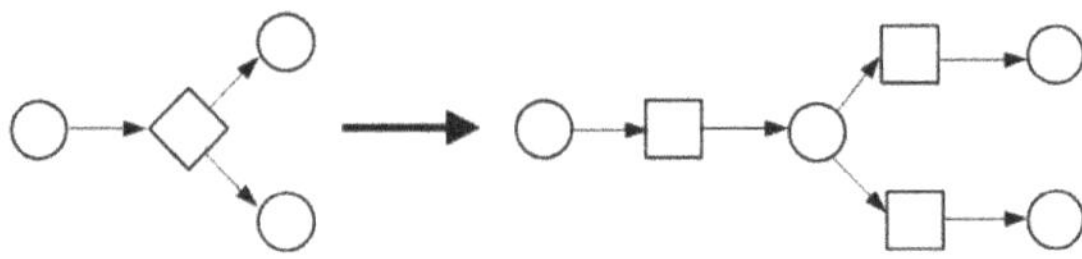

Fig. 1. Replacement of the or-construct (*diamond*) by standard constructs

represented by a diamond. In fact the model is made in Yasper, a Petri net tool (see [12] for details). The semantics of an or-transition is that it can fire as soon as there is a token on one of its input places and that will produce a token for exactly one of its output places. It is easy to replace the or-construct by standard constructs: the or-transition is replaced by one new place, and a new transition is added for each input or output place of the or-transition — connecting that place with the newly added one (see Fig. 1).

Next we describe the process in more detail. The process starts with the intake activity. Then a doctor observes the patient and then the doctor makes a diagnosis. According to this diagnosis the patient is released (no illness or not treatable) or a plan is made for further investigations (testing) or a therapy is chosen. Each test or therapy has its own specific activities and according to the outcomes and the plan, it is decided to continue with testing or a therapy, or the patient goes back to the doctor for a new diagnosis, in which case the whole process may be repeated. This process is graphically described in Fig. 2. Since each activity is associated with a software function embodied in a module or component, a trace through this process model is at the same time a test run where we assume that if we call the software service associated with the action we are able to see if the function is correct or not. We will return to this example in Sect. 6 to illustrate a real application of our whole approach.

3 Modelling Framework for Testing

In this section, we introduce the basic definitions to be used in our test procedure. We consider software systems consisting of a set of components running as a sequential process. We use labelled transition systems, which can be seen as a subclass of Petri nets, to model such process.

Definition 1 (Labelled Transition System). *A* labelled transition system *(LTS) is a triple $L = (S, T, R)$, where*

1. *S is a non-empty finite set whose elements are called* states*,*
2. *T is a non-empty finite set whose elements are called* transitions*,*
3. *$R \subseteq S \times T \times S$ is a ternary relation such that for all $t \in T$ there exist $s, s' \in S$ such that $(s, t, s') \in R$,*
4. *there is exactly one state $i \in S$ (called the* initial state*) such that there is no triple $(s, t, i) \in R$,*
5. *there is at least one state $f \in S$ (called* final states*) such that there is no triple $(f, t, s) \in R$,*

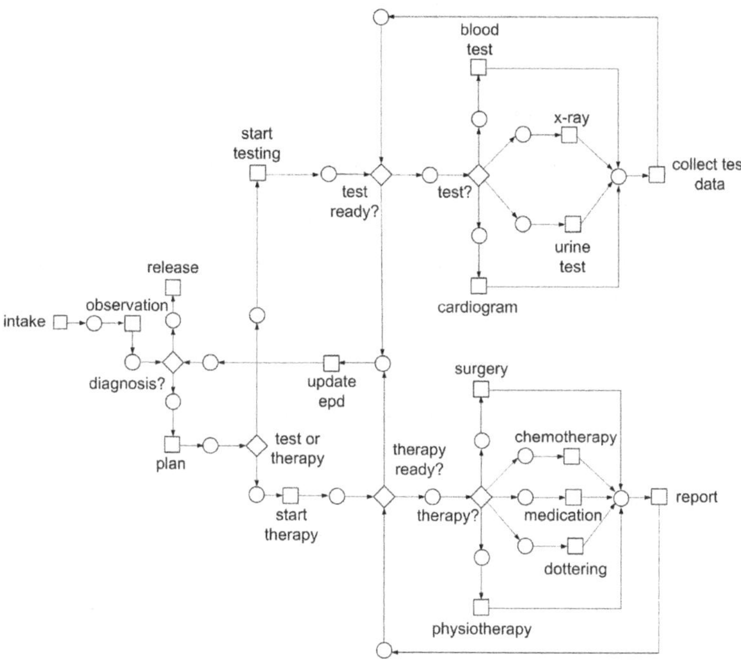

Fig. 2. Generic medical workflow of a hospital

6. *for any state* $s \in S$ *there is a sequence* $(s_1, t_1, s_2, \dots, s_n, t_n, s_{n+1})$ *such that* $(s_k, t_k, s_{k+1}) \in R$ *for all* $1 \le k \le n$, $s_1 = i$, *and* $s_{n+1} = s$, i.e., *any state is reachable from the initial one.*

When we do not want to specify the name of a transition we say that there is an arc *from* s *to* s', $s, s' \in S$. *Given an LTS, for all* $s \in S$ *we define* $\bullet s = \{u \in S \mid \exists t \in T : (u, t, s) \in R\}$ *and* $s\bullet = \{v \in S \mid \exists t \in T : (s, t, v) \in R\}$ *as the* preset *and the* postset *of* s, *respectively. A* path *in an LTS is either the empty sequence, denoted by* ε, *or a sequence* $p = (s_1, t_1, \dots, s_n, t_n, s_{n+1})$ *such that for all* $1 \le k \le n$, $(s_k, t_k, s_{k+1}) \in R$. *A* subpath *of a path* p *is a subsequence* p' *of* p *starting and ending with a state. A path* p *is said to be* linear *if for all* s_k, $1 < k < n+1$, *it follows that* $|\bullet s_k| = |s_k \bullet| = 1$. *We say that a path* $p{=}(s_1, t_1, \dots, s_n, t_n, s_{n+1})$ *is a* cycle *if* $s_1 = s_{n+1}$. *An LTS is* acyclic *if it does not contain cycles. An LTS is said to be a* one-path *LTS if* $|s\bullet| = 1$ *for all non-final states* s.

The next step is to present the new concepts needed for our test purposes. First we define what an error is. The main assumption is to represent software components or modules as transitions that either behave correctly or have an error. We define an error as a symbolic marking or labelling of a transition.

Definition 2 (Error). *A symbolic marking of transitions in an LTS is a function* $M : T \to \{0, 1\}$ *such that*

$$M(t) = \begin{cases} 1, & \textit{if } t \textit{ is error marked} \\ 0, & \textit{if } t \textit{ is error free} \end{cases}$$

The set $\mathcal{D} = \{t \mid M(t) = 1\}$ *is called* error set.

This function is unknown to the tester and it is the result of a random process (see Sect. 5). When an error is repaired, the marking of the transition at hand is changed from 1 to 0. We assume that we do not introduce new errors during the repair process and thus the number of errors in the system decreases as long as the system is being tested.

In our model we discover an error if and only if we visit an error marked transition. As soon as an error is discovered, it is repaired before we continue testing. The error finding process consists of executing a path from the initial state of the system to either a state with empty postset, to a repeated state or to an error marked transition. We refer to this path as run.

Definition 3 (Run). *Let* $L = (S, T, R)$ *be an LTS with a unique initial state* i. *A* run σ *in* L *is a path* $(i, t_1, \ldots, s_n, t_n, s_{n+1})$. *A run is said to be* successful *if* $s_k \neq s_j$, *for all* $k \neq j$, $1 \leq k \leq n$, $1 \leq j \leq n$, $M(t_r) = 0$, $1 \leq r \leq n$, *and either* $|s_{n+1} \bullet| = \varnothing$ *or there exists exactly one* $1 \leq k \leq n$ *such that* $s_k = s_{n+1}$. *A run is said to be* failure *if* $s_k \neq s_j$, *for all* $k \neq j$, $1 \leq k \leq n$, $1 \leq j \leq n$, $M(t_r) = 0$, *for all* $1 \leq r < n$, *and* $M(t_n) = 1$. *We denote by* Σ *the set of all runs in* L.

We now define a special test procedure that can be regarded as a probability distribution on the branching points of the LTS. We call it walking function.

Definition 4 (Walking Function). *Let* $L = (S, T, R)$ *be an LTS. A* walking function *for* L *is a function* $w : T \to [0, 1]$ *such that for all non-final states* $s \in S$, $\sum_{t \in s\bullet} w(t) = 1$. *We denote by* $\mathcal{W}$ *the set of all walking functions.*

Note that each transition t in an LTS has exactly one incoming state s, thus the sum in definition of walking function is well-defined. Initially all the transitions are weighted with non-zero probabilities and therefore all the transitions are executable. When the system is in a certain state the next transition to be executed is chosen by a weighted random drawing based on the walking function. After each successful run the walking function may be updated in order to produce a new one. This new walking function assigns probability zero to some already executed transitions so that for the next execution those transitions will not fire. Note that a zero probability transition can also be considered as a non-existing transition. The update of the walking function is done by the following procedure.

Definition 5 (Walking Function Update). *Let* $L = (S, T, R)$ *be an LTS. A function* $U : \mathcal{W} \times \Sigma \to \mathcal{W}$ *such that if* $w(t) = 0$ *for some* $t \in T$, *then* $w'(t) = 0$, *where* $U(w, \sigma) = w'$, *is called a* walking function update *(WFU) function for* w.

Therefore, an update means that no transitions are added but transitions may get blocked. A detailed description of both walking function and WFU function as well as a proof of exhaustiveness for the test procedure are given in Sect. 4.

Since exhaustive testing is not always feasible in practice, we need to define a stopping criterion that allows us to stop before we have tested all transitions.

Definition 6 (Stopping Set). *Let $\mathcal{H} = \{0,1\}^*$ be the set of all finite sequences of* 0 *and* 1. *If $\prec$ denotes the proper prefix relation, a set $\mathcal{A} \subset \mathcal{H}$ is a* stopping set *if and only if*

1. *for all $a, b \in \mathcal{A}$ we have $\neg(a \prec b)$,*
2. *for all $h \in \mathcal{H}$ there exists $a \in \mathcal{A}$ such that $h \prec a \vee a \prec h$.*

A procedure determining a stopping set is called stopping rule.

Note that the first condition states that when a sequence that stops the procedure is found, that sequence is not continued. The second condition states that any sequence has a stopping moment either in the past or possibly in the future. In Sect. 5 we define concrete stopping sets for our test procedure. Our test procedure consists basically of four steps: collecting tested transitions, keeping a record of the error marked transitions encountered during testing, updating the LTS by using a WFU function and defining a stopping rule.

4 Walking Strategy

In this section, we first describe a general WFU and then a more efficient update for a special subclass of LTS. After each successful run, we want to increase the probability of visiting new transitions. For that reason, for the next run we discard some already visited parts of the LTS, in such a way that the reduced system remains an LTS. We show that after a finite number of updates all the transitions are visited, so that the updating procedure is exhaustive. At the end of this section we compare the two algorithms for acyclic LTS.

4.1 Walking Function Update for Labelled Transition Systems

First we give an informal description of a WFU function for LTS and successful runs. Let $L = (S, T, R)$ be an LTS with walking function w. If L is a one-path LTS, then we stop after the first successful run since we reach the final state. Therefore, we assume that our system is not one-path. Given a successful run $\sigma = (i, t_1, \ldots, s_n, t_n, s_{n+1})$ in L we look for the last state, say s_k, in the sequence σ with at least two outgoing arcs. Since L is not a one-path LTS such a state always exists. Note that s_{n+1} is either a state with no outgoing arcs or a state that we encounter twice in σ. We update w to a new walking function w' by setting $w'(t_k) = 0$. With this we avoid to run t_k the next time we reach s_k. We do the same for transitions after t_k until we reach a state with more than one incoming transition if any. The formal description of the WFU function is given in Algorithm 1. An example of the application of the WFU function is described in Fig. 3. Suppose that $(s_0, t_0, s_1, t_1, s_2, t_2, s_1)$ is a subpath of a successful run σ in L. We update w by setting $w'(t_2) = 0$ since s_2 is the last state in σ with more than one outgoing arc. Note that this is equivalent to removing t_2 from L.

Algorithm 1. WFU Function for an LTS and a Successful Run

```
input : L = (S,T,R), σ = (s_0, t_0, s_1, t_1, ..., t_n, s_{n+1}), w
output: w' = U(w, σ)

Var tail : Int
Var s : Int → S
Var w' : T → [0,1]
begin
    s_0 := i; tail := n; w' := w
    while (tail ≥ 0) ∧ (|s_tail •| ≤ 1) do
        tail := tail − 1
    end
    while (tail ≤ n ∧ |• s_tail| = 1) do
        w'(t_tail) := 0, tail := tail + 1
    end
end
```

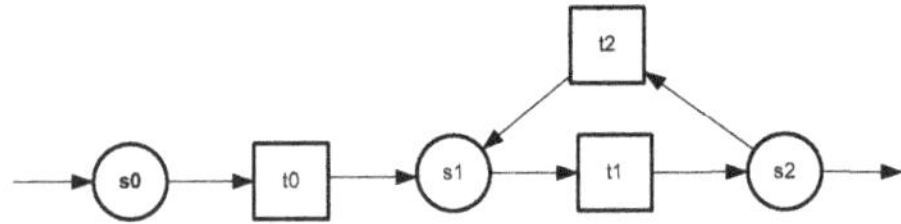

Fig. 3. LTS with a cycle. We remove t_2.

4.2 Validity of the Walking Function Update

We now study the validity of the update procedure. The next result shows that the resulting system after updating w remains an LTS.

Definition 7 (Reduced System). *Let $L = (S, T, R)$ be an LTS with WFU function U. Let w and σ be a walking function for L and a successful run, respectively. The* reduced system *L' w.r.t. $w' = U(w, \sigma)$ is the triple (S', T', R') such that $T' = \{t \in T \mid w'(t) > 0\}$, $S' = S \setminus \{s \in S \mid \bullet s \subset \tilde{T} \wedge s\bullet \subset \tilde{T}\}$, where $\tilde{T} = \{t \in T \mid w'(t) = 0\}$, and $R' = R \cap (S' \times T' \times S')$.*

Theorem 1. *Let $L = (S, T, R)$ be an LTS with WFU function U as defined by Algorithm 1. If w is a walking function for L, then for any successful run σ in L there exists at least one transition t in σ such that $U(w, \sigma)(t) = 0$. Moreover, the reduced system L' w.r.t. U and w remains an LTS and after a finite number of updates we test all transitions.*

Proof. If L is a one-path LTS, then after a successful run we stop our procedure and we do not update w. Assume that L is not one-path and denote by $\sigma = (i, t_0, s_1, \ldots, t_n, s_{n+1})$ a successful run in L. Since L is not a one-path LTS, there exists a state s_k in σ, with $0 \leq k \leq n$, such that $|s_k \bullet| > 1$. According to Algorithm 1 we choose the last state in the sequence σ with more than one outgoing arc. We can assume without loss of generality that s_k is such a state.

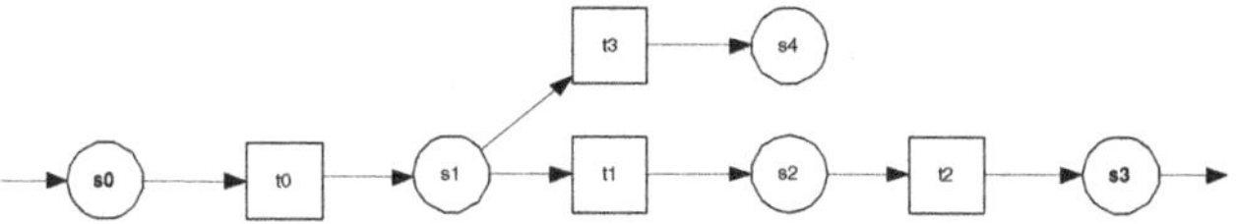

Fig. 4. Failure run in an LTS. The WFU function cannot be applied.

We consider the path $p = (s_k, t_k, s_{k+1}, \ldots, t_n, s_{n+1})$. Therefore, we update w by setting $w'(t_k) = 0$. We now prove that the reduced system, denoted by L', remains an LTS. It suffices to verify that every state x not in p is reachable from the initial one. Note that x is also a state in L' and there exists a path v from i to x in L. If p and v have no states in common, then v is also a path in L' and we are done. Now assume that p and v have at least one state in common. Suppose first that $|s_{n+1} \bullet| = 0$. Obviously x is not reachable from s_{n+1} and since s_k is the last state with two outgoing arcs in σ, s_k is the only common state of p and v. Therefore, v is a path from i to x via s_k but not via t_k. Thus, v is also a path in L'. Suppose now that $|s_{n+1} \bullet| > 0$, i.e., s_{n+1} is observed twice in σ. If s_k is also in v, then two cases are possible. Either v is a path from i to x via s_k but not via t_k, in which case v is also a path in L', or v is a path from i to x via t_k which means (since s_k is the last state in σ with two outgoing arcs) that v passes through s_{n+1}. Therefore, there exists a path v' from i to x via s_{n+1} that is also a path in L'. Finally, if s_k is not in v, then there exists l with $k+1 \leq l \leq n+1$, such that $(s_l, t_l, \ldots, t_n, s_{n+1})$ is a subsequence of both p and v. In any case, s_{n+1} is also a state in v. Hence, there exists a path v' in L' from i to x via s_{n+1}. For the last statement recall that we discard at least one transition after a successful run. Failure runs may not reduce L, but since the number of error marked transitions is finite, after a finite number of runs we visit all the transitions and thus an exhaustive procedure is defined. □

Note that σ must be a successful run, otherwise Theorem 1 is not true. This is illustrated in Fig. 4. Suppose that $(s_0, t_0, s_1, t_1, s_2)$ is a subpath of a failure run σ in L. According to Algorithm 1, we would update the walking function w by setting $w'(t_1) = 0$. However, the reduced system would not be an LTS anymore because t_2 would be unreachable.

4.3 Walking Function Update for Acyclic Workflow Transition Systems

We now present a more efficient WFU function update for a special subclass of LTS. Since this subclass is in fact a special class of workflow Petri nets, we call it workflow transitions systems (WTS).

Definition 8 (Workflow Transition System). *A workflow transition system (WTS) is an LTS with the additional requirements that there is a unique final state f and that for every state $s \neq f$ there is a path from s to f.*

Algorithm 2. WFU Function for an Acyclic WTS and a Successful Run

```
input  : L = (S, T, R), σ = (s_0, t_0, s_1, t_1, ..., t_n, s_{n+1}), w
output: w' = U(w, σ)

Var head; current : Int
Var s : Int → S
Var w' : T → [0, 1]
begin
    s_0 := i; s_{n+1} := f; head := 0; current := 0; w' := w
    while (current ≤ (n + 1)) do
        while (| • s_current| = 1) do
            if (|s_current • | > 1) then
                head := current
            endif
            current := current + 1
        end
        for (x = head to current)
        w(t_x) := 0
    end
end
```

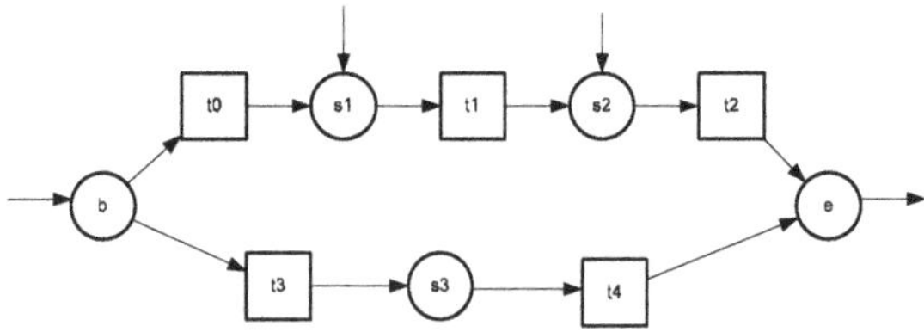

Fig. 5. Acyclic WTS where s_1 and s_2 have only one outgoing arc. We remove t_0.

We first give an informal description of the WFU function for acyclic WTS. Let $W = (S, T, R)$ be an acyclic WTS with walking function w. We assume that W is not one-path since testing one-path WTS is also trivial. Given a successful run σ in W we look for the first state, say s, in σ with at least two outgoing arcs. Since W is not one-path such a state always exists. Setting s as a marker, called "head", we move forward through σ. If the next state has exactly one incoming and one outgoing arc, then we move to the following state. If we reach a state, say s', with at least two outgoing arcs but only one incoming, then we set s' as "head". We continue the same procedure until we find a state, say $\tilde{s}$, with at least two incoming arcs. Such a state always exists because there is exactly one final state, there are no cycles and the final state can be reached from any other state. We update w to a new walking function w' by setting $w'(t') = 0$, where t' is any transition in σ between s' and $\tilde{s}$. Therefore, we avoid to run again the sequence comprised between t' and $\tilde{t}$ the next time we reach s'. When this update has been done we continue moving forward through σ looking for a

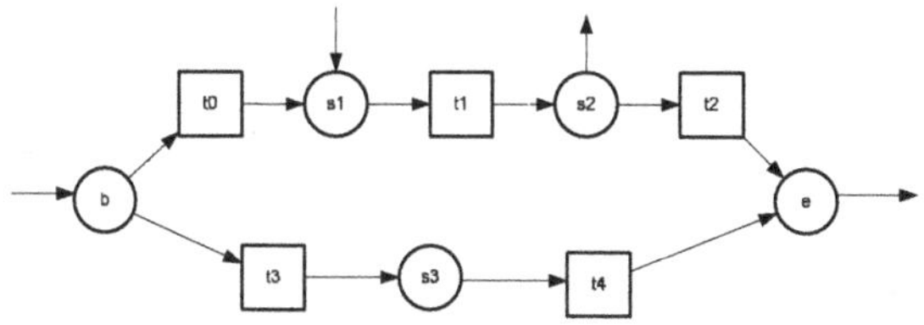

Fig. 6. Acyclic WTS where s_1 has only one outgoing arc and s_2 has two outgoing arcs. We remove t_0 and t_2.

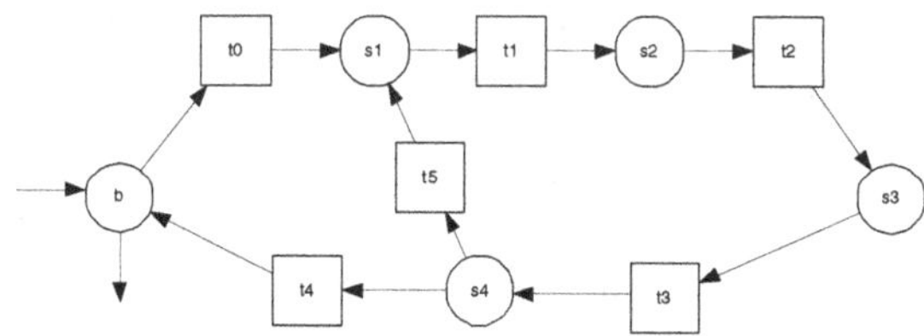

Fig. 7. Cyclic WTS. The WFU function cannot be applied.

new "head" and applying the same procedure until we reach the final state f. Note that the workflow property is guaranteed because of acyclicity. The formal description of this WFU function is given in Algorithm 2. An example of its application is shown in Fig. 5. Suppose that $(b, t_0, s_1, t_1, s_2, t_2, e)$ is a subpath of a successful run σ in W. We update w by setting $w'(t_0) = 0$. Note that this is equivalent to removing t_0 from W. Similarly, in the situation illustrated in Fig. 6, we update w by setting $w'(t_0) = 0$ and $w'(t_2) = 0$. If in both cases (b, t_3, s_3, t_4, e) was a subpath of σ, then we would update w by setting $w'(t_3) = 0$ and $w'(t_4) = 0$. Note that the update procedure is valid only for an acyclic WTS. Suppose that $(b, t_0, s_1, \ldots, s_4, t_4, b)$ is a cycle as it is shown in Fig. 7, and subpath of σ. According to Algorithm 2 we would update w by setting $w'(t_0) = 0$. However, the reduced system is not a WTS anymore because t_5 would be unreachable.

4.4 Validity of the Walking Function Update for Acyclic WTS

Similarly to the general case, we now study the validity of the procedure for an acyclic WTS. Reduced WTS are defined in a similar way as in Definition 8, therefore we skip a formal definition here.

Theorem 2. *Let $W = (S, T, R)$ be an acyclic WTS with WFU function U as defined by Algorithm 2. If w is a walking function for W, then for a successful run σ in W there exists at least one transition t in σ such that $U(w, \sigma)(t) = 0$. Moreover, the reduced system W' w.r.t. U and w remains a WTS and after a finite number of updates we visit all transitions.*

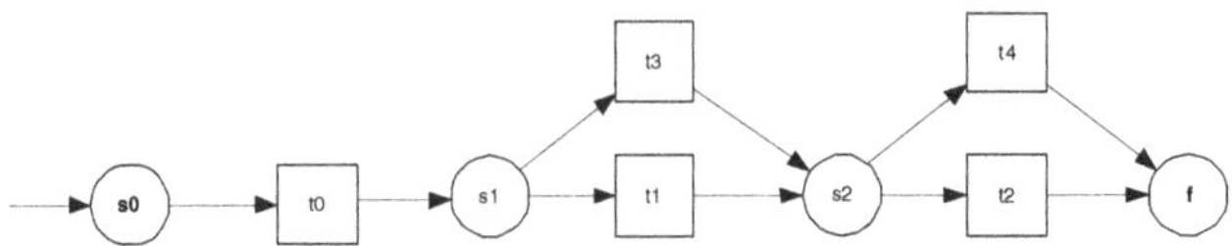

Fig. 8. Acyclic WTS. Transitions t_1 and t_2 are removed by Algorithm 2. Only t_2 is removed by Algorithm 1.

Note that the update procedure may be applied several times moving forward through a successful run until the final state is reached. However, we present a proof for the case where the system is reduced only once. Given this proof, the proof for multiple reductions is straightforward.

Proof. If W is a one-path WTS, then after a successful run we stop our procedure and we do not update w. Assume that W is not a one-path WTS and denote by $\sigma = (i, t_0, s_1, \ldots, t_n, f)$ a successful run in W. Since W is not a one-path WTS, there exists a state s_k in σ, with $0 \leq k \leq n$, such that $|s_k \bullet| > 1$. We can assume without loss of generality that s_k is the "head" marker in Algorithm 2 and s_l, with $k < l \leq n$, be the first state in σ after s_k with more than one incoming arc. We consider the path $p = (s_k, t_k, s_{k+1}, \ldots, t_{l-1}, s_l)$. Note that p is a linear subpath of σ. Therefore, we update w by setting $w'(t_k) = \cdots = w'(t_{l-1}) = 0$. We now prove that the reduced system, denoted by W', remains a WTS. Since we do not introduce new transitions, it is enough to verify the existence of paths to f. Consider an arbitrary state x in W that is not in p. Therefore, x is also a state in W' and there exists a path v from i to x and from x to f in W. If p is not a subpath of v, then v is also a path in W' and we are done. Suppose now that p is a subpath of v. Either p is a subpath from i to x or from x to f. Suppose that it is a subpath from i to x. Since p is a linear path and passes via s_l to x and $|\bullet s_l| > 1$, there exists at least another path from i to s_l such that p is not a subpath of it (due to acyclicity). Assume now that p is a subpath from x to f. Since $|s_k \bullet| > 1$ there exists at least another path from s_k to f such that p is not a subpath of it (again due to acyclicity). Therefore, W' is a WTS. The final statement follows as in the proof of Theorem 1. □

4.5 Algorithm Comparison

We now illustrate with a simple example the advantage of using Algorithm 2 for acyclic WTS. We have shown in Sect. 4.2 that Algorithm 1 is valid for general LTS. Therefore, if we do not have any information about whether the system is acyclic or not we apply Algorithm 1. However, if we know that the system is an acyclic WTS it is more efficient to use Algorithm 2 since after a successful run it reduces at least the same number of transitions as Algorithm 1. This is depicted in Fig. 8. Suppose the path $\sigma = (i, t_0, s_1, t_1, s_2, t_2, f)$ is a successful run. According to Algorithm 1 we update the walking function w by setting $w'(t_2) = 0$, i.e., the system is reduced by one transition. Nevertheless, if we apply Algorithm 2, then we update w by setting $w'(t_1) = 0$ and $w'(t_2) = 0$, reducing thus the system by two transitions.

5 Statistical Release Procedure

In Sect. 4 we have presented a procedure based on the structure of the net that allows for exhaustive testing. When exhaustive testing is not feasible in practice, statistical procedures must be considered. We propose a statistical release procedure that only makes use of the information collected during the walking phase, namely the total number of transitions in an LTS, the number of distinct tested transitions and the number of tested error marked transitions, denoted by N, n and s, respectively. We assume that each transition is independently marked as an error with probability θ. Therefore, if $L = (S, T, R)$ denotes an LTS and $N = |T|$, then the (unknown) total number of error marked transitions in L, denoted by D, is binomially distributed with parameters N and θ. Our stopping rule determines the probability of having at most k remaining errors when we decide to stop testing. Thus, if we fix k and a confidence level $1 - \alpha$, our problem consists of visiting the minimal number of transitions such that the probability of having at most k remaining errors is greater than or equal to $1 - \alpha$. We study two approaches to this problem according to the chosen point of view in statistics: one based on classical statistics (frequentist approach) and one based on Bayesian statistics. At the end of the section we carry out a comparison between the two approaches in order to establish our preference for the Bayesian approach when we present a practical application of our procedures in Sect. 6.

5.1 Frequentist Approach

This is the classical estimation problem approach in statistics. We must provide point estimates of the parameters and also confidence intervals. Since D is binomially distributed with parameters N and θ, the Maximum Likelihood estimate of θ is given by $\hat{\theta} = s/n$. The highest estimated value for θ is the upper bound of its one-sided confidence interval and it is given by $\theta_u = \hat{\theta} + z_\gamma \sqrt{\hat{\theta}(1 - \hat{\theta})/n}$, where z_γ is the γ-quantile of the standard normal distribution. Therefore, the probability of having at most k remaining errors should be calculated using θ_u in order to have the best reliability. Hence, for a fixed α, our problem consists of calculating the minimal value of n such that

$$\mathrm{P}\left[s \le D \le s + k \mid \theta_u\right] = \sum_{d=s}^{s+k} \binom{N}{d} (\theta_u)^d (1 - \theta_u)^{N-d} \ge 1 - \alpha \,. \tag{1}$$

Thus, $\mathcal{A} = \{\mathbf{x} \subset \mathcal{H} \mid \mathrm{P}\left[s \le D \le s + k \mid \theta_u\right] \ge 1 - \alpha\}$ is a stopping set according to Definition 6, since as n increases to N (and thus s increases to d) the probability $\mathrm{P}\left[s \le D \le s + k \mid \theta_u\right]$ will always tend to 1. Thus, the stopping criterion will always be met.

5.2 Bayesian Approach

In this approach, we consider the error probability as a random variable Θ with a prior distribution function $F_\Theta(\theta)$. Denote by $\mathbf{X} = (X_1, \ldots, X_n)$ the output of the n tested transitions (error free or error marked) and let $\mathbf{x} = (x_1, \ldots, x_n)$ be their realizations. In this case, for a fixed α, we want to calculate the minimal value of n such that

$$\mathrm{P}\left[s \leq D \leq s+k | \mathbf{X} = \mathbf{x}\right] = \sum_{d=s}^{s+k} \mathrm{P}\left[D = d | \mathbf{X} = \mathbf{x}\right] \geq 1 - \alpha \,. \tag{2}$$

Application of the Bayes rule and the law of total probability yields

$$\mathrm{P}\left[D = d | \mathbf{X} = \mathbf{x}\right] = \frac{\mathrm{P}\left[\mathbf{X} = \mathbf{x} \mid D = d\right] \displaystyle\int_0^1 \mathrm{P}\left[D = d | \Theta = \theta\right] \, f_\Theta\left(\theta\right) \, d\theta}{\displaystyle\int_0^1 \mathrm{P}\left[\mathbf{X} = \mathbf{x} | \Theta = \theta\right] \, f_\Theta\left(\theta\right) \, d\theta} \,. \tag{3}$$

To calculate the probabilities in (3) note that $\mathrm{P}\left[\mathbf{X} = \mathbf{x} | D = d\right]$ is the result of a hypergeometric experiment where the order is taken into account, the random variable $D|_{\Theta=\theta}$ is binomially distributed with parameters N and θ and finally $\mathrm{P}\left[\mathbf{X} = \mathbf{x} | \Theta = \theta\right]$ is the result of a binomial experiment where the order is taken into account. Substitution in (3) yields

$$\mathrm{P}\left[D = d | \mathbf{X} = \mathbf{x}\right] = \binom{N-n}{d-s} \frac{\displaystyle\int_0^1 \theta^d (1-\theta)^{N-d} f_\Theta(\theta) \, d\theta}{\displaystyle\int_0^1 \theta^s (1-\theta)^{n-s} f_\Theta(\theta) \, d\theta} \,. \tag{4}$$

Since (2) can be computed, $\mathcal{A} = \{\mathbf{x} \subset \mathcal{H} | \mathrm{P}\left[s \leq D \leq s+k | \mathbf{X} = \mathbf{x}\right] \geq 1 - \alpha\}$ is a stopping set according to Definition 6. Note that as long as we observe $\mathbf{x}$ the posterior distribution of Θ can be computed (since we only need n and s). We can use the posterior distribution of Θ to update the prior in order to compute again (4), and so do (2). This procedure of collecting data and updating the distribution of Θ can be done in several stages, defining a fully sequential procedure. Note that in contrast to the binomial approach, the Bayesian rule can also be computed in case that $s = 0$. Moreover, in the next subsection we illustrate with a simple example why the Bayesian rule is preferred to the binomial rule also in case that $s \neq 0$.

5.3 Comparison

We now compare the binomial and the Bayesian stopping rules. We assume that Θ has a prior uniform distribution on the interval $(0, 1)$ since we assume total ignorance about possible values of θ. Note that if we had some prior knowledge about the parameter, this should be reflected in the prior distribution. For example, if we knew that the mean is concentrated about a certain value μ, then

Table 1. Values of k (remaining error marked transitions) obtained using the Bayesian and the binomial stopping rules for n (tested transitions) and s (tested error marked transitions) given, when $N = 3,000$ (total number of transitions), $1 - \alpha = 0.95$ (confidence level of the stopping procedure) and $1 - \gamma = 0.99, 0.95, 0.90$ (level at which the confidence intervals for θ are calculated)

n	s	Bayesian	BN ($\gamma = 0.01$)	BN ($\gamma = 0.05$)	BN ($\gamma = 0.1$)
500	5	55	69	59	54
1,000	12	42	61	53	49
1,500	16	27	46	40	37
2,000	19	17	36	31	28
2,500	21	8	27	23	22

one typical choice for prior distribution in Bayesian statistics is the Beta distribution with expected value μ. In the following example we consider a large LTS consisting of $N = 3,000$ transitions. We compare the Bayesian and the binomial stopping rules when the confidence level of the stopping procedure denoted by $1 - \alpha$, equals 0.95. Note that for the binomial rule it is also necessary to fix the level $1 - \gamma$ at which the confidence intervals for the error probability θ are calculated. We have chosen 0.01, 0.05 and 0.1 as typical values of γ. For some given values of the number of distinct tested transitions n and the number of tested error marked transitions s, the minimal number of remaining error marked transitions k needed to meet the stopping condition is shown in Table 1.

Note that γ does not play a fundamental role in the choice between the binomial and the Bayesian rule since the Bayesian rule performs better in general (especially in later stages of testing). This and the fact that only the Bayesian stopping rule is suitable in case we do not observe any errors during testing ($s = 0$), lead us to choose the Bayesian instead of the binomial rule for our calculations in the next section.

6 Application

In this section, we illustrate our approach with a real example using the model of the generic medical workflow of a hospital presented in Sect. 2. Although the net used in this example is small, it is enough to illustrate the whole procedure (random exhaustive testing, exhaustive testing using the reduction rules and the application of the statistical stopping rule) and to show how the approach will work in large cases.

The experiments carried out consist of the following. We have uniformly distributed five errors over the net, i.e., we have given a special label to five transitions in the net and all the transitions have the same probability of having this label. Note that this is a fairly high number of errors considering the total number of transitions of the net (22). We want to compare exhaustive random testing with our reduction procedure and to study the behaviour of the stopping rules. By exhaustive random testing we mean that the net is subjected to series

Table 2. Mean number of runs, standard deviation of runs and mean number of errors left comparing random testing and our reduction procedure for four different stopping rules: Error free (all the errors are discovered), Exhaustive (all the transitions are tested), Stop 0.90 and Stop 0.95 (the probability of having at most one remaining error is 0.90 and 0.95, respectively)

	Number of runs				Errors left	
	Mean		Std. dev.		Mean	
	Reduction	Random	Reduction	Random	Reduction	Random
Error free	13.25	35.40	1.75	20.25	–	–
Exhaustive	15.60	52.75	1.24	22.02	–	–
Stop (0.90)	12.75	32.25	1.33	12.00	0.60	0.45
Stop (0.95)	14.15	37.95	1.42	14.03	0.35	0.25

of runs from the initial state to either an error marked transition (failure run) or to the final state (successful run). On the other hand, exhaustive testing using our procedure consists of performing series of runs on the net according to Definition 3 and applying Algorithm 1 (although it is a WTS it is not acyclic) after each successful run. In both cases the choices at the branch points are made at random and we stop testing when we have tested all the transitions at least once. We have performed 20 paired experiments using exhaustive random testing and our reduction rules. Paired means here that the distribution of the errors is fixed beforehand and two experiments, one using random testing and one using our procedure, are performed for the same error configuration. We have recorded the number of runs needed to discover all the errors and the number of runs needed to reach exhaustiveness. We have also calculated when our stopping rule advises us to stop testing, in case that the probability of having at most one remaining error is 0.90 and 0.95. Finally we have also computed the number of errors left due to an early stop. The results using random exhaustive testing and our exhaustive test procedure are shown in Table 2. Note that the runs to error free are only possible in the experiment but not in reality since the number of errors in the system is unknown. We can extract two main conclusions from Table 2:

- The reduction algorithm is efficient: the algorithm is reducing exhaustive search in approximately 30%.
- The stopping rules are efficient: the stopping rules stop testing almost at the same level of error freeness. However, they have a small error, namely the remaining number of errors (on average 0.35 and 0.25 for the 0.95 rule and 0.60 and 0.45 for the 0.90 rule). Moreover, the stopping rules are reducing exhaustive search in about 40%. Note that the decrease in test effort due to the 0.90 stopping rule has the disadvantage of the increase of the average number of errors left.

The efficiency of the reduction algorithm and the stopping rules can be statistically supported via hypothesis testing. Let us consider the following random variables:

- X_1 ="number of runs to reach error freeness using our reduction algorithm"
- X_2 ="number of runs to stop testing using the 0.90 stopping rule and our reduction algorithm"
- X_3 = "number of runs to stop testing using the 0.95 stopping rule and our reduction algorithm"
- X_4 = "number of runs to reach error freeness using random testing"
- X_5 ="number of runs to stop testing using the 0.90 stopping rule and random testing"
- X_6 = "number of runs to stop testing using the 0.95 stopping rule and random testing"
- X_7 = "number of runs to exhaustiveness using random testing"
- X_8 = "number of runs to exhaustiveness using our reduction algorithm"

Since the observations are collected in pairs, to statistically quantify the performance of our stopping rules and our reduction algorithm we perform the following two sample paired tests:

1. H_0 : Expected value of X_2−Expected value of $X_1 = 0$
2. H_0 : Expected value of X_3−Expected value of $X_1 = 0$
3. H_0 : Expected value of X_5−Expected value of $X_4 = 0$
4. H_0 : Expected value of X_6−Expected value of $X_4 = 0$
5. H_0 : Expected value of X_7−Expected value of $X_8 = 0$

Note that to give a statistical proof of the efficiency of the stopping rules we have to test from Tests, 1 to 4 to cover all possible combinations (stopping rules 0.90 and 0.95, random testing and testing using our reduction procedure). In case we do not reject these null hypotheses we can conclude that the expected performance of the stopping procedure is at the level of error freeness with certain statistical confidence. On the other hand, to measure the efficiency of our algorithm we have to compare the runs to exhaustive testing using random testing and our reduction technique, i.e., we perform Test 5. In case we reject this null hypothesis we can quantify with certain statistical confidence the average improvement of the algorithm (in terms of testing effort) with respect to random testing. We have carried out such tests using all the collected data and the results, given in 95% confidence intervals, yield to not reject the null hypotheses for all the first four tests and rejection of the null hypothesis for Test 5. These results confirm with high reliability (95% confidence) our intuition from what we had observed in Table 2: the efficiency of the stopping rules, since on average they require the same test effort needed to find all the errors, and the efficiency of the reduction algorithm, since on average less test effort than with random testing is required to reach exhaustiveness.

7 Conclusion and Future Work

We have presented a test procedure for software systems consisting of a set of components running as one sequential process. Such software systems are modelled as labelled transition systems. We have defined an exhaustive procedure that uses the knowledge of the structure of the system and the results of prior testing. However, since exhaustive testing is not always feasible in practice, we have presented a statistical stopping criterion consisting of accepting with certain confidence a maximum number of remaining errors in the system. We have shown the efficiency of both the testing and the stopping procedures in comparison with random testing.

There are many natural extensions to this work. We are mainly interested in studying similar procedures for concurrent systems instead of sequential ones. We will consider errors located in the direction of the arcs or in the states, or that they are input dependent, meaning that for one input the transition can show an error but for another input the transition functions correctly. We can also introduce different kind of errors or correlations between them. Restarting the run not from the initial state but from the error marked transition is also a possible extension. These extensions must be also statistically modelled in order to define new statistical release procedures.

Acknowledgments. We gratefully acknowledge the insightful remarks and suggestions of the reviewers, which led to a substantial improvement of this paper.

References

1. Andrews, A., Offutt, J., Alexander, R.: Testing web applications by modeling with FSMs. Softw. Syst. Model 4(3), 326–345 (2005)
2. Belli, F., Budnik, C., White, L.: Event-based modelling, analysis and testing of user interactions: approach and case study. Software Testing, Verification and Reliability 16(1), 3–32 (2006)
3. Bernot, G., Gaudel, M.C., Marre, B.: Software testing based on formal specifications: a theory and a tool. Softw. Eng. J. 6(6), 387–405 (1991)
4. Brinksma, E.: A theory for the derivation of tests. In: van Eijk, P.H.J., Vissers, C.A., Diaz, M. (eds.) The Formal Description Technique LOTOS: Results of the ESPRIT/SEDOS Project, pp. 235–247. Elsevier Science Publishers, North-Holland (1989)
5. Brinksma, E., Tretmans, J.: Testing transition systems: an annotated bibliography. In: Cassez, F., Jard, C., Rozoy, B., Dermot, M., et al. (eds.) MOVEP 2000. LNCS, vol. 2067, pp. 187–195. Springer, Heidelberg (2001)
6. Chen, T., von Mayrhauser, A., Hajjar, A., Anderson, C., Sahinoglu, M.: How much testing is enough? Applying stopping rules to behavioral model testing. In: HASE 1999: The 4th IEEE International Symposium on High-Assurance Systems Engineering, Washington, DC, USA, pp. 249–256. IEEE Computer Society, Los Alamitos (1999)
7. Chow, T.: Testing software designs modeled by finite-state machines. IEEE Trans. Softw. Eng. 4(3), 178–187 (1978)
8. De Nicola, R., Hennessy, M.: Testing equivalence for processes. In: Díaz, J. (ed.) ICALP 1983. LNCS, vol. 154, pp. 548–560. Springer, Heidelberg (1983)
9. Denise, A., Gaudel, M.C., Gouraud, S.D.: A generic method for statistical testing. In: ISSRE 2004: Proceedings of the 15th International Symposium on Software Reliability Engineering, Washington, DC, USA, pp. 25–34. IEEE Computer Society, Los Alamitos (2004)

10. Di Bucchianico, A., Groote, J.F., van. Hee, K., Kruidhof, R.: Statistical certification of software systems. Comm. Stat. C 37(2), 346–359 (2008)
11. El-Far, I.K., Whittaker, J.A.: Model-based Software Testing. In: Marciniak, J.J. (ed.) Encyclopedia of Software Engineering. Wiley, Chichester (2001)
12. van Hee, K., Oanea, O., Post, R., Somers, L., van de Werf, J.M.: Yasper: a tool for workflow modeling and analysis. In: ACSD 2006: Proceedings of the 6th International Conference on Application of Concurrency to System Design, Washington, DC, USA, pp. 279–282. IEEE Computer Society, Los Alamitos (2006)
13. Howden, W.: Methodology for the generation of program test data. IEEE Trans. Softw. Eng. 24, 208–215 (1975)
14. Huang, J.: An approach to program testing. ACM Comp. Surveys 7(3), 113–128 (1975)
15. Lee, C., Nam, K., Park, D.H.: Optimal software release policy based on Markovian perfect debugging model. Comm. Statist. Theory Methods 30(11), 2329–2342 (2001)
16. Lee, D., Yannakakis, M.: Principles and methods of testing finite state machines-A survey. Proceedings of the IEEE 84, 1090–1126 (1996)
17. Milner, R.: A Calculus of Communicating Systems. LNCS, vol. 92. Springer, Heidelberg (1980)
18. Morali, N., Soyer, R.: Optimal stopping rules for software testing. Naval Research Logistics 50, 88–104 (2003)
19. Plotkin, G.D.: An operational semantics for CSP. In: Bjørner, D. (ed.) Formal Description of Programming Concepts II, pp. 199–223. North-Holland, Amsterdam (1983)
20. Reisig, W.: Petri Nets: An Introduction. Springer, New York (1985)
21. Thevenod-Fosse, P., Waeselynck, H., Crouzet, Y.: Software statistical testing. In: Randell, B., Laprie, J.C., Kopetz, H., Littlewood, B. (eds.) Predictably Dependable Computing Systems, pp. 253–272. Springer, Heidelberg (1995)
22. Tretmans, J.: A Formal Approach to Conformance Testing. PhD thesis, University of Twente, Enschede, The Netherlands (1992)
23. Zhu, H., Hall, P.A.V., May, J.H.R.: Software unit test coverage and adequacy. ACM Comput. Surv. 29(4), 366–427 (1997)

Assessing State Spaces Using Petri-Net Synthesis and Attribute-Based Visualization

H.M.W. (Eric) Verbeek, A. Johannes Pretorius, Wil M.P. van der Aalst, and Jarke J. van Wijk

Technische Universiteit Eindhoven
PO Box 513, 5600 MB Eindhoven, The Netherlands
{h.m.w.verbeek, a.j.pretorius, w.m.p.v.d.aalst, j.j.v.wijk}@tue.nl

Abstract. State spaces are commonly used representations of system behavior. A state space may be derived from a model of system behavior but can also be obtained through process mining. For a good understanding of the system's behavior, an analyst may need to assess the state space. Unfortunately, state spaces of realistic applications tend to be very large. This makes this assessment hard. In this paper, we tackle this problem by combining Petri-net synthesis (i.e., regions theory) and visualization. Using Petri-net synthesis we generate the attributes needed for attribute-based visualization. Using visualization we can assess the state space. We demonstrate that such an approach is possible and describe our implementation using existing tools. The only limiting factor of our approach is the performance of current synthesis techniques.

Keywords: state spaces, visualization, attributes, Petri-net synthesis.

1 Introduction

State spaces are popular for the representation and verification of complex systems [7]. System behavior is modeled as a number of *states* that evolve over time by following *transitions*. Transitions are "source-action-target" triplets where the execution of an *action* triggers a change of state. By analyzing state spaces more insights can be gained into the systems they describe.

In many cases, state spaces can be directly linked to a model that has some form of formal/executable semantics (e.g. Petri nets, process algebras, state charts, EPCs [20], UML-ADs [17], MSCs [18], BPEL [6], YAWL [2], etc.). If such a model does not allow for a more direct analysis, the state space allows for a "brute force" analysis by considering all states and transitions. However, many state spaces cannot be linked to some formal model, either because the formal model is not available for some reason, or because the formal model does not exist at all. As examples of the latter, the state space may be based on the analysis of program code, the merging of different low-level models, or as the result of process mining [1,4]. Although the approach presented in this paper is generic, we will devote special attention to state spaces obtained through process mining, as we think that especially in the process mining area our approach looks promising.

K. Jensen, W. van der Aalst, and J. Billington (Eds.): ToPNoC I, LNCS 5100, pp. 152–171, 2008.

Process mining techniques are applicable to a wide range of systems. These systems may be pure information systems (e.g. ERP systems) or systems where the hardware plays a more prominent role (e.g. embedded systems). The only requirement is that the system produces *event logs*, thus recording (parts of) the actual behavior. An example is the "CUSTOMerCARE Remote Services Network" of Philips Medical Systems (PMS). This is a worldwide internet-based private network that links PMS equipment to remote service centers. Any event that occurs within an X-ray machine (e.g. moving the table, setting the deflector, etc.) is recorded and analyzed. Another example is the Common Event Infrastructure (CEI) of IBM. CEI offers a unified way of storing events in the context of middleware and web services. Using CEI it is possible to record all kinds of business events. Process mining techniques are then used to discover models by analyzing these event logs. An example is the α-algorithm, which constructs a Petri net model describing the behavior observed in the event log [5]. However, most techniques that directly discover models from event logs have a "model bias" and tend to either overgeneralize or produce incorrect results (e.g. a model with deadlocks). Therefore, several approaches do not try to construct the model directly, but construct a state space first. Classical approaches stop when the state space is constructed [9] while more recent approaches use multiple steps to obtain a higher level model [3,24].

State spaces tend to be very large. The state explosion problem is well-known, especially in the presence of concurrency. Therefore, many researchers try to reduce the state space or handle it more efficiently. Nevertheless, the most popular analysis approach is still to specify and check requirements by inspecting the state space, e.g. model checking approaches [12]. For this approach to be successful, the premise is that all requirements are known. When this is not the case, the system cannot be verified.

In such cases, one approach is to directly inspect the state space with the aim of gaining insight into the behavior it describes. *Interactive visualization* provides the user with a visual representation of the state space and with controls to change this view, i.e., through interaction the user can take different perspectives on the state space. We argue that interactive visualization offers three advantages:

1. By giving visual form to an abstract notion, communication among analysts and with other stakeholders is enhanced.
2. Users often do not have precise questions about the systems they study, they simply want to "get a feeling" for their behavior. Visualization allows them to start formulating hypotheses about system behavior.
3. Interactivity provides the user with a mechanism for analyzing particular features and for answering questions about state spaces and the behavior they describe.

Attribute-based visualization enables users to analyze state spaces in terms of attributes associated with every state [23]. Users typically understand the meaning of this data and can use this as a starting point for gaining further insights. For example, by clustering on certain data, the user can obtain a summary view on the state space, where details on the non-clustered data have been left out. Based on such a view, the user can come to understand how the system behaves with respect to the clustered data.

Attribute-based visualization is only possible if states have meaningful attributes. When the model is obtained through process mining this is not the case. Event logs typically only refer to events and not to states. Therefore, state spaces based on event logs do not provide intuitive descriptions of states other than the actions they relate to. Hence, the challenge is to generate meaningful attributes. In this paper we investigate the possibility of automatically deriving attribute information for visualization purposes. To do so, we use existing synthesis techniques to generate a Petri net from a given state space [10,13,14,21,22]. The places of this Petri net are considered as new derived state attributes.

The remainder of the paper is structured as follows. Section 2 provides a concise overview of Petri nets, the *Petrify* tool, the *DiaGraphica* tool, and the *ProM* tool. The *Petrify* tool implements the techniques to derive a Petri net from a state space, *DiaGraphica* is an attribute-based visualization tool, while the *ProM* tool implements process mining techniques and provides the necessary interoperability between the tools. Section 3 discusses the approach using both *Petrify* and *DiaGraphica*. Section 4 shows, using a small example, how the approach works, whereas Sect. 5 discusses the challenges we faced while using the approach. Finally, Sect. 6 concludes the paper.

2 Preliminaries

2.1 Petri Nets

A classical Petri net can be represented as a triplet (P, T, F) where P is the set of places, T is the set of Petri net transitions[1], and $F \subseteq (P \times T) \cup (T \times P)$ the set of arcs. For the state of a Petri net only the set of places P is relevant, because the network structure of a Petri net does not change and only the distribution of tokens over places changes. A state, also referred to as a *marking*, corresponds to a mapping from places to natural numbers. Any state s can be presented as $s \in P \rightarrow \{0, 1, 2, \ldots\}$, i.e., a state can be considered as a multiset, function, or vector. The combination of a Petri net (P, T, F) and an initial state s is called a marked Petri net (P, T, F, s). In the context of state spaces, we use places as attributes. In any state the value of each place attribute is known: $s(p)$ is the value of attribute $p \in P$ in state s.

A Petri net also comes with an unambiguous visualization. Places are represented by circles or ovals, transitions by squares or rectangles, and arcs by lines. Using existing layout algorithms, it is straightforward to generate a diagram for this, for example, using *dot* [15].

[1] The transitions in a Petri net should not be confused with transitions in a state space, i.e., one Petri net transition may correspond to many transitions in the corresponding state space. For example, many transitions in Fig. 2 refer to the Petri net transition $t1$ in Fig. 3.

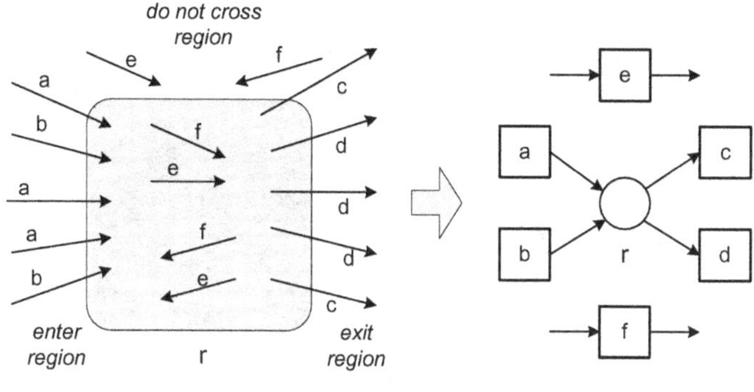

(a) State space with region r. (b) Petri net with place r.

Fig. 1. Translation of regions to places

2.2 Petrify

The *Petrify* [11] tool is based on the classical *Theory of Regions* [10,14,22]. Using regions it is possible to synthesize a finite transition system (i.e., a state space) into a Petri net.

A (labeled) transition system is a tuple $TS = (S, E, T, s_i)$ where S is the set of states, E is the set of events, $T \subseteq S \times E \times S$ is the transition relation, and $s_i \in S$ is the initial state. Given a transition system $TS = (S, E, T, s_i)$, a subset of states $S' \subseteq S$ is a *region* if for all events $e \in E$ one of the following properties holds:

- All transitions with event e *enter the region*, i.e., for all $s_1, s_2 \in S$ and $(s_1, e, s_2) \in T$: $s_1 \notin S'$ and $s_2 \in S'$; or
- All transitions with event e *exit the region*, i.e., for all $s_1, s_2 \in S$ and $(s_1, e, s_2) \in T$: $s_1 \in S'$ and $s_2 \notin S'$; or
- All transitions with event e *do not "cross" the region*, i.e., for all $s_1, s_2 \in S$ and $(s_1, e, s_2) \in T$: $s_1, s_2 \in S'$ or $s_1, s_2 \notin S'$.

The basic idea of using regions is that each region S' corresponds to a place in the corresponding Petri net and that each event corresponds to a transition in the corresponding Petri net. Given a region all the events that *enter* the region are the transitions producing tokens for this place and all the events that *exit* the region are the transitions consuming tokens from this place. Figure 1 illustrates how regions translate to places. A region r referring to a set of states in the state space is mapped onto a place: a and b enter the region, c and d exit the region, and e and f do not cross the region.

In the original theory of regions many simplifying assumptions are made, e.g. elementary transitions systems are assumed [14] and in the resulting Petri net there is one transition for each event. Many transition systems do not satisfy such assumptions. Hence many refinements have been developed and implemented in tools like *Petrify* [10,11]. As a result it is possible to synthesize a Petri net for

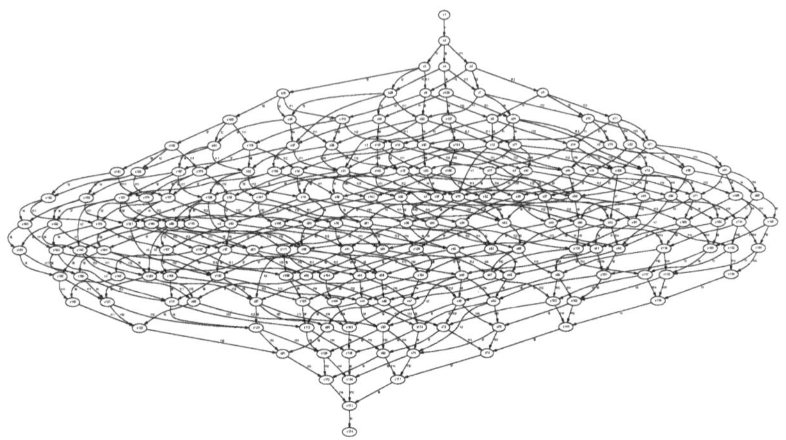

Fig. 2. State space visualization with off-the-shelf graph-drawing tools

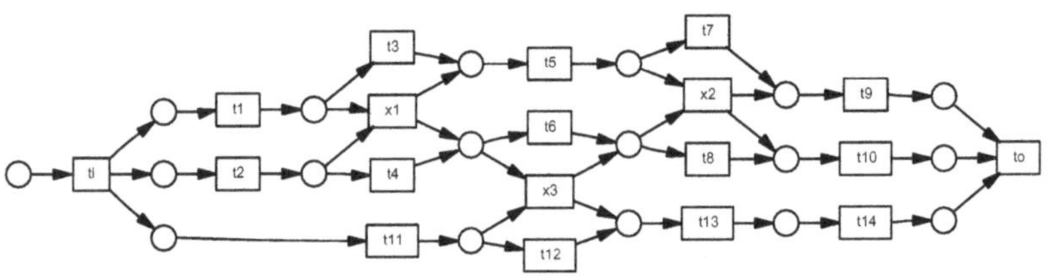

Fig. 3. Petri net synthesized from the state space in Fig. 2

any transition system. Moreover, tools such as *Petrify* provide different settings to balance compactness and readability and one can specify desirable properties of the target model. For example, one can specify that the Petri net should be free-choice. For more information we refer the reader to [10,11].

With a state space as input *Petrify* derives a Petri net for which the reachability graph is bisimilar [16] to the original state space. We already mentioned that the Petri net shown in Fig. 3 can be synthesized from the state space depicted in Fig. 2. This Petri net is indeed bisimilar to the state space. For the sake of completeness we mention that we used *Petrify* version 4.2 (`www.lsi.upc.es/petrify/`) with the following options: `-d2` (debug level 2), `-p` (generate a pure Petri net), `-dead` (do not check for the existence of deadlock states), and `-ip` (show implicit places).

2.3 DiaGraphica

DiaGraphica is a prototype for the interactive visual analysis of state spaces with attributes and can be downloaded from `www.win.tue.nl/~apretori/diagraphica/`. It builds on a previous work [23] and addresses the gap between the semantics that users associate with attributes that describe states and their

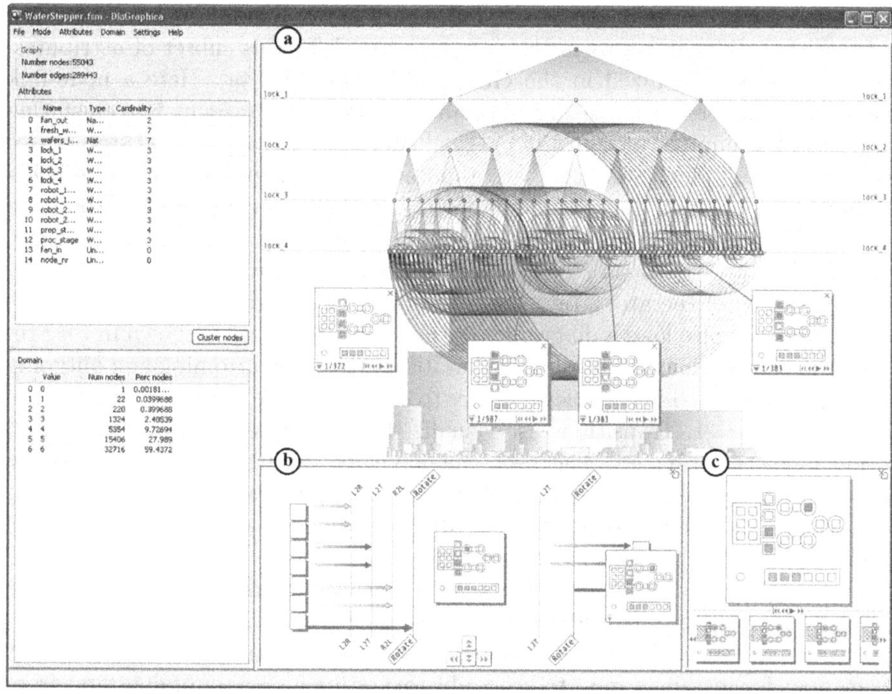

Fig. 4. DiaGraphica incorporates a number of correlated visualizations that use parameterized diagrams

visual representation. To do so, the user can define custom diagrams that reflect associated semantics. These diagrams are incorporated into a number of correlated visualizations.

Diagrams are composed of a number of shapes such as ellipses, rectangles and lines. Every shape has a number of Degrees Of Freedom (DOFs) such as position and color. It is possible to link a DOF with a state attribute, which translates to the following in the context of this paper. Suppose we have a state space that has been annotated with attributes that correspond to the markings of the places in its associated Petri net. It is possible to represent this Petri net with a diagram composed out of a number of circles, squares and lines corresponding to its places, transitions and arcs. Now, we can parameterize a circle (place) in this diagram by linking, for example, its color with the attribute representing the marking of the corresponding places. As a result, the color of the circle will reflect the actual marking of the corresponding place. For example, the circle could be white if the place contains no tokens, green if it contains one token, and red if it contains more than one tokens.

DiaGraphica has a file format for representing parameterized diagrams. This facility makes it possible to import Petri nets generated with *Petrify* as diagrams.

Parameterized diagrams are used in a number of correlated visualizations. As starting point the user can perform attribute based clustering. First, the user selects a subset of attributes. Next, the program partitions all states into clusters that differ in terms of the values assumed for this subset of attributes. The results are visualized in the cluster view (see Fig. 4a). Here a node-link diagram, a bar tree and an arc diagram are used to represent the clustering hierarchy, the number of states in every cluster, and the aggregated state space [23]. By clicking on clusters they are annotated with diagrams where the DOFs of shapes are calculated as outlined above. A cluster can contain more than one state and it is possible to step through the associated diagrams. Transitions are visualized as arcs between clusters. The direction of transitions is encoded by the orientation of the arcs which are interpreted clockwise.

The user can also load a diagram into the simulation view as shown in Fig. 4b. This visualization shows the "current" state as well as all incoming and outgoing states as diagrams. This enables the user to explore a local neighborhood around an area of interest. Transitions are visualized by arrows and an overview of all action labels is provided. The user can navigate through the state space by selecting any incoming or outgoing diagram, by using the keyboard or by clicking on navigation icons. Consequently, this diagram slides toward the center and all incoming and outgoing diagrams are updated.

The inspection view enables the user to inspect interesting diagrams more closely and to temporarily store them (see Fig. 4c). First, it serves as a magnifying glass. Second, the user can use this view as a temporary storage facility. Users may, for instance, want to keep a history, store a number of diagrams from various locations in the state space to compare, or keep diagrams as seeds for further discussions with colleagues. These are visualized as a list of diagrams through which the user can scroll.

Diagrams can be seamlessly moved between different views by clicking on an icon on the diagram. To maintain context, the current selection in the simulation or inspection view is highlighted in the clustering hierarchy.

2.4 ProM

ProM is an open-source plug-able framework that provides a wide range of process mining techniques [1,25]. Given event logs of different systems, *ProM* is able to construct different types of models (ranging from plain state spaces to colored Petri nets). Moreover, *ProM* can be used to convert models from one notation into another, e.g. translate an Event-driven Process Chain (EPC) [20] into a Petri net or a state space. *ProM* offers connections to *Petrify* and *DiaGraphica* in various ways. For example, a state space mined by *ProM* can be automatically converted into a Petri net by *Petrify* and then loaded into *ProM* and *DiaGraphica*.

3 Using Petrify to Obtain Attributed States Described by Attributes

The behavior of systems can be captured in many ways. For instance, as an *event log*, as a formal *model* or as a *state space*. Typically, system behavior is

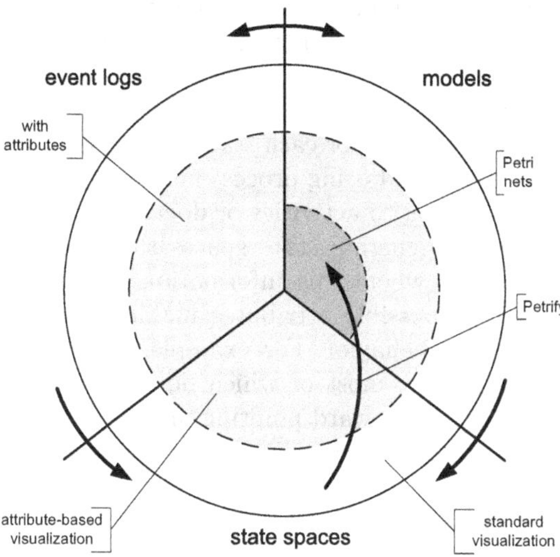

Fig. 5. The approach proposed in this paper

not directly described as a state space. However, as already mentioned in the introduction, it is possible to generate state spaces from process models (i.e., model-based state space generation) or directly from code or other artifacts. Moreover, using process mining techniques [4,5] event logs can be used to construct state spaces. This is illustrated in Fig. 5.

Both ways of obtaining state spaces are shown by the two arrows in the lower left and right of the figure. The arrow in the lower right shows that using model-based state space generation the behavior of a (finite) model can be captured as a state space. The arrow in the lower left shows that using process mining the behavior extracted from an event log can be represented as a state space [3]. Note that an event log provides execution sequences of a (possibly unknown) model. The event log does not show explicit states. However, there are various ways to construct a state representation for each state visited in the execution sequence, e.g. the prefix or postfix of the execution sequence under consideration. Similarly transitions can be distilled from the event log, resulting in a full state space.

Figure 5 also shows that there is a relation between event logs and models, i.e., a model can be used to generate event logs with example behavior and based on an event log there may be process mining techniques to directly extract models, e.g. using the α-algorithm [5] a representative Petri net can be discovered based on an event log with example behavior. Since the focus is on state space visualization, we do not consider the double-headed arrow at the top and focus on the lower half of the diagram.

We make a distinction between event logs, models and state spaces that have *descriptive attributes* and those that do not (inner and outer sectors of Fig. 5). For example, it is possible to model behavior simply in terms of transitions without providing any further information that describes the different states that a system can be in. Figure 2 shows a state space where nodes and arcs have labels but without any attributes associated to states. In some cases it is possible to attach attributes to states. For example, in a state space generated from a Petri net, the token count for each state can be seen as a state attribute. When a state space is generated using process mining techniques, the state may have state attributes referring to activities or documents recorded earlier.

It is far from trivial to generate state spaces that contain state attributes from event logs or models where this information is absent. Moreover, there may be an abundance of possible attributes making it difficult to select the attributes relevant for the behavior. For example, a variety of data elements may be associated to a state, most of which do not influence the occurrence of events. Fortunately, as the upward pointing arrow in Fig. 5 shows, tools like *Petrify* can *transform a state space without attributes into a state space with attributes.*

Consider the state space in Fig. 2. Since it does not have any state attributes, we cannot employ attribute-based visualization techniques. When we perform synthesis, we derive a Petri net that is guaranteed to be bisimilar to this state space. That is, the behavior described by the Petri net is equivalent to that described by the state space [11]. Figure 3 shows a Petri net derived using *Petrify*.

Note that the approach, as illustrated in Fig. 5, does not require starting with a state space. It is possible to use a model or event log as a starting point. Using process mining an event log can be converted into a state space [3,24]. Any process model (e.g. Petri net) can also be handled as input, provided that its state space can be constructed within reasonable time. For a bounded Petri net, this state space is its reachability graph, which will be finite. The approach can also be extended for unbounded nets by using the coverability graph. In this case, $s \in P \rightarrow \{0, 1, 2, \ldots\} \cup \{\omega\}$ where $s(p) = \omega$ denotes that the number of tokens in p is unbounded. This can also be visualized in the Petri net representation. We also argue that our technique is applicable to other graphical modeling languages with some form of semantics, e.g. the various UML diagrams describing behavior. In the context of this paper, we use state spaces as starting point because of the many ways to obtain them (i.e., process mining, code analysis, model-based generation, etc.).

4 Proof of Concept

To demonstrate the feasibility of our approach, we now present a small case study, using the implementation of the approach as outlined above. Figure 6 illustrates the route we have taken in terms of the strategy introduced in Sect. 3.

4.1 Setting

The case study concerns a traffic light controller for the road intersection shown in Fig. 7, which corresponds to an existing road intersection in Eindhoven, The

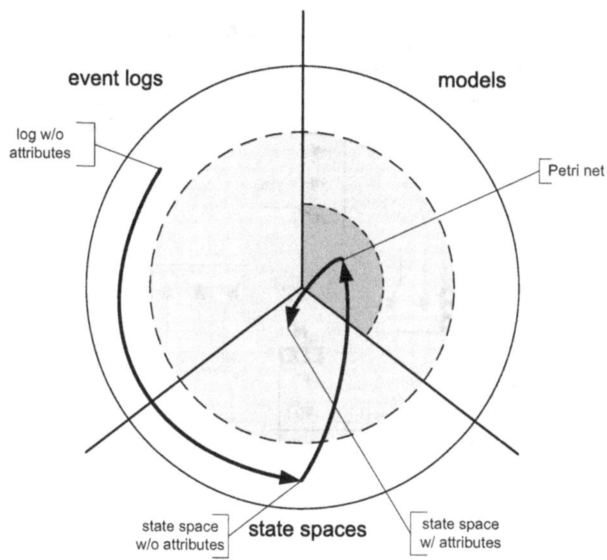

Fig. 6. The approach taken with the case study

Netherlands. As Fig. 7 shows, there are 12 different traffic lights on the intersection, labeled A through L. Traffic light A controls the two southbound lanes that take a right turn, whereas B controls the lane for the other directions; traffic light C controls all three westbound lanes; and so forth.

The case study starts with a log for the traffic light controller. This log is free of any noise and contains over 1,300,000 events without data attributes. Possible event labels in the log are start, end, Arg, Bgy, and Cyr, which have to following meaning:

start indicates that the controller has been started,
end indicates that the controller is about to stop,
Arg indicates that traffic light **A** has moved from **r**ed to **g**reen,
Bgy indicates that traffic light **B** has moved from **g**reen to **y**ellow (amber), and
Cyr indicates that traffic light **C** has moved from **y**ellow to **r**ed.

Figure 8 shows a small fragment of the log. It shows, that at some point in time, traffic light H moved from green to yellow, after which B moved first from green to yellow and then from yellow to red, and so forth.

A relevant question is whether the traffic light controller, according to the log, has behaved in a safe way. From Fig. 7 it is clear, that traffic lights A, B, and C should not all signal *go* (that is, show either green or yellow) at any given moment in time. Traffic lights A and B could signal *go* at the same time, but both are in conflict with C. Thus, if either A or B signal *go*, then C has to signal *stop* (that is, show red). The goal of our case study is to show how we can use our approach to answer the question whether the controller indeed has behaved in a safe way.

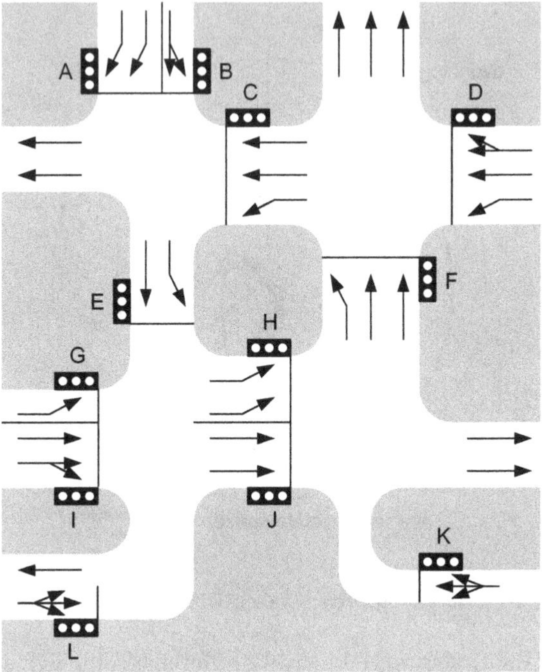

Fig. 7. A road intersection with traffic lights in Eindhoven

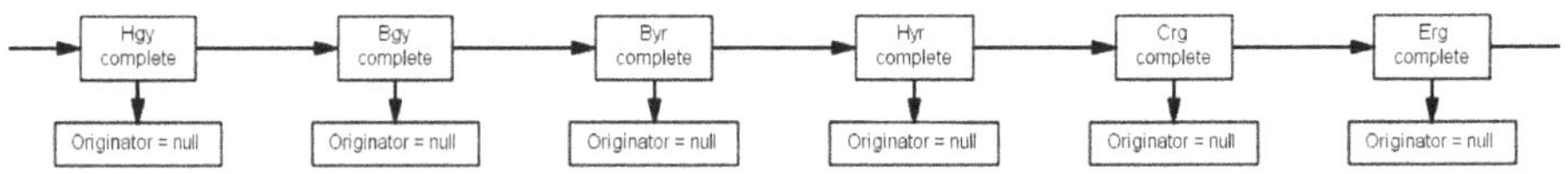

Fig. 8. A small fragment of the log visualized

4.2 Findings

Using process mining techniques, we constructed a state space from the event log. Figure 9 shows a visualization of a fragment of the entire state space, which contains 40,825 states and 221,618 edges. Note that this visualization does not help us to verify that the controller behaved in a safe way. Also note that, as we took a log as starting point, we cannot show that the controller will behave in a safe way in the future.

From the above state space, we constructed a Petri net using *Petrify*. This Petri net contains 26 transitions and 28 places and is shown in Fig. 10. As mentioned in Sect. 1, the place labels in the Petri net have no intuitive description. Therefore, these labels can only be used to identify places. The transitions labels, however, correspond one-to-one to the event labels that were found in the original log.

Fig. 9. A visualization of a fragment of the entire state space for the traffic light controller

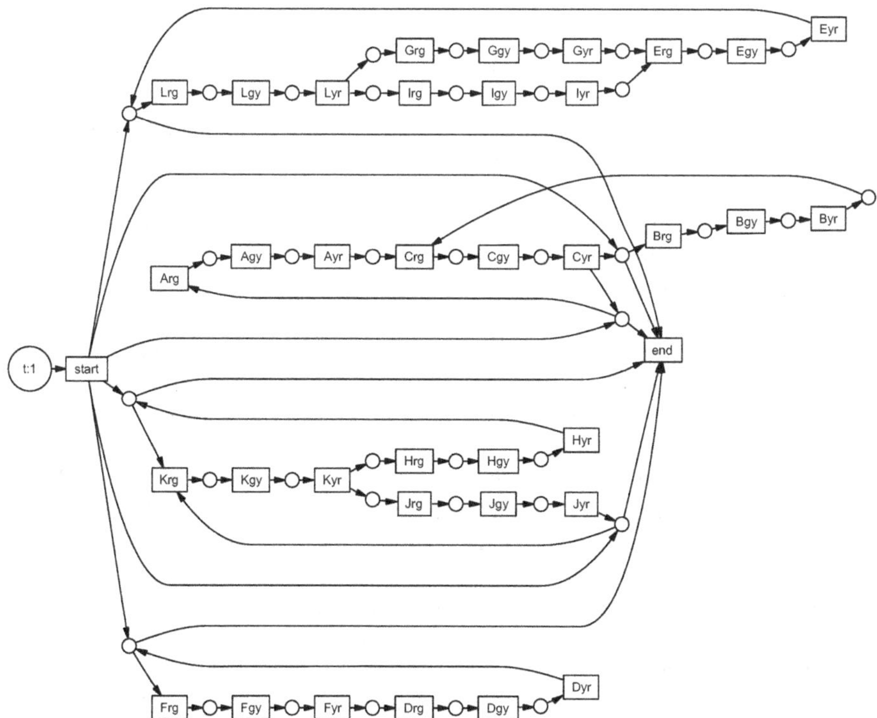

Fig. 10. The synthesized Petri net for the traffic light controller

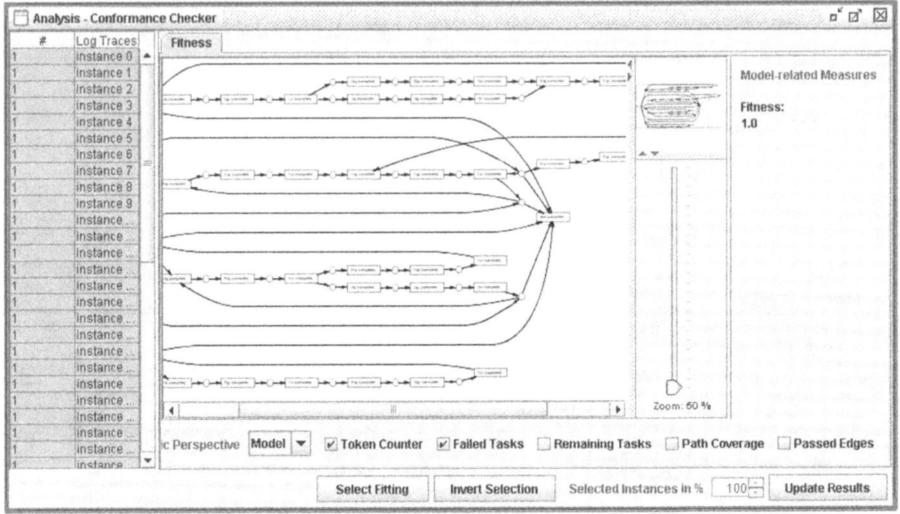

Fig. 11. The synthesized Petri net *fits* the log

Next, we tested whether the constructed Petri net can actually replay all instances present in the log. If some instance cannot be replayed by the Petri net, then some actual behavior is not covered by the Petri net, and we cannot make any claim that certain situations did not occur by looking at the Petri net only. Figure 11 shows that the Petri net can actually replay all behavior which is present in the log: Their fitness measure equals 1.0. Possibly, the Petri net can generate behavior which is not in the log, but at least the Petri net covers the behavior present in the log. As a result, we can use the Petri net to show that certain situations did not occur in the traffic light controller: If the situation is not possible according to the Petri net, it was not possible according to the log.

After having recreated the state space from the Petri net, which is guaranteed to be bisimilar to the original state space (that is, the state space we derived from the log), we can now use *DiaGraphica* to answer the question whether the controller behaved in a safe way. From the Petri net, we learn that the places p22, and p14 signal *go* for the traffic light A, p10 and p21 signal *go* for B, and p23 and p16 for C. Figure 12 shows the state space after we have abstracted from all places except the ones just mentioned. Note that the 40,825 states have been clustered in such a way that only 11 clusters remain. As a result, we can actually see some structure in this state space. For example, the rightmost cluster in Fig. 12 shows clearly that the other places are empty if place p23 contains a token. Thus, if traffic light C shows green, then A and B show red. Likewise, we can now show that the controller behaved in a safe way for the other conflicts as well. Figure 12 also shows the representation of the controller state using the Petri net layout in the right bottom corner, and possible predecessor and successor states. Using this, it is possible to navigate over individual states in the state space.

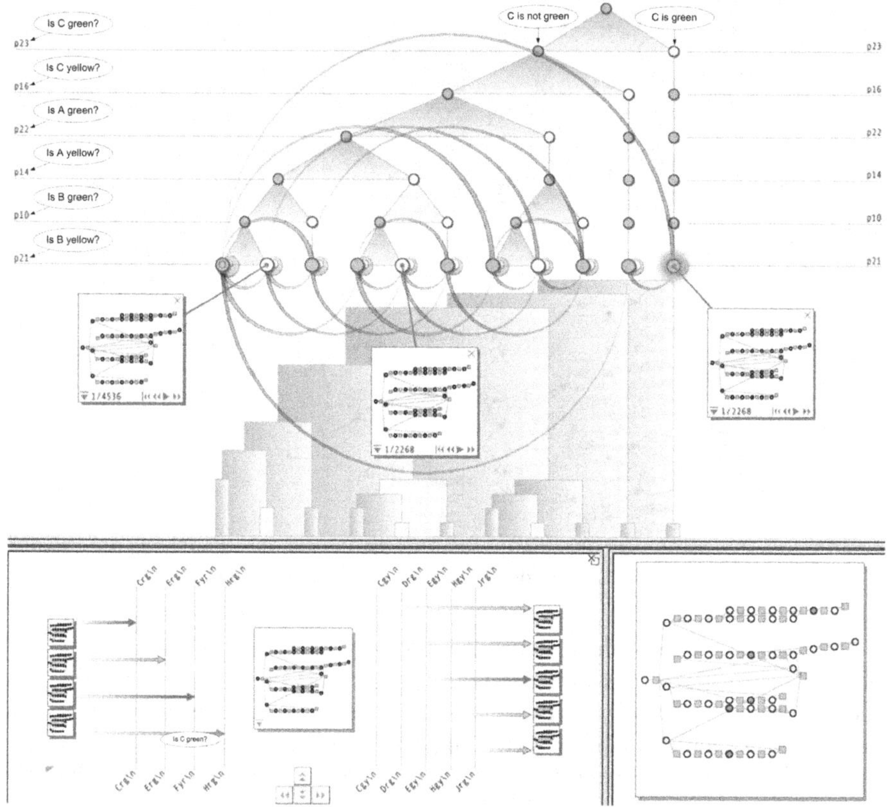

Fig. 12. Analyzing safeness using *DiaGraphica*

4.3 Conclusion

Using both process mining and Petri net synthesis techniques, we were able to convert a log that contains no data attributes into a state space that does contain data attributes: the synthesized places. Based on these attributes, we were able to verify that, according to the log, the controller has behaved in a safe way. Thus, in an automated way, we have been able to derive sensible attributes from this log, and using these attributes we are able to deduce a meaningful result.

5 Challenges

In the previous section, we showed how attribute-based visualization assisted us in providing new insights even if the corresponding state space is large. Given the many ways of obtaining state spaces (e.g. through process mining), the applicability and relevance of this type of visualization is evident. However, in order to attach attributes to states, our approach requires the automatic construction of a suitable Petri net.

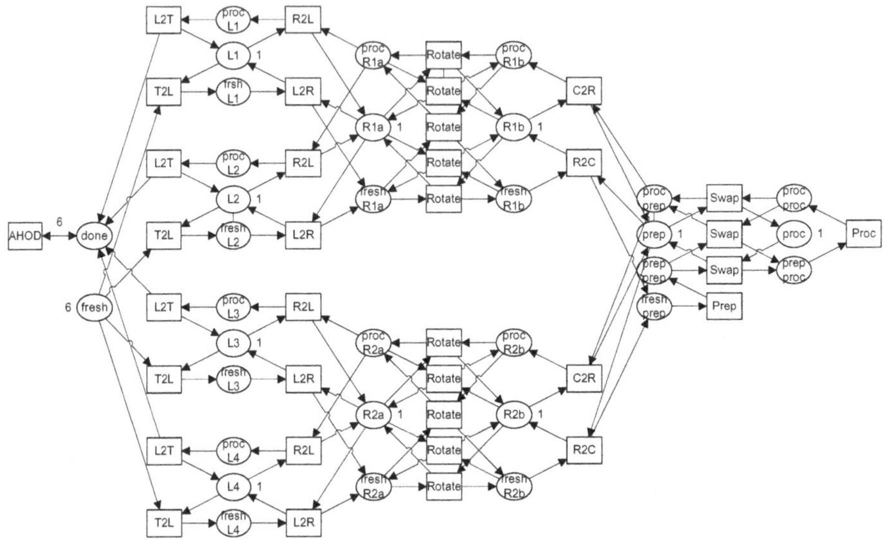

Fig. 13. A Petri net for the wafer stepper machine

Although the approach works well for some examples, we have found that the synthesis of Petri nets from arbitrary state spaces can be a true bottle-neck. The performance of current region-based approaches is poor in two respects: (1) the computational complexity of the algorithms makes wide-scale applicability intractable and (2) the resulting models are sometimes more complex than the original transition systems and therefore offer little insight. One of the key points is that synthesis works well if there is a lot of "true" and "full" concurrency. If a and b can occur in parallel in state s_1, there are transitions $s_1 \xrightarrow{a} s_2$, $s_1 \xrightarrow{b} s_3$, $s_2 \xrightarrow{b} s_4$, and $s_3 \xrightarrow{a} s_4$ forming a so-called "diamond" in the state space. Such diamonds allow for compact Petri nets that provide additional insights. Tools such as *Petrify* have problems dealing with large state spaces having "incomplete" diamonds.

To illustrate the problem we revisit the state space shown in Fig. 4 [19]. This state space contains 55,043 nodes and 289,443 edges and represents the behavior of a wafer stepper. Although the initial state space was not based on a Petri net model we discovered that it can be generated by the Petri net shown in Fig. 13. The wafer stepper machine consists of four locks (L1 – L4), two rotating robots (R1 and R2), a preparing station (Prep, and a processing station (Proc). Fresh wafers start at the left (place fresh), are moved to the right, are prepared, are processed, and are moved back to the left, where they end as processed wafers (place done). The visualization by DiaGraphica shown in Fig. 4 is not based on the Petri net depicted in Fig. 13, i.e., the state space was provided to us and the visualization was based on existing attributes in the state space and the diagram (cf. Fig. 4c) was hand-made based on domain knowledge.

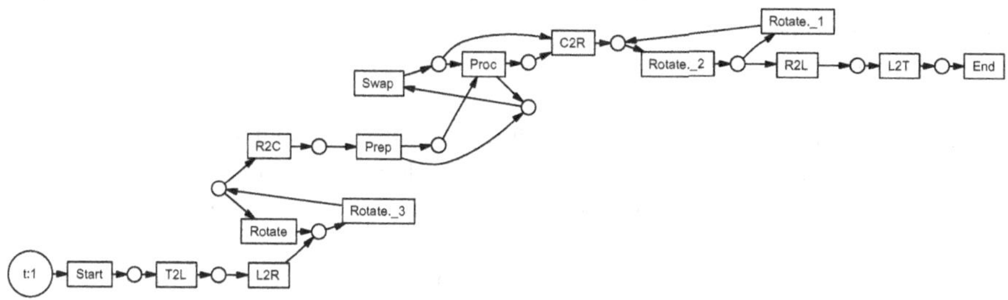

Fig. 14. A Petri net for the wafer stepper machine with only one wafer

Given the fact that DiaGraphica is able to nicely visualize the state space and that there exists a Petri net with a bisimilar state space, we expected to be able to apply the approach presented in this paper. Unfortunately, *Petrify* was unable to derive a Petri net as shown in Fig. 13 from the given state space. As a result, this state space could not be used to illustrate our approach. However, it might be of interest to know *why Petrify* failed. In this section, we try to answer this question. It should be noted that the problem is not specific for *Petrify*; it applies to all region based approaches [8,10,13,14,21,22].

Our first observation is that the places fresh and done are not safe, which might be a problem for *Petrify*. However, both places can be modeled in a straightforward way using six safe places, and hence, there exists a safe Petri net that corresponds to the given state space. Clearly, *Petrify* was unable to find this Petri net.

Second, we reduced the number of wafers in the system from six to one, that is, we generated a state space for the situation where only one wafer needs to be processed by the wafer stepper. In this case, *Petrify was* able to construct a suitable Petri net, which is shown in Fig. 14. This Petri net shows that the single wafer is first moved to a lock (T2L), moved to a robot (L2R), rotated by the robot (Rotate), moved to the preparing station (R2C), prepared (Prep), swapped to the processing station (Swap), processed (Proc), swapped back, moved to the robot, rotated by the robot, moved to the lock, and finally moved back onto the tray. Note that the structure around the transitions Prep, Proc, and Swap takes care of the fact that the wafer needs to be swapped both before and after the processing step. Apparently, *Petrify* preferred this solution above having two Swap transitions (like we have four Rotate transitions).

Having succeeded for one wafer, we next tried the same for two wafers. *Petrify* did construct a Petri net for this situation, but, unfortunately, this Petri net is too complex to be used.

Finally, we again tried the situation with two wafers, but with increased capacity for the robots, the preparing station, and the processing station. As a result, the wafers need not to wait for a resource (such as a robot or a preparing station) as these will always be available. Clearly, the net as shown in Fig. 14

corresponds to this system, where only its initial marking needs to be changed (two wafers instead of one). Unfortunately, *Petrify* was unable to construct such a net. Apparently, *Petrify* cannot generate a Petri net where multiple tokens follow an identical route.

The experiment using variants of the state space shown in Fig. 4 illustrates that classical synthesis approaches have problems when dealing with real-life state spaces. Typically, the application of regions is intractable and/or results in a Petri net of the same size as the original state space.

When applying synthesis approaches to state spaces generated through process mining another problem surfaces; *synthesis approaches assume that the state space is precise and complete.* However, the state space is based on an event log that only shows example behavior. In reality logs are seldom complete in the sense that all possible execution sequences are not necessarily included [5]. Consider for example ten parallel activities. To see all possible interleaving at least $10! = 3{,}628{,}800$ different sequences need to be observed. Even if all sequences have equal probability (which is typically not the case) much more sequences are needed to have some coverage of these 3,628,800 possible sequences. Hence, it is likely that some possibilities will be missing. Therefore, the challenge is not to create a Petri net that exactly reproduces the transition system or log. The challenge is to find a Petri net that captures the "characteristic behavior" described by the transition system.

If the system does not allow for a compact and intuitive representation in terms of a labeled Petri net, it is probably *not useful to try and represent the system state in full detail.* Hence more abstract representations are needed when showing the individual states. The abstraction does not need to be a Petri net. However, even in the context of regions and Petri nets, there are several straightforward *abstraction mechanisms.*

First of all, it is possible to split the sets of states and transitions into interesting and less interesting. For example, in the context of process mining states that are rarely visited and/or transitions that are rarely executed can be left out using abstraction or encapsulation. There may be other reasons for removing particular transitions, e.g. the analyst rates them as less interesting. Using abstraction (transitions are hidden, i.e., renamed to τ and removed while preserving branching bisimilarity) or encapsulation (paths containing particular transitions are blocked), the state space is effectively reduced. The reduced state space will be easier to inspect and allows for a simpler Petri net4 representation.

Another approach is not to simplify the state space but to generate a model that serves as a simplified *over-approximation of the state space.* The complexity of a generated Petri net that *precisely* captures the behavior represented by the state space is due to the non-trivial relations between places and transitions. If places are removed from such a model, the resulting Petri net is still able to reproduce the original state space (but most likely also allows for more and even infinite behavior). In terms of regions this corresponds to only including the most "interesting" regions resulting in an over-approximation of the state space. Future research aims at selecting the right abstractions and over-approximations.

6 Conclusions and Future Work

In this paper we have investigated an approach for state space visualization with Petri nets. Using existing techniques we derive Petri nets from state spaces in an automated fashion. The places of these Petri are considered as newly derived attributes that describe every state. Consequently, we append all states in the original state space with these attributes. This allows us to apply a visualization technique where attribute-based visualizations of state spaces are annotated with Petri net diagrams.

The approach provides the user with two representations that describe the same behavior: state spaces and Petri nets. These are integrated into a number of correlated visualizations. By presenting a case study, we have shown that the combination of state space visualization and Petri net diagrams assists users in visually analyzing system behavior.

We argue that the combination of the above two visual representations is more effective than any one of them in isolation. For example, using state space visualization it is possible to identify all states that have a specific marking for a subset of Petri net places. Using the Petri net representation the user can consider how other places are marked for this configuration. If we suppose that the user has identified an interesting marking of the Petri net, he or she can identify all its predecessor states, again by using a visualization of the state space. Once these are identified, they are easy to study by considering their Petri net markings.

In this paper, we have taken a step toward state space visualization with automatically generated Petri nets. As we have shown in Sect. 4, the ability to combine both representations can lead to interesting discoveries. The approach also illustrates the flexibility of parameterized diagrams to visualize state spaces. In particular, we are quite excited about the prospect of annotating visualizations of state spaces with other types of automatically generated diagrams.

Finally, as indicated in Sect. 5, current synthesis techniques are not always suitable: If no elegant Petri net exists for a given state space, then *Petrify* will not be able to find such a net, and even if such a net exists, *Petrify* might fail to find it. In such a situation, allowing for some additional behavior in the Petri net, that is, by over-approximating the state space, might result in a far more elegant net. For example, the net as shown in Fig. 14 would be an acceptable solution for the wafer stepper state space containing six wafers. Furthermore, one single "sick" trace in a state space might prevent the construction of a suitable Petri net. Therefore, we are interested in automated abstraction techniques and over-approximations of the state space. Of course, there's also a downside: The state space corresponding to the resulting Petri net is no longer bisimilar to the original state space. Nevertheless, we feel that having an elegant approximation is better than having an exact solution that is of no use.

Acknowledgments

We are grateful to Jordi Cortadella for his kind support on issues related to the *Petrify* tool. Furthermore, we thank the anonymous reviewers for helping to improve the paper. Hannes Pretorius is supported by the Netherlands Organization for Scientific Research (NWO) under grant 612.065.410.

References

1. van der Aalst, W.M.P., van Dongen, B.F., Günther, C.W., Mans, R.S., Alves de Medeiros, A.K., Rozinat, A., Rubin, V., Song, M., Verbeek, H.M.W., Weijters, A.J.M.M.: ProM 4.0: Comprehensive Support for Real Process Analysis. In: Kleijn, J., Yakovlev, A. (eds.) ICATPN 2007. LNCS, vol. 4546, pp. 484–494. Springer, Heidelberg (2007)
2. van der Aalst, W.M.P., ter Hofstede, A.H.M.: YAWL: yet another workflow language. Information Systems 30(4), 245–275 (2005)
3. van der Aalst, W.M.P., Rubin, V., van Dongen, B.F., Kindler, E., Günther, C.W.: Process mining: a two-step approach using transition systems and regions. BPM Center Report BPM-06-30, BPMcenter.org (2006)
4. van der Aalst, W.M.P., van Dongen, B.F., Herbst, J., Maruster, L., Schimm, G., Weijters, A.J.M.M.: Workflow mining: A Survey of issues and approaches. Data and Knowledge Engineering 47(2), 237–267 (2003)
5. van der Aalst, W.M.P., Weijters, A.J.M.M., Maruster, L.: Workflow mining: discovering process models from event logs. IEEE Transactions on Knowledge and Data Engineering 16(9), 1128–1142 (2004)
6. Alves, A., Arkin, A., Askary, S., Barreto, C., Bloch, B., Curbera, F., Ford, M., Goland, Y., Guízar, A., Kartha, N., Liu, C.K., Khalaf, R., Koenig, D., Marin, M., Mehta, V., Thatte, S., Rijn, D., Yendluri, P., Yiu, A.: Web Services Business Process Execution Language Version 2.0 (OASIS Standard). WS-BPEL TC OASIS (2007), `http://docs.oasis-open.org/wsbpel/2.0/wsbpel-v2.0.html`
7. Arnold, A.: Finite Transition Systems. Prentice-Hall, Englewood Cliffs (1994)
8. Bergenthum, R., Desel, J., Lorenz, R., Mauser, S.: Process Mining Based on Regions of Languages. In: Alonso, G., Dadam, P., Rosemann, M. (eds.) BPM 2007. LNCS, vol. 4714, pp. 375–383. Springer, Heidelberg (2007)
9. Cook, J.E., Wolf, A.L.: Discovering models of software processes from event-based data. ACM Transactions on Software Engineering and Methodology 7(3), 215–249 (1998)
10. Cortadella, J., Kishinevsky, M., Lavagno, L., Yakovlev, A.: Synthesizing Petri Nets from State-Based Models. In: Proceedings of the 1995 IEEE/ACM International Conference on Computer-Aided Design (ICCAD 1995), pp. 164–171. IEEE Computer Society, Los Alamitos (1995)
11. Cortadella, J., Kishinevsky, M., Lavagno, L., Yakovlev, A.: Deriving Petri nets from finite transition systems. IEEE Transactions on Computers 47(8), 859–882 (1998)
12. Dams, D., Gerth, R.: Abstract interpretation of reactive systems. ACM Transactions on Programming Languages and Systems 19(2), 253–291 (1997)
13. Darondeau, P.: Unbounded petri net synthesis. In: Desel, J., Reisig, W., Rozenberg, G. (eds.) Lectures on Concurrency and Petri Nets. LNCS, vol. 3098, pp. 413–438. Springer, Heidelberg (2004)

14. Ehrenfeucht, A., Rozenberg, G.: Partial (Set) 2-Structures - Part 1 and Part 2. Acta Informatica 27(4), 315–368 (1989)
15. Gansner, E.R., Koutsofios, E., North, S.C., Vo, K.-P.: A technique for drawing directed graphs. IEEE Transactions on Software Engineering 19(3), 214–230 (1993)
16. van Glabbeek, R.J., Weijland, W.P.: Branching time and abstraction in bisimulation semantics. Journal of the ACM 43(3), 555–600 (1996)
17. Object Management Group. OMG Unified Modeling Language 2.0. OMG (2005), `http://www.omg.com/uml/`
18. Harel, D., Thiagarajan, P.S.: Message sequence charts. In: UML for Real: Design of Embedded Real-Time Systems, Norwell, MA, USA, pp. 77–105. Kluwer Academic Publishers, Dordrecht (2003)
19. Hendriks, M., van den Nieuwelaar, N.J.M., Vaandrager, F.W.: Model checker aided design of a controller for a wafer scanner. Int. J. Softw. Tools Technol. Transf. 8(6), 633–647 (2006)
20. Keller, G., Nüttgens, M., Scheer, A.W.: Semantische Processmodellierung auf der Grundlage Ereignisgesteuerter Processketten (EPK). Veröffentlichungen des Instituts für Wirtschaftsinformatik, Heft 89 (in German), University of Saarland, Saarbrücken (1992)
21. Lorenz, R., Juhas, G.: Towards Synthesis of Petri Nets from Scenariose. In: Donatelli, S., Thiagarajan, P.S. (eds.) ICATPN 2006. LNCS, vol. 4024, pp. 302–321. Springer, Heidelberg (2006)
22. Nielsen, M., Rozenberg, G., Thiagarajan, P.S.: Elementary transition systems. In: Second Workshop on Concurrency and compositionality, Essex, UK, pp. 3–33. Elsevier Science Publishers Ltd., Amsterdam (1992)
23. Pretorius, A.J., van Wijk, J.J.: Visual analysis of multivariate state transition graphs. IEEE Transactions on Visualization and Computer Graphics 12(5), 685–692 (2006)
24. Rubin, V., Günther, C.W., van der Aalst, W.M.P., Kindler, E., van Dongen, B.F., Schäfer, W.: Process mining framework for software processes. In: Wang, Q., Pfahl, D., Raffo, D.M. (eds.) ICSP 2007. LNCS, vol. 4470, pp. 169–181. Springer, Heidelberg (2007)
25. Verbeek, H.M.W., van Dongen, B.F., Mendling, J., van der Aalst, W.M.P.: Interoperability in the ProM Framework. In: Latour, T., Petit, M. (eds.) Proceedings of the EMOI-INTEROP Workshop at the 18th International Conference on Advanced Information Systems Engineering (CAiSE 2006), pp. 619–630. Namur University Press (2006)

Directed Unfolding of Petri Nets

Blai Bonet[1], Patrik Haslum[2], Sarah Hickmott[3], and Sylvie Thiébaux[2]

[1] Universidad Simón Bolívar, Departamento de Computación, Caracas, Venezuela,
[2] National ICT Australia & The Australian National University, Canberra, Australia
[3] National ICT Australia & The University of Adelaide, Adelaide, Australia

Abstract. The key to efficient on-the-fly reachability analysis based on unfolding is to focus the expansion of the finite prefix towards the desired marking. However, current unfolding strategies typically equate to blind (breadth-first) search. They do not exploit the knowledge of the marking that is sought, merely entertaining the hope that the road to it will be short. This paper investigates *directed unfolding*, which exploits problem-specific information in the form of a heuristic function to guide the unfolding towards the desired marking. In the unfolding context, heuristic values are estimates of the distance between configurations. We show that suitable heuristics can be automatically extracted from the original net. We prove that unfolding can rely on heuristic search strategies while preserving the finiteness and completeness of the generated prefix, and in some cases, the optimality of the firing sequence produced. We also establish that the size of the prefix obtained with a useful class of heuristics is never worse than that obtained by blind unfolding. Experimental results demonstrate that directed unfolding scales up to problems that were previously out of reach of the unfolding technique.

1 Introduction

The Petri net unfolding process, originally introduced by McMillan [1], has gained the interest of researchers in verification (see e.g. [2]), diagnosis [3] and, more recently, planning [4]. All have reasons to analyse reachability in distributed transition systems, looking to unfolding for some relief of the state explosion problem. Unfolding a Petri net reveals all possible partially ordered runs of the net, without the combinatorial interleaving of independent events. Whilst the unfolding can be infinite, McMillan identified the possibility of a finite prefix with all reachable states. Esparza et al. [5] generalised his approach, to produce the now commonly used ERV unfolding algorithm. This algorithm involves a search, but does not mandate a specific search strategy. Typically, it has been implemented as a breadth-first search, using the length of paths to select the next node to add and to determine cut-off events.

Of the various unfolding-based reachability techniques, experimental results indicate on-the-fly analysis to be most efficient for proving the reachability of a single marking [6]. Nevertheless, generating the complete prefix up to a particular state via breadth-first search quickly becomes impractical when the unfolding is wide or the shortest path to the state is deep. Unfortunately, it has not been

K. Jensen, W. van der Aalst, and J. Billington (Eds.): ToPNoC I, LNCS 5100, pp. 172–198, 2008.

obvious what other strategies could be used in the ERV algorithm and recent results have shown that the use of depth-first search in a simpler unfolding algorithm is incorrect [7]. In this paper, we investigate *directed unfolding*, a strategy that takes advantage of information about the sought marking to guide the search. The reason why such an informed strategy has not been considered before may be that unfolding is typically used to prove the absence of deadlocks: this has set the focus on making the entire prefix smaller rather than on reducing the part of the search space explored to reach a particular marking. However, as demonstrated below, information about the goal marking can help also in the case when this marking is not reachable.

Inspired by heuristic search in artificial intelligence, particularly in the area of automated planning, directed unfolding exploits problem-specific information in the form of a heuristic function to guide search towards the desired marking. Specifically, the heuristic estimates the shortest distance from a given marking to the desired one, and is used to implement a search strategy where choices are explored in increasing order of their estimated distance. If the heuristic is sufficiently informative, this order provides effective guidance towards the marking sought. Whilst the order is not always adequate, in the sense defined in [5], it still guarantees finiteness and completeness of the generated prefix. Interestingly, our proof relies on the observation that adequate orders are stronger than necessary for these purposes, and introduces the weaker notion of semi-adequate ordering.

Using heuristics, automatically extracted from the representation of a transition system, to guide search has significantly improved the scalability of automated planning [8–10]. We show that heuristic values can be similarly calculated from a Petri net. If the chosen heuristic is *admissible* (meaning it never overestimates the shortest distances) then directed unfolding finds the *shortest* path to the target marking, just like breadth-first search. Moreover, a slightly stronger property than admissibility guarantees that the prefix produced is never larger than the prefix obtained by breadth-first search. Using inadmissible heuristics, completeness and correctness are preserved, and performance is often dramatically improved at the expense of optimality. Altogether, directed unfolding can solve much larger problems than the original breadth-first ERV algorithm. Moreover, its implementation requires only minor additions.

The paper is organised as follows. Section 2 is an overview of Place/Transition nets, unfoldings, and on-the-fly reachability analysis. Section 3 describes the ideas behind directed unfolding and establishes its theoretical properties. In Sect. 4, we show how to automatically extract a range of heuristics from the Petri net description. In Sect. 5 presents experimental results and Sect. 6 concludes with remarks about related and future work.

2 Petri Nets, Unfolding and Reachability Analysis

2.1 Place/Transition Petri Nets

Petri nets provide a factored representation of discrete-event systems. States are not enumerated and flattened into single unstructured entities but rather

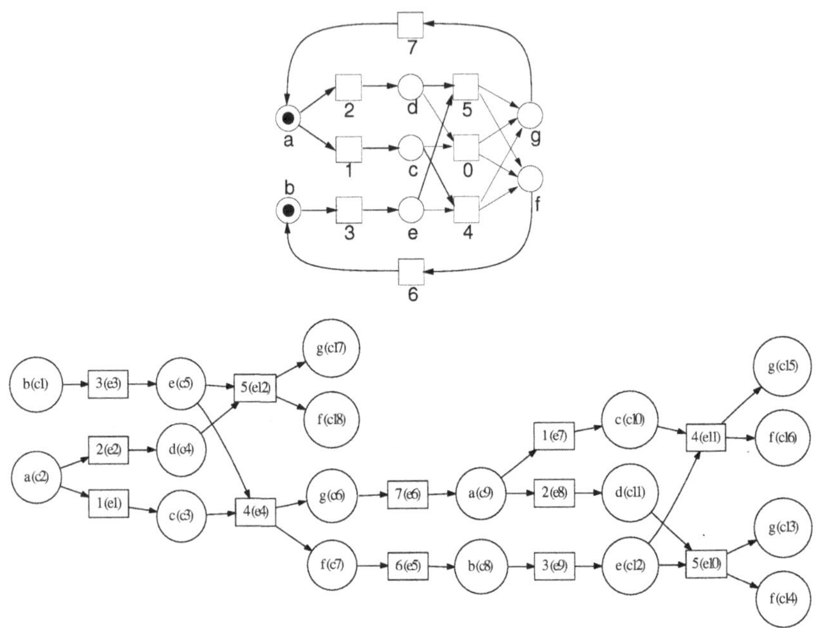

Fig. 1. Example of a Place/Transition Net (*top*) and its unfolding (*bottom*)

explicitly factorized into variables (places) such that the temporal relations between variables become transitions that produce and consume markers in the net. We consider the so-called *Place/Transition* (P/T) nets, and describe them only briefly; a detailed exposition can be found in [11].

A P/T-net (top part of Fig. 1) consists of a net N and its initial marking M_0. The net is a directed bipartite graph where the nodes are places and transitions (depicted as circles and squares, respectively). Typically, places represent the state variables and transitions the events of the underlying discrete-event system. The dynamic behaviour is captured by the flow relation F between places and transitions and vice versa. The *marking* of a P/T-net represents the state of the system. It assigns to each place zero or more tokens (depicted as dots).

Definition 1. *A P/T-net is a 4-tuple* (P, T, F, M_0) *where* P *and* T *are disjoint finite sets of places and transitions, respectively,* $F : (P \times T) \cup (T \times P) \to \{0, 1\}$ *is a flow relation indicating the presence (1) or absence (0) of arcs, and* $M_0 : P \to \mathbb{N}$ *is the initial marking.*

The *preset* ${}^\bullet x$ of node x is the set $\{y \in P \cup T : F(y, x) = 1\}$, and its *postset* $x^\bullet$ is the set $\{y \in P \cup T : F(x, y) = 1\}$. The marking M enables a transition t if $M(p) > 0$ for all $p \in {}^\bullet t$. The occurrence, or *firing*, of an enabled transition t absorbs a token from each of its preset places and puts one token in each postset place. This corresponds to a state transition in the modeled system, moving the net from M to the new marking M' given by $M'(p) = M(p) - F(p, t) + F(t, p)$

for each p; this is denoted as $M \xrightarrow{t} M'$. A *firing sequence* $\sigma = t_1 \dots t_n$ is a legal sequence of transition firings, i.e., there are markings $M_1, \dots, M_n$ such that $M_0 \xrightarrow{t_1} M_1 \cdots M_{n-1} \xrightarrow{t_n} M_n$; this is denoted as $M_0 \xrightarrow{\sigma} M_n$. A marking M is *reachable* if there exists a firing sequence σ such that $M_0 \xrightarrow{\sigma} M$. In this paper, we only consider 1-bounded nets, meaning that all reachable markings assign at most one token at each place.

2.2 Unfolding

Unfolding is a method for reachability analysis which exploits and preserves concurrency information in the Petri net. It a partially ordered structure of events that represents all possible firing sequences of the net from the initial marking.

Unfolding a P/T-net produces a pair $U = (ON, \varphi)$ where $ON = (B, E, F')$ is an occurrence net, which is a P/T-net without cycles, self conflicts or backward conflicts (defined below), and φ is a homomorphism from ON to N that associates the places/transitions of ON with the places/transitions of the P/T-net.

A node x is in self conflict if there exist two paths to x which start at the same place and immediately diverge. A backward conflict happens when two transitions output to the same place. Such cases are undesirable since in order to decide whether a token can reach a place in backward conflict, it would be necessary to reason with disjunctions such as from which transition the token came. Therefore, the process of unfolding involves breaking all backward conflicts by making independent copies of the places involved in the conflicts, and thus the occurrence net ON may contain multiples copies of places and transitions of the original net which are identified with the homomorphism.

In the occurrence net ON, places and transitions are called conditions B and events E, respectively. The initial marking M_0 defines a set of initial conditions B_0 in ON such that the places initially marked are in 1–1 correspondence with the conditions in B_0. The set B_0 constitutes the "seed" of the unfolding.

The bottom part in Fig. 1 shows a prefix of the unfolding of the P/T-net in the top part. Note the multiple instances of place g, for example, due to the different firing sequences through which it can be reached (multiple backward conflicts). Note also that transition 0 does not appear in the unfolding, as there no firing sequence that enables transition 0.

2.3 Configurations

To understand how a prefix of an unfolding is built, the most important notions are that of a configuration and local configuration. A *configuration* represents a possible partially ordered run of the net. It is a finite set of events C such that:

1. C is causally closed: $e \in C \Rightarrow e' \in C$ for all $e' \leq e$,
2. C contains no forward conflict: ${}^\bullet e_1 \cap {}^\bullet e_2 = \emptyset$ for all $e_1 \neq e_2$ in C;

where $e' \leq e$ means there is a directed path from e' to e in ON. If these two conditions are met, the events in a configuration C can be ordered into a firing sequence with respect to B_0. For instance, in the finite prefix in Fig. 1, {e1, e3, e4} is a configuration, while {e1, e4} and {e1, e2} are not since the former is not causally closed and the latter has a forward conflict.

A configuration C can be associated with a final marking Mark(C) of the original P/T-net by identifying which conditions will contain a token after the events in C are fired from the initial conditions; i.e., $\text{Mark}(C) = \varphi((B_0 \cup C^\bullet)\setminus {}^\bullet C)$ where $C^\bullet$ (resp. ${}^\bullet C$) is the union of postsets (resp. presets) of all events in C. In other words, the marking of C identifies the resultant marking of the original P/T-net when only the transitions labelled by the events in C occur. For instance, in Fig. 1, the marking of configuration {e1, e3, e4, e5} is {g, b}. The *local configuration* of an event e, denoted by $[e]$, is the minimal configuration containing event e. For example, [e5] = {e1, e3, e4, e5}. A set of events can occur in the same firing sequence iff the union of their local configurations is a configuration.

2.4 Finite Complete Prefix

The unfolding process involves identifying which transitions are enabled by those conditions, currently in the occurrence net, that can be simultaneously marked. These are referred to as the possible next events. A new instance of each is added to the occurrence net, as are instances of the places in their postsets.

The unfolding process starts from the seed B_0 and extends it iteratively. In most cases, the unfolding U is infinite and thus cannot be built. However, it is not necessary to build U entirely, but only a *complete finite prefix* β of U that contains all the information in U. Formally, a prefix β of U is *complete* if for every reachable marking M, there exists a configuration $C \in \beta$ such that $\text{Mark}(C) = M$, and for every transition t enabled by M there is an event $e \notin C$ with $\varphi(e) = t$ such that $C \cup \{e\}$ is a configuration.

The key for obtaining a complete finite prefix is to identify those events at which the unfolding can be ceased without loss of information. Such events are referred to as *cut-off events* and can be defined in terms of an *adequate order* on configurations [1,5,12]. In the following, $C \oplus E$ denotes a configuration that extends C with the finite set of events E disjoint from C; such E is called an extension of configuration C.

Definition 2 (Adequate Orderings). *A strict partial order $\prec$ on finite configurations is an* adequate order *if and only if*

(a) $\prec$ is well founded, i.e., it has no infinite descending chains,
(b) $C_1 \subset C_2 \Rightarrow C_1 \prec C_2$, and
(c) $\prec$ is weakly *preserved by finite extensions; i.e., if $C_1 \prec C_2$ and $\text{Mark}(C_1) = \text{Mark}(C_2)$, then for all finite extension E_2 of C_2, there exist a finite extension E_1 of C_1 that is structurally isomorphic*[1] *to E_2, and $C_1 \oplus E_1 \prec C_2 \oplus E_2$.*

Without threat to completeness, we can cease unfolding from an event e, if it takes the net to a marking which can be caused by some other already unfolded

[1] Two extensions E and E' are structurally isomorphic if the labelled digraphs induced by the two sets of events and their adjacent conditions are isomorphic [12].

Algorithm 1. The ERV Unfolding Algorithm (and ERV/fly variant)

Input: a P/T-net (P, T, F, M_0) (and transition t_R for ERV/fly).
Output of ERV: complete finite prefix β.
Output of ERV/fly: finite prefix β with event e_R, with $\varphi(e_R) = t_R$, if t_R is reachable,
finite prefix β with no event e_R, with $\varphi(e_R) = t_R$, otherwise.

1. Initialise the prefix β with the conditions in B_0
2. Initialise the priority queue with the events possible in B_0
3. Initialise the set *cut-off* to $\emptyset$
4. **while** the queue is not empty **do**
5.   Remove event e in the queue (minimal with respect to $\prec$)
6.   [[only for ERV/fly]] **if** $h([e]) = \infty$ **then terminate** (t_R is not reachable)
7.   **if** $[e]$ contains no event in *cut-off* **then**
8.   Add e and conditions for its postset to β
9.   [[only for ERV/fly]] **if** $\varphi(e) = t_R$ **then terminate** (t_R is reachable)
10.   Identify the *new* possible next events and insert them in the queue
11.   **if** e is a cut-off event in β with respect to $\prec$ **then**
12.   Update *cut-off* := *cut-off* $\cup \{e\}$
13.   **endif**
14.   **endif**
15. **endwhile**

event e' such that $[e'] \prec [e]$. This is because the events (and thus marking) which proceed from e will also proceed from e'. Relevant proofs can be found in [5,12].

Definition 3 (Cut-off Events). *Let $\prec$ be an adequate order and β a prefix. An event e is a* cut-off event in β with respect to $\prec$ *iff β contains some event e' such that Mark$([e])$ = Mark$([e'])$ and $[e'] \prec [e]$.*

2.5 The ERV Algorithm

Algorithm 1 shows the well-known ERV algorithm for unfolding P/T-nets [5] (and a variant, called ERV/fly, which will be discussed later). ERV maintains a queue of events, sorted in increasing order with respect to $\prec$. At each iteration, a minimal event in the queue is processed, starting with checking whether its local configuration contains any cut-off event with respect to $\prec$ in the prefix β under construction. If not, the event is added to the prefix along with conditions for its postset, and the new possible next events enabled by the new conditions are inserted in the queue. The algorithm terminates when all queue events have been processed (the ERV/fly variant has two additional conditions for earlier termination). This is the ERV algorithm exactly as it is described in [5].

It is important to mention certain details about the implementation of the algorithm. First, the order $\prec$ is used *both to order the queue and to identify the cut-off events.* As noted in [5], this implies that if the ordering $\prec$ is total, the check at line 11 in Algorithm 1 ("e is a cut-off event in β with respect to $\prec$") can be replaced by the simpler check: "β contains a local configuration $[e']$ such that Mark($[e]$) = Mark($[e']$)", since with a total order, $[e'] \prec [e]$ for any event e that is dequeued after e'. This optimisation may be important if evaluating $\prec$ is expensive (this, however, is not the case for any order we consider in this paper). Second, it is in fact not necessary to insert new events that are causal successors of a cut-off event into the queue – which is done in the algorithm as described – since they will only be discarded when dequeued. While this optimisation makes no difference to the prefix generated, it may have a significant impact on both runtime and memory use. For optimizations related to the generation of possible next events see [13].

Besides the explicit input parameters, the ERV and ERV/fly algorithms implicitly depend on an order $\prec$ (and also on a function h for ERV/fly). Whenever this dependency needs to be emphasized, we will refer to both algorithms as ERV[$\prec$] and ERV/fly[$\prec, h$], respectively. Again, note that whatever order this may be, *it is used both to order the queue and to identify cut-off events.*

MOLE[2] is a freeware program that implements the ERV algorithm for 1-bounded P/T-nets. MOLE uses McMillan's [1] cardinality-based ordering ($C \prec_m C'$ iff $|C| < |C'|$), further refined into a total order [5]. Note that using this order equates to a breadth-first search strategy. MOLE implements the optimisation described above, i.e., successors of cut-off events are never placed on the queue.

The prefix in Fig. 1 is the complete finite prefix that MOLE generates for our example. The events e10, e11, and e12 are all cut-off events. This is because each of their local configurations has the same marking as the local configuration of event e4, i.e., $\{\mathsf{f}, \mathsf{g}\}$, and each of them is greater than the local configuration of e4 with respect to the adequate order implemented by MOLE.

2.6 On-The-Fly Reachability Analysis

We define the *reachability problem* (also often called coverability problem) for 1-bounded P/T-nets as follows:

> REACHABILITY: Given a P/T-net (P, T, F, M_0) and a subset $P' \subseteq P$, determine whether there is a firing sequence σ such that $M_0 \xrightarrow{\sigma} M$ where $M(p) = 1$ for all $p \in P'$.

This problem is PSPACE-complete [14].

Since unfolding constructs a complete finite prefix that represents every reachable marking by a configuration, it can be used as the basis of an algorithm for deciding REACHABILITY. However, deciding if the prefix contains any configuration that leads to a given marking is still NP-complete [6]. If we are interested in solving multiple REACHABILITY problems for the same net and initial marking, this is still an improvement. Algorithms taking this approach have been designed using mixed-integer linear programming [15], stable models for Logic Programs [16], and other methods [6,17].

However, if we are interested in the reachability of just one single marking, the form of completeness offered by the prefix constructed by unfolding is unnecessarily strong: we require only that the target marking is represented by some

[2] `http://www.fmi.uni-stuttgart.de/szs/tools/mole/`

configuration if it is indeed reachable. We will refer to this weaker condition as *completeness with respect to the goal marking.* This was recognised already by McMillan, who suggested an on-the-fly approach to reachability. It involves introducing a new transition t_R to the original net with ${}^\bullet t_R = P'$ and $t_R{}^\bullet = \{p_R\}$ where p_R is a *new place.* [3] The net is then unfolded until an event e_R, such that $\varphi(e_R) = t_R$, is retrieved from the queue. At this point we can conclude that the set of places P' is reachable. If unfolding terminates without identifying such an event, P' is not reachable. If $[e_R]$ is not required to be the shortest possible firing sequence, it is sufficient to stop as soon as e_R is generated as one of the possible next events, but to guarantee optimality, even with breadth-first unfolding, it is imperative to wait until the event is pulled out of the queue. Experimental results have shown the on-the-fly approach to be most efficient for deciding the reachability of a single marking [6].

The ERV/fly variant of the ERV unfolding algorithm embodies two "short cuts", in the form of conditions for earlier termination, which are motivated by the fact that we are interested only in completeness with respect to the goal marking. The first is simply to adopt McMillan's on-the-fly approach, stopping when an instance of transition t_R is dequeued. The second depends on a property of the heuristic function h, and will be discussed in Sect. 3.3.[4]

3 Directing the Unfolding

In the context of the reachability problem, we are only interested in checking whether the transition t_R is reachable. An unfolding algorithm that does not use this information is probably not the best approach. In this section, we aim to define a *principled method* for using this information during the unfolding process in order to solve the reachability problem more efficiently. The resulting approach is called "directed unfolding" as opposed to the standard "blind unfolding".[5]

The basic idea is that for deciding REACHABILITY, the unfolding process can be understood as a *search process* on the quest for t_R. Thus, when selecting events from the queue, we should favour those "closer" to t_R as their systematic exploration results in a more efficient search strategy. This approach is only possible if the prefix constructed is guaranteed to be complete, in the sense that it will, eventually, contain an instance of t_R if it is reachable.

We show that the ERV algorithm can be used with the same definition of cut-off events when the notion of adequate orderings is replaced by a weaker notion

[3] Strictly speaking, to preserve 1-safeness, it is also necessary to add a new place complementary to p_R to ${}^\bullet t_R$ to avoid multiple firings of t_R.

[4] In addition, for completeness with respect to a single goal marking, it is not necessary to insert cut-off events into the prefix at all, since any marking represented by the local configuration of a cut-off event is by definition already represented by another event. This optimisation may not have a great impact on runtime, at least if the previously described optimisation of not generating successors of cut-off events is already in place, but may reduce memory requirements.

[5] The term "directed" has been used elsewhere to emphasize the informed nature of other model checking algorithms [18].

that we call *semi-adequate* orderings. This is prompted by the observation that the definition of adequate orderings is a sufficient but not a necessary condition for a sound definition of cut-off events. Indeed, just replacing condition (*b*) in Definition 2 by a weaker condition opens the door for a family of semi-adequate orderings that allow us to direct the unfolding process.

3.1 Principles

As is standard in state-based search, our orderings are constructed upon the values of a function f that maps configurations into non-negative numbers (including infinity). Such functions f are composed of two parts $f(C) = g(C)+h(C)$ in which $g(C)$ refers to the "cost" of C and $h(C)$ estimates the distance from $\mathrm{Mark}(C)$ to the *target marking* $\{p_R\}$. For the purposes of the present work, we will assume a fixed function $g(C) = |C|$, yet other possibilities also make sense, e.g. when transitions are associated with costs, and the cost of a set of transitions is defined as the sum of the costs of the transitions in the set.

The function $h(C)$ is a non-negative valued function on configurations, and is required to satisfy:

1. $h(C) = 0$ if $\mathrm{Mark}(C)$ contains a condition c_R such that $\varphi(c_R) = p_R$ where p_R is the new place in $t_R{}^\bullet$, and
2. $h(C) = h(C')$ whenever $\mathrm{Mark}(C) = \mathrm{Mark}(C')$.

Such functions will be called *heuristic functions on configurations.* Note that the function which assigns value 0 to all configurations is a heuristic function. We will denote this function $h \equiv 0$. For two heuristic functions, $h \leq h'$ denotes the standard notion of $h(C) \leq h'(C)$ for all configurations C.

Let h be a heuristic and, for $f(C) = |C| + h(C)$, define the ordering $\prec_h$ as follows:

$$C \prec_h C' \text{ iff } \begin{cases} f(C) < f(C') & \text{if } f(C) \neq f(C') \\ |C| < |C'| & \text{if } f(C) = f(C'). \end{cases}$$

Observe that $\prec_{h\equiv 0}$ is the strict partial order $\prec_m$ on configurations used by McMillan [1], which can be refined into the total order defined in [5].

Let us define $h^*(C) = |C'| - |C|$, where $C' \supseteq C$ is a configuration of minimum cardinality that contains an instance of t_R if one exists, and ∞ otherwise. (By "an instance of t_R" we mean of course an event e_R such that $\varphi(e_R) = t_R$.) We then say that h is an *admissible heuristic* if $h(C) \leq h^*(C)$ for all finite configurations C. Likewise, let us say that a finite configuration C^* is *optimal* if it contains an instance of t_R, and it is of minimum cardinality among such configurations. By f^* we denote $|C^*|$ if an optimal configuration exists (i.e., if t_R is reachable) and ∞ otherwise. In the following, $\mathsf{ERV}[h]$ denotes $\mathsf{ERV}[\prec_h]$.

Theorem 1 (Main). *Let h be a heuristic function on configurations. Then,* $\mathsf{ERV}[h]$ *computes a finite and complete prefix of the unfolding. Furthermore, if h is admissible, then* $\mathsf{ERV}[h]$ *finds an optimal configuration if t_R is reachable. Both claims also hold for any semi-adequate ordering that refines $\prec_h$.*[6]

[6] Ordering $\prec'$ refines $\prec$ iff $C \prec C'$ implies $C \prec' C'$ for all configurations C and C'.

Note that this result by no means contradicts a recent proof that unfolding with depth-first search is incorrect [7]. Not only do heuristic strategies have a "breadth" element to them which depth-first search lacks, but, more importantly, the algorithm shown incorrect differs from the ERV algorithm in that when identifying cut-off events it only checks if the prefix contains a local configuration with identical marking but does not check whether the ordering $\prec$ holds.

Optimal configurations are important in the context of diagnosis since they provide shortest firing sequences to reach a given marking, e.g. a faulty state in the system. A consequence of Theorem 1 is that the MOLE implementation of the ERV algorithm, which equates using a refinement of $\prec_{h\equiv 0}$ into a total order [5], finds shortest firing sequences. In the next two sections, we will give examples of heuristic functions, both admissible and non-admissible, and experimental results on benchmark problems. In the rest of this section, we provide the technical characterization of semi-adequate orderings and their relation to adequate ones, as well as the proofs required for the main theorem. We also provide a result concerning the size of the prefixes obtained.

3.2 Technical Details

Upon revising the role of adequate orders when building the complete finite prefix, we found that condition (*b*), i.e., $C \subset C' \Rightarrow C \prec C'$, in Definition 2 is only needed to guarantee the finiteness of the generated prefix. Indeed, let n be the number of reachable markings and consider an infinite sequence of events $e_1 < e_2 < \cdots$ in the unfolding. Then, there are $i < j \leq n + 1$ such that $\text{Mark}([e_i]) = \text{Mark}([e_j])$, and since $[e_i] \subset [e_j]$, condition (*b*) implies $[e_i] \prec [e_j]$ making $[e_j]$ into a cut-off event, and thus the prefix is finite [5]. A similar result can be achieved if condition (*b*) is replaced by the weaker condition that in every infinite chain $e_1 < e_2 < \cdots$ of events there are $i < j$ such that $[e_i] \prec [e_j]$. To slightly simplify the proofs, we can further weaken that condition by asking that the local configurations of these events have equal markings.

Definition 4 (Semi-Adequate Orderings). *A strict partial order $\prec$ on finite configurations is a* semi-adequate order *if and only if*

(*a*) *$\prec$ is well founded, i.e., it has no infinite descending chains,*
(*b*) *in every infinite chain $C_1 \subset C_2 \subset \cdots$ of configurations with equal markings there are $i < j$ such that $C_i \prec C_j$, and*
(*c*) *$\prec$ is* weakly *preserved by finite extensions.*

Theorem 2 (Finiteness and Completeness). *If $\prec$ is a semi-adequate order, the prefix produced by* ERV[$\prec$] *is finite and complete.*

Proof. The completeness proof is identical to the proof of Proposition 4.9 in [5, p. 14] which states the completeness of the prefix computed by ERV for adequate orderings: this proof does not rely on condition (*b*) at all. The finiteness proof is similar to the proof of Proposition 4.8 in [5, p. 13] which states the finiteness of the prefix computed by ERV for adequate orderings. If the prefix is not finite, then by the version of König's Lemma for branching processes [19], an infinite chain $e_1 < e_2 < \cdots$ of events exists in the prefix. Each event e_i defines a configuration $[e_i]$ with marking Mark($[e_i]$), and since the number of markings is finite, there is at least one marking that appears infinitely often in the chain. Let $e'_1 < e'_2 < \cdots$ be an infinite subchain such that Mark($[e'_1]$) = Mark($[e'_j]$) for all $j > 1$. By condition (*b*) of semi-adequate orderings, there are $i < j$ such that $[e'_i] \prec [e'_j]$ that together with Mark($[e'_i]$) = Mark($[e'_j]$) make e'_j into a cut-off event and thus the chain cannot be infinite. □

Clearly, if $\prec$ is an adequate order, then it is a semi-adequate order. The converse is not necessarily true. The fact that $\prec_h$ is semi-adequate is a consequence of the monotonicity of $g(C) = |C|$, i.e., $C \subset C' \Rightarrow g(C) < g(C')$, and that configurations with equal markings have identical h-values.

Theorem 3 (Semi-Adequacy of $\prec_h$). *If h is a heuristic on configurations, $\prec_h$ is a semi-adequate order.*

Proof. That $\prec_h$ is irreflexive and transitive is direct from definition.

For well-foundedness, first observe that if C and C' are two configurations with the same marking, then $C \prec_h C'$ iff $|C| < |C'|$. Let $C_1 \succ_h C_2 \succ_h \cdots$ be an infinite descending chain of *finite* configurations with markings $M_1, M_2, \ldots$, respectively. Observe that not all C_i's have $f(C_i) = \infty$ since, by definition of $\prec_h$, this would imply $\infty > |C_1| > |C_2| > \cdots \geq 0$ which is impossible. Similarly, at most finitely many C_i's have infinite f value. Let $C'_1 \succ_h C'_2 \succ_h \cdots$ be the subchain where $f(C'_i) < \infty$ for all i, and $M'_1, M'_2, \ldots$ the corresponding markings. Since the number of markings is finite, we can extract a further subsubchain $C''_1 \succ_h C''_2 \succ_h \cdots$ such that Mark(C''_1) = Mark(C''_j) for all $j > 1$. Therefore, $|C''_1| > |C''_2| > \cdots \geq 0$ which is impossible since all C''_i's are finite.

For condition (*b*), let $C_1 \subset C_2 \subset \cdots$ be an infinite chain of finite configurations with equal markings. Therefore, $val \doteq h(C_1) = h(C_j)$ for all $j > 1$, and also $|C_1| < |C_2|$. If $val = \infty$, then $C_1 \prec_h C_2$. If $val < \infty$, then $f(C_1) = |C_1| + val < |C_2| + val = f(C_2)$ and thus $C_1 \prec_h C_2$.

Finally, if $C_1 \prec_h C_2$ have equal markings and the extensions E_1 and E_2 are isomorphic, the configurations $C'_1 = C_1 \oplus E_1$ and $C'_2 = C_2 \oplus E_2$ also have equal markings, and it is straightforward to show that $C'_1 \prec_h C'_2$. □

Proof (of Theorem 1). That ERV[h] computes a complete and finite prefix is direct since, by Theorem 3, $\prec_h$ is semi-adequate and, by Theorem 2, this is enough to guarantee finiteness and completeness of the prefix.

For the second claim, assume that t_R is reachable. Then, the prefix computed by ERV contains at least one instance of t_R. First, we observe that until e_R is dequeued, the queue always contains an event e such that $[e]$ is a prefix of an optimal configuration C^*. This property holds at the beginning (initially, the queue contains all possible extensions of the initial conditions) and by induction remains true after each iteration of the while loop. This is because if e is dequeued then either $e = e_R$, or a successor of e will be inserted in the queue which will satisfy the property, or it must be the case that e is identified as a cut-off event by ERV. But the latter case implies that there is some e' in the prefix built so far such that $\mathrm{Mark}([e']) = \mathrm{Mark}([e])$ and $f([e']) < f([e])$. This in turn implies that $h([e']) = h([e])$, and thus $||[e']|| < ||[e]||$ which contradicts the assumption on the minimality of C^*.

For proof by contradiction, suppose that ERV dequeues a instance e_R of t_R such that $[e_R]$ is not optimal, i.e., not of minimum cardinality. If e is an event in the queue, at the time e_R is dequeued, such that $[e]$ is a subset of an optimal configuration C^*, then

$$f([e]) \ = \ ||[e]|| + h([e]) \ \leq \ ||[e]|| + h^*([e]) \ = \ ||[e]|| + |C^*| - ||[e]|| \ = \ |C^*| .$$

On the other hand, since $[e_R]$ is non-optimal by supposition, $f([e_R]) = ||[e_R]|| > |C^*|$. Therefore, $f([e_R]) > f([e])$ and thus $[e] \prec_h [e_R]$ and e_R could not have been pulled out of the queue before e.

Observe that the proof does not depend on how the events with equal f-values are ordered in the queue. Thus, any refinement of $\prec_h$ also works. □

3.3 Size of the Finite Prefix

As we have already remarked, to solve REACHABILITY using unfolding we require only that the prefix is complete with respect to the sought marking, i.e., that it contains a configuration representing that marking iff the marking is reachable. This enables us to take certain "short cuts", in the form of conditions for earlier termination, in the unfolding algorithm, which results in a smaller prefix being constructed. In this section, we show first that these modifications preserve the completeness of the algorithm, and the guarantee of finding an optimal solution if the heuristic is admissible. Second, under some additional assumptions, we show a result relating the size of the prefix computed by directed on-the-fly unfolding to the informedness of the heuristic.

Before proceeding, let us review the modifications made in the variant of the ERV algorithm which we call ERV/fly (for ERV on-the-**fly**). The first "short cut" is adopting the on-the-fly approach, terminating the algorithm as soon as an instance of the target transition t_R is added to the prefix. For the second, if the heuristic h has the property that $h(C) = \infty$ implies $h^*(C) = \infty$ (i.e., it is not possible to extend C into a configuration containing an instance t_R), then the unfolding can be stopped as soon as the f-value of the next event retrieved from the queue is ∞, since this implies that t_R is unreachable. We call heuristics that satisfy this property *safely pruning*. Note pruning safety is a weaker requirement than admissibility, in the sense that an admissible heuristic is always safely pruning.

Monotonicity is another well-known property of heuristic functions, which is stronger than admissibility. A heuristic h is *monotonic* iff it satisfies the triangle inequality $h(C) \leq |C'| - |C| + h(C')$, i.e., $f(C) \leq f(C')$, for all finite $C' \supseteq C$. If h is monotonic, the order $\prec_h$ is in fact adequate [4]. Even though admissibility does not imply monotonicity, it is in practice difficult to construct good admissible heuristics that are not monotonic. The admissible heuristic $h^{\max}$, described in the next section, is also monotonic.

Although ERV/fly depends on an order $\prec$ and a heuristic h, we consider only the case of $\prec_h$ and h for the same heuristic. Thus, we denote with ERV/fly$[h]$ the algorithm ERV/fly$[\prec_h, h]$, and with $\beta[h]$ the prefix computed by ERV/fly$[h]$. We first establish the correctness of the modified algorithm, and then relate the size of the computed prefix to the informedness of the heuristic.

Theorem 4. *Let h be a safely pruning heuristic function on configurations. Then,* ERV/fly$[h]$ *computes a finite prefix of the unfolding that is complete with respect to the goal marking, and this prefix is contained in that computed by* ERV$[h]$. *Furthermore, if h is admissible, then* ERV/fly$[h]$ *finds an optimal configuration if t_R is reachable. Both claims also hold for* ERV/fly$[\prec, h]$ *where $\prec$ is any semi-adequate order that refines $\prec_h$.*

Proof. ERV/fly$[h]$ is exactly ERV$[h]$ plus two conditions for early termination. As long as neither of these is invoked, ERV/fly$[h]$ behaves *exactly* like ERV$[h]$. If the positive condition (an instance of t_R is dequeued, line 9 in Algorithm 1) is met, t_R is clearly reachable and the the prefix computed by ERV/fly[h] contains a witnessing event. If the negative condition (the h-value of the next event in the queue is ∞, line 6 in Algorithm 1) is met, then the h-value of every event in the queue must be ∞. Since h is safely pruning, this implies none can be extended to a configuration including an instance of t_R. Thus, ERV$[h]$ will not find an instance of t_R either (even though it continues dequeueing these events, inserting them into the prefix and generating successor events until the queue is exhausted). Since ERV$[h]$ is complete, t_R must be unreachable.

As in ERV$[h]$, both claims hold also for any refinement of $\prec_h$. □

If the heuristic h does not assign infinite cost to any configuration, the negative condition can never come into effect and ERV/fly$[h]$ is simply a directed version of McMillan's on-the-fly algorithm. In particular, this holds for $h \equiv 0$.

The next result is that when heuristics are monotonic, improving the informedness of the heuristic can only lead to improved performance, in the sense of a smaller prefix being constructed. In particular, this implies that for any monotonic heuristic h, *the prefix $\beta[h]$ is never larger than that computed by* ERV/fly$[h \equiv 0]$, *regardless of whether the goal transition t_R is reachable or not.* This is not particularly surprising: it is well known in state space search, that – all else being equal – directing the search with a monotonic heuristic cannot result in a larger part of the state space being explored compared to blind search.

In order to compare the sizes of the prefixes computed with two different heuristics, we need to be sure that both algorithms *break ties when selecting events from the queue in a consistent manner.* For a formal definition, consider two instances of ERV/fly: ERV/fly$[h_1]$ and ERV/fly$[h_2]$. We say that a pair of events (e, e') is an inconsistent pair for both algorithms if and only if

1. $[e] \not\prec_{h_i} [e']$ and $[e'] \not\prec_{h_i} [e]$ for $i \in \{1, 2\}$,
2. there was a time t_1 in which e and e' were in the queue of ERV/fly$[h_1]$, and e was dequeued before e', and
3. there was a time t_2, not necessarily equal to t_1, in which e and e' were in the queue of ERV/fly$[h_2]$, and e' was dequeued before e.

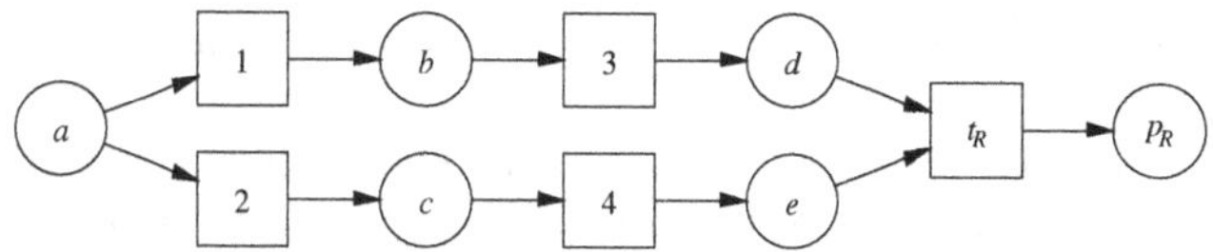

Fig. 2. Example net with an unreachable goal transition (t_R)

We say that ERV/fly$[h_1]$ and ERV/fly$[h_2]$ break ties in a consistent manner if and only if there are no inconsistent pairs between them.

Theorem 5. *If h_1 and h_2 are two monotonic heuristics such that $h_1 \leq h_2$, and* ERV/fly$[h_1]$ *and* ERV/fly$[h_2]$ *break ties in a consistent manner, then every event in $\beta[h_2]$ is also in $\beta[h_1]$.*

Since the all-zero heuristic is monotonic, it follows that the number of events in the prefix computed by ERV/fly$[h]$, for any other monotonic heuristic h, is never greater than the number of such events in the prefix computed by ERV/fly$[h \equiv 0]$, i.e., McMillan's algorithm (although this can, in the worst case, be exponential in the number of reachable states). As noted earlier, for completeness with respect to the goal marking, it is not necessary to insert cut-off events into the prefix (since the marking represented by the local configuration of such an event is already represented by another event in the prefix).

Although the same cannot, in general, be guaranteed for inadmissible heuristics, we demonstrate experimentally below that in practice, the prefix they compute is often significantly smaller than that found by blind ERV/fly, even when the target transition is not reachable. The explanation for this is that all the heuristics we use are safely pruning, which enables us to terminate the algorithm earlier (as soon as the h-value of the first event in the queue is ∞) without loss of completeness.

To illustrate, consider the example net in Fig. 2. Suppose initially only place a is marked: at this point, a heuristic such as $h^{\max}$ (defined in the next section) estimates that the goal marking $\{p_R\}$ is reachable in 3 steps (the max length of the two paths). However, as soon as either transition 1 or 2 is taken, leading to a configuration in which either place b or c is marked, the $h^{\max}$ estimate becomes ∞, since there is then no way to reach one of the two goal places.

Pruning safety is a weaker property than admissibility, as it pertains only to a subset of configurations (the dead-end configurations from which the goal is unreachable). Most heuristic functions satisfy it; in particular, so do all the specific heuristics we consider in this paper. Moreover, the heuristics we consider all have equal "pruning power", meaning they assign infinite estimated cost to the same set of configurations. There exist other heuristics, for example those based on pattern databases [20, 21], that have much greater pruning power.

Proof of Theorem 5

Recall that f^* denotes the size of an optimal configuration if one exists, and ∞ otherwise.

Lemma 1. *If h is admissible, all events in $\beta[h]$ have f-value $\leq f^*$.* □

Proof. If t_R is not reachable, $f^* = \infty$ and the claim holds trivially. Suppose t_R is reachable. Before the first event corresponding to t_R is dequeued, the queue always contains an event e part of the optimal configuration, which, due to admissibility, has $f([e]) \leq f^*$ (see proof of Theorem 1 (ii)). Thus, the f-value of the first event in the queue cannot be greater than f^*. When an instance of t_R is dequeued, ERV/fly$[h]$ stops. □

Lemma 2. *Let h be a monotonic heuristic. (i) If $e < e'$, i.e., e is a causal predecessor of e', then $f([e]) \leq f([e'])$. (ii) Let β' be any prefix of $\beta[h]$ (i.e., β' is the prefix constructed by* ERV/fly*[h] at some point before the algorithm terminates). If e is an event in β', then every event e' such that $h([e']) < \infty$, $[e'] - \{e'\}$ contains no cut-off event in β' with respect to $\prec_h$, and $[e'] \prec_h [e]$, is also in β'.* □

Proof. (i) Consider two events, e and e', such that $e < e'$, i.e., e is a causal predecessor of e'. Since $[e']$ is a finite extension of $[e]$, the definition of monotonicity states that $h([e]) \leq ||[e']|| - ||[e]|| + h([e'])$, which implies that $||[e]|| + h([e]) \leq ||[e']|| + h([e'])$, i.e., that $f([e]) \leq f([e'])$. Thus, in any causal chain of events $e_1 < \cdots < e_n$, it holds that $f([e_1]) \leq \cdots \leq f([e_n])$.

(ii) Let e and e' be events such that e is in β', $h([e']) < \infty$, $[e'] - \{e'\}$ contains no cut-off event in β' with respect to $\prec_h$, and $[e'] \prec_h [e]$. We show that e' must be dequeued before e. Since $[e']$ cannot contain any cut-off event, other than possibly e' itself, it will be added to the prefix when it is dequeued, because, at this point, e' cannot be in the set of recognised cut-off event (the set *cut-off* is only updated on line 12 in the algorithm). Since $e \in \beta'$, this implies that $e' \in \beta'$.

Either e' itself or some ancestor e'' of e' is in the queue at all times before e' is dequeued. By (i), $f([e'']) \leq f([e']) < \infty$ for every causal ancestor e'' of e', and since $||[e'']|| < ||[e']||$ we have $[e''] \prec_h [e']$ and therefore $[e''] \prec_h [e]$ (by transitivity of $\prec_h$). Thus, all ancestors of e' must be dequeued before e and, since their local configurations contain no cut-off events, added to the prefix. Thus, e' must be put into the queue before e is dequeued, and, since $[e'] \prec_h [e]$, it is dequeued before e. □

Lemma 3. *For any heuristic h, the event e is a cut-off event in prefix β with respect to $\prec_h$ if and only if e is a cut-off event in β with respect to $\prec_m$, where $\prec_m$ is McMillan's order, i.e., $[e] \prec_m [e']$ if and only if $||[e]|| < ||[e']||$.* □

Proof. If e is a cut-off event in β with respect to $\prec_h$, then there exists an event e' in β such that $\text{Mark}([e']) = \text{Mark}([e])$ and $[e'] \prec_h [e]$. The former implies that $h([e']) = h([e])$. The latter implies that either $f([e']) < f([e])$, or $f([e']) = f([e])$ and $||[e']|| < ||[e]||$. Both imply $||[e']|| < ||[e]||$ and so $[e'] \prec_m [e]$.

If e is a cut-off event in β with respect to $\prec_m$, then there is e' such that $\text{Mark}([e']) = \text{Mark}([e])$ and $||[e']|| < ||[e]||$. The former implies that $h([e']) = h([e])$. Therefore, $f([e']) < f([e])$ and so $[e'] \prec_h [e]$. □

Lemma 4. *For any monotonic heuristic h, an event $e \in \beta[h]$ is a cut-off with respect to $\prec_h$ in $\beta[h]$ iff e is a cut-off in the prefix β' built by* ERV/fly*[h] up to the point when e was inserted.* □

Proof. That e remains a cut-off event in the final prefix $\beta[h]$ if it was in β' is obvious.

If the h-value of the first event on the queue is ∞, ERV/fly terminates, without inserting the event into the prefix. Thus, since $e \in \beta[h]$, $h([e]) < \infty$.

If e is a cut-off event in $\beta[h]$ with respect to $\prec_h$, there exists an event $e' \in \beta[h]$ such that $\text{Mark}([e']) = \text{Mark}([e])$, $[e'] \prec_h [e]$, and $[e']$ contains no cut-off event. The first two properties of e' are by definition of cut-off events. For the last, suppose $[e']$ contains a cut-off event: then there is another event $e'' \in \beta[h]$, with the same marking and such that $[e''] \prec_h [e']$ (and thus by transitivity $[e''] \prec_h [e]$). If $[e'']$ contains a cut-off event, there is again another event, with the same marking and less according to the order: the recursion finishes at some point because the order $\prec_h$ is well-founded and the prefix $\beta[h]$ is finite. Thus, there is such an event whose local configuration does not contain a cut-off event: call it e'. Consider the prefix $\beta' \oplus \{e\}$ (i.e., the prefix immediately after e was inserted): since it contains e, by Lemma 2(*ii*) it also contains e'. □

Since ERV/fly never inserts into the prefix an event e such that $[e]$ contains an event that is a cut-off in the prefix at that point, it follows from Lemma 4 that if h is a monotonic heuristic, the final prefix $\beta[h]$ built by ERV/fly[h] upon termination contains no event that is the successor of a cut-off event.

Proof (of Theorem 5). Let f_1 and f_2 denote f-values with respect to h_1 and h_2, respectively, i.e., $f_1([e]) = |[e]| + h_1([e])$ and $f_2([e]) = |[e]| + h_2([e])$.

We show by induction on $|[e]|$ that every event $e \in \beta[h_2]$ such that $[e] - \{e\}$ contains no cut-off event in $\beta[h_2]$ with respect to $\prec_{h_2}$, *i.e.,*, such that e is not a *post*-cut-off event, is also in $\beta[h_1]$. As noted, by Lemma 4, ERV/fly directed with a monotonic heuristic never inserts any post-cut-off event into the prefix. Thus, it follows from the above claim that every event that may actually be in $\beta[h_2]$ is also in $\beta[h_1]$.

For $|[e]| = 0$ the claim holds because there are no such events in $\beta[h_2]$. Assume that it holds for $|[e]| < k$. Let $e \in \beta[h_2]$ with $[e] - \{e\}$ containing no cut-off events and $|[e]| = k$. By inductive hypothesis, all causal ancestors of e are in $\beta[h_1]$.

Ancestors of e are not cut-off events in $\beta[h_2]$ with respect to $\prec_{h_2}$ (if any of them were e would be a post-cut-off event). Assume some ancestor e' of e is a cut-off event in $\beta[h_1]$ with respect to $\prec_{h_1}$. Then, there is $e'' \in \beta[h_1]$ such that $\text{Mark}([e'']) = \text{Mark}([e'])$, $[e''] \prec_{h_1} [e']$ and $[e'']$ contains no cut-off event in $\beta[h_1]$ with respect to $\prec_{h_1}$ (by the same reasoning as in the proof of Lemma 4). If some event $e''' \in [e'']$ is a cut-off event in $\beta[h_2]$ with respect to $\prec_{h_2}$, then there exists an event e^4 in $\beta[h_2]$, with equal marking, $[e^4] \prec_{h_2} [e''']$, and such that $[e^4]$ contains no cut-off event. But $|[e^4]| < |[e''']| < |[e'']| < |[e']| < k$, so by the inductive hypothesis, e^4 is also in $\beta[h_1]$, and because $[e^4] \prec_{h_2} [e''']$ implies that $[e^4] \prec_{h_1} [e''']$ (by Lemma 3), this means that e''' is a cut-off event in $\beta[h_1]$ with respect to $\prec_{h_1}$. This contradicts the choice of e'' as an event such that

$[e'']$ contains no cut-off events in $\beta[h_1]$ with respect to $\prec_{h_1}$. Therefore, because $\|[e'']\| < \|[e']\|$, which implies $[e''] \prec_{h_2} [e']$ (by Lemma 3), it follows from Lemma 2 that e'' is in $\beta[h_2]$. This makes e' a cut-off event in $\beta[h_2]$ with respect to $\prec_{h_2}$, contradicting the fact that e was chosen to be a non-post-cut-off event in $\beta[h_2]$. Thus, no ancestor of e is a cut-off event in $\beta[h_1]$ with respect to $\prec_{h_1}$. It remains to show that e must be dequeued by $\mathsf{ERV/fly}[h_1]$ before it terminates: since ancestors of e are not cut-off events in $\beta[h_1]$ with respect to $\prec_{h_1}$, it follows from Lemma 4 that they are not cut-off events in the prefix built by $\mathsf{ERV/fly}[h_1]$ at that point either, and therefore that, when dequeued, e is inserted into $\beta[h_1]$ by $\mathsf{ERV/fly}[h_1]$.

First, assume that t_R is reachable. By Theorem 4, there is an instance e_R^1 of t_R in $\beta[h_1]$ and an instance e_R^2 of t_R in $\beta[h_2]$ with $\|[e_R^1]\| = \|[e_R^2]\| = f^*$. By Lemma 1, $f_2([e]) \leq f_2([e_R^2]) = f^*$ and thus, since $h_1([e]) \leq h_2([e])$, $f_1([e]) \leq f^*$. We do an analysis by cases:

- If $f_1([e]) < f^*$, then $[e] \prec_{h_1} [e_R^1]$ and, by Lemma 2, e is in $\beta[h_1]$.
- If $f_1([e]) = f^*$ and $\|[e]\| < \|[e_R^1]\|$, then $[e] \prec_{h_1} [e_R^1]$ and e is in $\beta[h_1]$.
- If $f_1([e]) = f^*$, $\|[e]\| = \|[e_R^1]\|$ and $e = e_R^1$, then e is in $\beta[h_1]$.
- $f_1([e]) = f^*$, $\|[e]\| = \|[e_R^1]\|$ and $e \neq e_R^1$: e was in the queue of $\mathsf{ERV/fly}[h_1]$ when e_R^1 was dequeued because all causal ancestors of e were in $\beta[h_1]$ at that time (because their f-values are all less than or equal to f^* and the size of their local configurations is strictly smaller). Thus, $\mathsf{ERV/fly}[h_1]$ chose to dequeue e_R^1 before e (and terminated). We show that $\mathsf{ERV/fly}[h_2]$ must have chosen to dequeue e before e_R^1 even though e_R^1 was in the queue of $\mathsf{ERV/fly}[h_2]$, and thus the two algorithms do not break ties in a consistent manner, contradicting the assumptions of the theorem. All causal ancestors e' of e_R^1 satisfy $[e'] \prec_{h_2} [e_R^2]$ and therefore, by Lemma 2, are in $\beta[h_2]$. Hence, when e is dequeued by $\mathsf{ERV/fly}[h_2]$, e_R^1 is in the queue. It cannot be in $\beta[h_2]$ since this would imply termination of $\mathsf{ERV/fly}[h_2]$ before adding e. Thus, $\mathsf{ERV/fly}[h_2]$ chose e over e_R^1.

Next, assume that t_R is unreachable. In this case, $\mathsf{ERV/fly}[h_1]$ can terminate only when the queue is empty or the h-value of the first event in the queue is ∞. The former cannot happen before $\mathsf{ERV/fly}[h_1]$ dequeues e, because all ancestors of e are in $\beta[h_1]$ and thus e was inserted into the queue of $\mathsf{ERV/fly}[h_1]$. Since $e \in \beta[h_2]$, $h_2([e]) < \infty$ (recall that $\mathsf{ERV/fly}$ never inserts an event with infinite h-value into the prefix), and therefore $h_1([e]) < \infty$. Thus, the latter also cannot happen before $\mathsf{ERV/fly}[h_1]$ dequeues e, because e was in the queue of $\mathsf{ERV/fly}[h_1]$ and its h-value is less than ∞. □

4 Heuristics

A common approach to constructing heuristic functions, both admissible and inadmissible, is to define a *relaxation* of the search problem, such that the relaxed problem can be solved, or at least approximated, efficiently, and then use the cost of the relaxed solution as an estimate of the cost of the solution to the real problem, i.e., as the heuristic value [22]. The problem of extending a configuration C of the unfolding into one whose marking includes the target place p_R is equivalent to the problem of reaching p_R starting from Mark(C): this is the problem that we relax to obtain an estimate of the distance to reach p_R from C.

The heuristics we have experimented with are derived from two different relaxations, both developed in the area of AI planning. The first relaxation is to assume that the cost of reaching each place in a set of places is independent of the others. For a transition t to fire, each place in ${}^\bullet t$ must be marked: thus, the estimated distance from a given marking M to a marking where t can fire is $d(M, {}^\bullet t) = \max_{p \in {}^\bullet t} d(M, \{p\})$, where $d(M, \{p\})$ denotes the estimated distance from M to any marking that includes $\{p\}$. For a place p to be marked – if it is not marked already – at least one transition in ${}^\bullet p$ must fire: thus, $d(M, \{p\}) = 1 + \min_{t \in {}^\bullet p} d(M, {}^\bullet t)$. Combining the two facts we obtain

$$d(M, M') = \begin{cases} 0 & \text{if } M' \subseteq M \\ 1 + \min_{t \in {}^\bullet p} d(M, {}^\bullet t) & \text{if } M' = \{p\} \\ \max_{p \in M'} d(M, \{p\}) & \text{otherwise} \end{cases} \quad (1)$$

for the estimated distance from a marking M to M'. Equation (1) defines only estimated distances to places that are reachable, in the relaxed sense, from M; the distance to any place that is not is taken to be ∞. A solution can be computed in polynomial time, by solving what is essentially a shortest path problem. We obtain a heuristic function, called $h^{\max}$, by $h^{\max}(C) = d(\text{Mark}(C), \{p_R\})$, where $t_R{}^\bullet = \{p_R\}$. This estimate is never greater than the actual distance, so the $h^{\max}$ heuristic is admissible.

In many cases, however, $h^{\max}$ is too weak to effectively guide the unfolding. Admissible heuristics in general tend to be conservative (since they need to ensure that the distance to the goal is not overestimated) and therefore less discriminating between different configurations. Inadmissible heuristics, on the other hand, have a greater freedom in assigning values and are therefore often more informative, in the sense that the relative values of different configurations is a stronger indicator of how "promising" the configurations are. An inadmissible, but often more informative, version of the $h^{\max}$ heuristic, called h^{sum}, can be obtained by substituting $\sum_{p \in M'} d(M, \{p\})$ for the last clause of Eq. (1). h^{sum} dominates $h^{\max}$, i.e., for any C, $h^{\text{sum}}(C) \geq h^{\max}(C)$. However, since the above modification of Eq. (1) changes only estimated distances to places that are reachable, in the relaxed sense, h^{sum} is still safely pruning, and in fact has the same pruning power as $h^{\max}$.

The second relaxation is known as the *delete relaxation*. In Petri net terms, the simplifying assumption made in this relaxation is that a transition only requires the presence of a token in each place in its preset, but does not consume those tokens when fired (put another way, all arcs leading into a transition are assumed to be read-arcs). This implies that a place once marked will never be unmarked, and therefore that any reachable marking is reachable by a "short" transition sequence. Every marking that is reachable in the original net is a subset of a marking that is reachable in the relaxed problem. The delete-relaxed problem

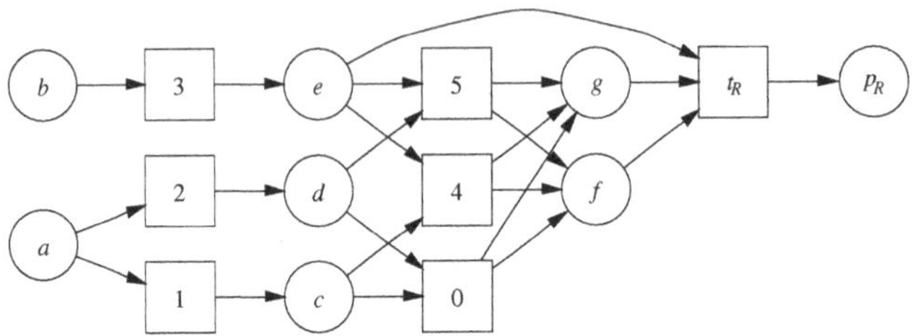

Fig. 3. Relaxed plan graph corresponding to the P/T-net in Fig. 1

has the property that a solution – if one exists – can be found in polynomial time. The procedure for doing this constructs a so called "relaxed plan graph", which may be viewed as a kind of unfolding of the relaxed problem. Because of the delete relaxation, the construction of the relaxed plan graph is much simpler than unfolding a Petri net, and the resulting graph is conflict-free[7] and of bounded size (each transition appears at most once in it). Once the graph has been constructed, a solution (configuration leading to p_R) is extracted; in case there are multiple transitions marking a place, one is chosen arbitrarily. The size of the solution to the relaxed problem gives a heuristic function, called h^{FF} (after the planning system FF [9] which was the first to use it). Figure 3 shows the relaxed plan graph corresponding to the P/T-net in Fig. 1: solutions include, e.g. the sequences $2, 3, 5, t_R$; $1, 3, 4, t_R$; and $1, 2, 0, 3, t_R$. The FF heuristic satisfies the conditions required to preserve the completeness of the unfolding (in Theorem 1) and it is safely pruning, but, because an arbitrary solution is extracted from the relaxed plan graph, it is not admissible. The heuristic defined by the size of the *minimal* solution to the delete-relaxed problem, known as h^+, is admissible, but solving the relaxed problem optimally is NP-hard [23].

The relaxing assumption of independence of reachability underlying the $h^{\max}$ heuristic is implied by the delete relaxation. This means $h^{\max}$ can also be seen as an (admissible) approximation of h^+, and that $h^{\max}$ is dominated by h^{FF}. However, the independence relaxation can be generalised by considering dependencies between sets of places of limited size (e.g. pairs), which makes it different from the delete relaxation [24].

5 Experimental Results

We extended Mole to use the $\prec_h$ ordering with the $h^{\max}$, h^{sum}, and h^{FF} heuristics. In our experiments below we compare the resulting directed versions of Mole with the original (breadth-first) version, and demonstrate that the former can solve much larger instances than were previously within the reach of

[7] Technically, delete relaxation can destroy the 1-boundedness of the net. However, the exact number of tokens in a place does not matter, but only whether the place is marked or not, so in the construction of the relaxed plan graph, two transitions marking the same place are not considered a conflict.

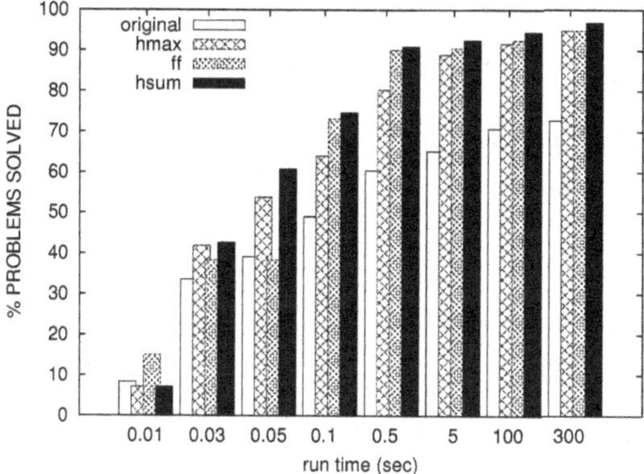

Fig. 4. Results for DARTES Instances

the unfolding technique. We found that the additional tie-breaking comparisons used by MOLE to make the order strict were slowing down all versions (including the original): though they do – sometimes – reduce the size of the prefix, the computational overhead quickly consumes any advantage. (As an example, on the unsolvable random problems considered below, the total reduction in size amounted to less than 1%, while the increase in runtime was around 20%.) We therefore disabled them in all experiments.[8] Experiments were conducted on a Pentium M 1.7 GHz with a 2 Gb memory limit. The nets used in the experiments can be found at `http://rsise.anu.edu.au/~thiebaux/benchmarks/petri`.

5.1 Petri Net Benchmarks

First, we tested directed MOLE on a set of standard Petri net benchmarks representative of Corbett's examples [25]. However, in all but two of these, the blind version of MOLE is able to decide the reachability of any transition in a matter of seconds. The two problems that presented a challenge are DARTES, which models the communication skeleton of an Ada program, and DME12. [9]

DARTES is the one where heuristic guidance shows the greatest impact. Lengths of the shortest firing sequences required to reach each of the 253 transitions in this problem reach over 90 events, and the breadth-first version could not solve any instance with a shortest solution length over 60. Overall, the undirected version is able to decide 185 of the 253 instances (73%), whereas the version directed by h^{sum} solves 245 (97%). The instances solved by each directed version is a strict superset of those solved by the original. Unsurprisingly, all the solved problems were positive decisions (the transitions were reachable). Figure 4 presents the percentage of reachability problems decided by each version of MOLE within increasing time limits. The breadth-first version is systematically outperformed by all directed versions.

[8] Thus, our breadth-first MOLE actually implements McMillan's ordering [1].

[9] It has since been pointed out to us that the DME12 problem is not 1-safe, and thus not suitable for either blind or directed MOLE.

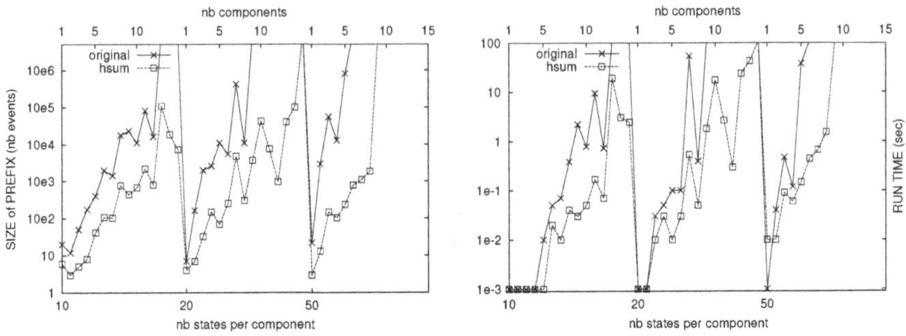

Fig. 5. Results for first set of Random P/T-nets

In the DME12 benchmark, blind MOLE finds solutions for 406 of the 588 transitions, and runs out of memory on the rest. Solution lengths are much shorter in this benchmark: the longest found by the blind version is 29 steps. Thus, it is more difficult to improve over breadth-first search. Nevertheless, MOLE directed with $h^{\max}$ solves an additional 26 problems, one with a solution length of 37. MOLE with the h^{sum} and h^{FF} performs worse on this benchmark.

5.2 Random Problems

To further investigate the scalability of directed unfolding, we implemented our own generator of random Petri nets. Conceptually, the generator creates a set of component automata, and connects them in an acyclic dependency network. The transition graph of each component automaton is a sparse, but strongly connected, random digraph. Synchronisations between pairs of component automata are such that only one (the dependent) automaton changes state, but can only do so when the other component automaton is in a particular state. Synchronisations are chosen randomly, constrained by the acyclic dependency graph. Target states for the various automata are chosen independently at random. The construction ensures that every choice of target states is reachable. We generated random problems featuring $1 \ldots 15$ component automata of 10, 20, and 50 states each. The resulting Petri nets range from 10 places and 30 transitions to 750 places and over 4,000 transitions.

Results are shown in Fig. 5. The left-hand graph shows the number of events pulled out of the queue. The right-hand graph shows the run-time. To avoid cluttering the graphs, we show only the performance of the worst and best strategy, namely the original one, and h^{sum}. Evidently, directed unfolding can solve much larger problems than blind unfolding. For the largest instances we considered, the gap reached over 2 orders of magnitude in speed and 3 in size. The original version could merely solve the easier half of the problems, while directed unfolding only failed on 6 of the largest instances (with 50 states per component).

In these problems, optimal firing sequences reach lengths of several hundreds events. On instances which we were able to solve optimally using $h^{\max}$, h^{FF}

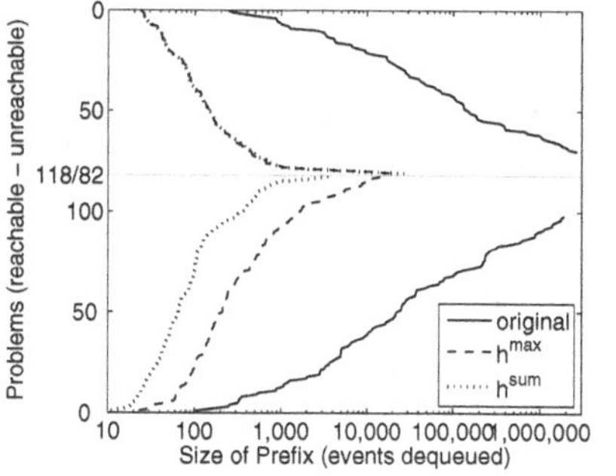

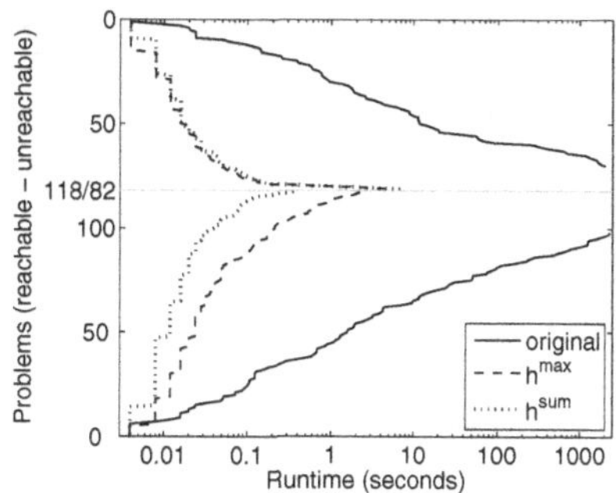

Fig. 6. Results for second set of Random P/T-nets

produced solutions within a couple transitions of the optimal. Over all problems, solutions obtained with h^{sum} were a bit longer than those obtained with h^{FF}.

With only a small modification, viz. changing the transition graph of each component automaton into a (directed) tree-like structure instead of a strongly connected graph, the random generator can also produce problems in which the goal marking has a fair chance of being unreachable. To explore the effect of directing the unfolding in this case, we generated 200 such instances (each with 10 components of 10 states per component), of which 118 turned out to be reachable and 82 unreachable, respectively. Figure 6 shows the results, in the form of distribution curves (prefix size on the left and run-time on the right; note that scales are logarithmic). The lower curve is for solvable problems, while the upper, "inverse" curve, is for problems where the goal marking is not reachable. Thus, the point on the horizontal axis where the two curves meet on the vertical is where, for the hardest instance, the reachability question has been answered.

As expected, h^{sum} solves instances where the goal marking is reachable faster than h^{max}, which is in turn much faster than blind unfolding. However, also in those instances where the goal marking is not reachable, the prefix generated by directed unfolding is significantly smaller than that generated by the original algorithm. In this case, results of using the two heuristics are nearly indistinguishable. This is due to the fact that, as mentioned earlier, their pruning power (ability to detect dead end configurations) is the same.

5.3 Planning Benchmarks

To assess the performance of directed unfolding on a wider range of problems with realistic structure, we also considered some benchmarks from the 4th International Planning Competition. These are described in PDDL (the Planning Domain Definition Language), which we translate into 1-bounded P/T-nets as explained in [4]. Note that runtimes reported below do not include the time for this translation.

The top two rows of Fig. 7, show results for 29 instances from the IPC-4 domain AIRPORT (an airport ground-traffic control problem) and 30 instances from the IPC-4 domain PIPESWORLD (a petroleum transportation problem), respectively. The corresponding Petri nets range from 49 places and 18 transitions

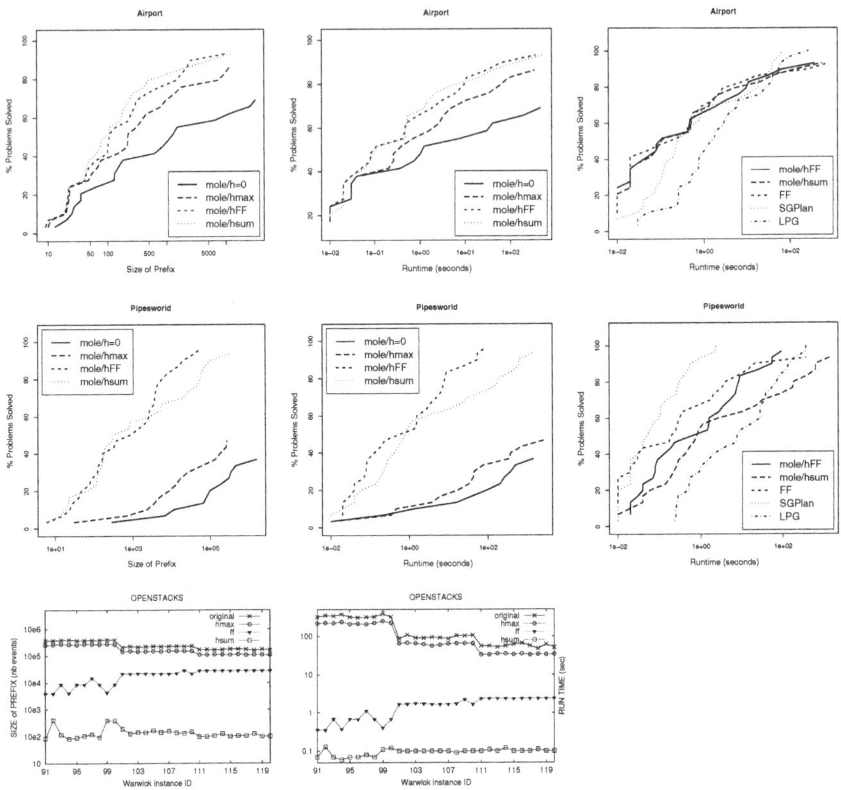

Fig. 7. Results for Planning Benchmarks AIRPORT (*top row*) and PIPESWORLD (*middle row*), and the OPENSTACKS problem (*bottom row*)

(AIRPORT instance 1) to 3,418 places and 2,297 transitions (AIRPORT instance 28). The length of optimal solutions, where known, range from 8 to over 160.

Graphs in the first and second columns show cumulative distributions of the number of dequeued events and runtime, respectively, for four different configurations of MOLE: using no heuristic (i.e., $h \equiv 0$), $h^{\max}$, h^{FF} and h^{sum}. Evidently, directed unfolding is much more efficient than blind, in particular when using the inadmissible h^{FF} and h^{sum} heuristics. The original version of MOLE fails to solve 9 instances in the AIRPORT domain, running out of either time (600s) or memory (1 Gb), while MOLE with $h^{\max}$ solves all but 4 and MOLE with h^{FF} and h^{sum} all but 2 instances (only one instance remains unsolved by all configurations). In the PIPESWORLD domain, blind MOLE solves only 11 instances, while guided with h^{FF} it solves all but 1.

Graphs in the last column compare the runtimes of the two faster, suboptimal, MOLE configurations with three domain-independent planning systems that are representative of the state-of-the-art. Note that these planning systems implement many sophisticated techniques besides heuristic search guidance. Also, all three are *incomplete*, in the sense that they are not guaranteed to find a solution even when one exists. While the directed unfolder is generally not the fastest, it is not consistently the slowest either. Moreover, with the h^{FF} heuristic, MOLE is very good at finding short solutions in the PIPESWORLD domain: in 14 of the 30 instances it finds solutions that are shorter than the best found by any suboptimal planner that participated in the competition, and only in one instance does it find a longer solution. In the AIRPORT domain, all planners find solutions of the same length.

The last row of Fig. 7 shows results for an encoding of the OPEN STACKS problem (a production scheduling problem) as a planning problem. A different encoding of this problem (which disabled all concurrency) was used in the fifth planning competition. The corresponding Petri nets all have 65 places and 222 transitions, but differ in their initial markings. Optimal solution lengths vary between 35 and 40 firings. This is an optimisation problem: solving it optimally is NP-complete [26], but only finding any solution is quite trivial. We include this benchmark specifically to illustrate that restricting search to optimal solutions can be very costly. The gap between suboptimal and optimal length unfolding is spectacular: MOLE using the h^{sum} heuristic consistently spends around 0.1 seconds solving each problem, while with the admissible $h^{\max}$ heuristic or no heuristic at all it requires over 50s. This shows that directed unfolding, which unlike breadth-first search is not confined to optimal solutions, can exploit the fact that non-optimal OPENSTACKS is an easy problem.

6 Conclusion, Related and Future Work

We have described directed unfolding, which incorporates heuristic search straight into an on-the-fly reachability analysis technique specific to Petri nets. We proved that the ERV unfolding algorithm can benefit from using heuristic search strategies, whilst preserving finiteness and completeness of the generated prefix. Such strategies are effective for on-the-fly reachability analysis, as they significantly reduce the prefix explored to find a desired marking or to prove that none exists. We demonstrated that suitable heuristic functions can be automatically extracted from the original net. Both admissible and non-admissible heuristics can be used, with the former offering optimality guarantees. Experimental results show that directed unfolding provides a significant performance improvement over the original breadth-first implementation of ERV featured in MOLE.

Edelkamp and Jabbar [27] recently introduced a method for directed model-checking Petri nets. It operates by translating the deadlock detection problem into a metric planning problem, solved using off-the-shelf heuristic search planning methods. These methods, however, do not exploit concurrency in the powerful way that unfolding does. In contrast, our approach combines the best of heuristic search and Petri net reachability analysis. Results on planning benchmarks show that directed unfolding with inadmissible heuristics is competitive (in the sense of not being consistently outperformed) with some of the current state-of-the-art domain-independent planners.

The equivalent of read-arcs is a prominent feature of many planning problems. In our translation to Petri nets, these are represented by the usual "consume-and-produce" loop, which forces sequencing of events that read the same place and thus may reduce the level of concurrency (although this does not happen in the two domains we used in our experiments; they are exceptional in that respect). We believe that a treatment of read-arcs that preserves concurrency, such as the use of place replication [28], is essential to improve the performance of directed unfolding applied to planning in the general case, and addressing this is a high priority item on our future work agenda.

In this paper, we have measured the cost of a configuration C by its cardinality, i.e., $g(C) = |C|$. Or similarly, $g(C) = \sum_{e \in C} c(e)$ with $c(e) = 1 \; \forall e \in E$. These results extend to transitions having arbitrary non-negative cost values, i.e., $c : E \to \mathbb{R}$. Consequently, using any admissible heuristic strategy, we can find the minimum cost firing sequence leading to t_R. As in the cardinality case, the algorithm is still correct using non-admissible heuristics, but does not guarantee optimality. The use of unfolding for solving optimisation problems involving cost, probability and time, is a focus of our current research.

We also plan to use heuristic strategies to guide the unfolding of higher level Petri nets, such as coloured nets [29]. Our motivation, again arising from our work in the area of planning, is that our translation from PDDL to P/T-nets is sometimes the bottleneck of our planning via unfolding approach [4]. Well developed tools such as PUNF[10] could be adapted for experiments in this area.

Acknowledgments. It was our colleague Lang White who first recognised the potential of exploring the connections between planning and unfolding-based reachability analysis; we are very thankful and much endebted to him. Many thanks to several of the UFO-07 participants for very insightful discussions. In particular, thanks to Eric Fabre, Victor Khomenko, and Walter Vogler, whose comments helped to significantly improve this paper. The TopNoc reviewers also provided insightful comments, for which we are thankful. Thanks also to Jussi Rintanen and John Slaney for their help with various aspects of this work at some stage or another, and to Stefan Schwoon for his help with MOLE. The authors thank NICTA and DSTO for their support via the DPOLP project. NICTA is funded through the Australian Government's *Backing Australia's Ability* initiative, in part through the ARC.

References

1. McMillan, K.L.: Using unfoldings to avoid the state explosion problem in the verification of asynchronous circuits. In: Probst, D.K., von Bochmann, G. (eds.) CAV 1992. LNCS, vol. 663, pp. 164–177. Springer, Heidelberg (1993)
2. Esparza, J.: Model checking using net unfoldings. Science of Computer Programming 23(2-3), 151–195 (1994)

---

[10] http://homepages.cs.ncl.ac.uk/victor.khomenko/tools/tools.html

3. Benveniste, A., Fabre, E., Jard, C., Haar, S.: Diagnosis of asynchronous discrete event systems, a net unfolding approach. IEEE Trans. on Automatic Control 48(5), 714–727 (2003)
4. Hickmott, S., Rintanen, J., Thiébaux, S., White, L.: Planning via Petri net unfolding. In: Proc. of 20th Int. Joint Conference on Artificial Intelligence, pp. 1904–1911. AAAI Press, Menlo Park (2007)
5. Esparza, J., Römer, S., Vogler, W.: An improvement of McMillan's unfolding algorithm. Formal Methods in System Design 20(3), 285–310 (2002)
6. Esparza, J., Schröter, C.: Unfolding based algorithms for the reachability problem. Fundamentia Informatica 46, 1–17 (2001)
7. Esparza, J., Kanade, P., Schwoon, S.: A negative result on depth first unfolding. Software Tools for Technology Transfer (2007)
8. Bonet, B., Geffner, H.: Planning as heuristic search. Artificial Intelligence 129(1-2), 5–33 (2001)
9. Hoffmann, J., Nebel, B.: The FF planning system: fast plan generation through heuristic search. Journal of Artificial Intelligence Research 14, 253–302 (2001)
10. McDermott, D.: Using regression-match graphs to control search in planning. Artificial Intelligence 109(1-2), 111–159 (1999)
11. Murata, T.: Petri nets: properties, analysis and applications. Proceedings of the IEEE 77(4), 541–580 (1989)
12. Chatain, T., Khomenko, V.: On the well-foundedness of adequate orders used for construction of complete unfolding prefixes. Information Processing Letters 104, 129–136 (2007)
13. Khomenko, V., Koutny, M.: Towards an efficient algorithm for unfolding Petri nets. In: Larsen, K.G., Nielsen, M. (eds.) CONCUR 2001. LNCS, vol. 2154, pp. 366–380. Springer, Heidelberg (2001)
14. Cheng, A., Esparza, J., Palsberg, J.: Complexity results for 1-safe nets. In: Shyamasundar, R.K. (ed.) FSTTCS 1993. LNCS, vol. 761, pp. 326–337. Springer, Heidelberg (1993)
15. Melzer, S.: Verifikation Verteilter Systeme Mittels Linearer–und Constraint-Programmierung. PhD thesis, Technische Universität München (1998)
16. Heljanko, K.: Using Logic Programs with stable model semantics to solve deadlock and reachability problems for 1-safe Petri nets. In: Cleaveland, W.R. (ed.) TACAS 1999. LNCS, vol. 1579, pp. 240–254. Springer, Heidelberg (1999)
17. Khomenko, V., Koutny, M.: LP deadlock checking using partial order dependencies. In: Palamidessi, C. (ed.) CONCUR 2000. LNCS, vol. 1877, pp. 410–425. Springer, Heidelberg (2000)
18. Edelkamp, S., Lluch-Lafuente, A., Leue, S.: Directed explicit model checking with HSF-SPIN. In: Dwyer, M.B. (ed.) SPIN 2001. LNCS, vol. 2057, pp. 57–79. Springer, Heidelberg (2001)
19. Khomenko, V., Koutny, M., Vogler, W.: Canonical prefixes of Petri net unfoldings. Acta Informatica 40(2), 95–118 (2003)
20. Edelkamp, S.: Planning with pattern databases. In: Proc. 6th European Conf. on Planning. LNCS, pp. 13–24. Springer, Heidelberg (2001)
21. Haslum, P., Bonet, B., Geffner, H.: New admissible heuristics for domain-independent planning. In: Proc. 20th National Conf. on Artificial Intelligence, pp. 1163–1168. AAAI Press / MIT Press (2005)
22. Pearl, J.: Heuristics: Intelligent Search Strategies for Computer Problem Solving. Addison-Wesley, Reading (1984)
23. Bylander, T.: The computational complexity of propositional STRIPS planning. Artificial Intelligence 69(1-2), 165–204 (1994)

24. Haslum, P., Geffner, H.: Admissible heuristic for optimal planning. In: Proc. 6th International Conf. on Artificial Intelligence Planning and Scheduling, Breckenridge, CO, pp. 140–149. AAAI Press, Menlo Park (2000)
25. Corbett, J.C.: Evaluating deadlock detection methods for concurrent software. IEEE Trans. on Software Engineering 22(3) (1996)
26. Linhares, A., Yanasse, H.H.: Connection between cutting-pattern sequencing, VLSI design and flexible machines. Computers & Operations Research 29, 1759–1772 (2002)
27. Edelkamp, S., Jabbar, S.: Action planning for directed model checking of Petri nets. Electronic Notes Theoretical Computer Science 149(2), 3–18 (2006)
28. Vogler, W., Semenov, A., Yakovlev, A.: Unfolding and finite prefix for nets with read arcs. In: Sangiorgi, D., de Simone, R. (eds.) CONCUR 1998. LNCS, vol. 1466, pp. 501–516. Springer, Heidelberg (1998)
29. Khomenko, V., Koutny, M.: Branching processes of high-level Petri nets. In: Garavel, H., Hatcliff, J. (eds.) TACAS 2003. LNCS, vol. 2619, pp. 458–472. Springer, Heidelberg (2003)

McMillan's Complete Prefix for Contextual Nets*

Paolo Baldan[1], Andrea Corradini[2], Barbara König[3], and Stefan Schwoon[4]

[1] Dipartimento di Matematica Pura e Applicata, Università di Padova, Padua, Italy
[2] Dipartimento di Informatica, Università di Pisa, Pisa, Italy
[3] Abteilung für Informatik und Angewandte Kognitionswissenschaft, Universität Duisburg-Essen, Duisburg, Germany
[4] Institut für Informatik (I7), Technische Universität München, Munich, Germany

Abstract. In a seminal paper, McMillan proposed a technique for constructing a finite complete prefix of the unfolding of bounded (i.e., finite-state) Petri nets, which can be used for verification purposes. Contextual nets are a generalisation of Petri nets suited to model systems with read-only access to resources. When working with contextual nets, a finite complete prefix can be obtained by applying McMillan's construction to a suitable encoding of the contextual net into an ordinary net. However, it has been observed that if the unfolding is itself a contextual net, then the complete prefix can be significantly smaller than the one obtained with the above technique. A construction for generating such a contextual complete prefix has been proposed for a special class of nets, called read-persistent. In this paper, we propose an algorithm that works for arbitrary semi-weighted, bounded contextual nets. The construction explicitly takes into account the fact that, unlike in ordinary or read-persistent nets, an event can have several different histories in general contextual net computations.

Keywords: Petri nets, read arcs, unfolding, complete finite prefix, verification.

1 Introduction

In recent years there has been a growing interest in the use of partial-order semantics to deal with the state-explosion problem when model checking concurrent systems. In particular, a thread of research that started with the seminal work by McMillan [11,12] proposes the use of the *unfolding* semantics as a basis for the verification of finite-state systems, modelled as Petri nets.

The unfolding of a Petri net, originally introduced in [15], is a safe, acyclic *occurrence* net that completely expresses its behaviour. For non-trivial nets the unfolding can be infinite even if the original net is *bounded*, i.e., it has a finite

* Research partially supported by EU IST-2004-16004 SENSORIA, MIUR Project ART, DFG project SANDS and CRUI/DAAD VIGONI "Models based on Graph Transformation Systems: Analysis and Verification".

K. Jensen, W. van der Aalst, and J. Billington (Eds.): ToPNoC I, LNCS 5100, pp. 199–220, 2008.

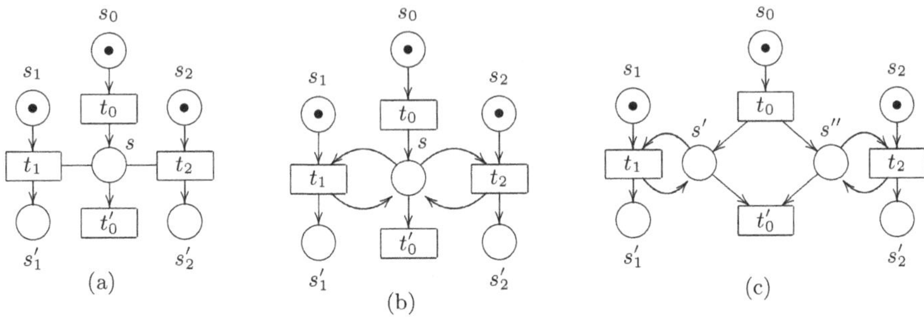

Fig. 1. (a) A safe contextual net; (b) its encoding by replacing read arcs with consume/produce loops; (c) its concurrency-preserving PR-encoding

number of reachable states. McMillan's algorithm constructs a *finite complete prefix*, i.e., a subnet of the unfolding such that each marking reachable in the original net corresponds to some concurrent set of places in such a prefix.

Contextual nets [14], also called nets with test arcs [5], activator arcs [9] or read arcs [18], extend ordinary nets with the possibility of checking for the presence of tokens without consuming them. The possibility of faithfully representing concurrent read accesses to resources allows one to model in a natural way phenomena like concurrent access to shared data (e.g. reading in a database) [17], to provide concurrent semantics to concurrent constraint programs [13], to model priorities [8] or to conveniently analyse asynchronous circuits [19].

When working with contextual nets, if one is interested only in reachable markings, it is well-known that read arcs can be replaced by consume/produce loops (see Fig. 1a and b), obtaining an ordinary net with the same reachability graph. However, when one unfolds the net obtained by this transformation, the number of transitions and places might explode due to the sequentialization imposed on readers. A cleverer encoding, proposed in [19] and hereafter referred to as the *place-replication encoding* (*PR-encoding*), consists of creating "private" copies of the read places for each reader (see Fig. 1c). In this way, for safe nets the encoding does not lead to a loss of concurrency, and thus the explosion of the number of events and places in the unfolding can be mitigated.

A construction that applies to contextual nets and produces an unfolding that is itself a contextual (occurrence) net has been proposed independently by Vogler, Semenov and Yakovlev in [19] and by the first two authors with Montanari in [3]. In particular, the (prefixes of the) unfolding obtained with this construction can be much smaller than in both encodings mentioned above.

Unfortunately, as discussed in [19], McMillan's construction of the finite complete prefix does not extend straightforwardly to the whole class of contextual nets. The authors of [19] propose a natural generalization of McMillan's algorithm which takes into account some specific features of contextual nets, but they show that their approach only works for contextual nets that are *read-persistent*, i.e., where there is no interference between preconditions and context conditions:

any two transitions t_1 and t_2 such that t_1 consumes a token that is read by t_2 cannot be enabled at the same time. Similarly, the algorithm proposed in [2], where McMillan's approach was generalised to graph grammars, is designed for a restricted class of grammars, which are the graph-grammar-theoretical counterpart of read-persistent nets.

The algorithms of [19] and [2] fail on non-read-persistent systems because, in general, a transition of a contextual occurrence net can have more than one possible *causal history* (or *local configuration*, according to [19]): this happens, for example, when a transition consumes a token which could be read by another transition. In this situation, McMillan's original *cut-off* condition (used by the algorithms in [19] and [2]) is not adequate anymore, because it considers a single causal history for each event (see also the example discussed in Sect. 3).

In this paper, we present a generalization of McMillan's construction that applies to arbitrary bounded *semi-weighted* contextual nets, i.e., Place/Transition contextual nets where the initial marking and the post-set of each transition are sets rather than proper multisets: this class of nets strictly includes safe contextual nets. The proposed algorithm explicitly takes into account the possible histories of events, and generates from a finite bounded semi-weighted contextual net a finite complete prefix of its unfolding. The same constructions and results could have been developed for general weighted contextual nets, at the price of some technical (not conceptual) complications.

As in McMillan's original work, the key concept here is that of a cut-off event, which is, roughly, an event in the unfolding that, together with its causal history, does not contribute to generating new markings. We prove that the natural generalisation of the notion of cut-off that takes into account all the possible histories of each event is theoretically fine, in the sense that the maximal cut-off-free prefix of the unfolding is complete. However, this characterisation is not constructive in general, since an event can have infinitely many histories. We show how this problem can be solved by restricting, for each event, to a finite subset of "useful" histories, which really contribute to generating new states.

The interest of this approach is twofold. From a theoretical point of view, the resulting algorithm extends [19] since it applies uniformly to the full class of contextual nets (and, for read-persistent nets, it specialises to [19]). From a practical point of view, with respect to the approach based on the construction of the complete finite prefix of the PR-encoding, we foresee several improvements. For safe nets the proposed technique produces a smaller unfolding prefix (once the histories recorded for generating the prefix are disregarded) and it has a comparable efficiency (we conjecture that the histories considered when unfolding a safe contextual net correspond exactly to the events obtained by unfolding its PR-encoding). Additionally, our technique appears to be more efficient for non-safe nets and it looks sufficiently general to be extended to other formalisms able to model concurrent read accesses to part of the state, like graph transformation systems, for which the encoding approach does not seem viable.

The paper is structured as follows. In Sect. 2, we introduce contextual nets and their unfolding semantics. In Sect. 3, we characterise a finite complete prefix of the unfolding for finite-state contextual nets, relying on a generalised notion of cut-off and in Sect. 4 we describe an algorithm for constructing a complete finite prefix. Finally, in Sect. 5 we draw some conclusions.

2 Contextual Nets and Their Unfolding

In this section, we introduce the basics of marked contextual P/T nets [17,14] and we review their unfolding semantics as defined in [19,3].

2.1 Contextual Nets

We first recall some notation for multisets. Let A be a set; a *multiset* of A is a function $M : A \to \mathbb{N}$. It is called finite if $\{a \in A : M(a) > 0\}$ is finite. The set of finite multisets of A is denoted by $\mu_* A$. The usual operations on multisets, like multiset union $\oplus$ or multiset difference $\ominus$, are used. We write $M \leq M'$ if $M(a) \leq M'(a)$ for all $a \in A$. If $M \in \mu_* A$, we denote by $[\![M]\!]$ the multiset defined, for all $a \in A$, as $[\![M]\!](a) = 1$ if $M(a) > 0$, and $[\![M]\!](a) = 0$ otherwise. A *multirelation* $f : A \leftrightarrow B$ is a multiset of $A \times B$. It is called *finitary* if $\{b \in B : f(a,b) > 0\}$ is a finite set for all $a \in A$, i.e., if any element $a \in A$ is related to finitely many elements $b \in B$. A finitary multirelation f induces in an obvious way a function $\mu f : \mu_* A \to \mu_* B$, defined as $\mu f(M)(b) = \sum_{a \in A} M(a) \cdot f(a,b)$ for $M \in \mu_* A$ and $b \in B$. In the sequel we will implicitly assume that all multirelations are finitary. A *relation* $r : A \leftrightarrow B$ is a multirelation r where multiplicities are bounded by one, namely $r(a,b) \leq 1$ for all $a \in A$ and $b \in B$. Sometimes we shall write simply $r(a,b)$ instead of $r(a,b) = 1$.

Definition 1 ((marked) contextual net). *A* (marked) contextual Petri net (c-net) *is a tuple* $N = \langle S, T, F, C, m \rangle$, *where*

- S *is a set of* places *and* T *is a set of* transitions*;*
- $F = \langle F_{pre}, F_{post} \rangle$ *is a pair of finitary multirelations* $F_{pre}, F_{post} : T \leftrightarrow S$*;*
- $C : T \leftrightarrow S$ *is a finitary relation, called the* context relation*;*
- $m \in \mu_* S$ *is a finite multiset, called the* initial marking.

In general, any multiset of S *is called a* marking. *The c-net is called* finite *if* T *and* S *are finite sets. Without loss of generality, we assume* $S \cap T = \emptyset$. *Moreover, we require that for each transition* $t \in T$, *there exists a place* $s \in S$ *such that* $F_{pre}(t,s) > 0$.

In the following, when considering a c-net N, we will implicitly assume that $N = \langle S, T, F, C, m \rangle$.

Given a finite multiset of transitions $A \in \mu_* T$ we write ${}^\bullet A$ for its *pre-set* $\mu F_{pre}(A)$ and $A^\bullet$ for its *post-set* $\mu F_{post}(A)$. Moreover, $\underline{A}$ denotes the *context* of A, defined as $\underline{A} = [\![\mu C(A)]\!]$. The same notation is used to denote the functions from S to the powerset $\mathcal{P}(T)$, i.e., for $s \in S$ we define ${}^\bullet s = \{t \in T : F_{post}(t,s) > 0\}$, $s^\bullet = \{t \in T : F_{pre}(t,s) > 0\}$, $\underline{s} = \{t \in T : C(t,s)\}$.

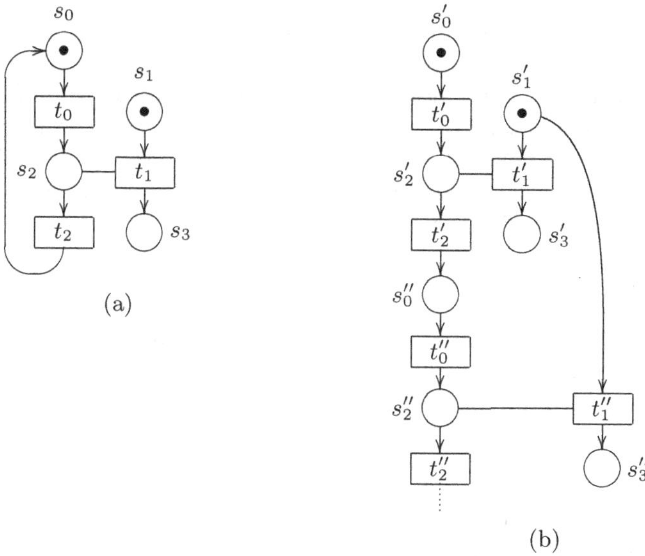

Fig. 2. (a) A contextual net N_0 and (b) its unfolding $\mathcal{U}_a(N_0)$

An example of a contextual net, inspired by [19], is depicted in Fig. 2a. Read arcs are drawn as undirected lines. For instance, referring to transition t_1 we have ${}^\bullet t_1 = s_1$, $t_1{}^\bullet = s_3$ and $\underline{t_1} = s_2$.

For a finite multiset of transitions A to be enabled at a marking M, it is sufficient that M contains the pre-set of A and one *additional* token in each place of the context of A. This corresponds to the intuition that a token in a place (like s in Fig. 1a) can be used as context concurrently by many transitions; instead, if read arcs are replaced by consume/produce loops (as in Fig. 1b) the transitions needing a token in place s can fire only one at a time.

Definition 2 (enabling, step). *Let N be a c-net. A finite multiset of transitions $A \in \mu_* T$ is* enabled *at a marking $M \in \mu_* S$ if ${}^\bullet A \oplus \underline{A} \leq M$. In this case, the execution of A in M, called a* step *(or a* firing *when it involves just one transition), produces the new marking $M' = M \ominus {}^\bullet A \oplus A^\bullet$, written as $M\,[A\rangle\, M'$.*

A marking M of a c-net N is called *reachable* if there is a finite sequence of steps leading to M from the initial marking, i.e., $m\,[A_0\rangle\, M_1\,[A_1\rangle\, M_2 \ldots [A_n\rangle\, M$.

Definition 3 (bounded, safe and semi-weighted nets). *A c-net N is called n-*bounded *if for any reachable marking M each place contains at most n tokens, namely $M(s) \leq n$ for all $s \in S$. It is called* safe *if it is 1-bounded and F_{pre}, F_{post} are relations (rather than general multirelations). A c-net N is called* semi-weighted *if the initial marking m is a set and F_{post} is a relation.*

Observe that requiring F_{pre} (resp. F_{post}) to be relations amounts to asking that for any transition $t \in T$, the pre-set (resp., post-set) of t is a set, rather than a general multiset.

We recall that considering semi-weighted nets is essential to characterise the unfolding construction, in categorical terms, as a coreflection [4]. However, in this paper, the choice of taking semi-weighted nets rather than general weighted nets is only motivated by the need of simplifying the presentation: while the presentation extends smoothly from safe to semi-weighted nets, considering general weighted nets would require some technical complications in the definition of the unfolding (Definition 11), related to the fact that an occurrence of a place would not be completely identified by its causal history.

2.2 Occurrence c-Nets

Occurrence c-nets are safe c-nets satisfying certain acyclicity and well-foundedness requirements. To define what this means, we will next introduce the notions of causality and asymmetric conflict.

Causality is defined as for ordinary nets, with an additional clause stating that transition t causes t' if it generates a token in a context place of t'.

Definition 4 (causality). *Let N be a safe c-net. The* causality relation *in N is the least transitive relation $<$ on $S \cup T$ such that*

1. *if $s \in {}^\bullet t$ then $s < t$;*
2. *if $s \in t^\bullet$ then $t < s$;*
3. *if $t^\bullet \cap \underline{t'} \neq \emptyset$ then $t < t'$.*

Given $x \in S \cup T$, we write $\lfloor x \rfloor$ for the set of causes *of x in T, defined as $\lfloor x \rfloor = \{t \in T : t \leq x\} \subseteq T$, where $\leq$ is the reflexive closure of $<$.*

For instance, in Fig. 2a, the three cases of Definition 4 are exemplified by $s_0 < t_0$, $t_0 < s_2$, and $t_0 < t_1$.

We say that a transition t is in *asymmetric conflict* with t', denoted $t \nearrow t'$, if *whenever both t and t' fire in a computation, t fires before t'*. The paradigmatic case is when transition t' consumes a token in the context of t, i.e., when $\underline{t} \cap {}^\bullet t' \neq \emptyset$, as for transitions t_1' and t_2' in Fig. 2b (see [4,16,10,19]). This situation cannot be captured adequately by the standard causality and conflict relations, and it is the reason of the possible existence of several causal histories for an event, the phenomenon typical of contextual nets mentioned in the introduction.

Note that the fact that *whenever both t and t' fire, t fires before t'* trivially holds when $t < t'$, because t cannot follow t' in a computation, and (with t and t' in interchangeable roles) also when t and t' have a common precondition, since they will never fire in the same computation. For technical convenience the definition of relation $\nearrow$ takes into account these two situations as well, with the consequence that an ordinary symmetric conflict amounts to an asymmetric conflict in both directions.

Definition 5 (asymmetric conflict). *Let N be a safe c-net. The* asymmetric conflict relation *in N is the binary relation $\nearrow$ on T defined as*

$$t \nearrow t' \quad \textit{iff} \quad \underline{t} \cap {}^\bullet t' \neq \emptyset \ \textit{or} \ (t \neq t' \ \wedge \ {}^\bullet t \cap {}^\bullet t' \neq \emptyset) \ \textit{or} \ t < t'.$$

For $X \subseteq T$, $\nearrow_X$ denotes the restriction of $\nearrow$ to X, i.e., $\nearrow_X = \nearrow \cap (X \times X)$.

As an example, consider Fig. 2b. There, we have $t'_1 \nearrow t'_2$ because t'_1 in order to fire requires a token on s'_2, which is consumed by t'_2; moreover, $t'_1 \nearrow t''_1$ (and vice versa) because both transitions consume a token from s'_1; and finally, $t'_0 \nearrow t'_2$, because the former is a causal predecessor of the latter.

An occurrence c-net is a safe c-net that exhibits an acyclic behaviour, satisfying suitable conflict-freeness requirements.

Definition 6 (occurrence c-nets). *An* occurrence c-net *is a safe c-net N such that*

- *each place $s \in S$ is in the post-set of at most one transition, i.e., $|{}^\bullet s| \leq 1$;*
- *the* causal relation $<$ *is irreflexive and its reflexive closure $\leq$ is a partial order, such that $\lfloor t \rfloor$ is finite for any $t \in T$;*
- *the* initial marking *is the set of $\leq$-minimal places, i.e., $m = \{s \in S : {}^\bullet s = \emptyset\}$;*
- *$\nearrow_{\lfloor t \rfloor}$ is acyclic for all $t \in T$.*

An example of an occurrence c-net can be found in Fig. 2b. The last condition of Definition 6 corresponds to the requirement of irreflexivity for the conflict relation in ordinary occurrence nets. In fact, if a transition t has a $\nearrow$ cycle in its causes then it can never fire, since in an occurrence c-net, the order in which transitions appear in a firing sequence must be compatible with the asymmetric conflict relation. This intuitive interpretation of cycles of asymmetric conflict as conflicts over sets of transitions is formalised as follows:

Definition 7 (conflict). *Let N be a c-net. The* conflict *relation $\# \subseteq \mathcal{P}(T)$ associated to N is defined as follows, where A is any finite subset of T:*

$$\frac{t_0 \nearrow t_1 \nearrow \ldots \nearrow t_n \nearrow t_0}{\#\{t_0, t_1, \ldots, t_n\}} \qquad\qquad \frac{\#(A \cup \{t\}) \quad t \leq t'}{\#(A \cup \{t'\})}$$

In ordinary nets, only symmetric conflicts can occur: they are represented by cycles of asymmetric conflicts of length two.

The notion of concurrency is the natural generalisation of the one for ordinary nets. Note that, because of the presence of contexts, some places that a transition needs in order to fire (the contexts) can be concurrent with the places it produces.

Definition 8 (concurrency relation). *Let N be an occurrence c-net. A finite set of places $M \subseteq S$ is called* concurrent, *written $conc(M)$, if*

1. *$\forall s, s' \in M.\ \neg(s < s')$;*
2. *$\lfloor M \rfloor = \bigcup\{\lfloor s \rfloor : s \in M\}$ is conflict-free, i.e., $\neg\# A$ for any $A \subseteq \lfloor M \rfloor$.*

It can be shown that, as for ordinary occurrence nets, a set of places M is concurrent if and only if there is some reachable marking in which all the places of M contain one token.

From now on, consistently with the literature, we shall often call the transitions of an occurrence c-net *events*.

Definition 9 (configuration). *Let N be an occurrence c-net. A set of events $C \subseteq T$ is called a* configuration *if*

1. *$\nearrow_C$ is acyclic;*
2. *$\{t' \in C : t' \nearrow t\}$ is finite for all $t \in C$;*
3. *C is left-closed w.r.t. $<$, i.e., for all $t \in C$, $t' \in T$, $t' < t$ implies $t' \in C$.*

We denote by $Conf(N)$ the set of all configurations of N, equipped with the ordering defined as $C \sqsubseteq C'$, if $C \subseteq C'$ and $\neg(t' \nearrow t)$ for all $t \in C, t' \in C' \setminus C$.

Furthermore, two configurations C_1, C_2 are said to be in conflict *$(C_1 \# C_2)$ when there is no $C \in Conf(N)$ such that $C_1 \sqsubseteq C$ and $C_2 \sqsubseteq C$.*

The notion of configuration characterises the possible (concurrent) computations of an occurrence c-net. It can be proved that a subset of events C is a configuration if and only if the events in C can all be fired, starting from the initial marking, in any order compatible with $\nearrow$. Observe that this includes also the infinite computations, as C is not required to be finite.

The relation $\sqsubseteq$ is a computational order of configurations: $C \sqsubseteq C'$ if C can evolve and become C'. Remarkably, this order is not simply subset inclusion since a configuration C cannot be extended with an event t' if $t' \nearrow t$ for some $t \in C$, since t' cannot fire after t in a computation. Two configurations are in (symmetric) conflict if they do not have a common extension. More concretely $C_1 \# C_2$ when there exists $t_1 \in C_1$ and $t_2 \in C_2 \setminus C_1$ such that $t_2 \nearrow t_1$, or the symmetric condition holds.

To illustrate the definition, consider again Fig. 2b. The set $C_1 = \{t'_0, t'_2\}$ is a configuration because t'_0 can fire first and then t'_2. Also $C_2 = \{t'_0, t'_1, t'_2\}$ is a configuration; its events can fire in the order t'_0, t'_1, t'_2. However, $C_1 \sqsubseteq C_2$ does not hold even though $C_1 \subseteq C_2$ because t'_1 must necessarily fire before t'_2 in any computation containing both events.

Notice also that all three conditions in Definition 9 are necessary. For instance, $\{t'_1, t''_1\}$ is not a configuration in Fig. 2b because it violates Condition 1, as it contains a conflict, and, e.g. $\{t'_2\}$ is not a configuration because it violates Condition 3: it does not represent a complete computation. The need for Condition 2 is slightly trickier to explain. Consider the (infinite) occurrence net in Fig. 3. For each $i \geq 1$, since $s' \in \underline{t_i}$, we have $t_i \nearrow t'$. Therefore, the set $\{t'\} \cup \{\, t_i \mid i \geq 1\,\}$ is not a configuration: it does not represent a computation because its elements cannot be ordered in such a way that t' will eventually fire.

Given a configuration C and an event $t \in C$, the *history of t in C* is the set of events that *must* precede t in the (concurrent) computation represented by C. For ordinary nets the history of an event t coincides with the set of causes $\lfloor t \rfloor$, independently of the configuration where t occurs. Instead, for c-nets, due to the presence of asymmetric conflicts between events, an event t that occurs in more than one configuration may have different histories. The next definition formalises this fact.

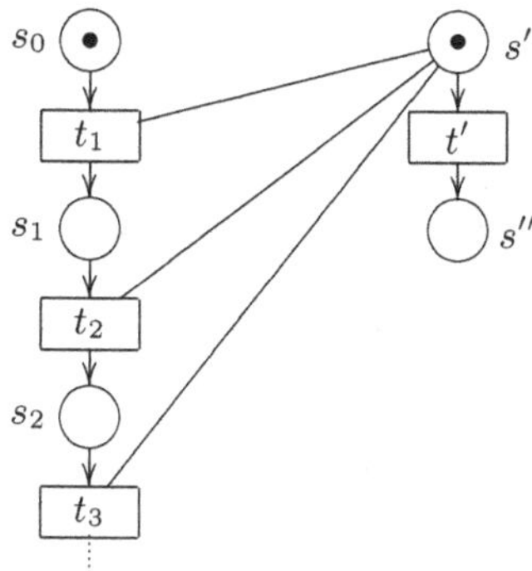

Fig. 3. Occurrence net illustrating condition 2 of Definition 9

Definition 10 (history). *Let N be an occurrence net. Given a configuration C and an event $t \in C$, the* history *of t in C, denoted by $C[\![t]\!]$, is defined as*

$$C[\![t]\!] = \{t' \in C : t'(\nearrow_C)^* t\}.$$

The set of all histories of an event t, namely, $\{C[\![t]\!] : C \in Conf(N) \ \wedge \ t \in C\}$ is denoted by $Hist(t)$.

For instance, in Fig. 2b, we have $t'_0 \nearrow t'_2$ and $t'_1 \nearrow t'_2$. There are several configurations containing t'_2, such as $C_1 = \{t'_0, t'_2\}$, $C_2 = \{t'_0, t'_1, t'_2\}$, and $C_3 = \{t'_0, t'_2, t''_0\}$, and t'_2 has two histories: $H_1 = C_1[\![t'_2]\!] = C_3[\![t'_2]\!] = \{t'_0, t'_2\}$, and $H_2 = C_2[\![t'_2]\!] = \{t'_0, t'_1, t'_2\}$. In history H_2 event t'_1 fires, using the token on s'_2 in its context, while in H_1 t'_1 did not fire.

2.3 Unfolding

Given a semi-weighted c-net N, an *unfolding* construction allows one to obtain an occurrence c-net $\mathcal{U}_a(N)$ that describes the behaviour of N [3,19]. As for ordinary nets, each event in $\mathcal{U}_a(N)$ represents a particular firing of a transition in N, and places in $\mathcal{U}_a(N)$ represent occurrences of tokens in the places of N. The unfolding is equipped with a mapping to the original net N, relating each place (event) of the unfolding to the corresponding place (transition) in N.

The unfolding, which is abstractly characterised as the maximal branching process of a net [6], can be constructed inductively by starting from the initial marking of N and then by adding, at each step, an occurrence of each transition of N that is enabled by (the image of) a concurrent subset of the places already generated.

Intuitively, our definition gives each place and event a "canonical" name. Each place in the unfolding is a pair whose second element points to the place of the original net it corresponds to. In order to distinguish different occurrences of tokens, the first component records the "history" of the token, i.e., the event that generates it. Similarly, each event is a triple recording the precondition and context used in the firing, and the corresponding transition in the original net.

$$\frac{s \in m}{s' = \langle \emptyset, s \rangle \in S' \qquad s' \in m' \qquad f_S(s') = s}$$

$$\frac{t \in T \quad M_p, M_c \subseteq S' \quad \mu f_S(M_p) = {}^\bullet t \quad \mu f_S(M_c) = \underline{t} \quad conc(M_p \cup M_c)}{t' = \langle M_p, M_c, t \rangle \in T' \qquad {}^\bullet t' = M_p \qquad \underline{t'} = M_c \qquad f_T(t') = t}$$

$$\frac{t' = \langle M_p, M_c, t \rangle \in T' \quad t^\bullet = \{s_1, \ldots, s_n\}}{s'_i = \langle t', s_i \rangle \in S' \qquad t'^\bullet = \{s'_1, \ldots, s'_n\} \qquad f_S(s'_i) = s_i}$$

Fig. 4. The inductive rules defining the unfolding of a c-net

Definition 11 (unfolding). *Let $N = \langle S, T, F, C, m \rangle$ be a semi-weighted c-net. The unfolding $\mathcal{U}_a(N) = \langle S', T', F', C', m' \rangle$ of the net N is the (minimal) occurrence c-net defined by the inductive rules in Fig. 4. The rules define also the* folding morphism *$f_N = \langle f_T, f_S \rangle : \mathcal{U}_a(N) \to N$ consisting of a pair of functions $f_T : T' \to T$ and $f_S : S' \to S$ mapping the unfolding to the original net.*

As said before, places and events in the unfolding of a c-net represent tokens and firings of transitions in the original net, respectively. Initially, a new place with empty history $\langle \emptyset, s \rangle$ is generated for each place s in the initial marking. Moreover, a new event $t' = \langle M_p, M_c, t \rangle$ is inserted in the unfolding whenever we can find a concurrent set of places (precondition M_p and context M_c) that corresponds, in the original net, to a marking that enables t. For each place s_i in the post-set of such t, a new place $\langle t', s_i \rangle$ is generated, belonging to the post-set of t'. The folding morphism f maps each place (event) of the unfolding to the corresponding place (transition) in the original net.

An initial part of the unfolding of the net N_0 in Fig. 2a is represented in Fig. 2b. The folding morphism from $\mathcal{U}_a(N_0)$ to N_0 is implicitly represented by the name of the items in the unfolding.

The unfolding is complete with respect to the behaviour of the original net in the following sense.

Proposition 1 (completeness of the unfolding). *Let N be a c-net and let $\mathcal{U}_a(N) = \langle S', T', F', C', m' \rangle$ be its unfolding. A marking $M \in \mu_* S$ is coverable in N iff there exists a concurrent subset $X \subseteq S'$ such that $M = \mu f_S(X)$.*

The above notion of completeness, which will be used in the rest of the paper, is slightly weaker than that of [11,19], for example. In fact, the notion of completeness for unfolding prefixes considered in the mentioned papers imposes, not only that every marking reachable in the original net N is represented in the prefix, but also that every transition firable in N has a representative in the prefix. The results could be easily adapted to this stronger notion of completeness.

3 Defining a Complete Finite Prefix

To obtain a finite prefix of the unfolding that is still complete in the sense of Proposition 1, the idea is to avoid including "useless" events in the unfolding,

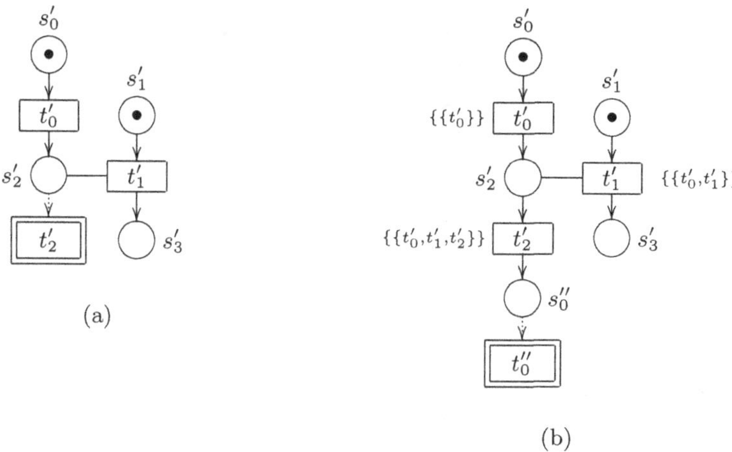

Fig. 5. (a) An incomplete and (b) a complete enriched prefix for the net in Fig. 2

where useless means events that do not contribute to generating new markings. To this aim McMillan introduced the notion of "cut-off" for ordinary nets, which is roughly an event whose history does not generate a new marking. Then the complete finite prefix is the greatest prefix without cut-offs. This definition of cut-off event has to be adapted to the present framework, since for contextual nets an event may have different histories, or, using McMillan terminology, different local configurations.

Considering only the minimal history of an event, i.e., its set of causes, in the definition of cut-off leads to a finite but not necessarily complete prefix, as observed in [19]. For instance, consider net N_0 in Fig. 2a. According to the ordinary definition of cut-off, in its unfolding $\mathcal{U}_a(N_0)$ shown in Fig. 2b the event t'_2 would be a cut-off since its minimal history $\{t'_0, t'_2\}$ generates a marking corresponding to the initial marking. Graphically, cut-offs are marked by using double lines. Thus the largest prefix without cut-offs would be the net O_0 in Fig. 5a, which is not complete since it does not "represent" the marking $s_0 \oplus s_3$, reachable in N_0.

Considering instead *all* the possible histories of an event leads to a characterisation of a prefix which is finite and complete, even if this characterisation is not constructive since there can be infinitely many possible histories for a single event (see [2] or the net depicted in Fig. 3). In the present paper, we suggest to record for each event only a subset of histories which are considered "useful to produce new markings".

To formalise this fact we introduce a notion of occurrence net decorated with possible histories for the involved events.

Definition 12 (enriched occurrence net). *An* enriched occurrence net *is a pair $E = \langle N, \chi \rangle$, where N is an occurrence net and $\chi : T \to \mathcal{P}(\mathcal{P}(T))$ is a function such that for any $t \in T$, $\emptyset \neq \chi(t) \subseteq Hist(t)$.*

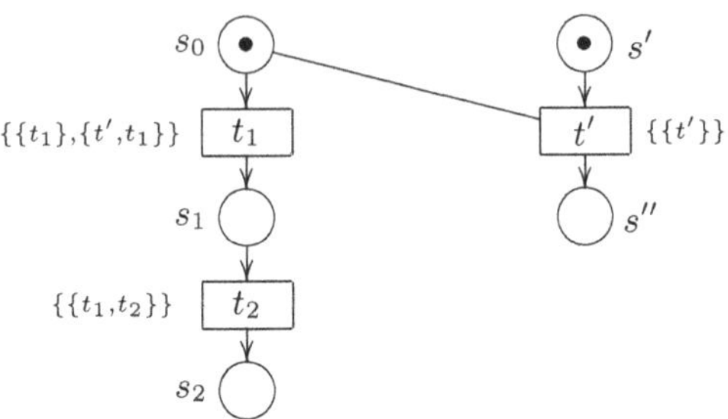

Fig. 6. Occurrence net illustrating Definition 12

The enriched occurrence net E is called closed *if for all $t, t' \in T$, for any $C \in \chi(t)$ if $t' \in C$ then $C[\![t']\!] \in \chi(t')$.*

A configuration of E is a configuration $C \in Conf(N)$ such that $C[\![t]\!] \in \chi(t)$ for all $t \in C$. The set of configurations of E is denoted by $Conf(E)$.

As an example, consider the enriched occurrence net in Fig. 6, where for any event t the set of histories $\chi(t)$ is indicated next to the event. Note that this net is closed. Instead, removing the history $\{t_1\}$ from $\chi(t_1)$ would result in a net that is not closed. In fact, since $\{t_1, t_2\} \in \chi(t_2)$, transition t_2 can be fired in a computation after firing only t_1. Thus t_1 must be firable alone. This would be in contradiction with the fact that the only remaining history of t_1 is $\{t', t_1\}$, which says that transition t_1 can be fired only after t'. Concerning the notion of configuration, note that for the net in Fig. 6, $\{t', t_1\}$ is a configuration while $\{t', t_1, t_2\}$ is not.

Often, given an enriched occurrence net E we will denote its components by N_E and χ_E. If the enriched net is E_i, we will denote its components N_i and χ_i.

From now on, $N = \langle S, T, F, C, m \rangle$ is a fixed semi-weighted c-net, $\mathcal{U}_a(N) = \langle S', T', F', C', m' \rangle$ is its unfolding, and $f_N : \mathcal{U}_a(N) \to N$ is the folding morphism.

Definition 13 (enriched event, enriched prefix). *An* enriched event *of the unfolding is a pair $\langle t, H_t \rangle$, where $t \in T'$ is an event of the unfolding, and $H_t \in Hist(t)$ is one of its histories. An* enriched prefix *of the unfolding $\mathcal{U}_a(N)$ is any* closed *enriched occurrence net E such that N_E is a prefix of $\mathcal{U}_a(N)$. We will say that the enriched prefix E contains an enriched event $\langle t, H_t \rangle$ and write $\langle t, H_t \rangle \in E$ if $t \in T_E$ and $H_t \in \chi_E(t)$.*

An example of an enriched prefix of $\mathcal{U}_a(N_0)$ in Fig. 2b is given in Fig. 5b.

A generalisation of the natural prefix ordering over occurrence nets can be defined on enriched occurrence nets.

Definition 14 (prefix ordering). *Given two enriched occurrence nets E_1 and E_2, we say that E_1 is a* prefix *of E_2, written $E_1 \preceq E_2$, if N_1 is a prefix of N_2, and for any $t \in T_1$, $\chi_1(t) \subseteq \chi_2(t)$.*

Lemma 1 (enriched prefixes form a lattice). *The set of closed enriched prefixes of $\mathcal{U}_a(N)$ endowed with the prefix ordering $\preceq$ is a complete lattice.*

Proof. Let $\{E_i\}_{i \in I}$ be a set of enriched prefixes of $\mathcal{U}_a(N)$. Then, we claim that their least upper bound $\bigsqcup_{i \in I} E_i$ is $E = \langle N_E, \chi_E \rangle$, where N_E is the component-wise union of the nets N_i, and, for any event t in N, $\chi_E(t) = \bigcup_{\{i \in I : t \in N_i\}} \chi_i(t)$.

Clearly, E is a well-defined enriched prefix. We only need to show that E is closed. Then the fact that it is the greatest lower bound for $\{E_i\}_{i \in I}$ is obvious. Let t be an event in N, let $C \in \chi_E(t)$ and take a $t' \in C[\![t]\!]$. We have to prove that $C[\![t']\!] \in \chi_E(t')$. Now, since $\chi_E(t) = \bigcup_{\{i \in I : t \in N_i\}} \chi_i(t)$, clearly $C \in \chi_{E_j}(t)$ for some $j \in I$. Since E_j is closed, this implies $C[\![t']\!] \in \chi_{E_j}(t')$ and therefore, $C[\![t']\!] \in \bigcup_{\{i \in I : t \in N_i\}} \chi_i(t') = \chi_E(t')$. □

Additionally, it is easy to prove that given two enriched prefixes E_1 and E_2

$$E_1 \preceq E_2 \quad \text{iff} \quad \mathit{Conf}(E_1) \subseteq \mathit{Conf}(E_2).$$

A configuration of $\mathcal{U}_a(N)$ represents a computation in the unfolding itself, which in turn maps, via the folding morphism, to a computation of N. Hence we can define the marking of N after a finite configuration of the unfolding.

Definition 15 (marking after a configuration). *Let $C \in \mathit{Conf}(\mathcal{U}_a(N))$ be a finite configuration. We denote by $\mathit{mark}(C)$ the marking of N after C, defined as $\mu f_S(m' \oplus \bigoplus_{t \in C} t^\bullet \ominus \bigoplus_{t \in C} {}^\bullet t)$.*

The notion of cut-off is now defined for enriched events, thus taking histories explicitly into account.

Definition 16 (cut-off). *An enriched event $\langle t, H_t \rangle$ of the unfolding $\mathcal{U}_a(N)$ is called a* cut-off *if $\mathit{mark}(H_t) = m$, the initial marking of N, or there is another enriched event $\langle t', H_{t'} \rangle$ of $\mathcal{U}_a(N)$ satisfying*

(1) $\mathit{mark}(H_t) = \mathit{mark}(H_{t'})$ and
(2) $|H_{t'}| < |H_t|$.

Let E be an enriched prefix of the unfolding. We say that E contains a cut-off if some enriched event $\langle t, H_t \rangle \in E$ is a cut-off in the full unfolding $\mathcal{U}_a(N)$. The enriched event $\langle t, H_t \rangle \in E$ is called a local cut-off *in E if $\mathit{mark}(H_t) = m$ or there is an enriched event $\langle t', H_{t'} \rangle \in E$ satisfying (1) and (2) above.*

A different notion of cut-off which refines the one originally proposed by McMillan by using *adequate orders* over configurations has been introduced in [7]. We are confident that this improvement can be integrated seamlessly into our framework.

Note that the notion of cut-off is based on a quantification over all the enriched events of the full unfolding and as such it is not effective. For an enriched event, being a cut-off is a global property, independent of the specific prefix of the unfolding we are considering. Clearly, every local cut-off in an enriched prefix E is also a cut-off. This simple observation will be used several times in the sequel.

Definition 17 (truncation). *The* truncation *$\mathcal{T}_a(N)$ of the unfolding is an enriched occurrence net defined as the greatest enriched prefix (w.r.t. prefix ordering $\preceq$) of the unfolding which does not contain cut-offs.*

The above definition is well-given thanks to the lattice structure of the set of enriched prefixes ordered by $\preceq$. However, it is not yet constructive. In Sect. 4, we will present an algorithm for computing a complete finite prefix, possibly larger than the truncation, using the notion of local cut-off.

We say that a configuration C of the unfolding includes a cut-off if for some $t \in C$, the enriched event $\langle t, C[\![t]\!]\rangle$ is a cut-off. The next fundamental lemma shows that configurations of the unfolding containing cut-offs can be disregarded without losing information about the reachable markings.

Lemma 2 (cut-off elimination). *Let $C \in \mathit{Conf}(\mathcal{U}_a(N))$ be a finite configuration. There exists a finite configuration C' without cut-offs such that $\mathit{mark}(C) = \mathit{mark}(C')$.*

Proof. We show that if C contains a cut-off then we can obtain a configuration C' such that $\mathit{mark}(C) = \mathit{mark}(C')$ and $|C'| < |C|$. Then the desired result immediately follows.

In fact, let $t \in C$ be an event such that $\langle t, C[\![t]\!]\rangle$ is a cut-off. According to Definition 16 there are two possibilities: (a) $\mathit{mark}(C[\![t]\!]) = m$ or (b) there exists an event t' in the unfolding and $H_{t'} \in \mathit{Hist}(t')$ such that $\mathit{mark}(C[\![t]\!]) = \mathit{mark}(H_{t'})$ and $|H_{t'}| < |C[\![t]\!]|$.

Let us define $H = \emptyset$ in case (a) and $H = H_{t'}$ in case (b). Hence in both cases

$$\mathit{mark}(C[\![t]\!]) = \mathit{mark}(H) \text{ and } |H| < |C[\![t]\!]|. \tag{1}$$

We show by induction on $k = |C| - |C[\![t]\!]|$ that we can find a configuration C', with $H \sqsubseteq C'$, such that $\mathit{mark}(C) = \mathit{mark}(C')$ and $|C'| - |H| = |C| - |C[\![t]\!]|$, thus, by (1), $|C'| < |C|$.

($k = 0$) Obvious, since $C = C[\![t]\!]$ one can just choose $C' = H$.
($k \to k+1$) In this case $C \setminus C[\![t]\!] \neq \emptyset$. Let $t_1 \in C \setminus C[\![t]\!]$, maximal w.r.t. $(\nearrow_C)^*$.

Therefore, $C_1 = C \setminus \{t_1\}$ is a configuration and $C_1[\![t]\!] = C[\![t]\!]$, by the choice of t_1. Thus by induction hypothesis there exists a configuration C_1' s.t. $H \sqsubseteq C_1'$ and

$$\mathit{mark}(C_1) = \mathit{mark}(C_1') \quad \text{and} \quad |C_1'| - |H| = |C_1| - |C_1[\![t]\!]|.$$

Since $\mathit{mark}(C_1') = \mathit{mark}(C_1)$, the event $f_N(t_1)$, executable in $\mathit{mark}(C_1)$, is still executable in $\mathit{mark}(C_1')$ and thus C_1' can be extended with an event t_1' in such a way that $C' = C_1' \cup \{t_1'\}$ satisfies all the requirements. □

Using the lemma above we can show that the truncation is a complete prefix of the unfolding.

Theorem 1 (completeness). *The truncation $\mathcal{T}_a(N)$ is a complete prefix of the unfolding, i.e., for any reachable marking M of N there is a finite configuration C of $\mathcal{T}_a(N)$ such that $\mathit{mark}(C) = M$.*

Proof. From the completeness of the (full) unfolding (see Proposition 1) it follows that we can find a finite configuration $C \in \mathit{Conf}(\mathcal{U}_a(N))$ such that

$mark(C) = M$. By Lemma 2, there exists a finite configuration C' in $Conf(\mathcal{U}_a(N))$ such that $mark(C') = mark(C)$, which does not contain cut-offs. Such a configuration must be a configuration of $\mathcal{T}_a(N)$. Otherwise, we could construct a cut-off-free prefix of the unfolding greater than $\mathcal{T}_a(N)$. In fact, C' itself can be seen as an enriched prefix E of $\mathcal{U}_a(N)$, where N_E is the subnet of the unfolding including the events in C' and $\chi_E(t) = \{C'[\![t]\!]\}$ for any $t \in C'$. Thus, if C' were not a configuration of $\mathcal{T}_a(N)$, the enriched prefix $\mathcal{T}_a(N) \sqcup E$ would be larger than $\mathcal{T}_a(N)$ and still without cut-offs, contradicting the definition of $\mathcal{T}_a(N)$. □

For finite n-bounded nets the number of reachable states of the net is finite and thus one can prove that the truncation of its unfolding is finite. We get this as a corollary of a more general result which will be also useful in proving the termination of the algorithm for the complete prefix.

Theorem 2 (finiteness). *Let N be a finite n-bounded c-net and let E be an enriched prefix of the unfolding free of local cut-offs. Then E is finite.*

Proof. For any event t in E let us fix a history $H_t \in \chi_P(t)$. By definition E is local cut-off free and thus for any t

$$\text{for any } t' \text{ in } T_E, \text{ if } mark(H_t) = mark(H_{t'}) \text{ then } |H_{t'}| \geq |H_t|.$$

Let $\mu^n S$ be the set of n-bounded markings and consider the function $\tau : T_E \to \mu^n S$, defined by $\tau(t) = mark(H_t)$. By the condition above, it is easy to see that $\tau(t_1) = \tau(t_2)$ implies $|H_{t_1}| = |H_{t_2}|$. Since the codomain of τ is finite, we can take the maximum k of the cardinalities $|H_t|$ for t in E.

Now, notice that for any event t clearly $depth(t) \leq |H_t| \leq k$. Hence E is included in the prefix of $\mathcal{U}_a(N)$ of depth k, which in turn is finite (since the initial marking is finite). □

Recalling that any local cut-off is a cut-off and thus that $\mathcal{T}_a(N)$ is free from local cut-offs we have the following.

Corollary 1. *Let N be a finite n-bounded net. The truncation $\mathcal{T}_a(N)$ is finite.*

For instance, consider the net N_0 and its unfolding $\mathcal{U}_a(N_0)$ in Fig. 2. The truncation $\mathcal{T}_a(N_0)$ is the enriched prefix depicted in Fig. 5b. Note that it includes the event t'_2. In fact, t'_2 has two possible histories: the minimal history $H_2 = \lfloor t'_2 \rfloor = \{t'_0, t'_2\}$ and $H'_2 = \{t'_0, t'_1, t'_2\}$. While $\langle t'_2, H_2 \rangle$ is a cut-off, the pair $\langle t'_2, H'_2 \rangle$ is not, and thus it is included in the truncation.

4 Computing the Prefix

In this section, we describe how to construct a prefix, possibly larger than $\mathcal{T}_a(N)$, but still finite and complete. The construction builds incrementally a finite prefix of the full unfolding of a semi-weighted c-net N by starting from the initial

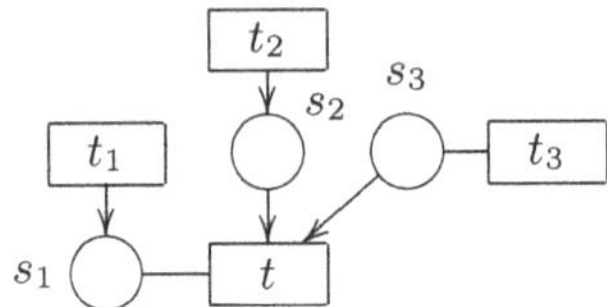

Fig. 7. Predecessors w.r.t. asymmetric conflict of an event t

marking and by iteratively adding new events representing occurrences of transitions of N. During the construction, for each event t in *Fin*, the currently built part of the prefix, we also record a current set of histories $\chi_{Fin}(t)$, thus making the prefix under construction an enriched occurrence net. We record in a set *pe* the enriched events which are candidates for being included in *Fin*, i.e., the pairs $\langle t, H\rangle$ where t is an event enabled in *Fin* and H is one of its current possible histories.

Let us first illustrate how the histories of an event t in a given enriched prefix E can be obtained from the histories of the events that are in direct asymmetric conflict with t. Consider a situation as in Fig. 7, which illustrates a part of the closed prefix E. A direct predecessor of t w.r.t. asymmetric conflict is either a cause (such as t_1, which produces a token that is read, or t_2, which produces a token that is consumed by t) or an event as t_3 that reads a token consumed by t.

The histories for t can be constructed as follows: for every direct cause t_i of t choose any history H_i of t_i, while for every transition t_j that is in direct asymmetric conflict with t (but not a cause) optionally take any history H_j. Whenever such histories are pairwise not in conflict (see Definition 9) then the set $H = \{t\} \cup \bigcup_i H_i$, the union of all such histories (and t), is called a *history for t consistent with E*.

Note that $H \in \mathit{Hist}(t)$ and furthermore adding H to E keeps the prefix closed, since for every transition $t' \in H$ the history $H[\![t']\!]$ is already contained in E. This is a consequence of the fact that for any t_i we have $H[\![t_i]\!] = H_i$ since no two histories in the union are in conflict.

The algorithm proceeds as follows. Again we use the notation of Definition 11.

Initialization. Start with $\mathit{Fin} := m'$ and let χ_{Fin} be the empty function. An event $t = \langle M_p, M_c, \hat{t}\rangle$ is enabled in *Fin* whenever $\mathit{conc}(M_p \cup M_c)$. Now let *pe* be the set of all pairs of the form $\langle t, H_t\rangle$, where t is an event enabled in *Fin* and H_t is a history of t consistent with *Fin*. Initially the only history of t is $\{t\}$.

Loop. While $\mathit{pe} \neq \emptyset$ do: Choose a pair $\langle t, H_t\rangle \in \mathit{pe}$ such that $|H_t|$ is minimal. Remove this pair from *pe* and consider the prefix Fin' obtained by inserting $\langle t, H_t\rangle$ in *Fin*, i.e.,

– if t is already present in *Fin* then add the history H_t to $\chi_{Fin}(t)$;
– otherwise add t to *Fin* and set $\chi_{Fin'}(t) := \{H_t\}$.

Then

- If $\langle t, H_t \rangle$ is a local cut-off in *Fin*$'$, do nothing and leave *Fin* unchanged.
- If $\langle t, H_t \rangle$ is not a local cut-off, set *Fin* := *Fin*$'$.
  Consider all events t' contained either in *Fin* or in *pe*: Whenever t' has a new history $H_{t'}$ consistent with the updated prefix *Fin*, arising from the insertion of H_t, then add $\langle t', H_{t'} \rangle$ to *pe*. (Note that a propagation phase is necessary to obtain all new histories.)
  If a new transition has been added to *Fin*, update *pe* by adding all events t which have become enabled in *Fin* in the last step together with all their histories consistent with *Fin*.

Note that whenever a new pair $\langle t', H_{t'} \rangle$ is added to *pe*, the size of $H_{t'}$ is larger than the size of the history H_t under consideration. This is due to the fact that these newly generated histories must include H_t. Observe also that all pairs $\langle t, H \rangle$ with $H \in \mathit{Hist}(t)$ are considered at some point, unless there exists a local cut-off $\langle t', H' \rangle$ such that $t' \in H$ and $H' = H[\![t']\!]$.

An efficient computation of the prefix should be based on suitable data structures. As observed above, a set of direct predecessors is needed for each event in order to update its histories. Furthermore, histories should not be stored explicitly, but via pointer structures containing references back to the histories they originated from. In addition, causality and conflict of histories can be computed incrementally.

It can be shown that at every iteration of the algorithm the prefix *Fin* does not contain local cut-offs. This can be used to prove the correctness and termination of the algorithm.

Lemma 3. *At every iteration of the algorithm Fin does not contain local cut-offs.*

Proof. (sketch) First observe that no local cut-off is inserted in *Fin*. Moreover, it cannot be the case that the history $H_{t'}$ of an event t' added to *Fin* at a certain step n later becomes a cut-off due to the insertion of other histories of events in the subsequent steps, since for each $H_{t''}$ inserted at step $n+k$ we have $|H_{t'}| \leq |H_{t''}|$ (see also the remark above). □

Theorem 3. *If the net N is finite and n-bounded the algorithm terminates and the prefix Fin it produces is complete.*

Proof. Termination is an immediate consequence of Lemma 3 and of Theorem 2.

Completeness follows by Theorem 1, using the fact that

$$\mathit{Conf}(\mathcal{T}_a(N)) \subseteq \mathit{Conf}(\mathit{Fin})$$

which is equivalent to $\mathcal{T}_a(N) \preceq \mathit{Fin}$, since both prefixes are closed. In fact, assume, by contradiction that there exists $C \in \mathit{Conf}(\mathcal{T}_a(N))$ such that $C \notin \mathit{Conf}(\mathit{Fin})$. Let $k(C)$ denote the set of events in C such that the enriched event $\langle t, C[\![t]\!] \rangle$ is not in *Fin*:

$$k(C) = \{t \mid t \in C \ \wedge \ \langle t, C[\![t]\!] \rangle \notin \mathit{Fin}\}.$$

By hypothesis $C \neq \emptyset$. Let $t \in k(C)$ be minimal in $k(C)$ with respect to $\nearrow_C$ and let $H_t = C[\![t]\!]$.

As in the proof of Theorem 1 we can see H_t as an enriched prefix E_t of the unfolding containing only the events in H_t, each one with its history in H_t.

Now, by construction, $C' = H_t \backslash \{t\} \in Conf(Fin)$ and $H_t \notin Conf(Fin)$. Therefore, by the way we defined the algorithm and from the construction procedure for new histories, we know that H_t must have been a history for t consistent with the prefix constructed up to a certain point. Thus, the only possible reason why H_t has not been included in *Fin* is that $\langle t, H_t \rangle$ was a local cut-off in the partial prefix. More formally, we know that $\langle t, H_t \rangle$ is a local cut-off in $Fin \sqcup H_t$.

Since any local cut-off is a cut-off, the enriched event $\langle t, H_t \rangle$, which is contained in $\mathcal{T}_a(N)$, would be a cut-off. But this contradicts the fact that $\mathcal{T}_a(N)$ is cut-off free. □

The complete prefix of a c-net can be much smaller than the complete prefix (constructed using McMillan's algorithm) for the net where read arcs are replaced by consume/produce loops. In fact, consider a net N_1^n analogous to the net in Fig. 1a but with n readers $t_1, \ldots, t_n$. Let N_2^n be obtained encoding N_1^n as an ordinary net by simply replacing read arcs with a consume/produce loops, as in Fig. 1b. The unfolding of net N_2^n includes $k_n = n + n(n-1) + \cdots + n!$ events corresponding to the readers, since each event does not only record the occurrence of a transition, but also its entire history, i.e., the sequence of all events occurring before. Similarly, there are $k_n + 1$ copies of event t_0'. Note that none of these events is a cut-off (according to McMillan's definition), since any two events generating the same marking have histories of equal size. Therefore the complete prefix computed for N_2^n is the unfolding itself. Instead, the complete enriched prefix obtained from N_1^n is the net N_1^n itself, thus it has $n+2$ transitions only; among them, $t_0, t_1, \ldots, t_n$ have one history each, while t_0' has 2^n histories. Even if still of exponential size, this prefix is much smaller than the complete prefix of N_2^n, essentially because the order in which the readers occurred does not need to be recorded. Moreover, the underlying net obtained by disregarding the histories is dramatically smaller in this case.

Now let N_3^n be the PR-encoding of N_1^n, as shown in Fig. 1c. The unfolding of N_3^n has one occurrence for each of the transitions $t_0, t_1, \ldots, t_n$ and 2^n occurrences of t_0', none of which is a cut-off (hence, also in this case, the complete prefix is the full unfolding). Thus there is a one-to-one correspondence between the histories in the enriched prefix of N_1^n and the events of the unfolding of N_3^n. Still, the size of the prefix of N_3^n is exponential in n while the size of the prefix of N_1^n, once the histories are disregarded, is linear.

We conjecture that what happens for N_1^n and N_3^n is a completely general fact, i.e., the histories of the complete enriched prefix of a *safe* c-net N are in one-to-one correspondence with the events of the complete finite prefix of the PR-encoding of N. In the case of non-safe nets, instead, the number of histories of the complete enriched prefix of N can be much smaller than the number of events of the complete finite prefix of the PR-encoding of N. As an example consider

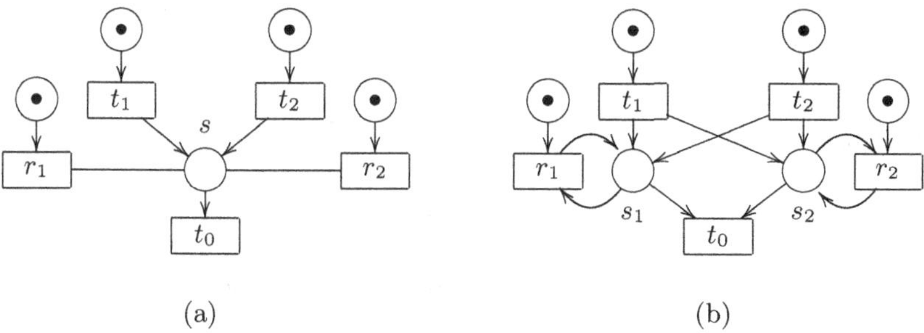

Fig. 8. A c-net N_4 and its PR-encoding

the net N_4 in Fig. 8a. Its truncation has two occurrences of transition t_0 (either t_0 is caused by t_1 or by t_2), each with four histories (which specify whether r_1 or r_2, or both, or none has been fired before). So in total we have eight histories.

Now consider the PR-encoding of N_4 in Fig. 8b. Unfolding the PR-encoding we obtain four occurrences of place s_1 (after firing t_1 or t_1, r_1 or t_2 or t_2, r_1) and analogously four occurrences of place s_2. All pairs of such places (one representing s_1 and the other s_2) are concurrent. Hence, we obtain $4 \cdot 4 = 16$ occurrences of transition t_0. An intuitive interpretation is as follows: the token in s is split into two half-tokens in s_1 and s_2. Then some of the transitions in the unfolding of the encoded net consume "half a token" produced by t_1 and "half a token" produced by t_2.

More generally, consider a net $N_4^{(h,k)}$ like N_4 one above, but with h writers $t_1, \ldots, t_h$ and k readers $r_1, \ldots, r_k$. The truncation of $N_4^{(h,k)}$ has h occurrences of t_0 with a total number of histories $h \cdot 2^k$, since t_0 can consume the token produced by any of the h writers, after it has been read by any subset of the k readers. Instead, the unfolding of the PR-encoding of $N_4^{(h,k)}$ includes $(h \cdot 2)^k$ occurrences of t_0, since each occurrence of t_0 consumes k tokens, and each of these tokens can be produced by any of the h writers and it could have possibly been produced/consumed by the corresponding reader.

We finally remark that histories are auxiliary information needed to build the prefix, but they can safely be disregarded at the end of the construction. For instance, histories are not needed for checking the coverability of a marking m' in a contextual prefix. Here, m' is coverable iff the set of causes $\lfloor m' \rfloor$ is a configuration, which amounts to checking for the absence of asymmetric-conflict cycles in $\lfloor m' \rfloor$. This can be done efficiently (linear in the size of the asymmetric-conflict relation) with topological sorting. Note that this can be an important advantage when a prefix is used for checking the coverability of a marking m of the original net N. It is well-known that m is coverable iff the complete prefix contains a marking m' such that (i) $\mu f_S(m') = m$ and (ii) m' is coverable. When a contextual prefix contains one marking m' with property (i), a non-contextual prefix of the corresponding PR-encoding may contain a large set of them, one for each history. An algorithm for coverability that works on contextual prefix just needs to consider m' whereas methods using non-contextual prefixes have the burden of dealing with the whole set.

5 Conclusions

We have presented an approach for computing finite complete prefixes of general contextual nets, which extends the approach proposed for the class of read-persistent nets in [19] and provides an alternative to the technique based on the PR-encoding of contextual nets as ordinary nets. Our work relies on the idea of dealing explicitly with the multiple histories that events can have in contextual net computations, due to the presence of asymmetric conflicts. Subsets of "useful" histories for events are recorded in the prefix during the construction and, correspondingly, a new notion of cut-off is considered. In the case of read-persistent nets every transition has a single history and hence our approach coincides with the one introduced in [19].

Our work shares some basic ideas with [20], where however the definition of cut-off is non-constructive, since it depends on all the possible histories that an event may have. In order to avoid this problem we introduced the (constructive) notion of local cut-off. Apart from that, the notion of cut-off in [20] is stronger than ours, which might lead to larger prefixes.

As witnessed by some examples in the paper, the complete prefix of a contextual net can be significantly smaller than that of an equivalent net where read arcs are replaced by consume/produce loops. The ability to generate smaller unfoldings comes with a price, i.e., during the construction of the prefix we have to record and evaluate additional information such as histories and asymmetric conflict. Still, we conjecture that the algorithm will never require more space or time than the ordinary algorithm applied to the PR-encoding of the net. More precisely, for safe nets, as discussed in Sect. 4, the histories in the prefix should correspond exactly to the events in the unfolding of the PR-encoding, and causality and conflict on histories should be the exact match to causality and conflict for transitions. Furthermore, we expect our technique to be strictly more efficient for non-safe nets as indicated by the example in the previous section.

From a more methodological perspective, let us stress that our approach can build a complete finite prefix for a large class of c-nets directly, without the need of resorting to an encoding. We think that this feature makes our approach more suitable than others to be extended to other classes of systems exhibiting concurrent read-only accesses, for which an encoding could either not be feasible or could cause a significant loss of concurrency.

In particular, we are interested in graph transformation systems (GTSs), a quite expressive formalism where reading and preserving part of the system state, in this case a graph, is an integral part of the model. We believe that our direct approach will be useful to generalise McMillan's approach to the full class of GTSs, while currently only its read-persistent subclass is dealt with in [2]. We are also interested in nets with inhibitor arcs. In this case, an encoding as c-nets would be feasible but it would cause (at least in the non-safe case) a loss of concurrency, and thus a direct approach could be preferable.

We plan to implement and test the algorithm for contextual nets in the framework of the Mole unfolder [1] that currently deals with ordinary nets. At present, with the limited goal of analyzing the size of the produced prefix, we implemented a prototype which given a safe c-net, converts the read arcs into consume/produce loops, builds its finite prefix, and then merges the occurrences of the same context places. A complete implementation of our algorithm is currently in progress. We expect that in order to obtain satisfactory experimental results about the complexity (in time and in space) of our algorithm, in comparison with others, first we will need to be able to deal with more refined notions of cut-offs based on adequate orders [7], and second we will have to design and implement efficient data structures for recording the sets of histories of an event during the construction of the prefix.

Acknowledgments. We are grateful to the anonymous referees for their insightful comments and suggestions on the submitted version of this paper.

References

1. The Mole unfolder, `http://www.fmi.uni-stuttgart.de/szs/tools/mole`
2. Baldan, P., Corradini, A., König, B.: Verifying finite-state graph grammars: an unfolding-based approach. In: Gardner, P., Yoshida, N. (eds.) CONCUR 2004. LNCS, vol. 3170, pp. 83–98. Springer, Heidelberg (2004)
3. Baldan, P., Corradini, A., Montanari, U.: An event structure semantics for P/T contextual nets: asymmetric event structures. In: Nivat, M. (ed.) FOSSACS 1998. LNCS, vol. 1378, pp. 63–80. Springer, Heidelberg (1998)
4. Baldan, P., Corradini, A., Montanari, U.: Contextual Petri nets, asymmetric event structures and processes. Information and Computation 171(1), 1–49 (2001)
5. Christensen, S., Hansen, N.D.: Coloured Petri nets extended with place capacities, test arcs and inhibitor arcs. In: Ajmone Marsan, M. (ed.) ICATPN 1993. LNCS, vol. 691, pp. 186–205. Springer, Heidelberg (1993)
6. Engelfriet, J.: Branching processes of Petri nets. Acta Informatica 28, 575–591 (1991)
7. Esparza, J., Römer, S., Vogler, W.: An improvement of McMillan's unfolding algorithm. Formal Methods in System Design 20, 285–310 (2002)
8. Janicki, R., Koutny, M.: Invariant semantics of nets with inhibitor arcs. In: Groote, J.F., Baeten, J.C.M. (eds.) CONCUR 1991. LNCS, vol. 527. Springer, Heidelberg (1991)
9. Janicki, R., Koutny, M.: Semantics of inhibitor nets. Information and Computation 123, 1–16 (1995)
10. Langerak, R.: Transformation and Semantics for LOTOS. PhD thesis, Department of Computer Science, University of Twente (1992)
11. McMillan, K.L.: Using unfoldings to avoid the state explosion problem in the verification of asynchronous circuits. In: Probst, D.K., von Bochmann, G. (eds.) CAV 1992. LNCS, vol. 663, pp. 164–174. Springer, Heidelberg (1993)
12. McMillan, K.L.: Symbolic Model Checking. Kluwer, Dordrecht (1993)

13. Montanari, U., Rossi, F.: Contextual occurrence nets and concurrent constraint programming. In: Ehrig, H., Schneider, H.-J. (eds.) Dagstuhl Seminar 1993. LNCS, vol. 776. Springer, Heidelberg (1994)
14. Montanari, U., Rossi, F.: Contextual nets. Acta Informatica 32(6), 545–596 (1995)
15. Nielsen, M., Plotkin, G., Winskel, G.: Petri Nets, event structures and domains, Part 1. Theoretical Computer Science 13, 85–108 (1981)
16. Pinna, G.M., Poigné, A.: On the nature of events: another perspective in concurrency. Theoretical Computer Science 138(2), 425–454 (1995)
17. Ristori, G.: Modelling Systems with Shared Resources via Petri Nets. PhD thesis, Department of Computer Science, University of Pisa (1994)
18. Vogler, W.: Efficiency of asynchronous systems and read arcs in Petri nets. In: Degano, P., Gorrieri, R., Marchetti-Spaccamela, A. (eds.) ICALP 1997. LNCS, vol. 1256, pp. 538–548. Springer, Heidelberg (1997)
19. Vogler, W., Semenov, A., Yakovlev, A.: Unfolding and finite prefix for nets with read arcs. In: Sangiorgi, D., de Simone, R. (eds.) CONCUR 1998. LNCS, vol. 1466, pp. 501–516. Springer, Heidelberg (1998)
20. Winkowski, J.: Reachability in contextual nets. Fundamenta Informaticae 51(1), 235–250 (2002)

Elasticity and Petri Nets

Jordi Cortadella[1], Michael Kishinevsky[2],
Dmitry Bufistov[1], Josep Carmona[1], and Jorge Júlvez[1]

[1] Universitat Politècnica de Catalunya, Jordi Girona, 1-3, 08034, Barcelona, Spain
[2] Intel Corporation, 2501 NW 229th Ave., Hillsboro, OR 97124, USA
jordicf@lsi.upc.edu, michael.kishinevsky@intel.com,
{dmitry,jcarmona,julvez}@lsi.upc.edu

Abstract. Digital electronic systems typically use synchronous clocks and primarily assume fixed duration of their operations to simplify the design process. Time elastic systems can be constructed either by replacing the clock with communication handshakes (asynchronous version) or by augmenting the clock with a synchronous version of a handshake (synchronous version). Time elastic systems can tolerate static and dynamic changes in delays (asynchronous case) or latencies (synchronous case) of operations that can be used for modularity, ease of reuse and better power-delay trade-off. This paper describes methods for the modeling, performance analysis and optimization of elastic systems using Marked Graphs and their extensions capable of describing behavior with early evaluation. The paper uses synchronous elastic systems (aka latency-tolerant systems) for illustrating the use of Petri nets, however, most of the methods can be applied without changes (except changing the delay model associated with events of the system) to asynchronous elastic systems.

1 Introduction

Synchronous systems dominate digital design practices in the areas of electronic system design and embedded systems. Such systems assume the presence of a global time reference — global clock — which significantly simplifies design tasks and enable usage of zero delay abstraction for computation and communication delays. When designing or analyzing a digital synchronous circuit, one implicitly assumes the existence of a master clock that determines the frequency at which computations are performed and input/output data are transferred.

The specification of synchronous systems typically rely on precise knowledge on latencies (i.e., delays as measured in number of clock cycles) of different computations. Such knowledge, that is typically required from early stages in design specifications, may make the design process highly inflexible to possible changes in communication and computation latencies or delays. In addition, it restricts the usage of adaptive, variable delay or latencies of components since static scheduling of such components is a much harder (or impossible) job and typically complicates the system description.

In contrast, these assumptions do not apply to software programs or distributed communication over Internet, for which one assumes that the response time will depend on a variety of factors beyond the control of the user: the current workload of the operating system, the cache hit ratio, the traffic on the network, etc.

K. Jensen, W. van der Aalst, and J. Billington (Eds.): ToPNoC I, LNCS 5100, pp. 221–249, 2008.

One could say that software programs and Internet communication are elastic, since they can adapt themselves to the specific characteristics of the resources required to execute them and to the environment that interacts with them.

With current and future nanotechnologies, circuits resemble more a distributed network of devices with variable computation and communication delays. For example, a factor like the temperature of a specific region of a chip may change the frequency of a local clock and the response time of a particular functional unit. However, conventional circuits are often not designed in a way that allows changing the timing behavior of some components arbitrarily without modifying the functional behavior of the system.

For several decades researchers have studied systems that are tolerant to the variability of different parameters of a circuit: delay, power supply, temperature. One line of research (that was used in many industrial designs) adopts frequency of the clock and voltage levels to changing operational parameters. The other natural way of improving the tolerance to variability in delays is to eliminate the clock from the system, making the entire system asynchronous.

1.1 Two Forms of Elastic Systems

Like a distributed network, the components of an asynchronous circuit talk to each other by means of handshake signals that commit to some protocol. Typically, there is a local bi-directional synchronization for each pair of components that must exchange data. In its minimal form, the synchronization is implemented by a pair of signals called request and acknowledge.

The term "elastic circuit" initially referred to pipelines that were tolerant to the variability of input data arrival and computation delays. For example, Sutherland [1] used the term elasticity in his Turing award lecture on micropipelines.

Asynchronous systems [2–5] imply additional design complexity, since they often encode information in signal transitions. Therefore, the asynchronous circuit must not produce glitches or other transient signal transitions that could result in misinterpretations of the information. It is important to entirely avoid spurious transitions (also called glitches or hazards) or to restrict glitches to the timing intervals during which the signal is not observed. Both constraints make the design of asynchronous circuits considerably more challenging than the synchronous one.

For this reason, several research efforts limit the elasticity of asynchronous systems to discrete multiples of a certain time interval, e.g. the period of a synchronous clock. Since the mid-1990's, this idea has evolved and reappeared in different forms under several names, such as synchronous emulation of asynchronous circuits [6], synchronous handshake circuits [7], latency-insensitive design [8, 9] or synchronous elastic systems [10–12]. In all these variants, the systems can tolerate changes to latencies of components, but events are synchronized to a common clock.

A synchronous elastic system resembles a conventional clock circuit, but every data item in it has an associated valid bit. Every functional unit can also issue a stop bit to stall the activity of the neighboring units when it is not ready to receive information. These bits implements a synchronous version of the handshake protocol optimized in comparison with an asynchronous request/acknowledge protocol thanks to the presence of the clock reference.

By incorporating synchronicity, the design of elastic systems becomes easier. As in regular synchronous circuits, signals must stabilize only by the end of the clock period and are allowed to have glitches. Therefore, the existing infrastructure and methods for synchronous design can be re-used for synchronous elastic circuits.

Elastic circuits pose new opportunities and challenges in the design of future digital systems. Their tolerance to variable latency motivates the design of functional units optimized for the most frequent cases (instead of the worst case), offering a better average delay and new design trade-offs. They enable dynamic changes in latencies (in a synchronous case) or delays (in the asynchronous case) and dynamic adaptation to different environmental scenarios (temperature, power supply, clock frequency, etc.). Layout synthesis can benefit from elasticity, since elasticity can be introduced into layout with few incremental changes enabling fine-tuning of the system for better power and performance. Elasticity introduces a certain degree of dynamic scheduling into system behavior making the optimal scheduling a more challenging problem. It also allows for new dimensions in high-level optimization and transformations.

1.2 Use of Petri Nets for Modeling Elastic Systems

It was discovered during the MIT MAC project [13–15] that Petri nets, with their capabilities for describing distributed asynchronous computations as collection of asynchronous concurrent behaviors, is a natural way of specifying asynchronous pipelined systems. Such description can then be used for performance analysis, synthesis, validation and other forms of formal reasoning. This line of research was further explored later by multiple research groups.

In this paper, we will illustrate how Petri nets can be used for modeling synchronous elastic systems (ES). The reader should keep in mind that we have chosen the synchronous version primarily for illustrative purpose and that methods for modeling of elastic systems with marked graphs (Sect. 3.1), for slack matching and buffer sizing (Sect. 4), and for performance modeling of systems with early evaluation (Sect. 6) can be applied equally well to the asynchronous implementation. The only adjustment that would be then required is to change the delay annotation of the Petri Nets events with other forms of delays (e.g. with real delay numbers to model continuous time domain instead of integers used for discrete time domain in synchronous systems). Methods for control optimization (Sect. 5) and for retiming and recycling (Sect. 7) rely on the synchronous nature of the systems.

Petri nets have been extensively used in asynchronous circuit design. In [16, 17], marked graphs are the underlying formalism to model the flow of data in asynchronous circuits. Signal transition graphs [18, 19] have also been used to specify asynchronous controllers. Several examples and areas illustrating synergies between hardware and Petri nets can be found in [20].

In this paper, we focus exclusively on the use of Marked Graphs and their new extension for modeling systems with early evaluation. This is because synchronous elastic systems can be adequately modeled with this sub-classes of Petri nets that is much easier to analyze and use for formal reasoning. When analyzing the performance, we will often assume that these systems are composed of equally-timed units (e.g. 1-cycle delays). This assumption is not a limitation, but just a simplification to improve the readability of the paper. The reader will soon realize that many of the methods discussed in the paper can be easily extended to units with different delays.

Most of the strategies use either linear or mixed-integer linear programming (MILP) to solve the stated problems. Linear programming (LP) problems can be solved in polynomial time [21], while mixed-integer linear programming problems are NP-complete problems for which several reliable solvers exist [22].

2 Elastic Systems

2.1 Introduction

Synchronous circuits are often modeled, at a certain level of abstraction, as machines that read inputs and write outputs at every cycle. The outputs at cycle i are produced according to a calculation that depends on the inputs at cycles $0,\ldots,i$. Computations and data transfers are assumed to take zero delay.

Latency-insensitive design [8] aims at relaxing this model by elasticizing the time dimension and decoupling the cycles from the calculations of the circuit. It enables the design of circuits tolerant to any discrete variation (in the number of cycles) of the computation and communication delays. With this modular approach, the functionality of the system only depends on the functionality of its components and not on their timing characteristics. The motivation for latency-insensitive design comes from the difficulties with timing and communication in nanoscale technologies. The number of cycles required to transmit data from a sender to a receiver is determined by the distance between them, and often cannot be accurately known until the chip layout is generated late in the design process. Traditional design approaches require fixing the communication latencies up front, and these are difficult to amend when layout information finally becomes available. Elastic circuits offer a solution to this problem. In addition, their modularity promises novel methods for microarchitectural design that can use variable-latency components and tolerate static and dynamic changes in communication latencies, while — unlike asynchronous circuits – still employing standard synchronous design tools and methods.

Figure 1a depicts the timing behavior of a conventional synchronous adder that reads input and produces output data at every cycle (boxes represent cycles). In this adder, the ith output value is produced at the ith cycle. Figure 1b depicts a related behavior of an elastic adder—a synchronous circuit too — in which data transfer occurs in some cycles and not in others. We refer to the transferred data items simply as data and we say that idle cycles contain bubbles.

Elasticization decouples cycle count from data count. In a conventional synchronous circuit, the ith data of a wire is transmitted at the ith cycle, whereas in a synchronous elastic circuit the ith data is transmitted at some cycle $k \geq i$.

Turning a conventional synchronous adder into a synchronous elastic adder requires a communication discipline that differentiates idle from non-idle cycles (bubbles from data). This communication is usually supported by a pair of wires that synchronizes the sender and the receiver.

In asynchronous circuits, synchronization is typically implemented by two wires called *request* (from sender to receiver) and *acknowledge* (from receiver to sender).

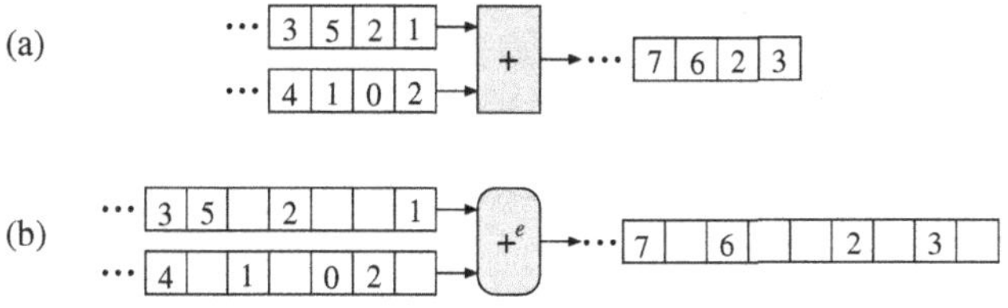

Fig. 1. a Conventional synchronous adder, **b** Synchronous elastic adder

In synchronous circuits, different nomenclatures have been used. In this paper we will call *valid* the wire from sender to receiver that indicates the validity of the data. We will also call *stop* the wire from receiver to sender that, when asserted, indicates that the receiver has not been able to accept data.

Different synchronization protocols for elasticity can be defined. In this paper we will focus on a specific one called Synchronous Elastic Flow (SELF) [11]. This protocol has been inspired on the theory of latency-insensitive design [8] and in some implementations of synchronous elastic pipelines [10].

In SELF, every input or output wire X in a synchronous component is associated to a *channel* in the elastic version of the same component. The channel is a triple of wires $< X, \mathsf{valid}_X, \mathsf{stop}_X >$, with X carrying the data and the other two wires implementing the control bits, as shown in Fig. 2b. Data is transferred on this channel when $\mathsf{valid}_X = 1$ and $\mathsf{stop}_X = 0$: the sender sends valid data and the receiver is ready to accept it.

Since elastic networks tolerate any variability in the latency of the components, empty FIFO buffers can be inserted in any channel, as shown in Fig. 2b, without changing the functional behavior of the network.

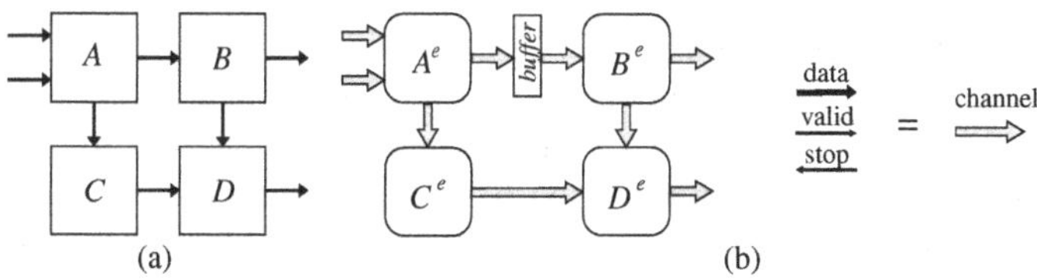

Fig. 2. a Synchronous network, **b** its elastic counterpart

2.2 Architectural View of Elastic Circuits

The FIFO buffers referred in the previous section will be called *Elastic Buffers* (EB). In elastic systems, the capacity of EBs has a direct impact on the performance. For an implementation of elasticity based on distributed control between neighboring blocks, EBs must have a capacity greater than 1 slot to avoid a degradation in performance. In particular for one-cycle propagation latency in the forward and backward directions, it has been proved that EBs with a capacity of two slots can guarantee the same performance as a non-elastic system [8].

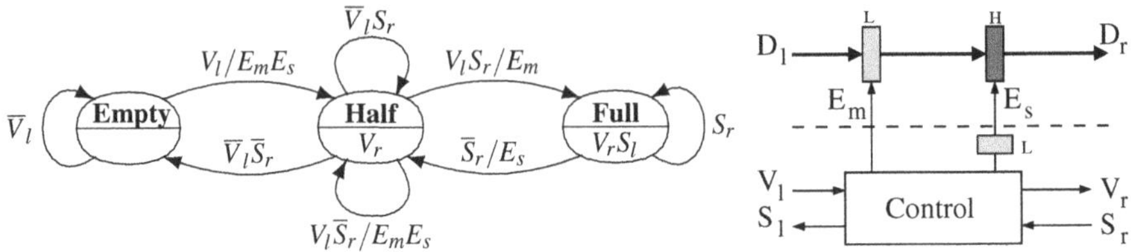

Fig. 3. Specification of the latch-based EB

There are different ways of implementing EBs. In [11], a latch-based implementation of EBs was proposed, in which each FIFO with capacity two was implemented with a pair of *Elastic Half-Buffers* (EHB). An EHB consists of a transparent latch and an associated handshake controller. An EB is composed of two EHBs in a similar way as flip–flops are implemented as a pair of transparent latches with opposite polarity (master and slave).

Figure 3 depicts the FSM specifications this scheme, where V and S represent the *valid* and *stop* signals of the handshakes and E represents the *enable* signal of the latch (transparent when high). The latches are labeled with the phase of the clock, L (active low) or H (active high). To simplify the drawing the clock lines are not shown. The enable signals must be AND-ed with the corresponding clock phase for a proper operation.

An enable signal for transparent latches must be emitted on the opposite phase and be stable during the active phase of the latch. Thus, the E_s signal for the slave latch is emitted on the L phase.

The FSM specification of Fig. 3 is similar to the specification of a two-slot FIFO: in the *Empty* state no valid data is captured in the data-path, in the *Half-full* state, an output slave latch keeps valid data, in the *Full* state — both latches keep valid data and the EB requests the sender to stop.

Let us show an architectural example of an elastic communication, with the circuit of Fig. 4. It represents part of a circuit where a sender provides data to a receiver. It is assumed a long distance between them, so EBs are inserted accordingly as shown in the figure. To make the example more general, data is processed between the latches (boxes named *CL*). White boxes represent the control part for each one of the EHBs. The example contains consecutive snapshots (left to right, top to bottom) of the consecutive states of the elastic circuit when the communication is taking place.

The situation initially is the following (top-left configuration in the figure): all but the second latch hold valid data, shown by the circles inside them. The valid bits are 1 in all the stages. The receiver is blocked, hence it has set the stop bit to 1, which has propagated two stages further towards the sender. The sender is not aware yet of the blocking of the receiver, due to the incoming stop bit with value 0. The next phase of the clock is H, so the next configuration contains the transmission into the second latch (labeled with H) of the data from the first L latch. Additionally, the stop bit has traveled one stage further towards the sender. The next phase of the clock (low) allows the sender to store data in the first L latch, and the stop bit has reached the sender. Stop bits are also known as back-pressure. After this phase, the whole channel is blocked

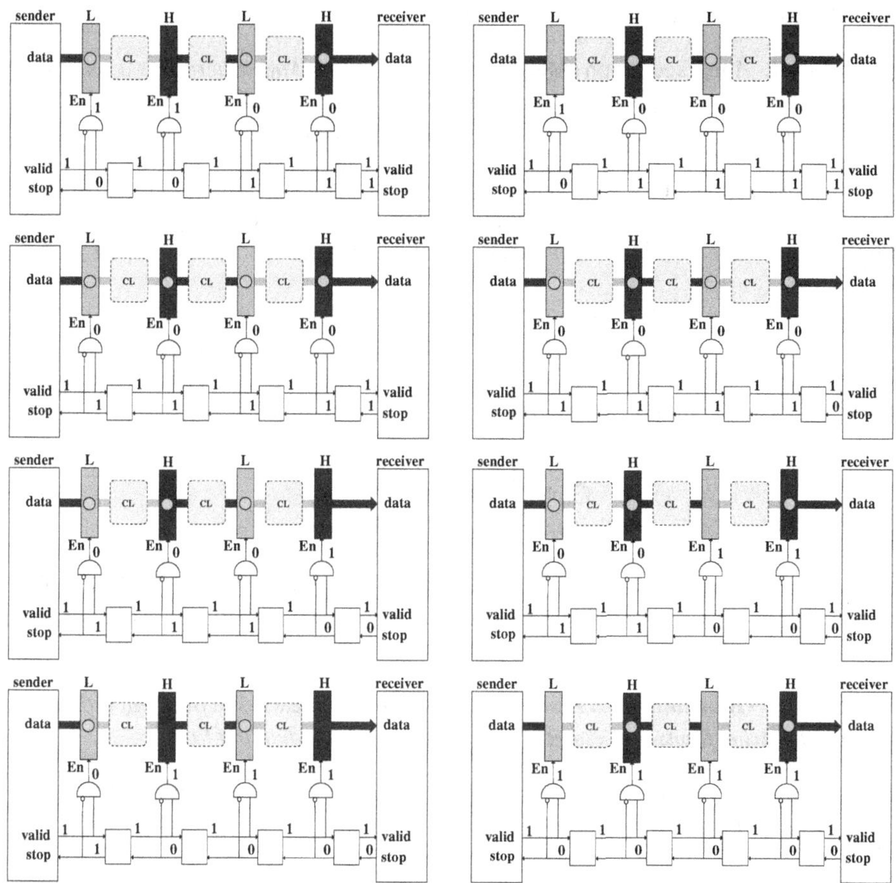

Fig. 4. Simulation of an elastic circuit

with data not processed by the receiver. New data coming from the sender must wait an arbitrary amount of time until the receiver is able to process the data on this channel. The forthcoming configurations in the figure (from the fourth to the eighth) show how the channel becomes available again when the receiver starts processing data from the full channel. Along consecutive stages, the unset stop bit travels towards the sender and the latches become enabled again.

3 Marked Graph Models for Synchronous Elasticity

This section presents the class of timed marked graphs that is used for modeling elastic systems. Although the paper is self-contained the reader can be referred to [23] for a survey on Petri nets.

3.1 Marked Graphs

Definition 1. *A* marked graph *(MG) is a tuple $G = (T, A, M_0)$, where T is a set of transitions (also called nodes), $A \subseteq T \times T$ is a set of directed arcs, and $M_0 : A \rightarrow \mathbb{N}$ is a marking that assigns an initial number of tokens to each arc.*

Without loss of generality, we model elastic systems with strongly connected MGs. For open systems interacting with an environment, it is possible to incorporate an abstraction of the environment into the model by a transition that connects the outputs with the inputs.

Given a transition $t \in T$, ${}^\bullet t$ and $t^\bullet$ denote the set of incoming and outgoing arcs of t, respectively. Given an arc $a \in A$, ${}^\bullet a$ and $a^\bullet$ refer to the source and target transition of a respectively. Let $\mathbb{C}$ be the $n \times m$ incidence matrix of the MG with rows corresponding to the n arcs and columns to the m transitions:

$$\mathbb{C}_{ij} = \begin{cases} -1 & \text{if } t_j \in a_i^\bullet \setminus {}^\bullet a_i \\ +1 & \text{if } t_j \in {}^\bullet a_i \setminus a_i^\bullet \\ 0 & \text{otherwise} \end{cases}$$

A transition t is *enabled* at a marking M if $M(a) > 0$ for every $a \in {}^\bullet t$. Any enabled transition t can fire. The firing of t removes one token from each input arc of t, and adds one token to each output arc of t.

Definition 2 (Reachability). *A marking M is said to be* reachable *from M_0 if there is a sequence of transitions that can fire starting from M_0 and leading to M.*

Definition 3 (Liveness). *An MG is said to be live if every node can eventually fire from any reachable marking.*

For the sake of notation, the total number of tokens in a subset $\phi \subseteq A$ at a given marking M is denoted by $M(\phi) = \sum_{a \in \phi} M(a)$. Some useful properties of strongly connected MGs [23] are:

Property 1 (Liveness). *An MG is* live *iff every cycle* $\mathbf{c}$ *is marked positively at M_0, i.e., $M_0(\mathbf{c}) > 0$.*

All the MGs considered throughout this paper are assumed to be live.

Property 2 (State equation and reachability). *A marking $M \geq 0$ is reachable from the initial marking M_0 iff the state equation*

$$M = M_0 + \mathbb{C} \cdot \sigma\ ,\ \sigma \geq 0 \tag{1}$$

is satisfied for some firing count vector σ (the j's component of σ corresponds to the number of times transition t_j has fired).

Property 3 (Cycles and reachability). *A marking M is reachable iff $M(\mathbf{c}) = M_0(\mathbf{c})$ for every cycle $\mathbf{c}$ of the MG.*

3.2 Timed Marked Graphs

Definition 4. *A timed marked graph (TMG) is a tuple $G = (T, A, M_0, \delta)$, where (T, A, M_0) is a MG, and $\delta : T \rightarrow \mathbb{R}^+ \cup \{0\}$ assigns a non-negative delay to every transition.*

In a TMG, a transition t fires $\delta(t)$ time units after becoming enabled. In order to correctly model the time behavior of the circuits, single server semantics is adopted, i.e., no multiple instances of the same transition can fire simultaneously. Notice that single server semantics is a particular case of infinite server semantics: the addition of a self-loop place with one token, i.e., a place p such that $p^\bullet = {}^\bullet p$ and $M_0(p) = 1$, around each transition guarantees single server semantics [24].

The average marking of an arc a, denoted as $\overline{M}(a)$, represents the average occupancy of the arc in steady state. Formally the average marking vector for all arcs is defined as:

$$\overline{M} = \lim_{\tau \to \infty} \frac{1}{\tau} \int_0^\tau M_\varphi d\varphi$$

where M_φ is the marking at time φ.

Performance Evaluation. We will measure the performance of a TMG as the throughput of its transitions. The throughput of a transition t, $\Theta(t)$, is the average number of times t fires per time unit, or cycle time, in the infinitely long execution of the system. Given that we are considering strongly connected TMGs, in the steady state all transitions have exactly the same throughput, Θ. We will describe two well-known methods to compute the throughput of a TMG.

Method 1. Each pair $\{a, a^\bullet\}$ of the TMG can be seen as a simple queuing system for which Little's formula [25] can be directly applied. Hence,

$$\overline{M}(a) = \overline{R}(a) \cdot \Theta \tag{2}$$

where $\overline{R}(a)$ is the average residence time at arc a, i.e., the average time spent by a token on the arc a [24]. The average residence time is the sum of the average waiting time due to a possible synchronization, and the average service time which in the case of TMGs is $\delta(a^\bullet)$. Therefore, the service time $\delta(a^\bullet)$ is a lower bound for the average residence time. This leads to the inequality:

$$\overline{M}(a) \geq \delta(a^\bullet) \cdot \Theta \quad \text{for every arc } a \tag{3}$$

The following LP Problem includes the constraint (3) for each arc, and the reachability condition for a estimated average marking $\widehat{M}$:

$$\begin{aligned} &\textit{Maximize}\ \ \Theta : \\ &\qquad \delta(a^\bullet) \cdot \Theta \leq \widehat{M}(a) \ \text{ for every } a \in A \\ &\qquad \widehat{M} = M_0 + \mathbb{C} \cdot \sigma \\ &\qquad \Theta \leq \min_{t \in T} \frac{1}{\delta(t)} \end{aligned} \tag{4}$$

The last constraint $\Theta \leq \min_{t \in T} 1/\delta(t)$ ensures single server semantics. Such constraint can be dropped if a self-loop arc with one token is introduced around each transition. The solution of LP (4) is the exact throughput of the TMG [24].

Method 2. If C is the set of simple directed cycles in an TMG, its throughput can be determined as [26]:

$$\Theta = \min \left\{ \min_{\mathbf{c} \in C} \frac{M_0(\mathbf{c})}{\sum_{t \in \mathbf{c}} \delta(t)}, \min_{t \in T} \frac{1}{\delta(t)} \right\} \tag{5}$$

As in (4), the term $\min_{t \in T} 1/\delta(t)$ enforces single server semantics. Many efficient algorithms for computing the throughput of an TMG exist that do not require an exhaustive enumeration of all cycles [27,28]. In practice, method 2 usually computes the throughput more efficiently than method 1.

Definition 5 (Critical cycle and arc). *A cycle* $\mathbf{c}$ *satisfying the equality* (5) *is called* critical. *An arc is called critical if it belongs to a critical cycle.*

3.3 Elastic Marked Graphs

Definition 6. *An* elastic marked graph *(EMG) is a tuple* $G = (T, A, M_0, \delta, L)$, *where* (T, A, M_0, δ) *is a TMG and:*

- $\delta : T \to \mathbb{N}^+$ *assigns a positive integer delay to every transition.*
- *For every arc* $a \in A$ *there exists a complementary arc* $a' \in A$ *satisfying the condition* ${}^\bullet a = a'^\bullet$ *and* ${}^\bullet a' = a^\bullet$. *A labeling function L maps all arcs of an EMG as forward or backward* $L : A \to \{F, B\}$ *such that* $L(a) = F$ *iff* $L(a') = B$.

The delay $\delta(t)$ of a given transition t represents the number of time cycles required by t to perform its computation. Thus, the class of EMGs can model adequately synchronous elastic systems. Typically, in the initial state of an elastic system there is at most one token on a forward arc.

Figure 5 shows an example of EMG. Given that in an EMG every arc a has a complementary arc a', for every pair $\{a, a'\}$, the equality $M(a) + M(a') = M_0(a) + M_0(a') = k$ is satisfied, where k is the capacity of the buffer $\{a, a'\}$. Semantically, the pair $\{a, a'\}$ represents the state of an EB. Assume that $L(a) = F$ and $L(a') = B$. We say that the

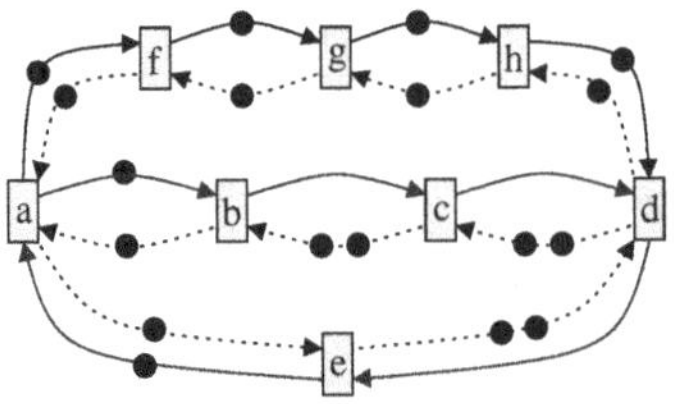

Fig. 5. An example of an elastic marked graph

EB is full when $M(a) = k$, $M(a') = 0$; when $M(a) = 0$, $M(a') = k$ we say that there is a *bubble* in the system. For instance, the EB represented by the arc pair $\{b,c\}$ in Fig. 5 is a bubble. $M(a)$ represents the number of information items inside the buffer, while $M(a')$ represents available free space in the state of the system that corresponds to the marking M. $M_0(a)$, and $M_0(a')$ represents the corresponding values at the time of system initialization after the reset.

4 Slack Matching

The performance of an elastic system may degrade because of unbalanced pipelines. This is a well-known problem in asynchronous design. In order to balance the pipelines and improve the performance empty buffers must be added [29–31]. This strategy is known as *slack matching*.

In this section, we present two transformations for slack matching of ES: buffer sizing and recycling. The main optimization considered here is *buffer sizing*, that consists on variations of the capacity of the EBs. At the end of the section, we will show that the insertion of bubbles (recycling) also may increase the throughput.

4.1 An Introductory Example

When tokens arrive at the input arcs of a join transition at different times, the early token will stall. The stalled event may generate further stalled events, i.e., it propagates backwards, which may degrade system performance. A very nice explanation of the nature of this phenomenon as well as the exact MILP for slack matching asynchronous design can be found in [31].

Here we try to give an intuitive understanding of the slack matching problem. For this purpose let us simulate the simple EMG depicted in Fig. 6. The EMG has the so called unbalanced fork–join structure. The fork transition is a, the join is c. The short branch is $\{a,c\}$ and the long one is $\{a,b,c\}$. All transitions have unit delay. The join transition c is not enabled at time stamp 0. This causes to stall the token on the arc $\{a,c\}$ by one time unit. The rest of the transitions are enabled and will fire. The resulting marking is shown at the configuration in time stamp 1. Now the EB that corresponds to the arc

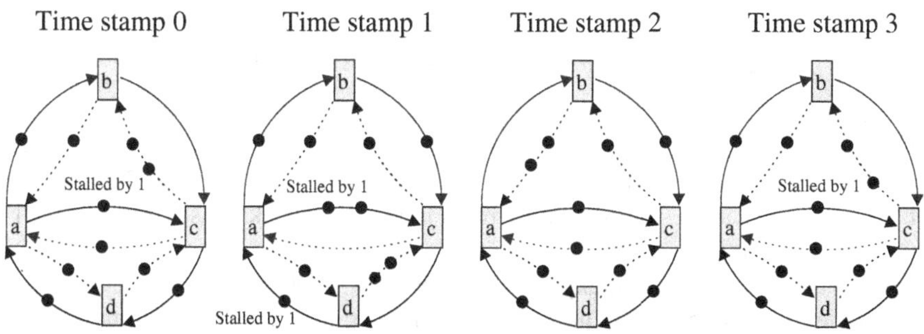

Fig. 6. A stall event backward propagation causes a throughput degradation

$\{a,c\}$ is full and cannot receive new data. Thus, in time stamp 1 transitions a and d are not enabled. This makes the token on the arc $\{d,a\}$ stall by one time unit. At time stamp 2 all transitions are enabled but b. At time stamp 3, the EMG is in the initial state. Each transition has fired twice during three time stamps. Hence, the throughput of the EMG is equal to 2/3. The critical cycle is $\{a,b,c\}$. It has two tokens and three arcs.

The EMG model allows us to identify when to balance the corresponding ES in order to avoid throughput degradation:

The backward propagation of stalled events leads to the ES throughput degradation iff there are backward arcs on all critical cycles of the corresponding EMG. In the provided example the critical cycle $\{a,b,c\}$ contains the backward arc $\{c,a\}$.

Buffer sizing and recycling transformations aim to make the throughput independent of backward edges. Hence, the maximum throughput that can be achieved by buffer sizing in a EMG is equal to the throughput of the "forward" TMG that is obtained by removing all backward arcs from the initial EMG.

4.2 MILP for Buffer Sizing

Buffer sizing adds tokens to backward arcs, i.e., it increases the capacities of the corresponding EBs.

For example, to remove the backward arc $\{c,a\}$ from the critical cycle in Fig. 6 it is enough to increase the capacity of the corresponding EB by one. Figure 7b shows the resulting EMG. The throughput is now equal to 3/4. The critical cycle $\{a,b,c,d\}$ contains only forward arcs. Tokens in the arc $\{d,a\}$ never stall.

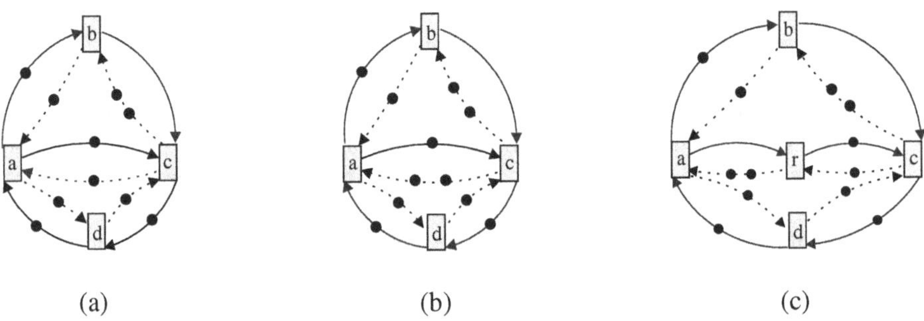

Fig. 7. a EMG from the Figure 6, **b** Buffer sizing, **c** Recycling

The maximum throughput can always be achieved by some proper buffer sizing, however to find a sizing with minimal storage elements overhead is an NP-complete problem [32]; this can be also shown by reducing the feedback arc set problem [33] to minimal buffer sizing.

Let us assume that the throughput of the "forward" TMG is known (it can be computed efficiently with the techniques presented in Sect. 3.2). Using an estimation of the average marking of the TMG, that was introduced in Sect. 3.2, one can encode the problem of buffer sizing with minimal storage elements overhead as the following MILP:

$$\begin{aligned} Minimize \ & \sum_{a\in A} \Delta M_0(a): \\ & \widehat{M} = M_0 + \Delta M_0 + \mathbb{C}\cdot\sigma, \\ & \widehat{M}(a) \geq \delta(a^\bullet)\cdot\Theta \text{ for every } a\in A, \\ & \Delta M_0 \in \mathbb{N}^{|A|}. \end{aligned} \tag{6}$$

Here Θ is throughput of the corresponding "forward" TMG. For each backward arc a, $\Delta M_0(a)$ contains the number of tokens that need to be added to a in order to reach the throughput Θ. The number $M_0(a) + \Delta M_0(a)$ represents the new marking of a. If a is a forward arc, then $\Delta M_0(a) = 0$ in the solution of (6). In [34], a similar MILP for minimal buffer sizing is presented, which is not based on the MGs theory.

The main disadvantage of buffer sizing is that it increases the complexity and consequently, the area and the combinational delay of the control logic of the ES are increased [35, 36].

4.3 Recycling for Slack Matching

In some situations, the throughput of an ES may be improved by inserting bubbles. Bubble insertion transformation is called *recycling*.

Figure 7c shows how the throughput of the EMG depicted in Fig. 6 can be increased by inserting the bubble $\{a, r\}$ between transitions a and c. The throughput of the resulting EMG is equal to 3/4, with critical cycles $\{a, b, c, d\}$ and $\{a, r, c, d\}$.

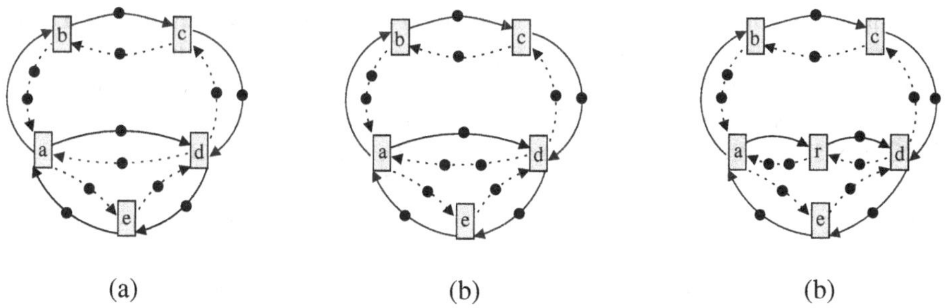

Fig. 8. Buffer sizing vs recycling

The main advantage of recycling with respect to buffer sizing is that no extra combinational logic in the control path is required. A weakness is that it may increase the response time of the system. Another drawback is that recycling may not achieve the maximum throughput improvement achieved by buffer sizing. An EMG where this happens is depicted in Fig. 8a. Assuming unit delays, the throughput in Fig. 8a is equal to 3/4, with the critical cycle $\{a,b,c,d\}$. The maximum throughput is given by the "forward" cycle $\{a,b,c,d,e\}$, and it is equal to 4/5. Applying buffer sizing, this throughput can be achieved by increasing the capacity of the buffer $\{a,d\}$, as shown in Fig. 8b.

From the EMG in Fig. 8a, let us try to achieve the same throughput improvement with recycling. Arc $\{d,a\}$ is the only backward arc in the critical cycle. Hence, channel $\{a,d\}$ is the only place where we can insert a bubble to balance the unbalanced fork–join $a-d$. The resulting EMG is depicted in Fig. 8c. It still has throughput $3/4$, due to the new critical cycle $\{a,r,d,e\}$.

In general, the insertion of bubbles in a critical cycle adds a zero-marked arc which may preclude to reach the maximum throughput.

In summary, buffer sizing and recycling are two optimization strategies that can be combined to improve the performance of an ES by removing stall event backward propagation. Depending on the structure of the circuit, buffer sizing can sometimes derive better results, but has a control overhead. For large circuits or circuits containing a regular structure, both transformations will likely lead to the same result.

5 Control Optimization

The main cost of elastizising a synchronous circuit is a control overhead. This section introduces a control simplification technique that reduces this overhead considerably while preserving the performance of the system. For simplicity, in this section we focus on synchronous elastic systems where all transitions have the same delay: $\delta(t_i) = \delta(t_j)$ for every $t_i, t_j \in T$. However, the reader will soon realize that the methods presented in this section can be easily extended to transitions with different delays.

5.1 An Introductory Example

The implementation of an elastic system maps an EMG to an asynchronous or a synchronous control circuit. For instance, Fig. 9a depicts the elastic circuit corresponding to part (events a, b and f) of the EMG drawn in Fig. 10a. The complexity of the circuit is typically linear in the size of the EMG (e.g. [11]). Therefore, reducing the size of an EMG contributes directly to the size reduction of the control circuit. Based on this fact, we focus on reducing the number of arcs in an EMG modeling an elastic system as this reduces the number of EBs and the number of channels in the fork and join controllers (that corresponds to transitions with multiple fan-out and fan-in, respectively).

For example, Fig. 9b corresponds to the sharing of transitions b and f from the EMG of Fig. 10 into a single transition. As a result of this sharing the implementation is simplified by removing one controller, one channel (a pair of handshake wires), and one EB, $F3$, in the data-path that is shared with $F2$.

The goal of this section is to identify a class of transformations that reduce the number of controllers while preserving the performance of the system. In particular, the firing of some transitions can be deliberately postponed in order to be synchronized to other transitions, allowing the sharing of their controllers without degrading the performance of the system.

As described in Sect. 3.2, the performance of an EMG can be measured by its throughput that is defined as the minimal ratio of the number of tokens to the delay across all simple cycles and can be efficiently computed [37]. Assuming that the delays of all transitions in Fig. 10a are equal to 1, the critical cycle is $\{a,b,c,d,e\}$ with

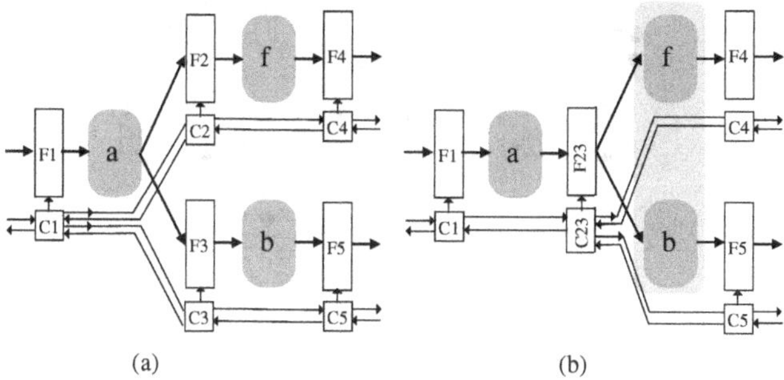

Fig. 9. Sharing a controller and an elastic FIFO

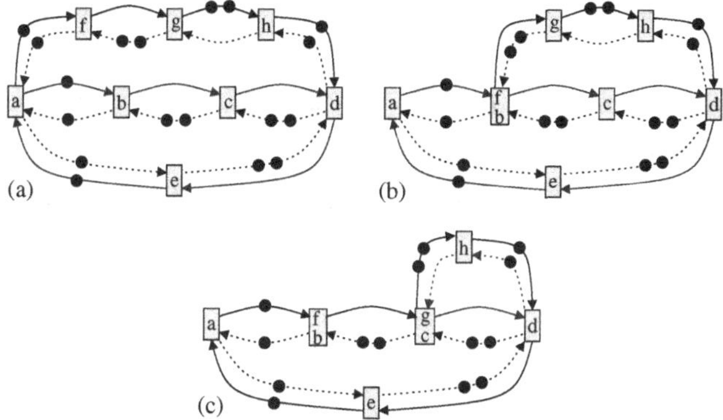

Fig. 10. An example of a elastic marked graph **a**, merging b and f **b**, and c and g **c**

a throughput $2/5$ (two tokens on the arcs of the cycle; delay of the cycle is five units). Since the initial marking of the arcs between a and b, and the arcs between a and f is the same, it is possible to merge transitions b and f (as shown in Fig. 10b) without affecting correctness of computation. The throughput of the system is the same $2/5$ and so is the critical cycle $\{a,\{b,f\},c,d,e\}$. Fig. 9b shows the corresponding implementation, simplified according to the merging of b and f.

Focusing on the new fork transition $\{b,f\}$ we again determine that the initial marking of arc pairs between $\{b,f\}$ and its successors c and g is the same and therefore it is possible to merge transitions c and g (as shown in Fig. 10c). However, the throughput of the system is degraded to $1/3$, with a new critical cycle $\{\{c,g\},d,h\}$.

5.2 A Sufficient Condition to Compute Mergeable Transitions

In the example above, the initial marking is used to decide whether two transitions can be merged: when the arcs from an adjacent fork transition have the same initial marking, then the transitions can be merged. The remainder of this section will present a strategy that uses a different marking (called *tight*) to compute mergeable transitions. A tight marking can be considered a variation of the average marking. It better exploits the

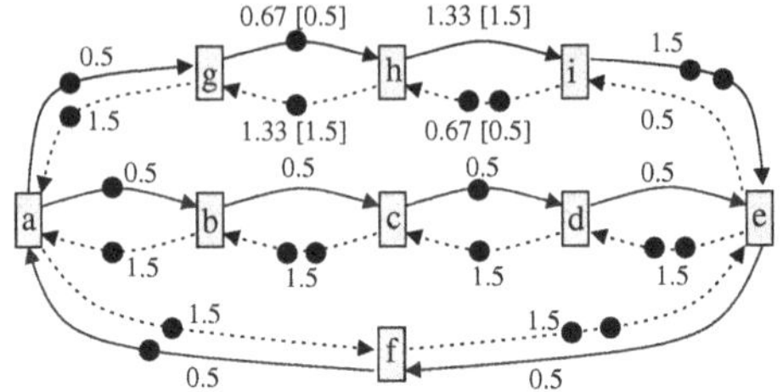

Fig. 11. An EMG illustrating a tight marking

flexibility of the system, in order to make the markings on the arcs as much as possible equal to maximize the sharing of controllers.

Formally, those pair of transitions that can be merged without degrading the performance of the system are defined:

Definition 7. *Transitions t_i and t_j are said to be* mergeable *if an* EMG $G < t_i, t_j >$ *obtained by merging transitions t_i and t_j in an* EMG *G has the same throughput as G.*

The formal definition of tight marking is the following:

Definition 8. *A marking $\tilde{M}$ is called a* tight *marking of an* EMG *if it satisfies:*

$$\tilde{M} = M_0 + \mathbb{C} \cdot \sigma \tag{7}$$

$$\forall\, a: \quad \tilde{M}(a) \geq \delta(a^\bullet) \cdot \Theta \tag{8}$$

$$\forall\, t\, \exists\, a \in {}^\bullet t: \quad \tilde{M}(a) = \delta(a^\bullet) \cdot \Theta \tag{9}$$

where $\tilde{M} \in \mathbb{R}^{|A|}$, $\sigma \in \mathbb{R}^{|T|}$, and Θ is the throughput of the EMG*. An arc a satisfying condition $\tilde{M}(a) = \delta(a^\bullet) \cdot \Theta$ is called* tight*.*

Therefore a tight marking satisfies the state equation (condition (7)) and no arc has marking less than $\delta(a^\bullet) \cdot \Theta$ (condition (8)). These two conditions are also satisfied by the average marking, and their relation with the system throughput has been described in Sect. 3.2. Additionally, the tight marking requires that every transition must have at least one tight incoming arc.

Let us consider the EMG in Fig. 11. It has a single critical cycle $\{a, b, c, d, e, f\}$ with a throughput 0.5. Each arc in Fig. 11 is labeled with one number if its average and tight markings coincide. When they are different the average marking is listed first and the tight marking is shown in square brackets. If the initial marking or the average marking are used, the only mergeable transitions are g and b (g and b are the only two transitions connected to the fork transition a such that $\overline{M}(ag) = \overline{M}(ab)$). However, if the tight marking is used instead, transitions h and c can be additionally merged.

The following theorem formalizes the above concepts on the tight marking [38]:

Theorem 1. *Let $\tilde{M}$ be a tight marking of an* EMG *G. Transitions t_i and t_j of G are mergeable if there exist arcs $a_i \in {}^\bullet t_i$ and $a_j \in {}^\bullet t_j$ such that:*

- $L(a_i) = L(a_j)$,
- $\tilde{M}(a_i) = \tilde{M}(a_j) = \delta(a_i^\bullet) \cdot \Theta$,
- *(${}^\bullet a_i = {}^\bullet a_j$) or (${}^\bullet a_i$ and ${}^\bullet a_j$ are mergeable).*

The first two conditions of Theorem 1 narrow the search space to tight arcs with the same label (forward or backward). The third condition defines iterative merging. These three conditions ensure the existence of an initialization, i.e., firing sequence of transitions, that produces a marking M in which $M(a_i) = M(a_j)$. Such an initialization corresponds to changing the initial marking of the EMG and can be acceptable in many, but not all, applications. After such initialization, transitions t_i and t_j can effectively be merged. This merging will make arcs a_i and a_j be identical, since $M(a_i) = M(a_j)$, $L(a_i) = L(a_j)$, ${}^\bullet a_i = {}^\bullet a_j$ and $a_i^\bullet = a_j^\bullet$, and hence they will be merged into a single arc.

A tight marking can be computed efficiently, as the following proposition states [38]:

Proposition 1. *A tight marking of a* EMG *can be computed by solving the following LP problem:*

$$\begin{aligned} &Maximize\ \Sigma\sigma : \\ &\qquad \delta(a^\bullet)\cdot\Theta \le \tilde{M}(a) \quad \textit{for every} \quad a \in A \\ &\qquad \tilde{M} = M_0 + \mathbb{C}\cdot\sigma \\ &\qquad \sigma(t_a) = k \end{aligned} \tag{10}$$

where t_a is a transition that belongs to a critical cycle and k is any real number. The last constraint guarantees the boundedness of the solution. Since the objective function $\Sigma\sigma$ is maximized, the obtained $\tilde{M}$ satisfies that for every transition t there exists an arc $a \in {}^\bullet t$ such that $\delta(t)\cdot\Theta = \tilde{M}(a)$.

The first two constraints of (10) can be transformed into:

$$\delta\cdot\Theta - M_0 \le \mathbb{C}\cdot\sigma \tag{11}$$

Since we are dealing with MGs, each row of the incidence matrix $\mathbb{C}$ contains a single positive $(+1)$ and a single negative (-1) value, while all other values are zeros. Therefore, Equation (11) is a system of *difference constraints* and hence the LP (10) can be efficiently solved by the Bellman–Ford algorithm [39].

The overall strategy for reducing an EMG involves the following steps:

1) Computation of the throughput of the system
2) Computation of a tight marking
3) Determine the sets of mergeable transitions by traversing the tight subgraph
4) Fire transitions to obtain the same marking in the input arcs of the mergeable transitions
5) Merge mergeable transitions and identical arcs.

6 Early Evaluation

In an early evaluation setting, operations can execute when enough information at the inputs has been received to determine the value at the outputs. The performance of elastic systems can be enhanced by using early evaluation. This section proposes an analytical model to estimate the performance of an early evaluated marked graph (see [40] for a preliminary work).

6.1 Motivation and Examples

The requirement that all input data must be available to compute a result is too strict in some cases. For example, if a functional unit computes $a = b * c$, it is not necessary to wait for both operands if one of them is already available and known to be zero. Therefore, the result $a = 0$ could be produced by an *early evaluation* of the expression. Early evaluation has been proposed and used in asynchronous design [41, 42].

Usual Petri nets are not capable of modeling early evaluation, since the enabling of transitions is based on AND-causality, i.e., all input conditions must be asserted. Causal Logic Nets from [43] extend Petri nets to allow transition enabling triggered by arbitrary logic guards associated with transitions. This section presents a new model of nets, called *multi-guarded nets* (GN), with the power of modeling early evaluation that associate with a single transition multiple logic guards selected non-deterministically. This non-deterministic selection models interaction of the control with conditions in the data-path.

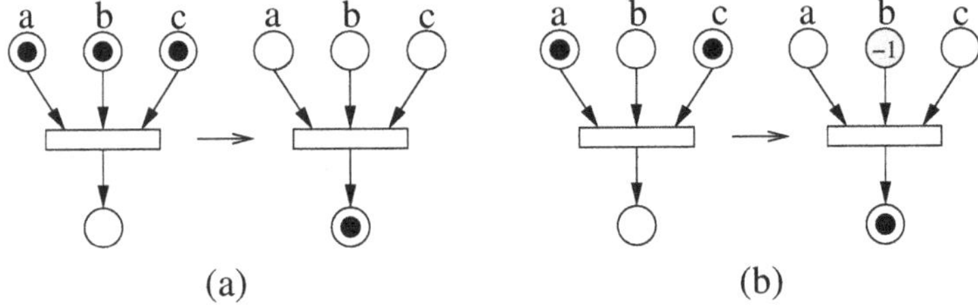

Fig. 12. Multi-guarded transitions: **a** AND-causality; **b** early firing with guard $\{c\}$

Figure 12a illustrates the usual firing rule in Petri nets (AND-causality). Early evaluation is modeled by *multi-guarded* transitions. A guard is a subset of arcs that can enable a transition. A multi-guarded transition has a set of guards from which one of them is chosen nondeterministically at each firing. Assume that the guards of the transition in Fig. 12b are $\{\{a\}, \{b\}, \{c\}\}$, and $\{c\}$ is the guard selected for the next firing. Given that arc c is positively marked, the transition is enabled and will fire. The firing of an early-enabled transition removes a token from every input arc. If an input arc is not positively marked, a *negative token* (-1) is placed in it. This negative token will be cancelled out when a *positive token* arrives at the arc.

Example 1. The most relevant example of a unit with early evaluation is the multiplexor: the output can be determined as soon as the information of the selected channel arrives, without waiting for the other channels.

Figure 13 depicts a marked graph with three cycles. The shadowed transitions t_1 and t_2 model two multiplexors. Their control signals are assumed not to be critical and are not depicted in the graph. Thus, the two input arcs of the multiplexors model the two input data. Associated to each input arc there is a guard and a real number in the interval $[0, 1]$ that indicates the probability for the guard to be selected. Each transition is assumed to have unit delay.

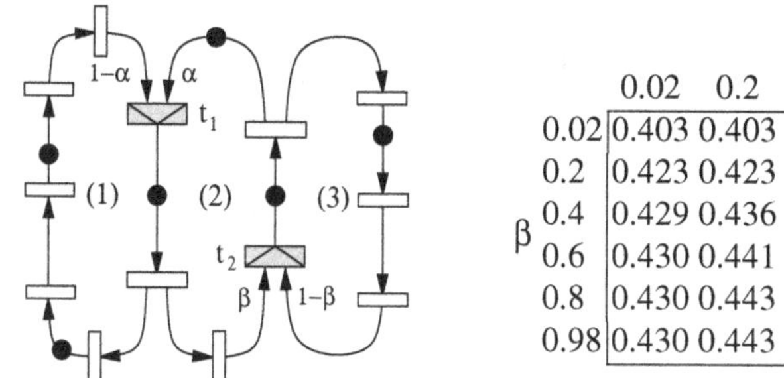

β \ α	0.02	0.2	0.4	0.6	0.8	0.98
0.02	0.403	0.403	0.403	0.403	0.403	0.403
0.2	0.423	0.423	0.424	0.424	0.425	0.426
0.4	0.429	0.436	0.442	0.447	0.451	0.453
0.6	0.430	0.441	0.454	0.465	0.480	0.487
0.8	0.430	0.443	0.460	0.479	0.507	0.530
0.98	0.430	0.443	0.461	0.488	0.527	0.584

Fig. 13. Throughput of a GN with probabilistic guards

Under a pure Petri net model with AND-causality, the performance of the system would be determined by the most stringent cycle. The throughput Θ_i (tokens/transitions) for each cycle is the following:

$$\Theta_1 = \frac{3}{7} = 0.429 \quad \Theta_2 = \frac{3}{5} = 0.6 \quad \Theta_3 = \frac{2}{5} = 0.4$$

Hence, the global throughput of the system would be 2/5. By incorporating early evaluation, the throughput can be increased, as shown in the table at the right-hand side of the figure. When β is close to 0, the system throughput tends to 0.4, i.e., it is almost completely determined by cycle (3). On the other hand, as α and β approach 1, the throughput increases and tends to 0.6, i.e., cycle (2) determines the system throughput. In general, the throughput lies between 0.4 and 0.6 depending on the probabilities at each multiplexor.

One could think of computing the throughput of the early evaluation system as a weighted sum of the throughputs of the individual loops, i.e., for the above example such a sum would be $\alpha \cdot \beta \cdot \frac{3}{5} + (1-\alpha) \cdot \beta \cdot \frac{3}{7} + \alpha \cdot (1-\beta) \cdot \frac{2}{5} + (1-\alpha) \cdot (1-\beta) \cdot \frac{2}{5}$. Nevertheless, this method is incorrect, since loops may affect each other in a complex interplay.

6.2 Approximate Models for Early Evaluation

Definition 9. *A timed multi-guarded marked graph (TGMG) is a tuple $N = \langle T, A, M_0, \delta, H, \alpha \rangle$ where:*

- *$\langle T, A, M_0, \delta \rangle$ is a timed marked graph TMG working under single server semantics.*
- *$H : T \to 2^{2^A}$ assigns a set of guards to every transition, such that the following condition is satisfied: Every transition t is assigned a set of guards $H(t)$, where every guard $g_i \in H(t)$ is a subset of the input arcs of t, i.e., $g_i \subseteq {}^\bullet t$, and $\bigcup_{g \in H(t)} g = {}^\bullet t$.*
- *α is a function that assigns a strictly positive probability to each guard such that for every guarded transition t: $\sum_{g \in H(t)} \alpha(g) = 1$.*

A guard $g \in H(t)$ is selected first in the initial marking, M_0, and then after each firing of t. The probability of selecting the guard $g \in H(t)$ is $\alpha(g)$. The selected guard of

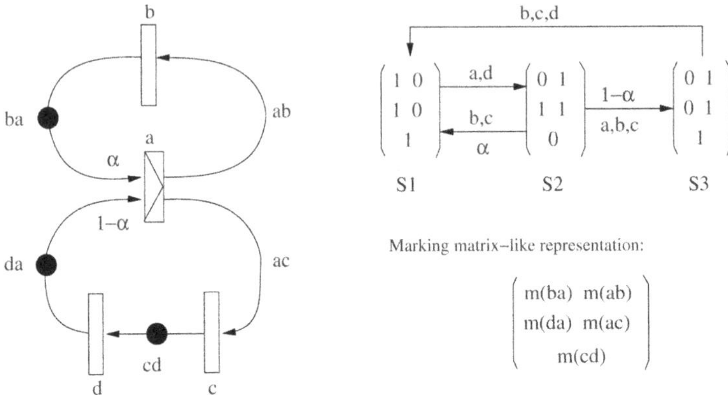

Fig. 14. A TGMG and its associated Markov chain

a transition t is *persistent*, i.e., it never changes between the firings of t. If the guard $g \in H(t)$ has been selected for the next firing of t, then t becomes enabled when every arc $a \in g$ has a token ($M(a) > 0$). If t is enabled, it fires $\delta(t)$ time units after becoming enabled. As in conventional transitions, the firing of t removes one token from every input place, and produces one token in every output place. A classical Petri net is simply a GN in which $H(t) = \{{}^\bullet t\}$, for every $t \in T$. Such transitions will be called *simple* transitions.

Analysis through Markov Chains. Due to the stochastic nature of selecting guards a TGMG can be viewed as a semi-Markov process [44]. In such a process, the sojourn time of a given state is the elapsed time between the arrival time to the state and the firing time of a transition from such a state.

Figure 14 shows a TGMG (delays of all transitions assumed to be 1) and the associated transition graph of the semi-Markov process. Each arc of the graph corresponds to one time unit. For simplicity, the transitions of the TGMG are named a, b, c, d and arcs ab, ba, ac, cd, da using pairs of names of preset–postset transitions. The states of this graph S_1, S_2, S_3 are the reachable markings. The matrix-like shape depicted at each state correspond to the marking at each state (see graphical explanation in Fig. 14). Arcs are labeled with probabilities to be taken (omitted if probability is 1) and a set of firing transitions.

The average time spent at each state (marking) at the steady state can be obtained by solving the set of linear equations corresponding to the semi-Markov process. Let Z_1, Z_2, Z_3 be the probabilities to be in the corresponding states S_1, S_2, S_3 in steady state. One can write a set of equations corresponding to the transitions of the process:

$$Z_2 = Z_1$$
$$Z_3 = (1-\alpha) \cdot Z_2$$
$$Z_1 + Z_2 + Z_3 = 1$$

The solution is:

$$Z_1 = Z_2 = \frac{1}{3-\alpha}, \quad Z_3 = \frac{1-\alpha}{3-\alpha}$$

Transition a is fired with probability 1 from S_1 and with probability $1-\alpha$ from S_2. Therefore, the steady state throughput of transition a is:

$$\Theta(a) = Z_1 + (1-\alpha)\cdot Z_2 = \frac{2-\alpha}{3-\alpha}$$

As in classical TMGs, the steady state throughput of a TGMG is the same for every transition [40], i.e., $\Theta(a) = \Theta(b) = \Theta(c) = \Theta(d)$.

6.3 Performance Estimation

The use of Markov chains allows one to compute the exact throughput of any bounded TGMG. However, it requires an exhaustive exploration of the reachability graph that is exponentially larger than the size of the bounded TGMG. This section presents a method to obtain an upper throughput bound via LP, i.e., the method has polynomial complexity.

For the sake of clarity, we will assume that every transition t has singleton guards, i.e., $|g| = 1$ for every $g \in H(t)$, or is simple, i.e., $H(t) = \{{}^\bullet t\}$. The set of transitions with singleton guards is denoted as T_1, and the set of simple transitions is denoted as T_2. Transitions with only one input arc can be included either in T_1 or in T_2. This assumption does not involve a loss of generality: a transition with non-singleton guards can be transformed to a transition with singleton guards with identical behavior [40].

Let $t \in T_2$. As explained in Sect. 3.2, Equation (3) is satisfied by each pair $\{a,t\}$ where $a^\bullet = t$. In other words, Equation (3) expresses linear relationships between the throughput of a simple transition and the average marking of its input arcs.

For each transition $t \in T_1$, it is also possible to establish a linear relationship between its throughput and the average marking of its input arcs. Let $t \in T_1$ and $prob(enab(t))$ be the probability of t to be enabled in steady state. In other words, $prob(enab(t))$ is the time ratio during which t is enabled. Since transitions have deterministic delays and operate under the single server semantics, the enabling operational law [45] for t is:

$$\delta(t)\cdot\Theta(t) = prob(enab(t)) \qquad \text{for any} \quad t \in T \tag{12}$$

After a number of algebraic manipulations, the value $prob(enab(t))$ can be expressed in terms of the marking of the input arcs of t. In particular, a useful expression is given by Theorem 2 [40]:

Theorem 2. *Let t be a transition with singleton guards, then:*

$$\delta(t)\cdot\Theta(t) = \sum_{a\in {}^\bullet t} \alpha(\{a\})\cdot\left(\overline{M}(a) - \sum_{i=2}^{\infty}(i-1)\cdot prob(M(a)=i)\right)$$

Corollary 1. *Let t be a transition with singleton guards. If the marking of its input arcs is 1-upperbounded then:*

$$\delta(t)\cdot\Theta(t) = \sum_{a\in {}^\bullet t} \alpha(\{a\})\cdot\overline{M}(a)$$

else:

$$\delta(t)\cdot\Theta(t) < \sum_{a\in {}^\bullet t} \alpha(\{a\})\cdot\overline{M}(a)$$

One can combine the constraints in Corollary 1 for transitions in T_1 and the constraint (3) for transitions in T_2 to build a LP Problem that maximizes a parameter ϕ, corresponding to the TGMG throughput. One scalar variable suffices since the throughput of all transitions is the same. The resulting LP can be expressed as:

$$\begin{aligned}
&\textit{Maximize}\ \ \phi : \\
&\quad \delta(t)\cdot\phi \le \sum_{a\in{}^\bullet t} \alpha(\{a\})\cdot\widehat{M}(a) \text{ for every } \ t\in T_1 \\
&\quad \delta(t)\cdot\phi \le \widehat{M}(a) \text{ for every } \ a\in{}^\bullet T_2 \\
&\quad \widehat{M} = M_0 + \mathbb{C}\cdot\sigma \\
&\quad \phi \le \min_{t\in T} 1/\delta(t)
\end{aligned} \tag{13}$$

The vector σ represents the firing count vector that drives the system from the initial marking, M_0, to the estimated average marking $\widehat{M}$. The constraint $\sigma \ge 0$ has been dropped since for any non-positive σ, a positive σ exists that delivers the same maximum value of ϕ (this is due to the fact that C is not a full rank matrix). The last constraint $\phi \le \min_{t\in T} 1/\delta(t)$ guarantees single server semantics.

The LP (13) always has solution since all its constraints must hold in the steady state. Given that the throughput variable, ϕ, is maximized, the obtained value is an upper throughput bound [40].

Theorem 3. *Let N be a* TGMG*. The solution of* (13) *gives an upper bound for the steady state throughput of the* TGMG*.*

Example 2. Consider again the 1-bounded TGMG from Fig. 14 (delays of all transitions assumed to be 1). The associated LP problem is:

$$\begin{array}{lll}
\multicolumn{2}{l}{\text{Maximize}\ \ \phi:} & \\
& \phi \le \overline{M}(ab) & \text{for transition } b \\
& \phi \le \overline{M}(ac) & \text{for transition } c \\
& \phi \le \overline{M}(cd) & \text{for transition } d \\
& \phi \le \alpha\cdot\overline{M}(ba) + (1-\alpha)\cdot\overline{M}(da) & \text{for transition } a \\
ba = & 1 + \overline{M}(b) - \overline{M}(a) & \text{for arc } ba \\
da = & 1 + \overline{M}(d) - \overline{M}(a) & \text{for arc } da \\
ab = & \overline{M}(a) - \overline{M}(b) & \text{for arc } ab \\
ac = & \overline{M}(a) - \overline{M}(c) & \text{for arc } ac \\
cd = & 1 + \overline{M}(c) - \overline{M}(d) & \text{for arc } cd
\end{array}$$

The solution to this problem is

$$\phi = \frac{2-\alpha}{3-\alpha}$$

which, in this case, corresponds exactly to the solution we have obtained with Markov chain analysis.

7 Retiming and Recycling

In this section, we will show how a well-known optimization technique (retiming [46]) can be combined with the insertion of empty buffers (recycling) for performance optimization. The EMG representation does not capture information about the combinational delay of a node, so in this section our representation of an elastic system is based on the *retiming graph* of Leiserson and Saxe [46].

7.1 An Introductory Example

In logic synthesis the usual representation of a synchronous sequential circuit is a set of combinational blocks interconnected via memory elements (registers). Figure 15a gives an example of a simple sequential circuit. This circuit has nine simple combinational blocks, denoted with lower case letters $a, b, \ldots, i$ and four registers R_1, R_2, R_3, R_4. Every gate computes some boolean function. The gate a is a usual representation of a NOR-gate, which implements a boolean function of two variables $f(x_1, x_2) = \overline{x_1 \vee x_2}$. The *delay* of the gate is the amount of time required to recompute the output value when some inputs are changed. A *combinational path* is a sequence of directly connected gates, i.e., without registers along the sequence. The sequence c, d, e, a from Fig. 15 is a combinational path, while the sequence a, b is not. The combinational path delay is the sum of the delays of its nodes. In order to have a well-defined physical design, combinational paths must not form cycles, i.e., each cycle must have at least one register.

Every time that the global clock signal (denoted as CLK on the figure) arrives, the registers become "transparent", i.e., the input data becomes output data. For example, the result computed by gate b during the previous clock cycle becomes the input for gate c. The amount of time between two consecutive clock signals (a *clock period*) should allow each gate to recompute its output value. In order to guarantee a correct functionality, the maximum combinational path delay of the circuit, which is called *cycle time*, should be less than or equal to the clock period.

The retiming technique represents sequential circuits as weighted directed graphs (retiming graph). The nodes of the graph model gates. Each node is labeled with its delay. A directed edge of the graph models an interconnection between gates, and is weighted with a register count. The register count is the number of registers along the

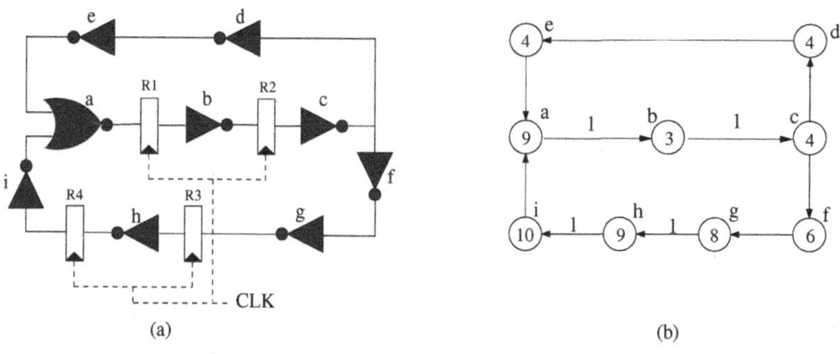

Fig. 15. a A synchronous sequential circuit, **b** its retiming graph

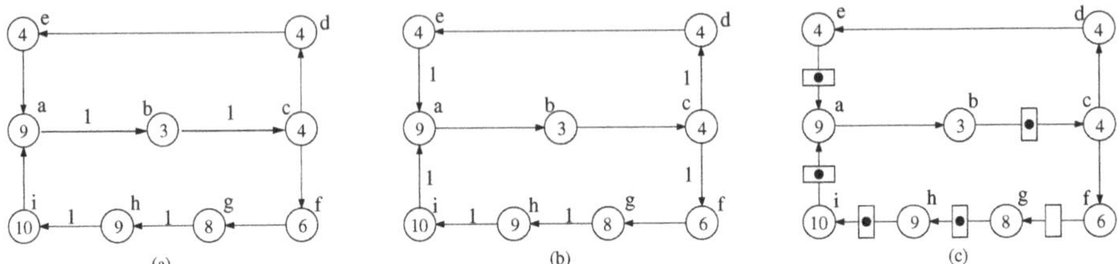

Fig. 16. a Retiming graph, **b** Min-delay retiming configuration, **c** Retiming and recycling

connection. Fig. 15b shows the corresponding retiming graph for the sequential circuit depicted on the Fig. 15a. The nodes (circles) are labeled with their delays. The edges are labeled with the corresponding register number, unlabeled edges have no registers. The delay of the combinational path c, f, g is equal to 18 time units, for path c, d, e, a it is equal to 21. The cycle time of the circuit with delays is equal to 21.

A retiming r on a given graph assigns an integer to each node of the graph. This assignment transforms the edge register count as follows: Assume that edge e has source node u, target node v and register count $w(e)$. Then, after applying retiming r, e will have register count $w'(e) = w(e) + r(v) - r(u)$. Let us exemplify this technique by applying the following retiming on the retiming graph in Fig. 16a: $r(a) = 1, r(c) = -1$, r is zero for the rest of the nodes. In order to apply $r(a) = 1$ it is enough to remove one register from each output edge of node a and add one register to each input edge of a; $r(c) = -1$ moves register across node c in opposite direction. Fig. 16b shows the resulting graph.

Retiming may change the cycle time and the number of registers in the circuit while preserving its sequential behavior. In the graph in the Fig. 16b the combinational path with the greatest delay is a, b, c. Then, the cycle time is equal to $9 + 3 + 4 = 16$ time units.

In order to describe an ES, we should be able to distinguish registers that contain valid data (dots) from empty registers (bubbles). For this purpose, we will add a new edge label into the retiming graph. This label represents the total number of registers (dots and bubbles) on the edge. The register count of the retiming graph now represents only the number of dots on the edge. Figure 16c shows an example. The empty boxes represent registers with non-valid data (register count = 1, dot count = 0), boxes with dots represent registers with valid data (register count = dot count = 1). There are two combinational paths that determine the cycle time: a, b and c, d, e. The cycle time is equal to 12 time units.

The bottom directed cycle has four dots and five registers. Therefore, it does not produce valid data every clock cycle, but four valid data every five cycles, i.e., its *processing rate* is $4/5$. The *effective cycle time* is given by its cycle time divided by its processing rate, this yields $12 \cdot 5/4 = 15$. This effective cycle time is better than the one of the original non-elastic circuit which was 16 (the processing rate of a system without bubbles is equal to one).

In this section, we show how the *minimal effective cycle time* of an ES represented as a retiming graph can be found. An exact solution of the retiming and recycling problem is specified with MILPs.

7.2 Marked Graphs and Retiming

The retiming graph (RG) is isomorphic to a TMG. Each combinational block corresponds to a node, each connection corresponds to an edge. The registers in the retiming graph are represented by tokens in the MG. This way, the firing rules of a MG coincide with the backward retiming rule: each time a node is retimed, registers are removed from the input edges and added to the output edges.

Definition 10 (Retiming Graph). *A RG is a TMG (N, E, R_0, δ). R_0 represents an initial assignment of registers with informative data (dots) to the edges of the graph.*

In Sect. 3.1 basic structural properties of a MG were introduced. The retiming interpretation of these properties is the following:

Retiming interpretation of liveness (Property 1, Sect. 3.1): *every cycle should have at least one register to avoid combinational cycles in the circuit netlist.*

Retiming interpretation of token preservation (Property 3, Sec. 3.1): This property has two directions. The $\Rightarrow$ direction corresponds to a well-known result in retiming: *A valid retiming preserves the number of registers at each cycle.* The important direction is $\Leftarrow$ that provides a new result for the theory of retiming [47]: *If an assignment of registers has the same number of registers at each cycle as the initial circuit, then the assignment is a valid retiming.*

Thus, we can reduce the retiming problem to a reachability problem in MGs.

In order to represent bubbles we associate another register assignment with a RG.

Definition 11 (Retiming and recycling configuration of a RG). *A retiming and recycling configuration (R&R) of a RG is a register assignment $R : E \to N$.*

An important question is: What is a valid R&R? The answer is easy: let us take any valid retiming configuration of the RG and let us add any arbitrary number of registers (bubbles) to every edge. That is, set register count R as follows: $R(e) = R_0(e) + k$, $k \in \mathbb{N}$. The resulting R&R is valid. Therefore, any integer vector R that satisfies to the following inequalities:

$$R \geq \widehat{R} = R_0 + \mathbb{C} \cdot \sigma \geq 0, \;\; R, \widehat{R} \in \mathbb{N}^{|E|} \tag{14}$$

is a valid R&R. In (14), $\mathbb{C}$ is the incidence matrix of the RG, $\widehat{R}$ represents the *retiming subset* of the solution (the registers containing only dots), and R represents registers containing dots and bubbles.

A bubble in a valid R&R is represented as follows: $R(e) = 1, \widehat{R}(e) = 0$, e.g. edge (f, g) in Fig, 16c. If the edge e has two registers and only one dot then it has the followings register counts: $R(e) = 2, \widehat{R}(e) = 1$. The register counts of an edge without registers are $R(e) = 0, \widehat{R}(e) = 0$. The difference between both vectors, $R - \widehat{R}$, represents the vector of registers containing the bubbles introduced by recycling.

Let $\tau(R)$ be the cycle time of R, i.e., the greatest delay of the path without registers in the RG. For instance, the cycle time of the R&R in Fig. 16c is equal to 12. Let $\Theta(R)$ be the throughput of R, i.e., the minimal dots to registers ratio of all directed cycles of the RG[1]. The cycle ratios for the top and bottom cycles of Fig. 16c are 1 and

[1] This throughput model assumes that backward arcs of the corresponding EMG do not constraint the throughput. This always can be achieved by proper buffer sizing (see Sect. 4).

4/5, respectively. Therefore, $\Theta(R) = 4/5$. The main performance measure of R is the *effective cycle time*. The effective cycle time of a R (ξ(R)) is the ratio of its cycle time and the throughput.

Now we give an overview of the strategy to find, for a given RG, a R with the minimal effective cycle time. The reader can refer to [47] for details.

7.3 Basic MILPs for Retiming and Recycling

Given a cycle time τ_c and a throughput $\Theta_c, 0 < \Theta_c \leq 1$. A registers assignment R is a valid R&R with $\tau(R) \leq \tau_c$ and $\Theta(R) \geq \Theta_c$ if it satisfies the following three sets of inequalities:

$$\mathrm{RR}(\tau_c, \Theta_c) \equiv \begin{cases} R \geq R_0 + \mathbb{C} \cdot \sigma_1 \geq 0, \\ R \cdot \Theta_c \leq R_0 + \mathbb{C} \cdot \sigma_2, \\ \texttt{Path\_Constraints}(R, \tau_c), \\ R \in \mathbb{N}^{|E|}, \sigma_1 \in \mathbb{Z}^{|N|} \end{cases} \tag{15}$$

The first set of the inequalities guarantees that R is valid (see (14)). The second set of the inequalities guarantees that the throughput of R is at least equal to Θ_c. They can be derived using MG performance theory [24] or the linear programming formulation of the minimal cycle ratio problem [28]. The $\texttt{Path\_Constraints}(R, \tau_c)$ is a set of linear inequalities that guarantees the delay of all combinational paths is at most τ_c [47].

7.4 Minimal Effective Cycle Time

Among all R&R configurations that satisfy constraints (15), the ones with minimal cycle time can be found with the following MILP:

$$\begin{aligned} &\mathit{Minimize} \ \ \tau : \\ &\quad \text{subject to } \mathrm{RR}(\tau, \Theta_c) \end{aligned} \tag{16}$$

Similarly, the throughput can be maximized (cycle time τ_c is constant):

$$\begin{aligned} &\mathit{Maximize} \ \ \Theta : \\ &\quad \text{subject to } \mathrm{RR}(\tau_c, \Theta) \end{aligned} \tag{17}$$

Problem (17) with Θ being a variable is neither linear nor convex. However, the throughput constraints in (15) can be modified as follows:

$$\frac{1}{\Theta} \cdot R_0 \geq R + \mathbb{C} \cdot \sigma_2'$$

Then, after substituting $x = \frac{1}{\Theta}$, the throughput can be maximized with the following MILP:

$$\begin{aligned} &\mathit{Minimize} \ \ x : \\ &\qquad R \geq R_0 + \mathbb{C} \cdot \sigma_1 \geq 0, \\ &\qquad R_0 \cdot x \geq R + \mathbb{C} \cdot \sigma_2, \\ &\qquad \texttt{Path\_Constraints}(R, \tau_c), \\ &\qquad R \in \mathbb{N}^{|E|}, \sigma_1 \in \mathbb{Z}^{|N|} \end{aligned} \tag{18}$$

Let $R(\tau,\Theta)$ be a R&R with cycle time τ and throughput Θ. We say that $R_1(\tau_1,\Theta_1)$ is dominated by $R_2(\tau_2,\Theta_2)$ iff $\Theta_1 = \Theta_2$ and $\tau_2 < \tau_1$. If R_1 is dominated by R_2 then $\xi(R_1) > \xi(R_2)$ and R_1 cannot provide the minimal effective cycle time. We say that $R(\tau,\Theta)$ is non-dominated if it is not dominated by any another configuration. Using MILPs (16) and (18) we can find all non-dominated R&R configurations and consequently the minimal effective cycle time.

8 Conclusions and Open Problems

When the behavior derived from the structure of a circuit is modeled at a low level of granularity, concepts like concurrency and elasticity appear in a natural way. The analysis of such systems can take advantage of the strong analogy between the structure and the behavior of a circuit and the structure and token flow of a Petri net.

This paper has reviewed several problems of elastic circuits that can be abstracted and reduced to problems in Petri nets, mainly marked graphs. The variability of computation and communication latencies and the increasing demand in relaxing the strong requirements imposed by global clocks open the door to new design paradigms with more complex models.

This is an area in which the sinergism between two worlds can be exploited. The existing knowledge in the theory of Petri nets can be effectively used to model and reason about problems that are actually emerging in the area of digital circuit design.

Open Problems. Several extensions of the models used in this paper can lead to a more accurate description of an elastic system. Two main extensions on the model might be considered for this purpose: (a) introduce early evaluated nodes in the problems considered in Sects. 4, 5 and 7, and (b) incorporate variable latencies in the nodes of the EMG.

An EMG extended with variable latencies on the nodes captures the variability of some nodes, by associating a probability function to the delays of the transitions. The methods proposed in this paper must be revised to handle these extensions.

References

1. Sutherland, I.E.: Micropipelines. Communications of the ACM 32(6), 720–738 (1989)
2. Muller, D.E., Bartky, W.S.: A theory of asynchronous circuits. In: Proceedings of an International Symposium on the Theory of Switching, April 1959, pp. 204–243. Harvard University Press (1959)
3. Martin, A.J.: Compiling communicating processes into delay-insensitive VLSI circuits. Distributed Computing 1(4), 226–234 (1986)
4. Sparsø, J., Furber, S. (eds.): Principles of Asynchronous Circuit Design: A Systems Perspective. Kluwer Academic Publishers, Dordrecht (2001)
5. Cortadella, J., Kishinevsky, M., Kondratyev, A., Lavagno, L., Yakovlev, A.: Logic synthesis of asynchronous controllers and interfaces. Springer, Heidelberg (2002)
6. O'Leary, J., Brown, G.: Synchronous emulation of asynchronous circuits. IEEE Transactions on Computer-Aided Design 16(2), 205–209 (1997)

7. Peeters, A., van Berkel, K.: Synchronous handshake circuits. In: Proc. International Symposium on Advanced Research in Asynchronous Circuits and Systems, pp. 86–95. IEEE Computer Society Press, Los Alamitos (2001)
8. Carloni, L.P., McMillan, K.L., Sangiovanni-Vincentelli, A.L.: Theory of latency-insensitive design. IEEE Transactions on Computer-Aided Design 20(9), 1059–1076 (2001)
9. Carloni, L.P., Sangiovanni-Vincentelli, A.L.: Coping with latency in SoC design. IEEE Micro, Special Issue on Systems on Chip 22(5), 12 (2002)
10. Jacobson, H.M., Kudva, P.N., Bose, P., Cook, P.W., Schuster, S.E., Mercer, E.G., Myers, C.J.: Synchronous interlocked pipelines. In: Proc. International Symposium on Advanced Research in Asynchronous Circuits and Systems, pp. 3–12 (April 2002)
11. Cortadella, J., Kishinevsky, M., Grundmann, B.: Synthesis of synchronous elastic architectures. In: Proc. ACM/IEEE Design Automation Conference, pp. 657–662 (July 2006)
12. Cortadella, J., Kishinevsky, M.: Synchronous elastic circuits with early evaluation and token counterflow. In: Proc. ACM/IEEE Design Automation Conference, pp. 416–419 (June 2007)
13. Dennis, J.B.: Modular asynchronous control structures for a high performance processor. In: Project MAC Conf. on Concurrent Systems and Parallel Computation, pp. 55–80 (1970)
14. Dennis, J.B., Patil, S.S.: Speed-independent asynchronous circuits. In: Proc. Hawaii International Conf. System Sciences, pp. 55–58 (1971)
15. Misunas, D.: Petri nets and speed independent design. Communications of the ACM 16(8), 474–481 (1973)
16. Linder, D.H., Harden, J.C.: Phased logic: supporting the synchronous design paradigm with delay-insensitive circuitry. IEEE Transactions on Computers 45(9), 1031–1044 (1996)
17. Cortadella, J., Kondratyev, A., Lavagno, L., Sotiriou, C.: Desynchronization: synthesis of asynchronous circuits from synchronous specifications. IEEE Transactions on Computer-Aided Design 25(10), 1904–1921 (2006)
18. Rosenblum, L.Y., Yakovlev, A.V.: Signal graphs: from self-timed to timed ones. In: Proceedings of International Workshop on Timed Petri Nets, Turin, Italy, July 1985, pp. 199–207. IEEE Computer Society Press, Los Alamitos (1985)
19. Yoeli, M.: Specification and verification of asynchronous circuits using marked graphs. In: Voss, K., Genrich, H.J., Rozenberg, G. (eds.) Concurrency and Nets, Advances in Petri Nets, pp. 605–622. Springer, Heidelberg (1987)
20. Yakovlev, A., Gomes, L., Lavagno, L. (eds.): Hardware Design And Petri Nets. Kluwer Academic Publishers, Dordrecht (2000)
21. Schrijver, A.: Theory of Linear and Integer Programming. John Wiley & Sons, Chichester (1998)
22. CPLEX, `http://www.ilog.com/products/cplex`
23. Murata, T.: Petri Nets: properties, analysis and applications. Proceedings of the IEEE, 541–580 (April 1989)
24. Campos, J., Silva, M.: Structural techniques and performance bounds of stochastic Petri net models. In: Rozenberg, G. (ed.) APN 1992. LNCS, vol. 609. Springer, Heidelberg (1992)
25. Little, J.D.C.: A proof of the queueing formula $L = \lambda W$. Operations Research 9, 383–387 (1961)
26. Ramamoorthy, C.V., Ho, G.S.: Performance evaluation of asynchronous concurrent systems using Petri nets. IEEE Trans. Software Eng. 6(5), 440–449 (1980)
27. Karp, R.: A characterization of the minimum cycle mean in a digraph. Discrete Mathematics 23, 309–311 (1978)
28. Dasdan, A., Irani, S.S., Gupta, R.K.: Efficient algorithms for optimum cycle mean and optimum cost to time ratio problems. In: Proc. 36th Design Automation Conference, pp. 37–42 (1999)
29. Williams, T.E.: Performance of iterative computation in self-timed rings. Journal of VLSI Signal Processing 7(1/2), 17–31 (1994)

30. Manohar, R., Martin, A.J.: Slack elasticity in concurrent computing. In: Jeuring, J. (ed.) MPC 1998. LNCS, vol. 1422, pp. 272–285. Springer, Heidelberg (1998)
31. Beerel, P.A., Kim, N.-H., Lines, A., Davies, M.: Slack matching asynchronous designs. In: Proc. of the 12th Int. Symp. on Asynchronous Circuits and Systems (2006)
32. Rodriquez-Beltran, J., Ramirez-Trevino, A.: Minimum initial marking in timed marked graphs. In: Proc. IEEE Int. Conf. on Systems, Man, and Cybernetics (SMC 2000), vol. 4, pp. 3004–3008 (October 2000)
33. Garey, M.R., Johnson, D.S.: Computers and Intractability: a Guide to the Theory of NP-Completeness. W.H. Freeman, New York (1979)
34. Lu, R., Koh, C.-K.: Performance optimization of latency insensitive systems through buffer queue sizing of communication channels. In: Proc. International Conf. Computer-Aided Design (ICCAD), pp. 227–231 (2003)
35. Lu, R., Koh, C.-K.: Performance analysis and efficient implementation of latency insensitive systems. ECE Technical Reports (March 2003)
36. Chelcea, T., Nowick, S.M.: Robust interfaces for mixed-timing systems. IEEE Trans. VLSI Syst. 12(8), 857–873 (2004)
37. Dasdan, A., Gupta, R.K.: Faster maximum and minimum mean cycle algorithms for system performance analysis. IEEE Transactions on Computer-Aided Design 17(10), 889–899 (1998)
38. Carmona, J., Júlvez, J., Cortadella, J., Kishinevsky, M.: Performance-preserving clustering of elastic controllers. Technical Report LSI-08-7-R, Department of Software, Universitat Politècnica de Catalunya (2007)
39. Cormen, T.H., Stein, C., Rivest, R.L., Leiserson, C.E.: Introduction to Algorithms. McGraw-Hill Higher Education, New York (2001)
40. Júlvez, J., Cortadella, J., Kishinevsky, M.: Performance analysis of concurrent systems with early evaluation. In: Proc. International Conf. Computer-Aided Design (ICCAD) (November 2006)
41. Brej, C.F., Garside, J.D.: Early output logic using anti-tokens. In: Int. Workshop on Logic Synthesis, pp. 302–309 (May 2003)
42. Reese, R.B., Thornton, M.A., Traver, C., Hemmendinger, D.: Early evaluation for performance enhancement in phased logic. IEEE Transactions on Computer-Aided Design 24(4), 532–550 (2005)
43. Yakovlev, A., Kishinevsky, M., Kondratyev, A., Lavagno, L., Pietkiewicz-Koutny, M.: On the models for asynchronous circuit behaviour with OR causality. Formal Methods in System Design 9(3), 189–233 (1996)
44. Wolff, R.W.: Stochastic Modeling and the Theory of Queues. Prentice-Hall, Englewood Cliffs (1989)
45. Chiola, G., Anglano, C., Campos, J., Colom, J.M., Silva, M.: Operational analysis of timed Petri nets and application to the computation of performance bounds. In: Baccelli, F., Jean-Marie, A., Mitrani, I. (eds.) Quantitative Methods in Parallel Systems, pp. 161–174. Springer, Heidelberg (1995); Also appears in Procs. PNPM 1993 (1993)
46. Leiserson, C.E., Saxe, J.B.: Retiming synchronous circuitry. Algorithmica 6(1), 5–35 (1991)
47. Bufistov, D., Cortadella, J., Kishinevsky, M., Sapatnekar, S.: A general model for performance optimization of sequential systems. In: Proc. International Conf. Computer-Aided Design (ICCAD), pp. 362–369 (November 2007)

Author Index